MENORCA

Ciutadella

Alaior

Maó

Pollença

Alcúdia

a

Artà

MALLORCA

Manacor

Llucmajor

Felanitx

Campos

Santanyí

CABRERA ISLAND

MENORCA
Pages 90–111

MALLORCA
Pages 42–89

0 km 20

0 miles 20

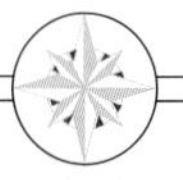

EYEWITNESS TRAVEL

MALLORCA
MENORCA & IBIZA

EYEWITNESS TRAVEL

MALLORCA
MENORCA AND IBIZA

MAIN CONTRIBUTOR: GRZEGORZ MICUŁA

LONDON, NEW YORK,
MELBOURNE, MUNICH AND DELHI
www.dk.com

PRODUCED BY Wydawnictwo Wiedza i Życie S.A., Warsaw
SENIOR GRAPHIC DESIGNER Paweł Pasternak
EDITORS Robert G. Pasieczny, Anna Moczar-Demko
GRAPHIC DESIGN Paweł Kamiński, Piotr Kiedrowski
TYPESETTING AND LAYOUT Paweł Kamiński,
Piotr Kiedrowski, Elżbieta Dudzińska
CARTOGRAPHY Magdalena Polak
PHOTOGRAPHY Bartłomiej Zaranek
ILLUSTRATIONS Bohdan Wróblewski,
Michał Burkiewicz, Monika Żylińska
CONTRIBUTORS Grzegorz Micuła, Katarzyna Sobieraj,
Robert G. Pasieczny, Eligiusz Nowakowski
CONSULTANT Carlos Cassas Marrodan

For Dorling Kindersley
TRANSLATOR Magda Hannay
EDITOR Matthew Tanner
SENIOR DTP DESIGNER Jason Little
PRODUCTION CONTROLLER Sarah Dodd

Reproduced by Colourscan, Singapore
Printed in Singapore by KHL Printing Co. Pte. Ltd.

First American edition, 2004
10 11 12 13 10 9 8 7 6 5 4 3 2 1

Published in the United States by DK Publishing,
375 Hudson Street, New York, New York 10014

Reprinted with revisions 2006, 2008, 2010

Published in Great Britain by Dorling Kindersley Limited.

ISSN 1542-1554
ISBN 978-0-75666-142-7

FLOORS ARE REFERRED TO THROUGHOUT IN ACCORDANCE WITH BRITISH USAGE; IE THE "FIRST FLOOR" IS THE FLOOR ABOVE GROUND LEVEL.

Front cover main image: View of Cala Pi de la Posada, Mallorca

The information in this Dorling Kindersley Travel Guide is checked regularly.

Every effort has been made to ensure that this book is as up-to-date as possible at the time of going to press. Some details, however, such as telephone numbers, opening hours, prices, gallery hanging arrangements and travel information are liable to change. The publishers cannot accept responsibility for any consequences arising from the use of this book, nor for any material on third party websites, and cannot guarantee that any website address in this book will be a suitable source of travel information. We value the views and suggestions of our readers very highly. Please write to: Publisher, DK Eyewitness Travel Guides, Dorling Kindersley, 80 Strand, London, WC2R 0RL, Great Britain.

◁ **Cala Morell, the most beautiful bay on the north coast of Menorca**

CONTENTS

Baroque sundial in one of Palma's palaces

INTRODUCING THE BALEARIC ISLANDS

Horse-cab ride through the streets of the old town, Palma

A sunny morning on the beach near S'Arenal harbour

Sign of a restaurant serving Mallorcan food

A stall selling watermelons at the weekly market in Inca

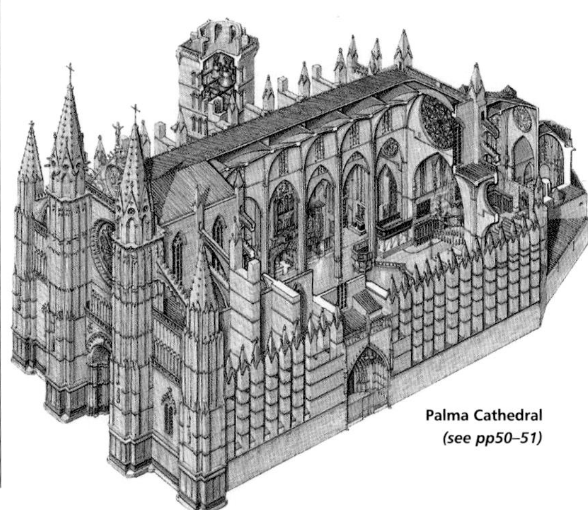

Palma Cathedral *(see pp50–51)*

HOW TO USE THIS GUIDE

This guide will help you to make the most of your visit to the Balearic Islands. The first section, Introducing the Balearic Islands, locates the islands geographically and gives an outline of their rich history and culture. Individual sections describe the main historic sights and star attractions on each of the four archipelago islands. Help with accommodation, restaurants, shopping, entertainment and many recreational activities can be found in the *Travellers' Needs* section, while the *Survival Guide* provides useful tips on everything you need to know, from money and language to getting around and seeking medical care.

THE BALEARIC ISLANDS AREA BY AREA

In this guide, each of the islands has been given its own chapter. Within each chapter there is an introduction, a pictorial map, and a detailed listing of all the best sights.

1 Introduction
This section provides a brief overview and history of each island, describing its history, geographical features and cultural characteristics as well as main tourist attractions.

Colour-coded thumb tabs identify pages devoted to individual islands.

A locator map indicates the position of the island within the archipelago.

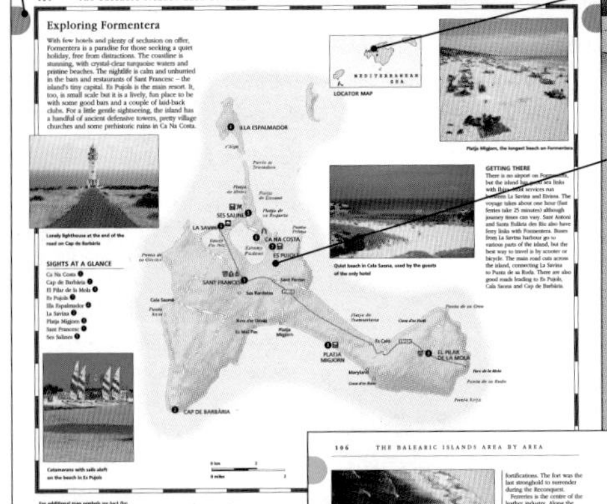
134 THE BALEARIC ISLANDS AREA BY AREA
FORMENTERA

Exploring Formentera

SIGHTS AT A GLANCE

GETTING THERE

2 Regional Map
This shows the main roads and topography of the island. It also locates all the sights that are later described in detail.

Boxes contain information about events and people associated with an area.

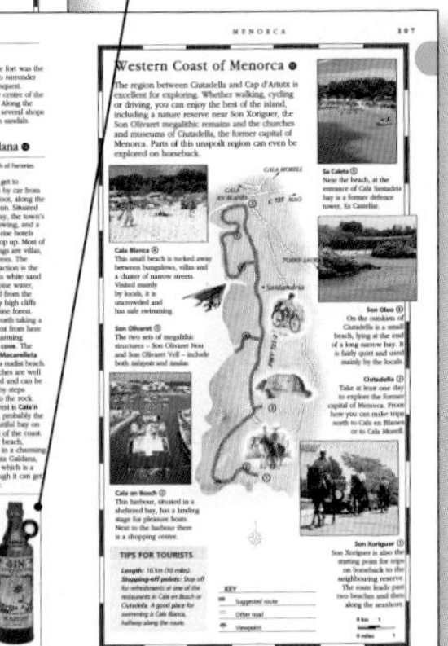
MENORCA 107

Western Coast of Menorca

TIPS FOR TOURISTS

3 Detailed Information
All the important sights on the islands are described individually. The address, phone number, opening hours, admission charges, how to get there and disabled access are given for each sight.

4 Major Towns

At least two pages are devoted to each major town, with a detailed description of the historic remains and local curiosities that are worth seeing.

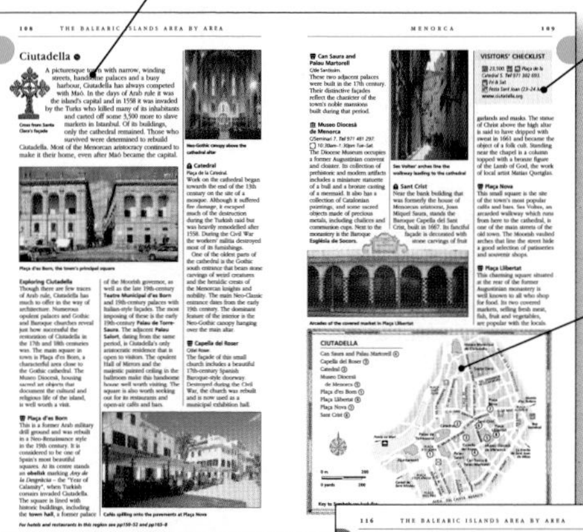

A Visitors' Checklist provides tourist and transport information, including opening hours of tourist attractions, admission charges, and details of local festivals and market days.

A Town Map shows the location of all the main sights within the town centre and provides tourist information on post offices and car parks.

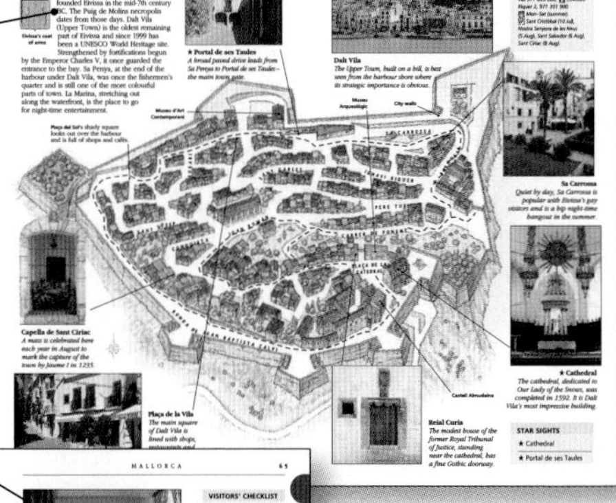

5 Street-by-Street Map

This gives a bird's-eye view of a particularly interesting sightseeing area described in the section.

Photographs illustrate the most interesting areas and the most impressive sights within an attraction.

Tourist information details length of suggested tour plus good stopping places.

6 Star Sights

At least one page is dedicated to each major sight. Historic buildings are dissected to reveal their interiors, and parks are illustrated to show the main attractions.

Star Attractions point out the best sights or exhibits that no visitor should miss.

Cut-outs show the sight in its surroundings and some parts of the interior.

INTRODUCING THE BALEARIC ISLANDS

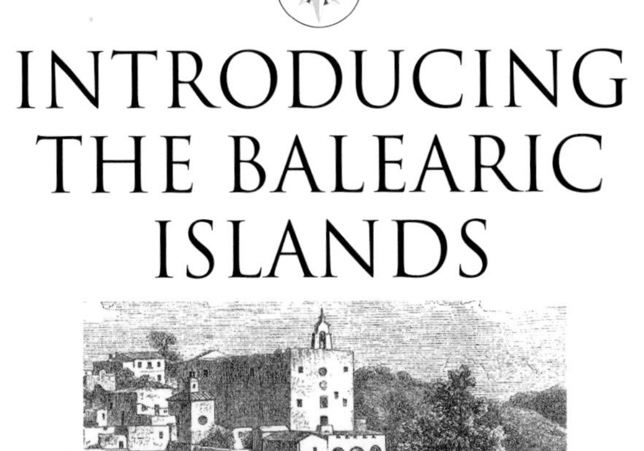

DISCOVERING THE BALEARIC ISLANDS

Each of the four main Balearic islands offers a variety of landscapes, from lively beaches and rocky coastlines to lush subtropical interiors. Mallorca's beaches are well known for package tourism, but more accommodation facilities are also appearing in the Serra de Tramuntana mountains and the towns of the verdant interior. Mallorca's capital, Palma, has a culture and history, as well as restaurants and nightlife, comparable to any mainland Spanish city. Beaches, coves, bays and spectacular countryside can be found on all four islands, in addition to history, arts and architecture, local customs and folklore, and superb gastronomy, wines and liquors.

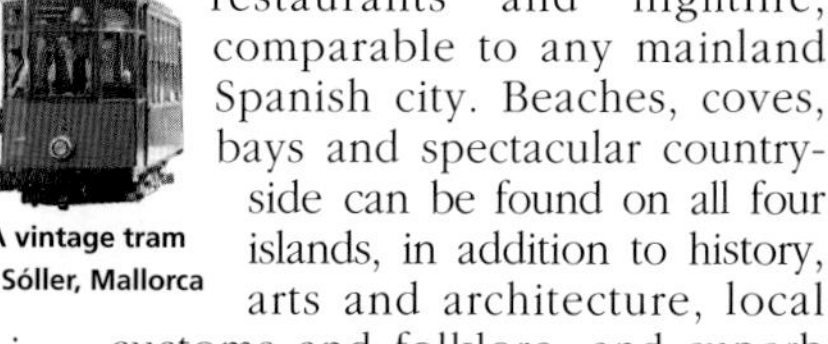

A vintage tram in Sóller, Mallorca

A panoramic view of the village of Deià, Mallorca

MALLORCA

- **Palma's rich architectural heritage**
- **Magaluf and S'Arenal's lively beach resorts**
- **Dramatic interior valleys surrounding Bunyola**

The largest of the Balearics, **Mallorca** *(see pp42–89)* also has the greatest diversity of landscape and culture. The cosmopolitan capital city, **Palma** *(see pp46–55)*, boasts an array of memorable sights. Its cathedral, **La Seu** *(see pp50–51)*, begun under Jaume I, is one of the most monumental in Europe, while its castle, the **Castell de Bellver** *(see p57)*, built for Jaume II in the 14th century, is a fine Gothic building. The **Banys Àrabs** *(see p55)*, a 10th-century *hammam*, is among the best-preserved bath houses in Spain.

Palma's museums and galleries, notably the Joan Miró Foundation on the outskirts of Palma in **Cala Major** *(see p58)*, as well as its restaurants and nightlife, are of an international standard.

Mallorca's famous resorts, such as **Magaluf** *(see p88)* and **S'Arenal** *(see p87)*, have long been synonymous with beach holidays for thousands European tourists. Quieter beaches can be found in and around the towns of **Andratx** *(see p60)*, **Sóller** *(see p69)*, **Pollença** *(see p74)* and **Alcúdia** *(see p75)*. The coastline becomes increasingly dramatic the further north you travel.

The mountain towns of **Valldemossa** *(see p66)* and **Deià** *(see p68)* are popular for their artistic associations. The great composer Frédéric Chopin spent time in Valldemossa with the French novelist George Sand who wrote about the town in *A Winter in Mallorca (see p67)*. English poet and novelist Robert Graves and French author Anaïs Nin both used idyllic Deià as a setting for their stories *(see p69)*.

Adventurous tourists visit the island's interior, using the panoramic **Train from Palma to Port de Sóller** *(see p70)* to stop at Bunyola, or the commuter line to reach Binissalem, centre of Mallorca's wine industry, and the large market town of **Inca** *(see p74)*. Other historic towns worth visiting include **Sineu** *(see pp76–7)* and **Montuïri** *(see pp87)*.

The Gothic cathedral of La Seu, towering over Palma, Mallorca

◁ **Hill-top village of Deià, where writer Robert Graves once lived**

An impressive Talayotic *taula* in Trepucó, Menorca

MENORCA

- A sedate pace of life
- Twin capitals: Maó and Ciutadella
- Exquisite beaches, bays and coves
- Extraordinary wealth of megalithic sites

The second-largest island of the Balearic archipelago, **Menorca** *(see pp90–111)* did not have an international airport until 1969, when Maó (Mahón) airport opened. If not quite stemming the tide of mass tourism, this relative inaccessibility kept – and continues to keep – Menorca a quieter place than its larger neighbour.

In the intervening decades, and with the recent rise of environmentally aware tourism, Menorca has settled into a more sedate rhythm. Its capital **Maó** *(see pp94–5)* and the former capital **Ciutadella** *(see pp108–9)* are both busy and cosmopolitan towns, with their own distinct architectural and cultural heritage, and a restaurant and nightlife scene less hectic than Palma but no less pleasant. Ciutadella, the older of the two, can claim the most impressive architecture, including a 13th-century cathedral and the beautiful Plaça d'es Born.

Outside the twin capitals, Menorca has suffered little of the development seen on Mallorca. The landscape is gentler, but equally picturesque. Some of its placid interior settlements, such as **Es Mercadal** *(see p101)*, date as far back as the 14th century, although most, including **Es Castell** *(see p98)* and **Ferreries** *(see p106)*, date from the 1600s. **Binibeca Vell** *(see p100)*, on the south-eastern coast, dates from as recently as 1972, and was built as a model of a living fishing village.

Menorca's coastline is dotted with tiny coves, bays and perfect beaches, while the island's interior has an impressive concentration of prehistoric Talayotic structures *(see p99)*.

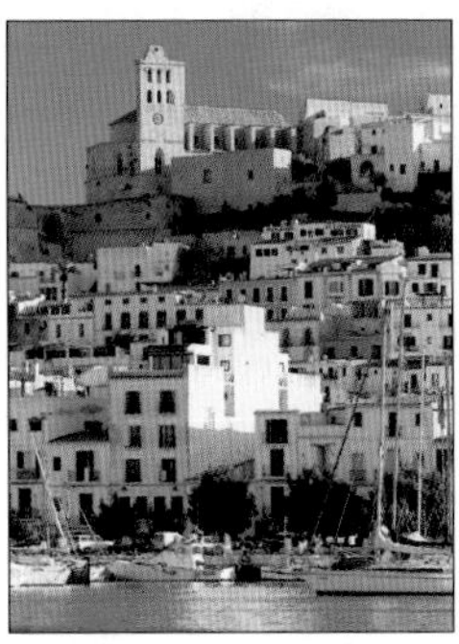

View from the harbour of the Upper Town of Eivissa, Ibiza

IBIZA

- World-famous nightlife
- Eivissa's historic past
- Quiet inland towns
- The unspoilt charm of Els Amunts

Long a favourite of hippies, **Ibiza** *(see pp112–31)* was the headquarters of the late 1980s "rave" culture. The hardcore elements have moved on, but the party continues at clubs such as Space and Manumission.

As Ibiza settles down, its older attractions are re-emerging, not least the walled Dalt Vila (Upper Town) of its capital, **Eivissa** *(see pp116–19)*, with its cathedral and some archaeological treasures dating as far back as the 7th century BC. Ibiza is the least verdant of the Balearics, but its rocky coastline conceals some extraordinarily beautiful beaches and coves.

Sant Antoni de Portmany *(see p123)* and **Santa Eulària des Riu** *(see p130)* are main nightlife centres, but interior towns such as **Sant Josep de sa Talaia** *(see pp122–3)* and **Sant Vicent de Sa Cala** *(see p129)* are almost unchanged.

Ibiza's mountain range, **Els Amunts** *(see p128)*, hosts a wild region of pine forests and olive and almond groves; few tourists venture here.

FORMENTERA

- Haven for walkers and nature lovers
- Untamed beaches
- A secluded paradise

Size and inaccessibility have kept **Formentera** *(see p132–9)* out of the mainstream. It is a place best explored by bicycle or on foot. The pocket-sized capital, **Sant Francesc** *(see p136)*, is just 3 km (2 miles) from the island's only harbour, **La Savina** *(see p136)*. Most tourist resorts are on the island's spectacular coastline. The larger beaches receive boatloads of day-trippers from Ibiza, but if you visit its quieter beaches, interior towns such as **El Pilar de la Mola** *(see p138)* and almost anywhere at night, Formentera will reward you with a great sense of peace and quiet.

Enjoying the sunshine on Platja Migjorn, Formentera

Putting the Balearic Islands on the Map

This little group of islands off the east coast of Spain is the Mediterranean's westernmost archipelago. An autonomous province, the Balearic Islands are 82 km (51 miles) from the Iberian Peninsula, a three-hour journey by ferry. The total area of the islands is slightly over 5,000 sq km (1,930 sq miles). Mallorca, the largest island, has an area of 3,640 sq km (1,405 sq miles). The smallest of the four main islands is Formentera.

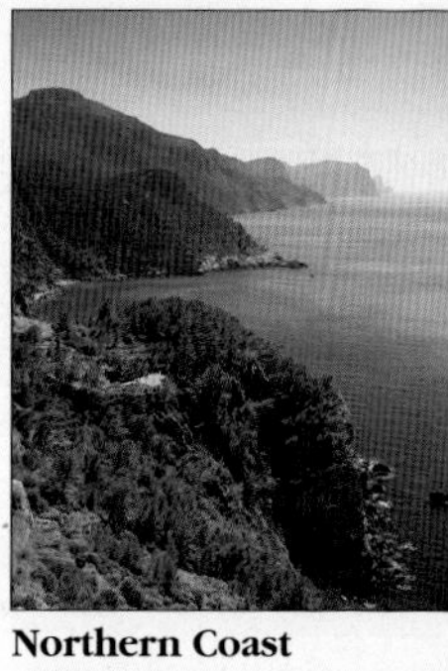

Northern Coast of Mallorca
The northern shores of the Balearic Islands descend steeply via craggy cliffs. There are few beaches here, but cliff-top trails are highly recommended.

Bird's-eye View of Eivissa, Ibiza
The old town at the centre of Ibiza is particularly interesting when viewed from above. A bird's-eye view reveals its maze of narrow streets and the layout of the city walls.

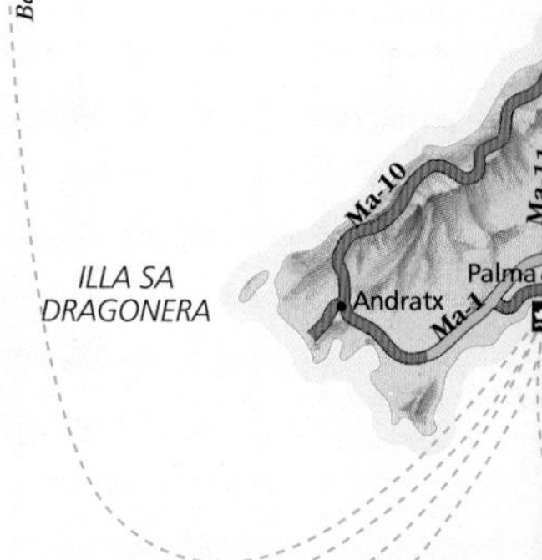

Formentera
El Mirador's restaurant terrace provides a stunning island view.

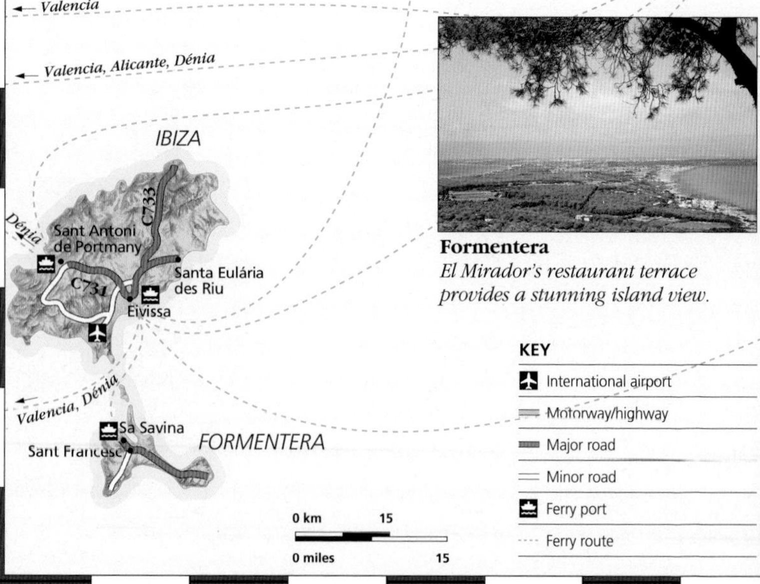

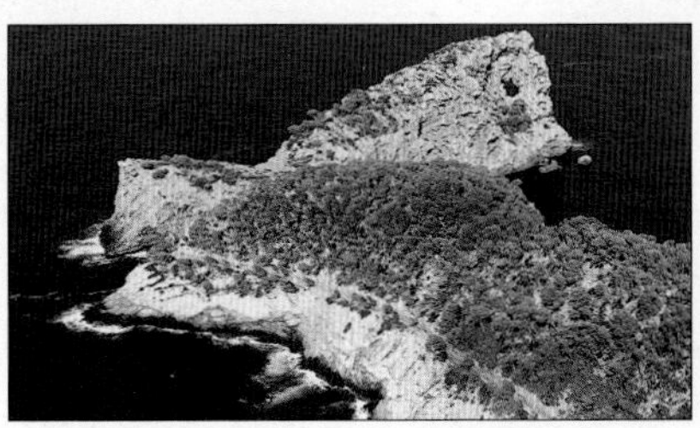

Sa Foradada, Mallorca
The picturesque cape jutting out into the sea near the Son Marroig estate of the Archduke Ludwig Salvator shows the true beauty of the Balearic coast, which some associate only with golden beaches. This landscape is typical of the northern shores of the islands.

Barcelona
Ciutadella
Me-1
Alaior
Mao
MENORCA
Pollença
Alcudia
Ma-13A
Ma-12
Artà
Capdepera
MALLORCA
Ma-15
Manacor
Llucmajor
Ma-14
Felanitx
Ma-17
Campos
Santanyí
Colònia
ant Jordi
Port
CABRERA ISLAND

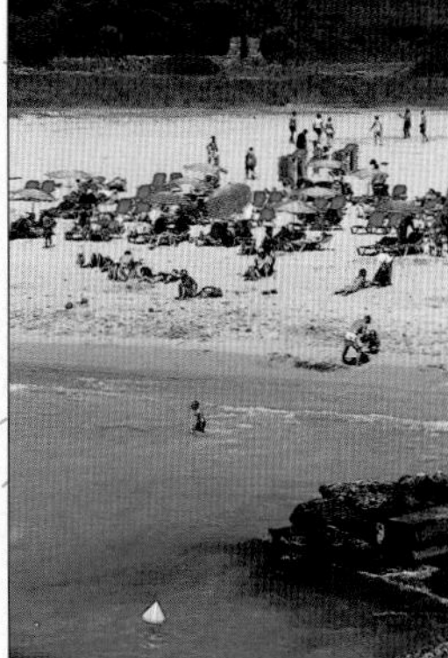

Cala en Porter
This Menorcan beach is reached either by road or via a steep set of steps. The water is shallow and there's plenty of sand, making it a popular spot for those travelling with children.

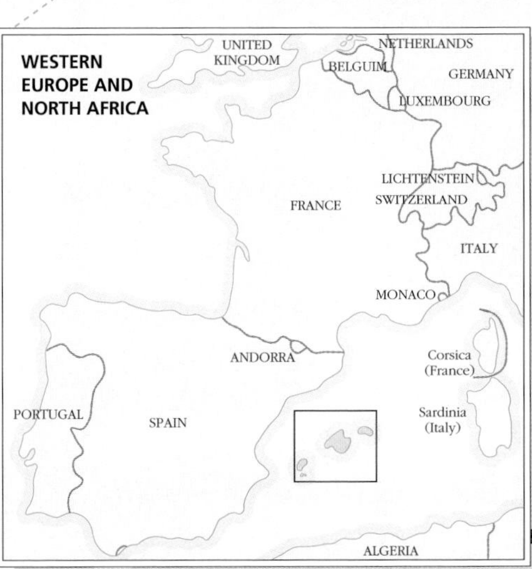

Location of the Archipelago
A short hop from Spain, the Balearic Islands are one of the most popular European resorts. Flights from northern Europe take less than three hours. As a result, the islands attract many visitors all the year round.

A PORTRAIT OF THE BALEARIC ISLANDS

The Balearic Islands are blessed by a hot Mediterranean sun that is tempered by cool sea breezes. Holidaymakers crowd onto the beaches every summer while the young make the most of the clubs and bars. Away from the resorts, time has moved at a gentler pace and inland the islands are quiet and undeveloped.

An ideal staging post between Europe and Africa, these beautiful islands have had their fair share of invaders, including the Phoenicians and the Romans who made the islands part of their Empire. In recent times, the islands have fallen to a full-scale invasion of tourists, which began in the 1960s.

The islands' nightlife, particularly on Ibiza and Mallorca, is legendary and attracts a young crowd. There is far more on offer than clubs however, and if chic cafés are more your thing, the Balearic Islands can supply these too. Indeed, the islands have proved to be popular with the rich and famous, many of whom have homes on the hillsides, away from the prying lenses of the paparazzi.

A clay whistle from Mallorca

Even before the influx of tourists, the islands' climate attracted celebrities. The composer Frédéric Chopin journeyed to Mallorca with his lover George Sand in the winter of 1838–9. Other artists, including the painter and sculptor Joan Miró and the poet Robert Graves, liked it so much that they settled down here.

Menorca is quieter than Mallorca or Ibiza. It has low-key resorts, golden beaches and a rocky landscape that is rich in fascinating prehistoric remains.

Formentera, 4 km (2 miles) south of Ibiza, is the smallest of the Balearic Islands. Tourism is still light though the island's population doubles in the summer as daytrippers come to enjoy what is still a rural haven.

Cala Tarida on the western shores of Ibiza

◁ Stone windmills and olive trees, typical features of the Mallorcan landscape

Rocky coast near Coves d'Artà in Mallorca

TOURIST PARADISE

It was in the early part of the 19th century that tourists first began to arrive on the Balearic Islands, and since that time the local economy has taken full advantage of the opportunities these new arrivals offered. Over 10 million visitors arrive every year to enjoy the islands' many attractions.

Mallorca, the largest island, is by far the most culturally rich, but the other islands are not short of attractions. Ibiza is famous as the clubbing capital of Europe; Menorca is an ideal resort for families, while those in search of peace and quiet head for Formentera.

Sweet and fragrant oranges from the Balearics

Portal of the main entrance to Palma's cathedral

You may even spot the occasional celebrity – Annie Lennox, Claudia Schiffer and Michael Schumacher all have homes on Mallorca, while Elle MacPherson, Roman Polanski and Noel Gallagher (to name but a few) have opted for life on Ibiza. The Balearic Islands are also very popular with politicians and royalty, including the Spanish royal family with their summer residence in Palma.

The Balearics have many fascinating historic sights ranging from Neolithic remains and castle ruins to stunning cathedrals and fine examples of British colonial architecture. Gourmets can delight in the famous Menorcan cheeses and Mallorcan wines, as well as sample the products of the local distilleries, including gin (inherited from the English) and the potent Ibizan herbal liqueurs. The famous *caldereta de llagosta* (Menorcan lobster stew) is not to be missed.

NATURAL TREASURES

The greatest riches of the archipelago are its landscape and natural beauty. The local authorities, hoping to preserve these assets for future generations, have issued several legal decrees which are aimed at protecting the natural environment. Currently, over 40 per cent of the archipelago is legally protected. There are a total of 82 areas of outstanding natural beauty, while the whole of Menorca is designated as a UNESCO Biosphere Reserve, with 18 designated sites that are currently assigned special protection. Mallorca's stunning Parc Natural de S'Albufera is a unique ornithological reserve and is one of southern Europe's most precious water marshes. Among Mallorca's other parks and nature reserves are Cala Mondragó and Dragonera Island.

Fishermen sorting the catch in Eivissa's harbour

Cabrera Island National Park, to the south of Mallorca, also enjoys special protection. The number of boats permitted to land here is strictly limited. This has halted the mass influx of tourists who come here to experience its unique natural beauty and swim in its crystal-clear waters. Here, it is not only the island's landscape that is protected, but also its surrounding waters. It is worth mentioning that one species of seal – the Mediterranean Monk Seal – once lived here, but is now almost extinct.

National parks can be explored on foot or by bicycle, using special trails and signposts. There are also organized tours. The natural wonders of the islands can also be seen outside the parks. Some charming places are to be found, particularly in the valleys of the Serra de Tramuntana mountain range in Mallorca and in the secluded coves of the northwestern part of the island, as well as along most of the coastline of Menorca. The Pitiusan (Pine Trees) archipelago, comprising Ibiza, Formentera and numerous neighbouring uninhabited rocky islands, forms a combined ecosystem visible from the air. A region of outstanding ecological value in Ibiza is the system of salt marshes, Ses Salines, which includes areas inhabited by thousands of birds. Since the Carthaginians discovered the islands these salt marshes have been used to supply salt extracted from sea water.

PEOPLE AND EVENTS

Although the impact of tourism has been far reaching, island customs and traditions have survived intact. This is particularly apparent in the rural areas, away from the resorts. To see this side of island life, you can visit a local farmers' market in one of the small inland towns, or sit down with the locals in a village bar.

Solemn procession held during Corpus Christi

Entrance to El Palacio Hotel in Eivissa

Another important element of island life is the numerous national, local and religious holidays and fiestas. Normally these are days devoted to the patron saints of local parishes, but they can also be held at the end of harvest time or to celebrate an anniversary of an important public event.

Popular national costume

A long calendar of fiestas begins in January with the Festa de Sant Antoni in Mallorca. Perhaps the most colourful is the Festa de Sant Joan in Ciutadella, Menorca (23–24 June), with horseback processions along the narrow streets, firework displays and a jousting tournament. *(See pp26–9 for more on fiestas and holidays).*

THE ARTS

The islands have long been a draw for artists. Frédéric Chopin came to Valldemossa on Mallorca, though the weather was far from ideal (one of his Mallorcan compositions was the *Raindrops Prelude*). The picturesque Mallorcan village of Deià was for many years the home of the English writer Robert Graves, whose guests included Pablo Picasso and the actors Alec Guinness and Peter Ustinov. The most famous artist associated with Mallorca, however, is Joan Miró, whose works can be seen in the Fundació Pilar i Joan Miró, on the outskirts of Palma.

SPORTS

The archipelago is famous for its water sports, particularly the many races held on the waters of the Badia de Palma. The most important of these are held under the patronage and with the participation of King Juan Carlos I. They are attended by leading members of the yachting world. The big events, including the King's Cup and Queen Sofia's Cup, are celebrated as public holidays.

Sun-worshippers on the beach in Son Xoriguer, Menorca

King Juan Carlos, a frequent visitor to the Balearics

Bullfights *(corridas)*, popular in mainland Spain, enjoy more limited popularity in the Balearics. A bullfight can be seen in one of the arenas in Mallorca, but the standard of shows is not high.

The true local passion is *fútbol* (football). Real Mallorca, based in Palma, is one of the leading Spanish sides and won the 1998 Spanish Cup. It is worth attending a match, not just as a sporting event but to enjoy the good-natured enthusiasm of the crowd.

Banner advertising a hippy market

Other sports strongly associated with the islands include yachting, windsurfing, horse riding and golf. Excellent golfing conditions exist in the islands, even in winter.

PRESENT-DAY BALEARICS

Once removed from the mainstream of international life, the Balearic Islands have now found themselves drawn in, thanks to tourism. Before World War I, they were visited by the English King Edward VII and the German Emperor Wilhelm II. This high-society tourism reached its peak in the 1930s, when the poet Adam Diehl built the luxurious Hotel Formentor on Pollença Bay. In the 1960s, Ibiza was "discovered" by hippies. Soon after, charter flights began operating to Mallorca. Mass tourism developed rapidly after the death of General Franco in 1975.

In 1983, the islands became an autonomous region of Spain. The authorities made Catalan and its local dialects (*Mallorquín* on Mallorca, *Menorquín* on Menorca and *Eivissenc* on Ibiza) the joint official language with Spanish and introduced strict control of the local economy.

Following a string of environmental protest marches in 1998 and 1999 an "eco-tax" was introduced in 2002. The tax, levied on visitors to the islands, was intended to tackle some of the environmental havoc that had been wreaked by unregulated tourism over the last 30 years. In its first year the tax's benefits included funding the demolishing of a number of unsightly hotels. The "eco-tax" was always controversial, however, and the government finally decided to scrap it in 2003.

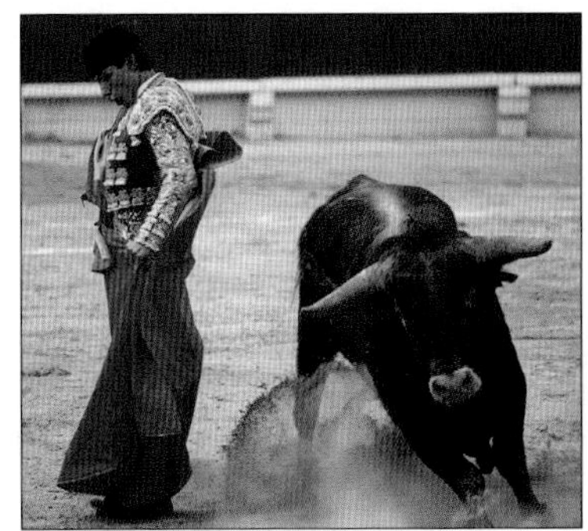

Bullfight in the Mallorcan arena

Architecture of the Balearic Islands

The Balearic Islands boast a rich and diverse architectural heritage. The sights worth seeing range from prehistoric chamber tombs to magnificent aristocratic mansions and palaces. Palma has the most to see, notably the fine Gothic cathedral which was renovated by Antoni Gaudí, while Menorca has many remains from the Talayotic period. Ibiza's houses, influenced by the Arabs, have inspired some of the greatest architects of the 20th century including Le Corbusier and Walter Gropius.

Main entrance to a residence in Els Calders in Mallorca

COUNTRY HOUSES

The typical village landscape is marked by low, often whitewashed houses. Built of the local stone, many have aged to a yellow-brown colour, blending with their surroundings. Thick walls and few openings ensure that the interior stays cool even on the hottest days. A farmstead often also includes some modest outbuildings; the whole surrounded by a garden and fields.

More modest homes *are often adjoined by farm buildings, with a small granary on top. Village houses are almost always single-storey dwellings.*

COUNTRY ESTATES

At the centre of each country estate was a fine *hacienda* (or *possessió*). Their owners vied with each other by building ever more extravagant dwellings attesting to their wealth and importance. The interiors were furnished with magnificent furniture and paintings. The accommodation included formal apartments, private rooms and domestic quarters. Some are now let as holiday homes.

Great country houses, *such as La Granja on Mallorca's southwest coast, belonged to wealthy landowning families and were run according to a feudal system.*

VILLAS

This form of architecture appeared on Mallorca in the 19th century. Villas, serving as summer residences, were built in line with the fashion of the day. Their numbers rose with the increasing popularity of the island.

Modern villas *are often owned by the rich and famous. They stand in beautiful, secluded spots on many of the islands.*

Old villas, *with their delightful architecture, can be seen in many large town centres and in seaside resorts on Mallorca.*

CHURCHES

Whitewashed churches are typical of Ibiza, although they can also be seen on Menorca and Formentera. Often they stand at the centre of the village or on a hillside at its outskirts. The entrance to the dark interior is usually preceded by a triple arcade.

The belfry *on a village church is usually a simple affair. It consists of a distinctive arcade rising above the façade, crowned with an iron cross and housing a bell.*

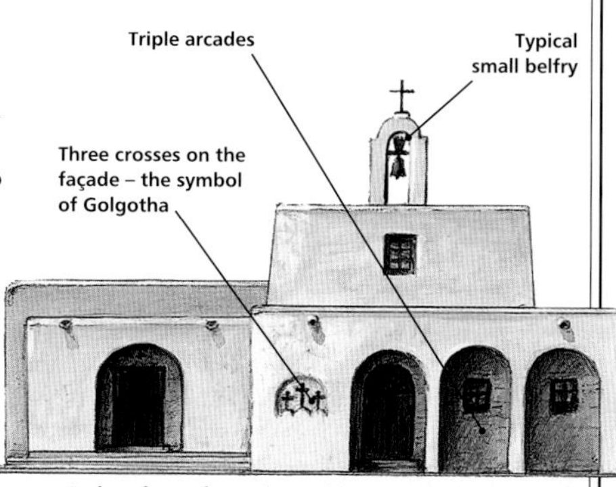

A church *is often adjoined by a single-storey parish building or a vestry. It may be surrounded by a low stone wall and feature an enclosed forecourt.*

WATCH TOWERS

The stone towers that can be seen along the coastline were built to protect the islands from attacks by pirates, mainly from North Africa, who raided the ports and inland towns. The towers stand in secluded, inaccessible spots, so that they could be easily defended. Most of the towers are deserted, and closed to visitors. A few are used as viewpoints.

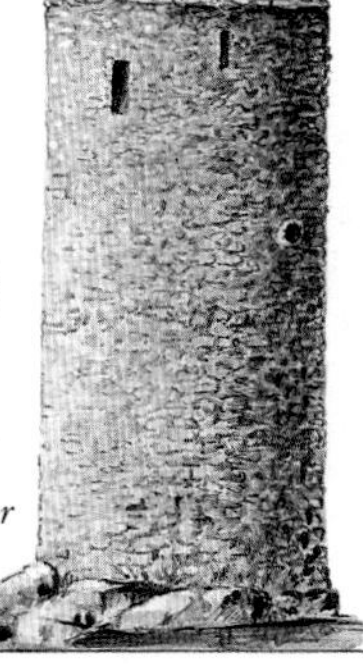

Towers on Mallorca *are slender. For extra protection, their entrances were high above the ground. Their walls feature narrow loop-holes.*

Towers on other islands *are lower. Built of stone, they resemble the fortresses built in the Canary Islands.*

WINDMILLS OF THE BALEARIC ISLANDS

Stone-built windmills are another typical feature of the Balearic landscape. Early mills were used to grind grain; later they were used to pump water. Most stone-built mills are no longer in use and are slowly falling into disrepair. Some have lost their sails, and they now resemble watchtowers. Others have been converted into restaurants, with the machinery and millstones serving as tourist attractions.

Windmills *were built mostly on the plains among green fields, and were used to grind corn or to drive the pumps of deep-water wells. Because they are cheaper to run than petrol-driven pumps, some farmers still use wind power to pump water even today.*

Typical windmills *were built near towns with food markets, and were used for grinding grain. Often the miller would actually live in the tower.*

Landscape and Wildlife of the Balearic Islands

Lilac crocus flower

Thanks to the huge variety of habitats, from mountains and cliffs to sandy beaches and wide plains, the Balearics have a wide diversity of wildlife including some rare birds and reptiles. Mallorca's characteristic terrain is *garrigue*, an open scrubland, interspersed with small pockets of forest. At higher altitudes the scrub is replaced by *maquis* – a mix of mainly rosemary, broom and laurel. Menorca, in particular, is noted for its wild flowers and shrubs while large swathes of Ibiza are covered by forests of pine.

Olive groves *are seen mainly in Mallorca, inland as well as near the coastline. Tree trunks and boughs are sometimes twisted into curious shapes.*

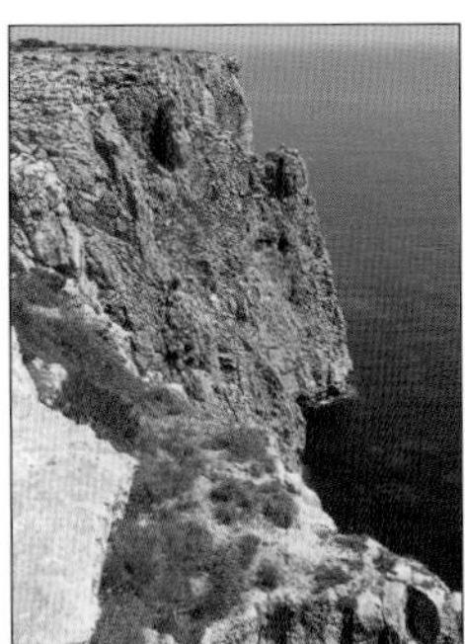

The northern shores *of the islands are mostly steep and craggy. Inland, the vegetation is dense and lush. There are few beaches and those that are accessible are rocky or pebbly. The northern shores have been less affected by tourism, and provide stunning views as well as excellent natural areas to explore.*

The craggy cliffs, sharp-edged and forbidding, appear inaccessible. Consisting of limestone, they are sparsely covered with vegetation.

Forests are rare on the islands. The largest woodland areas can be found in Mallorca. These are mainly pine forests, featuring Aleppo pine mixed with holm oak.

BALEARIC LANDSCAPE

Of all the Balearic Islands, Mallorca's landscape is the most diverse. As well as its many secluded coves, it has magnificent green plains and the Serra de Tramuntana mountain range.

Cove beaches *are one of the features that make the islands so attractive. Some are now resorts. Others can be difficult to reach, but their soft sands, gentle waves and clear water attract a steady flow of visitors.*

High mountains *are found only in the northern part of Mallorca. Puig Major – the highest peak in the Serra de Tramuntana – rises to a height of 1,445 m (4,740 ft).*

Coves with sandy beaches are typical of the Balearic Islands' landscape.

Macchia, an evergreen shrub, grows on the rocky mountain slopes.

FLORA

There are some 1,500 species of flowering plant on the islands, of which 50 or so are native. Some of them grow only in Mallorca and the Cabrera archipelago. Most flower in spring and at this time the islands are a blaze of colour. For the rest of the year, the islands are green, but the sun-bleached foliage is no longer quite so lush.

Common broom *is typical of Mediterranean flora. Its bright yellow flowers, which blossom in March, can be seen from afar.*

Small foxglove, *with its distinctive, thimble-like flower, is a highly ornamental plant. It is one of the plants native to the Balearic Islands. Few people realize that the species is also poisonous.*

Holm oak *is widespread throughout the islands. Its tough, evergreen leaves protect it against water loss.*

FAUNA OF THE BALEARIC ISLANDS

Fauna on the Balearic Islands includes a handful of native species, such as the rare Lilford's wall lizard. The islands are also home to some rare species of birds, including the black vulture, rock falcon and the Balearic shearwater. Several smaller mammals such as rabbits and hedgehogs are commonplace in the lowlands of the archipelago.

Rabbits *have easily adapted to the wide variety of landscapes on the islands, particularly since they have no natural predators.*

The Lilford's wall lizard *is one of the few endemic species living on the islands.*

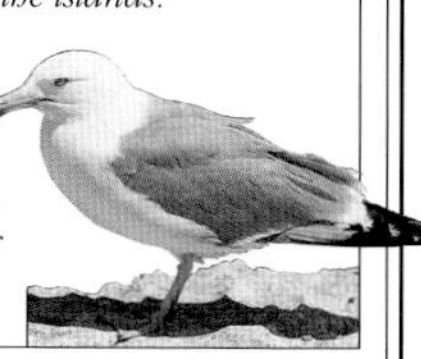

The Silver gull *is the most common bird inhabiting the coastal regions of the archipelago.*

The Underwater World

Some four million years ago, the Balearic archipelago was joined to the continent. The sinking seabed caused the islands to become separated from the mainland by the Balearic Sea. The coastline is topographically varied, featuring sandy beaches with shallows stretching far out into the sea, and cliffs with distinct layers of rock, full of cracks, niches and caves. Facing them, rising up from the sea, are small rocky islands and solitary rocks created by sea abrasion. In the coastal and offshore waters there is a rich variety of marine life.

Cardinal fish *live in small shoals. The tiny red fish can be seen mostly among sea grass or hiding near the entrances to underwater caves and grottoes.*

MARINE SPECIES

The waters surrounding the archipelago are too cold for coral reefs. The only variety found here is the soft gorgonia. The sea grass meadows are home to a variety of animals, from lugworms to fish. The rocky sea bed supports the richest variety of life. Here, you will find varieties of molluscs, starfish, lobster and fish – from the smallest goby to the giant grouper.

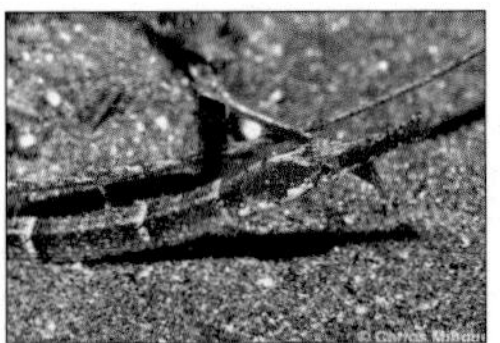

The great pipefish *hides among sea grass. It feeds on small marine animals, including crustaceans and fry, which it sucks in with its long snout. Pipefish eggs hatch inside the male's pouch.*

The cuttle-fish *is a predator that uses its long tentacles to catch its prey. It hunts while swimming or lying buried in the sand, almost invisible to its victim. The cuttle-fish can change its colour to blend in with the background. When threatened, it ejects an inky fluid that disorientates the attacker.*

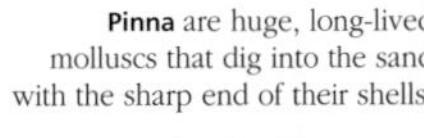

Pinna are huge, long-lived molluscs that dig into the sand with the sharp end of their shells.

Starfish *inhabit the coastal regions of the Balearic Islands, up to a depth of 35 m (115 ft). They live mainly on the rocky bottom, and are conspicuous by their red colour.*

The Lilford's wall lizard *can be seen everywhere, even close to beaches, in dry, sunny places. There are 22 known subspecies, which are spread throughout the archipelago.*

The Balearic shearwater, *also known as the "Moresque shearwater", is a common sight. It gathers food by sitting on the water and catching crustaceans, squid and small fish. The shearwater is native to the Balearic Islands and nests in large colonies.*

The Mediterranean monk seal was once a common sight in the archipelago but is now almost extinct.

Red clingfish *have no scales and attach themselves to the surfaces of rocks with a sucker situated between their ventral fins.*

The Haliotis clam prefers rocky bottoms close to the shore. This primitive snail is highly valued by gourmets.

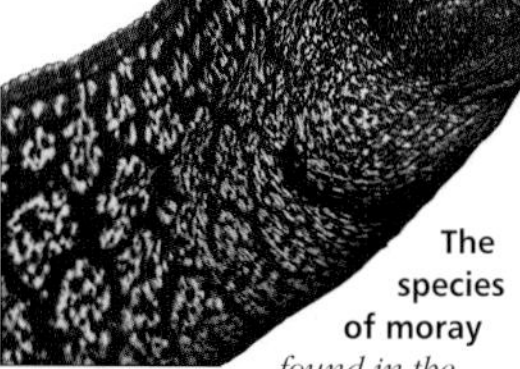

The species of moray *found in the Mediterranean has no venom, but its bite can be dangerous. Hidden amid rocks, it springs surprise attacks, feeding on fish and crustaceans.*

Mediterranean scallop

Gorgonia

Link wrasse

Amarela

The slipper lobster *is not as common as the cicada lobster, which is twice its size. Its body is covered with a hard shell and is armed with spikes, while its antennae have evolved into short, wide plates.*

The Dusky grouper *is, despite its fearsome size, a gentle fish. Because of this, and its sheer bulk, it presents an easy target for spear-fishing.*

THE BALEARIC ISLANDS THROUGH THE YEAR

The inhabitants of the Balearic Islands are deeply attached to their traditions, a fact that is reflected in the many religious feast days, or fiestas, they celebrate. Fiestas are generally associated with the cult of saints, particularly the patron of the local parish or the island. Though mostly religious, fiestas are an opportunity for people to enjoy themselves, with parades, music and much dancing. The most spectacular of these is the Festa de Sant Joan, which has been celebrated in Ciutadella, Menorca, since medieval times. In the resorts, fiestas are less conspicuous, but elsewhere everybody joins in the fun. During the fiesta, normal life stops and only minimal bus services run. It is also difficult to find hotel accommodation, so book in advance. Tourist information offices can provide details of local fiestas.

Children enjoying a fiesta in Mallorca

Almond blossom in early spring in Mallorca

SPRING

With the advent of spring, life in Spain moves out into the streets, and the café terraces fill with guests. This is a very beautiful time of year. Before the arrival of the summer heat, trees, flowers and wild herbs burst into flower. The famous Semana Santa (Holy Week) before Easter is a time of religious processions.

MARCH

Semana Santa
On Maundy Thursday in Palma, a procession leaves the church of La Sang at Plaça de Hospital, carrying a crucifix. On Good Friday, solemn processions are held in many towns, including Palma and Sineu (Mallorca) and Maó (Menorca). The sombre ceremony of laying in the tomb *(Davallament)* is held at the church of Nostra Senyora del Àngels, in Pollença. In Monastir de Lluc the faithful conduct a penitential Way of the Cross.

APRIL

Festa Sant Francesc *(2 Apr).* The popular feast of St Francis is celebrated throughout the islands, in parishes of which the saint is the patron.
Princess Sofia Trophy *(1st fortnight)*, Palma. One of the most important yachting regattas in the Balearics.
Festa Sant Jordi *(23 Apr).* Feast day of the patron saint of many towns and villages, celebrated on all the islands.

MAY

Festa de Maig *(1st Sun in May),* Santa Eulàlia, Ibiza. This springtime flower festival is one of the most colourful and beautiful fiestas in the Balearic Islands.
Festa de Nostra Senyora de la Victòria *(2nd Sun in May),* Sóller and Port de Sóller, Mallorca. Mock battles pit Christian against Moor, and are staged to mark the raid by Turkish pirates, on 11 May 1561.
Eivissa Medieval *(2nd Sun in May),* Eivissa, Ibiza. A new festival to celebrate the declaration of Dalt Vila as a World Heritage site in 1999 with dancing and concerts.
Festa de Primavera de Manacor *(27 May)*, Manacor. Spring Festival, the most important festival in Manacor, lasting until early June.

Princess Sofia Cup yachting regatta

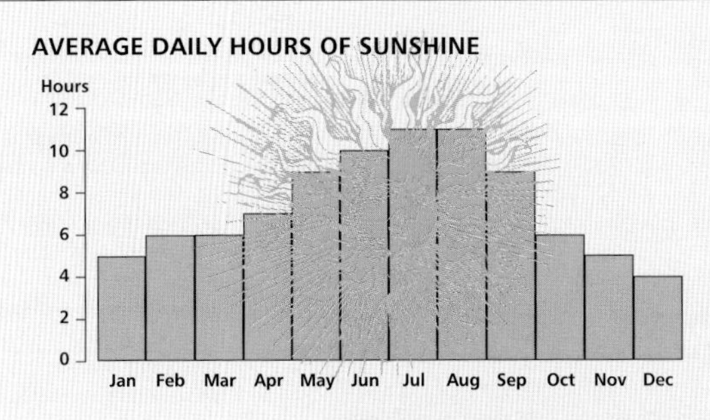

Hours of Sunshine
During July and August, there are nearly 11 hours of sunshine daily. Not surprisingly, these months coincide with the peak of the tourist season. Fewer sunny days occur in November, December and January. At this time of the year the islands are at their least attractive.

SUMMER

June marks the beginning of the peak tourist season in the Balearic Islands, which will last until September. It is ushered in by numerous cultural events, including concerts, festivals and folk group performances. The latter half of summer features various fiestas associated with gathering the harvest.

Beaches of Cala Millor, in Mallorca, crowded with holidaymakers

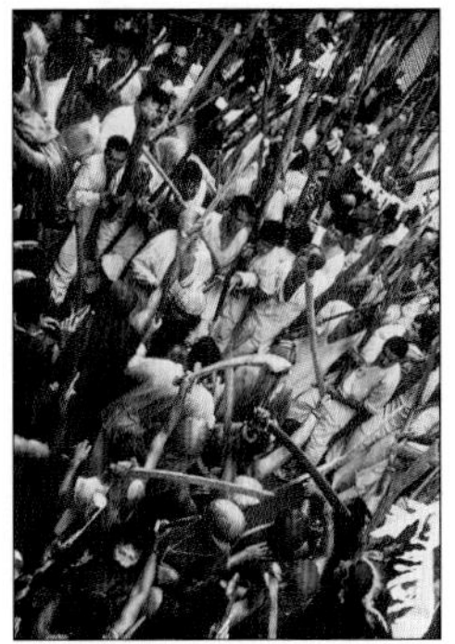
Festa de Nostra Senyora de la Victòria in Sóller

JUNE

Corpus Christi, Pollença, Mallorca. The Dance of Eagles, performed in the main square of the town, is followed by a procession.
Sant Antoni de Juny *(13 Jun),* Artà, Mallorca. A local feast featuring parades of people dressed as horses.
Sant Joan *(24 Jun),* Ciutadella, Menorca. King Juan Carlos's name day. Horses are a major feature. At its climax the horses rear up and the crowd attempts to support them.
Romeria de Sant Marçal *(30 Jun),* Sa Cabeneta, Mallorca. A fair where they sell *siurells.* Similar fairs are also held in Campos, Sineu, Felanitx and Manacor.

JULY

Día de Virgen de Carmen *(15–16 Jul).* The feast of the patron saint of sailors and fishermen, celebrated all over the islands with parades and a blessing of the fishing boats.
Passejada díes Bou i Carro Triunfal *(27–28 Jul),* Valldemossa, Mallorca. The feast of Catalina Thomàs. A bull is led through the streets of this small town, followed the next day by a procession of carts, with one girl playing the role of St Catalina.

AUGUST

Copa del Rey *(1st wk in Aug),* Palma, Mallorca. International yachting regattas held under the patronage of King Juan Carlos.
Sant Ciriac *(8 Aug),* Ibiza, Formentera. A feast held to commemorate the Spanish recapture of these islands.
Festa de Sant Lorenç *(2nd wk in Aug),* Alaior, Menorca. Riding displays in the streets.
Assumption of the Virgin *(15 Aug).* A festival celebrated throughout Spain.
Sant Bartomeu *(24 Aug).* Horse races in Capdepera; devil dances in Montuïri.
Sant Agustín *(28 Aug)* Felanitx, Mallorca. A joyful fiesta in honour of St Augustine, with dancing and horse-riding shows.

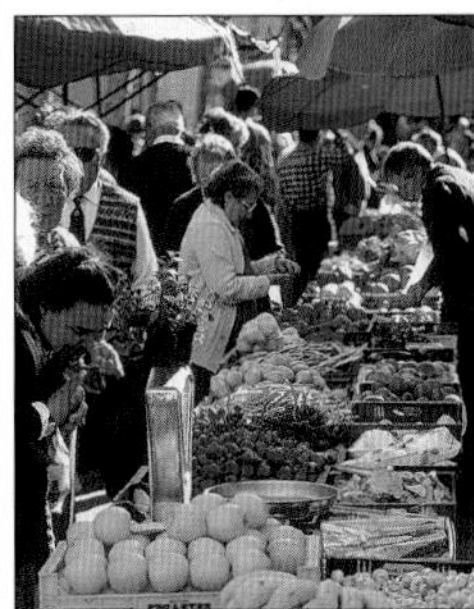
Busy fruit stalls at Pollença market in Mallorca

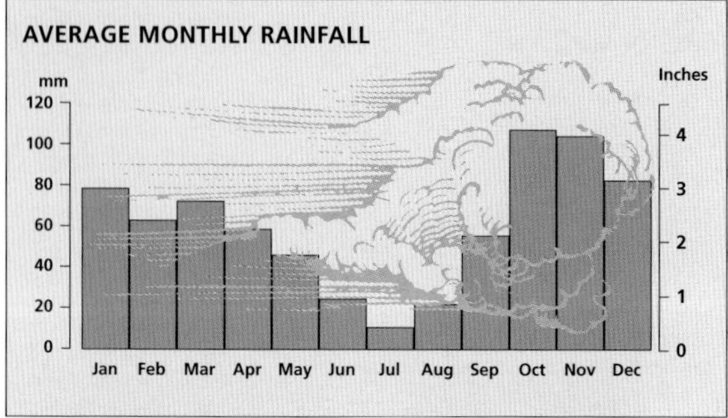

Rainfall
The lowest rainfall is in July; the highest between October and December. Storms are rare in the summer. Visitors should bear in mind that in the mountainous regions clouds may be thicker and rain more frequent than in the coastal areas.

Procession with crops, during Festa des Vermar in Binissalem

AUTUMN

After the summer scorchers, autumn days bring cool air and rain. With the passing of the peak holiday season, the resorts empty out. Harvest fiestas continue and the wine festivals come to the fore, particularly in Binissalem, Mallorca. The first juice extracted from the grape harvest is blessed and in some places wine is served free.

SEPTEMBER

Processió de la Beata *(1st Sun in Sep)*, Santa Margalida, Mallorca. A procession of colourful floats and people dressed in folk costumes honouring Sant Catalina – known as *beata* – the blessed one.
Diada de Mallorca *(12 Sep)*. Commemorates the signing of the Majorcan Statute of Rights by King Jaume II in 1276, with concerts, conferences and sporting events at sea and in the mountains.
Festa des Vermar *(last Sun in Sep)*, Binissalem, Mallorca. A grape-harvest festival with floats and open-air concerts.
Festa des Meló *(last Sun in Sep)*, Vilafranca de Bonany, Mallorca. Watermelon Festival, marking the end of harvest.

OCTOBER

Día de la Hispanidad *(12 Oct)*. Spanish National Holiday celebrating the discovery of the "New World" by Christopher Columbus, in 1492.

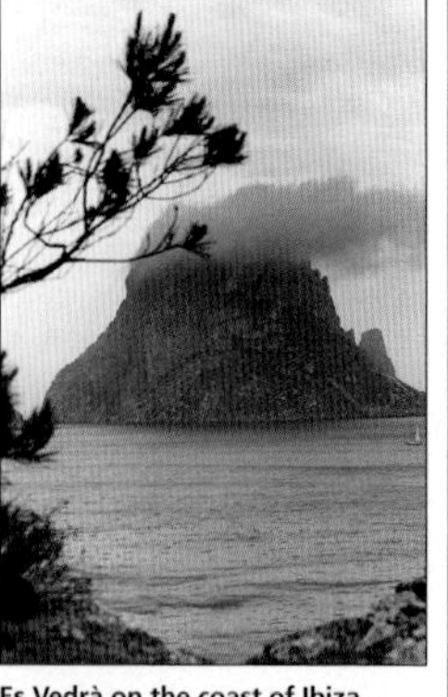
Es Vedrà on the coast of Ibiza, shrouded in clouds

La Beateta *(16 Oct)*. Fancy-dress procession in Palma. Fairs in Alcúdia, Campos, Felanitx, Porreres and Llucmajor. Raft races in Porto Portals.
Festa de Les Verges *(21 Oct)*, Palma. Festival where enormous quantities of *buñelos de vientyo* cakes are consumed and young people sing serenades in honour of Santa Ursula and the 11,000 virgins.
Festa d'Es Botifarró *(3rd Sun in Oct)*, Sant Joan, Mallorca. This fairly recent festival includes dancing and music to accompany the eating of large amounts of sausages *(berenada de butifarra)* and vegetable pies *(coca amb trampó)*.

NOVEMBER

Todos los Santos *(1 Nov)*. All Saints' Day and the following day – *Día dels difunts* (All Souls) – are a time when people visit the graves of relatives and friends.
Sant Carles *(4 Nov)*, Ibiza. Patron saint's day, celebrated throughout the island.
Dijous Bo *(3rd Thu in Nov)*, Inca, Mallorca. Important agricultural feast in Mallorca, featuring fairs and revelry.
Birthday of Junipero Serra *(24 Nov)*. Celebrated throughout the archipelago as the birthday of this Franciscan monk who founded the cities of San Diego, Los Angeles and San Francisco *(see p77)*.

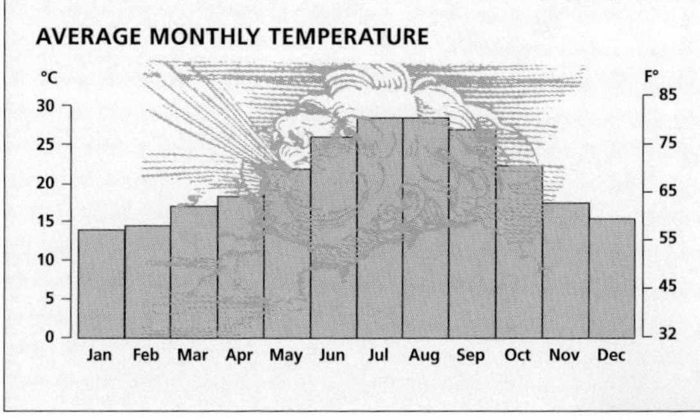

Temperature
Temperatures in the Balearic Islands rarely fall below zero. This happens only occasionally in December and early January. For this reason, many people enjoy out-of-season visits. Summer temperatures may soar to 40° C (104° F).

WINTER

The Balearic winter is not particularly severe. Nights are cold, but days are often sunny and mild. Christmas is a time of special celebration throughout Spain, with families gathering to participate in religious festivities.

Working in the fields during early spring

DECEMBER

Noche Buena *(24 Dec).* Christmas Eve is celebrated within the family circle, and often includes midnight mass. Numerous nativity plays and scenes are organized in Palma.
Santos Inocentes *(28 Dec).* The Spanish equivalent of Britain's April Fool's day.
Festa de l'Estandard *(31 Dec),* Palma, Mallorca. Feast commemorating the town's conquest by Jaume I, in 1229.

JANUARY

Revetlla i Beneides de Sant Antoni Abat *(16–17 Jan),* Mallorca. Fiesta with bonfires, parades and the blessing of animals. People wander between the bonfires, dressed in costumes, dancing and consuming large quantities of eel and vegetable pies.
Processo dels Tres Tocs *(17 Jan),* Ciutadella, Menorca. The Procession of the Three Strikes marks the victory of Alfonso III over the Muslims, in 1287.
Festa de Sant Sebastià *(20 Jan),* Pollença, Mallorca. Procession carrying a banner with the image of the saint and with two dancers, called *cavallets*, mounting wooden horses.

FEBRUARY

Carnival Parades *(Feb/Mar).* Fancy dress balls marking the end of Carnival, before Lent. The most spectacular fiesta, called *Sa Rua* (the Cavalcade), takes place in Palma and its surrounding resorts.

Carnival in Palma, Mallorca

PUBLIC HOLIDAYS

Año Nuevo *New Year's Day (1 Jan)*
Día de Reyes *Epiphany (6 Jan)*
Jueves Santo *Maundy Thursday (Mar/Apr)*
Viernes Santo *Good Friday (Mar/Apr)*
Día de Pascua *Easter (Mar/Apr)*
Fiesta de Trabajo *Labour Day (1 May)*
Corpus Christi *(early Jun)*
Asuncíon *Assumption of the Virgin (15 Aug)*
Día de la Hispanidad *National Day (12 Oct)*
Todos los Santos *All Saints' Day (1 Nov)*
Día de la Constitución *Constitution Day (6 Dec)*
Inmaculada Concepción *Immaculate Conception (8 Dec)*
Navidad *Christmas Day (25 Dec)*

Autumn fishing from a traditional Balearic boat

THE HISTORY OF THE BALEARIC ISLANDS

The Balearic Islands were often a target for conquest and this turbulent history has left behind numerous reminders. Consecutive waves of raiders continually destroyed the heritage of their predecessors and it was not until the conquest of the islands by Jaume I, in 1229, that a period of relative stability began. But even the centuries that followed were not a period of calm.

EARLIEST INHABITANTS

The earliest inhabitants of the Balearic Islands probably arrived from the Iberian Peninsula. Archaeological findings indicate that the islands were occupied by 4000 BC. Archaeological remains include flint tools, primitive pottery and artifacts made of horn, giving evidence that these early settlers were shepherds and hunters. As well as herding sheep, the earliest inhabitants of the Balearic Islands hunted the local species of mountain goat *(Myotragus balearicus)*, now extinct. Most archaeological finds were discovered in caves, which were used for shelter and also for ritual burials. The best preserved complex of caves, developed and extended by the Talayotic settlers, are the Cales Coves discovered near Cala en Porter, in Menorca.

The Beaker ware found in Deià, in Mallorca, represents a style known throughout Western Europe. Beaker People are so named because of their custom of placing pottery beakers in graves. The representatives of this culture were capable of producing excellent bronze tools and artifacts. They appeared in the islands around 2300 BC.

Terracotta bust dating from the Punic era

TALAYOTIC PERIOD

The mysterious structures made of giant stones found on the islands date from around 1300 BC. The most typical of the time, which also gave the period its name, is the *talayot* derived from the Arabic word *atalaya* meaning observation tower. These structures appear in greatest numbers in Menorca, with somewhat fewer in Mallorca. None has been found in Ibiza. Other common sights are *taulas* and *navetas* *(see p99)*. In southern Europe similar structures can be found only in Sardinia *(nuraghi)*.

These early inhabitants of the islands represented a relatively advanced civilization. Some of them lived in fortified settlements, such as Capocorb Vell, Mallorca, where over 30 stone houses and four massive *talayots* have been found.

TIMELINE

4000 BC Human occupation well established on the Balearic Islands

2300 BC Beaker culture flourishes in the Iberian Peninsula

1300 BC Beginning of the Talayotic civilization; development of Cales Coves

6000 BC | 4000 BC | 3000 BC | 2000 BC

Around 5000 BC Probable arrival of man can be dated from finds around Sóller and Valldemossa

Arrowhead dating from the Talayotic era

◁ **A painting of Maó harbour, Menorca, in the early 19th century**

Figurine, 5th century BC, from Torralba d'en Salord

PHOENICIANS, GREEKS AND CARTHAGINIANS

The Phoenicians arrived in the islands in the early part of the 1st millennium BC. They founded a trading settlement, Sanisera, on the northern coast of Menorca. Two hundred years later, the islands attracted the attention of the Greeks, who were exploring the western regions of the Mediterranean. The Greeks did not settle in the Balearics, as they lacked the metal ores that would have made the islands suitable for colonization. They were also discouraged by the hostile reception from the local inhabitants. But the archipelago owes its name to the Greeks. It derives from the Greek word *ballein* (to throw from a sling). The islanders were famed as outstanding sling-shots and, more than once, made life a misery for various raiders.

The Carthaginians also took an interest in trade in the western region of the Mediterranean. Carthaginian sailors started to explore the Balearic Islands in the early 7th century BC. In 654, they took Ibiza, where they founded the fortified capital of Eivissa (the famous Carthaginian general, Hannibal, was born on Ibiza). After conquering the entire archipelago, they founded new towns, including Jamna (Ciutadella) and Maghen (Maó) in Menorca.

The Balearic Islands played a strategic role during the Punic Wars. Following their defeat at Zama in 202 BC, the Carthiginians were crushed. Soon afterwards, they left Mallorca and Menorca but remained in Ibiza for a further 70 years.

Clay oil lamp from Roman times

ROMAN EMPIRE AND BYZANTIUM

The Romans conquered Ibiza in 146 BC. Meanwhile, the inhabitants of Mallorca and Menorca, taking advantage of the political upheavals, turned to piracy. This lasted until 123 BC, when the Roman Consul Quintus Metellus occupied the islands. He was awarded the honorary title of *Balearico* for his

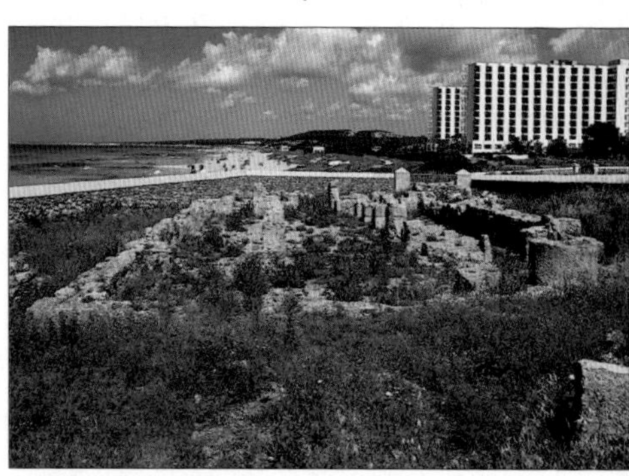

Ruins of the Christian basilica in Son Bou, Menorca

TIMELINE

800 BC Twilight of the Talayotic civilization. Greeks visit the islands

654 BC Carthaginians conquer Ibiza

202 BC Carthagini[…] defeated at Zama

1000 BC | 700 BC | 400 BC | 100 B[…]

Around 1000 BC Phoenician merchants arrive on the islands

146 BC Romans conquer Ibiza

Figurine of the goddess Tanit, 2nd century BC

deeds. Roman rule lasted for over 500 years and the islands were renamed: Balearis Major (Mallorca), Balearis Minor (Menorca) and Ebusus (Ibiza). The *Pax Romana* brought prosperity: Roman settlers planted vineyards, built roads and founded Palmeria and Pollentia, a settlement near Alcúdia in Mallorca. They also founded Portus Magonis (Maó) in Menorca, which subsequently became the island's capital and extended the Phoenician port, Sanisera, making it one of the biggest harbours of the empire.

A mosaic from the Calvià library, Mallorca, showing the conquest of Mallorca by Arabs in 904

By the 3rd century AD, the expansion of Christianity had begun on the islands. Roman rule was already in decline when, in 425, the Vandals invaded and destroyed both the Roman and Christian cultural heritages.

Subsequently, the Byzantine army led by Belisarius expelled the Vandal tribes from the Balearic Islands. For over 100 years the islands remained within the sphere of influence of the Byzantine Empire. This ensured their stability until the declining empire came under attack from the Arabs.

THE MOORS

The conquest of Menorca and Mallorca by the Emir of Cordoba at the beginning of the 10th century marks the beginning of Moorish influence over the islands, which lasted for more than three centuries. During this period the Muslims transformed the Balearic Islands, introducing new irrigation techniques, planting crops like rice and cotton and, on terraced hillsides, oranges, limes and olives. In 1114, Muslim rule was interrupted when an army of 70,000 Italian and Catalan soldiers attacked Ibiza and Mallorca. Supported by the pope, the Christian troops slaughtered most of the Muslims and set sail, filling their ships with spoils. The Moors quickly re-established themselves, however, and flourished once again under the rule of the Almoravids, a Berber dynasty from North Africa. Reminders of Moorish presence on the islands include the agricultural terraces, architecture and designs for embroidery and ceramics.

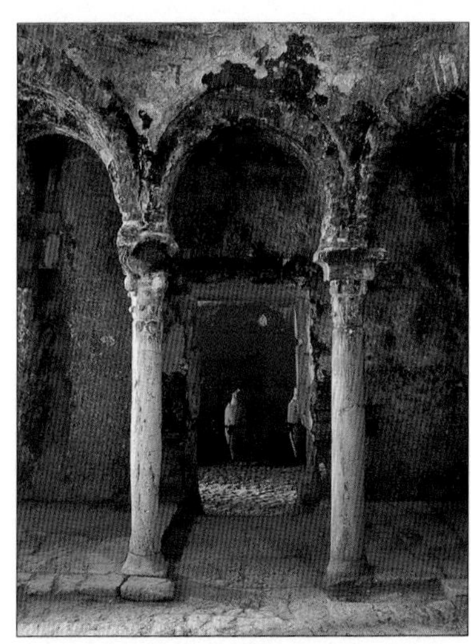

Arab Bath in Palma, one of few surviving relics of Muslim culture on the islands

Sacking of Pollentia by Vandals

707 First raids by the Arabs

798 Raid by Moorish pirates

1085 Islands gain the status of caliphate ruled by the Almoravids

AD 200 | 500 | 800 | 1100

426 Vandal invasion

533 Beginning of Byzantine rule over the archipelago

859 Vikings raid the islands

902 Mallorca becomes a member of the Cordoba Caliphate

1114 Mallorca invaded, unsuccessfully, by Christian army – "Small Crusade"

JAUME I

In September 1229, on the beach near Santa Ponça, Mallorca, the Catalan King Jaume I, later known as "El Conqueridor", landed with his army, which consisted of 16,000 soldiers and 1,500 cavalry. The pretext for the attack was the seizure of several Catalan vessels by the Emir of Mallorca. In the ensuing battle, Jaume I captured the capital and conquered the entire island. In 1232, he returned to Mallorca with a handful of soldiers. From there he sent delegates to Menorca, who were to negotiate a surrender. Meanwhile, Jaume I built a camp on the mountain slopes near Capdepera. In the evening he ordered numerous bonfires to be lit, to look as though a large army was preparing to attack. The ruse worked and the Moors surrendered Menorca to the king, who left them to rule the island as his vassals.

Cross in Santa Ponça, marking Jaume I's conquest

In 1230, Jaume I had issued the *Carta de Població* (People's Charter), which encouraged Catalans to settle on the conquered islands, granting them exemption from taxes and guaranteeing equality before the law to all its citizens. Special privileges were granted to Jews, in an effort to stimulate trade. After the king's death, his successors fought for the inheritance, which was finally won by Alfonso III.

Miniature with the image of Jaume I

ALFONSO AND HIS SUCCESSORS

Despite being nicknamed "The Liberal", Alfonso III massacred the rebels of Palma and the remaining fortresses after he had conquered them, a bloody deed that led to his excommunication from the Catholic church. Worse was to follow. In 1287, Alfonso III's army attacked and conquered Menorca. The Moslem defenders were sold into slavery or slaughtered. Medina Menurqua was renamed Ciutadella and its mosques turned into churches or destroyed. Following the death of Alfonso III in 1291 at the age of 25, Jaume II took control of Mallorca and Menorca. Jaume II, who had been crowned king of Mallorca and Menorca in 1276 before being deposed by Alfonso III, was an altogether more enlightened ruler. He and his successors presided over a "Golden Age" that saw great advances including the building of the Castell de Bellver and Palau de

TIMELINE

1229 Mallorca captured by the army of Jaume I who is hailed as "El Conqueridor"

1230 Declaration of *Carta de Població* (People's Charter) by Jaume I

1285 Palma conquered by Alfonso III

1200 | 1250 | 1300 | 135

1203 The Almohads assume rule over the archipelago

1233 Ramon Llull, philosopher and theologian, father of the Catalan language, is born in Palma

Statue of Alfonso III by the cathedral in Maó, Menorca

L'Almudaina, the establishment of a weekly market in Palma and the reintroduction of gold and silver coinage to stimulate trade. The next ruler of the archipelago was Jaume II's son, Sancho, who built a strong fleet to defend the islands against pirates. After his death, in 1324, control passed into the hands of his nephew, Jaume III, whose two-decade reign also marked a period of great prosperity. The "Golden Age" came to an abrupt end in 1344 when an Aragonese conquest, led by Pedro IV, landed on Mallorca and took it in only a week. The islands of Menorca and Ibiza soon suffered the same fate.

Painting of Saint George slaying the dragon, by Francesca Comesa

DECLINE AND FALL

Now part of the kingdom of Aragón, the Balearic Islands found themselves to be outside major politics. The economy soon suffered as a result of high taxes and in 1391 Mallorca was the scene of an uprising by the poorest parts of the community. In Menorca, the rivalry between Ciutadella and Maó ended in armed conflict. The economic position of the Balearic Islands was worsened further by the discovery and colonization of the Americas at the end of the 15th century, which shifted the hub of European trade to the shores of the Atlantic Ocean. This downturn led, in 1521, to a bloody revolt by peasants and craftsmen in Mallorca, which ended in the slaughter of many of the nobility and their supporters.

Throughout the 16th and 17th centuries, there were frequent pirate attacks. Many of the islands' fortifications date from this period including Eivissa's surviving defences and Maó's Fort San Felipe.

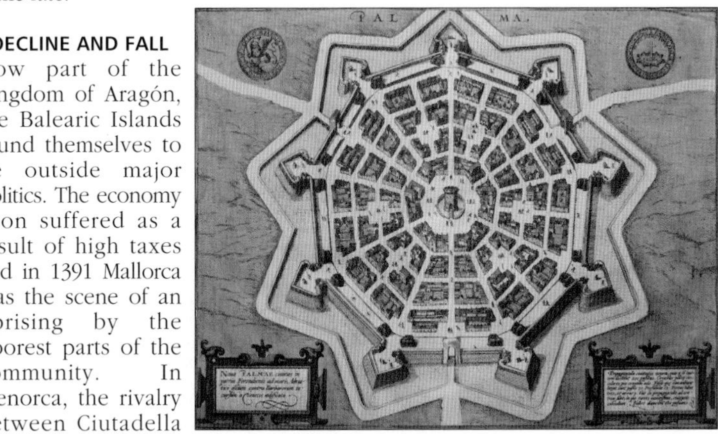

Ideal fortification layout of 16th-century Palma

Gothic rosette from a museum in Palma, Mallorca

1521 Armed insurrection of peasants and craftsmen

1531-1558 Devastating raids by Turkish pirates

1400 | 1450 | 1500 | 1550

1391 Insurrection of the poor in Mallorca

1479 Unification of Aragón and Castile

Barbarossa, the conqueror of Maó in 1535

Junipero Serra setting up a mission in California

UNDER BRITISH AND FRENCH RULE

During the 17th century, Menorca's harbours became the subject of Anglo-French rivalry. In 1708 the British occupied Maó's harbour, and subsequently the whole of Menorca. In 1756, the island was captured by the French, although they soon returned it to the British, in 1763, in exchange for Cuba and the Philippines. The government of the island changed hands several more times until, finally, in 1802, Menorca was handed over to Spain. The town of Sant Lluís, founded by the French, stands as a reminder of French rule.

The British colonial legacy on Menorca includes the building of the garrison town of Georgetown (now known as Villacarlos) and major improvements to the roads. The choice of Maó as Menorca's capital is thanks to the British governor, Richard Kane. Reminders of Georgian architecture, including the sash windows in Hanover Street, Maó, can still be seen today.

Composer Frédéric Chopin

THE 19TH CENTURY

The 19th century proved extremely difficult for the islands. The inhabitants were plagued by periods of famine and epidemics, Spanish was declared the official language, and many inhabitants of the Balearic Islands decided to emigrate. During the 19th century the islands acquired scheduled links with Barcelona and Valencia and the situation began to improve. In 1838, Chopin visited Mallorca and in 1867 Archduke Ludwig Salvator *(see p68)* settled here. At the same time, the development of agriculture, particularly almond-growing in Mallorca, and footwear production in Menorca, led to a rise in the standard of living. Catalan culture was also becoming popular and *Modernista* buildings, including designs by Antoni Gaudí, began to appear in Palma and other town centres.

FRANCO'S DICTATORSHIP

During the Spanish Civil War (1936–39), which originated in Morocco, the Balearic Islands were

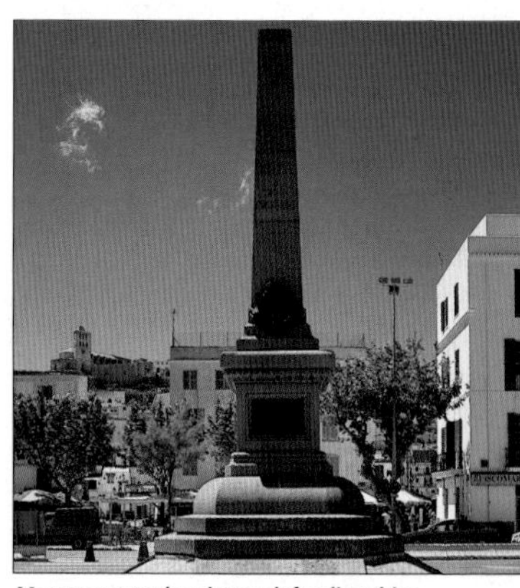

Monument to the pirates defending Ibiza

TIMELINE

1652 Islands devastated by horrific plague

1713 Junipero Serra born in the small town of Petra, in Mallorca

1756 Menorca conqu by the French

1600 | 1660 | 1720 | 178

1708 Menorca conquered by the British

1763 British regain Menorca

1802 M pass the ha the S

Baroque stone tablet from 1672

divided. Mallorca became an important base for the Fascists, while Menorca and Ibiza declared themselves for the Republicans. In retaliation, Italian planes bombed Ibiza. Menorca was the last stronghold of the Republicans. Following a peace deal, negotiated with the help of the British, 450 refugees left the island aboard *HMS Devonshire*, and the island was left under the control of Franco. Formentera, which had backed the Republicans, became the site of a concentration camp established by the Fascists, where some 1,400 people were imprisoned. Throughout the entire 40 years of Franco's dictatorship, the Catalan language and culture were suppressed, as elsewhere on the mainland.

Ionument at Monte Toro for hose killed in Morocco in 1925

MODERN TIMES

After Franco's death in 1975, a process of decentralization began. In 1983, the inhabitants of the islands succeeded in creating the Comunidad Autónoma de las Islas Baleares, and the islands became an autonomous region. This led to the introduction of Catalan in schools and offices and greater control of the local economy. Most of the money earned by the islands now remains here and is reinvested locally.

Initially, the most important factor driving the local economy was tourism. Where the hippies led, others followed. In 1966 Mallorca received one million tourists. By 2000 this number had grown to eight million and the islands, so poor until fairly recently, now boast the highest income per capita in the whole of Spain. This economic achievement has come at a price. Large numbers of foreigners, mainly German and British, have settled here, pushing up the cost of real estate, while the construction of a number of poor quality resorts has left a blot on the islands' otherwise idyllic landscape. Many jobs on the islands are now seasonal and there has been a general decline in traditional forms of employment. Factors such as these gave rise to a growing environmental movement and the introduction of an "eco tax" *(see p19)*, designed to sustain the islands' tourism. The tax was scrapped in 2003.

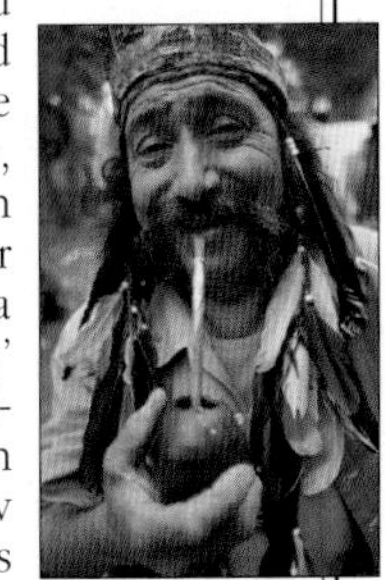

Hippy in colourful head gear

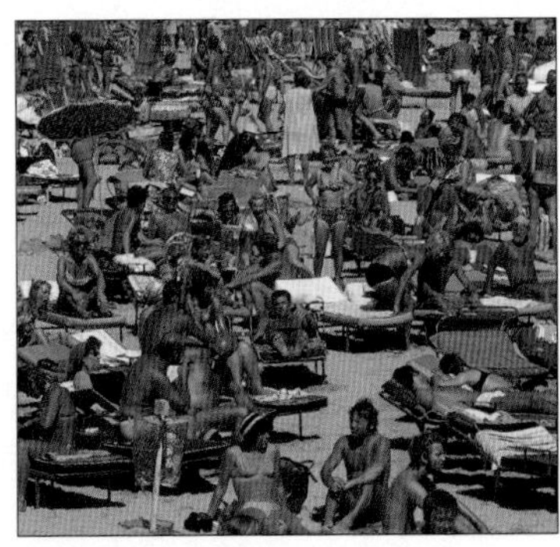

Mallorcan beaches filled with tourists

Archduke wig Salvator

1926 Argentinian poet Adan Diehl opens the Hotel Formentor

1975 Death of General Francisco Franco

1983 Creation of the Autonomous Community of the Balearic Islands

1840 | 1900 | 1960 | 2020

1867 Mallorca visited by Habsburg Archduke wig Salvator, subsequent promoter of the island

1936-1939 Spanish Civil War

1950 The first charter plane, from Germany, lands in Mallorca

Tourists in a hotel bar

THE BALEARIC ISLANDS AREA BY AREA

The Balearic Islands at a Glance

The hot climate, cooling sea breezes, lively resorts and excellent beaches make the Balearic Islands an ideal holiday destination. Those who want to rave choose Ibiza, with its frenetic clubs and all-night entertainment. Those who prefer a more sedate holiday can find peace and quiet on all the islands, where charming little towns and miles of empty trails are perfect for walking, riding and cycling. Mallorca's caves and grottoes can provide interesting exploration while Menorca's prehistoric structures offer a fascinating glimpse into life on the islands many thousands of years ago.

Palma *is the capital of Mallorca and of the Balearic Islands. Full of historic sights and throbbing with life, it is the archipelago's finest city.*

Cala Bassa's *Blue Flag beach is typical of Ibiza's beaches. Small, with fine, golden sand, it is hidden in a sheltered cove.*

Santa Eulària des Riu *is one of the loveliest resort towns in Ibiza. It has good restaurants and bars, plenty of shopping and a beautiful beach.*

FORMENTERA
(see pp132–139)

Platja Migjorn *is a narrow sandy beach, stretching over 5 km (3 miles) along the southern coast of Formentera. It is always possible to find an isolated spot.*

0 km 20

0 miles 20

◁ **Dawn over yachting marina in Port de Pollença in Mallorca**

Cap de Cavalleria *is the northernmost point of the Balearic Islands and one of Menorca's wildest regions. The road to the lighthouse on the headland runs through an undulating area. The steep cliffs here provide a nesting ground for a number of sea birds including the sea eagle and kite.*

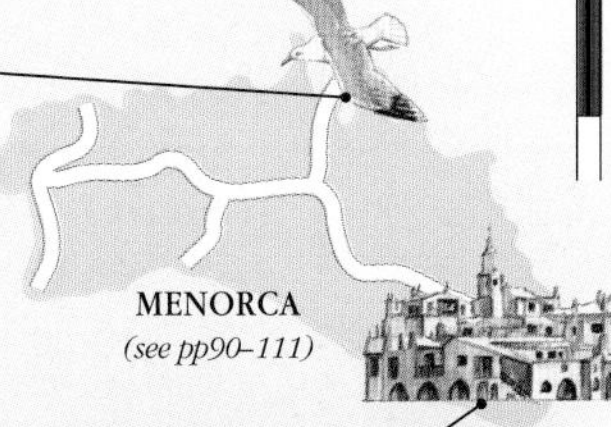

MALLORCA
(see pp42–89)

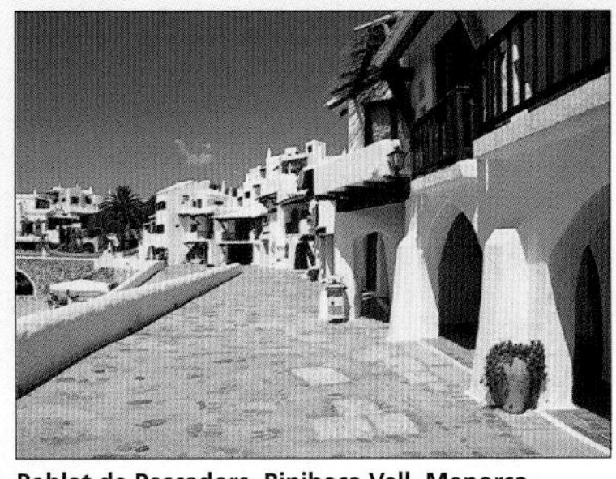

Poblat de Pescadors, Binibeca Vell, Menorca, *with its distinctive development of white houses, was purpose-built for holidaymakers to resemble a Mediterranean fishing village.*

Aqualand El Arenal, *in S'Arenal near Palma, is one of several water parks in Mallorca. With pools, water flumes and plenty of space, it provides a fun day out for the children.*

Cap de Formentor *is Mallorca's northernmost peninsula. It makes a good destination for a day-long excursion during which you can take in the cliff-top views or swim in one of the coves below. At the very tip of the peninsula is a lighthouse, which also serves at a viewing point.*

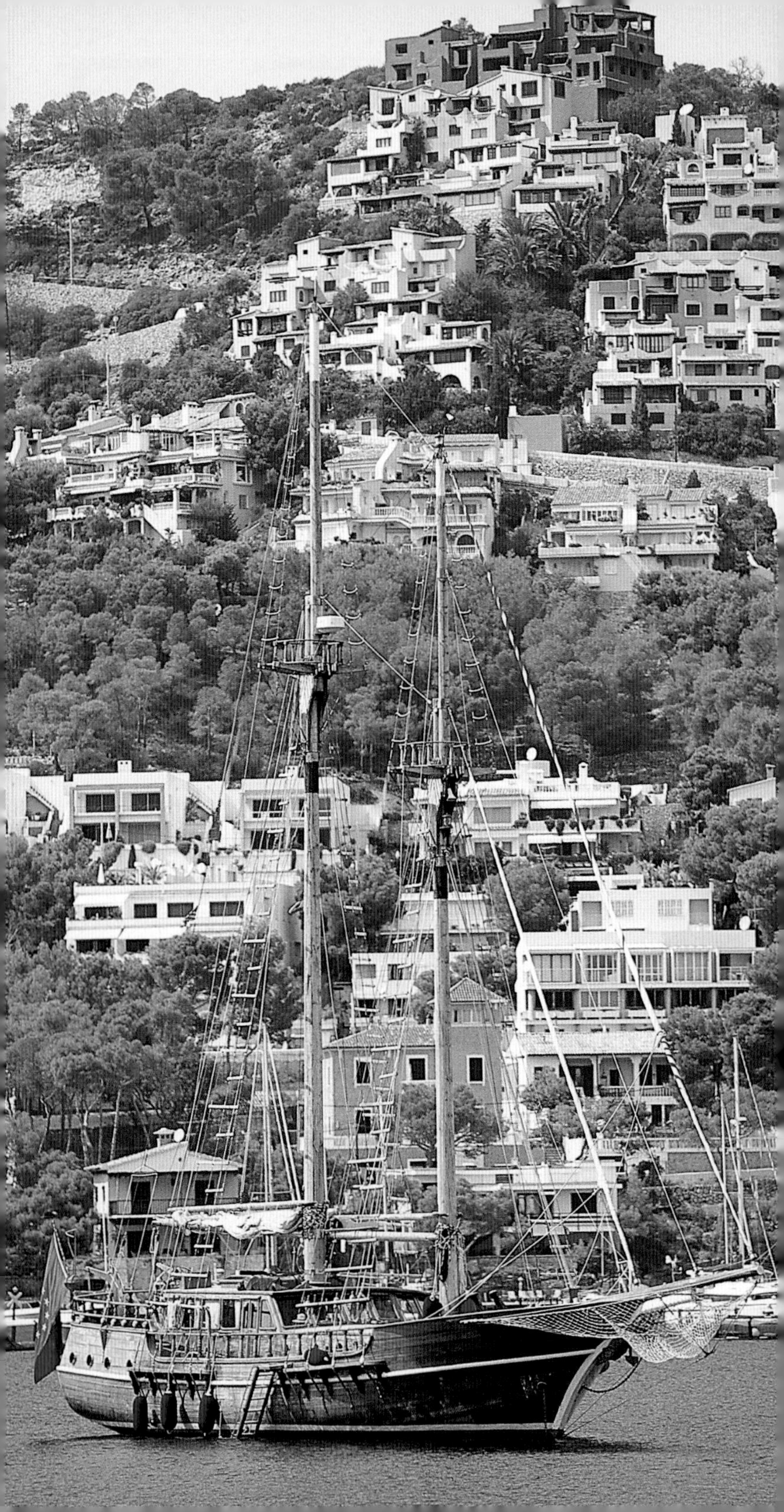

MALLORCA

Mallorca's landscape is incredibly diverse for such a small island, ranging from the fertile lowlands of the central region to the high peaks of the Serra de Tramuntana. Its warm climate, fine beaches and historic capital, Palma, make it one of the main European holiday centres. Venture away from the resorts and you also find picturesque inland villages, pine forests and peaceful coves.

With an area of 3,640 sq km (1,405 sq miles), and a population of around 846,000, of which nearly half live in Palma, Mallorca is the largest island of the Balearic archipelago. Consisting mainly of limestone, the terrain has a large number of cave systems, particularly in the wild central region of the Serra de Tramuntana and on the east coast. Some of these, such as the Coves d'Artà, can be visited as part of a guided tour. Elsewhere on the island, there is much to enjoy from stunning nature reserves and charming fishing villages to picturesque ruins and impressive country estates.

Wind-powered water pump

The climate here is typically Mediterranean, with dry summers and up to 650 mm (26 inches) of rainfall during the autumn-winter season. Cold winters are rare. The island has unique flora and fauna, with a wide variety of birds. Native species of flowers and flowering shrubs are also much in evidence though the cultivation of fields, vineyards and olive groves has partly displaced the natural vegetation.

The island has been known since ancient times and traces of Roman and Arab civilizations can still be seen. Once an independent kingdom, Mallorca became part of Aragón in the 14th century, and was later incorporated into Spain. Since 1983, the Balearic Islands have been an autonomous region of Spain.

Much of the island is virtually untouched by tourism. Mallorca offers wonderful beaches and nightlife for visitors who want a lively holiday, and rural retreats, peaceful coves and historic ruins for those seeking quiet.

Crowded beach in Cala Millor, the destination for many sun-seeking visitors

◁ Yacht moored in the shelter of Port d'Andratx, with dwellings rising steeply behind it

Exploring Mallorca

Most visitors to Mallorca come in search of sun and make the most of the nightclubs, discos, waterparks and the plentiful supply of clean beaches. Many also enjoy the historic towns and villages, particularly the winding streets of the island's capital, Palma, which has lots to see and a wide range of shops and restaurants. Visitors looking for the best beaches go to the Badia de Palma region or to the northeastern shores of the island.

LOCATOR MAP

Historic tram in the main square in Sóller

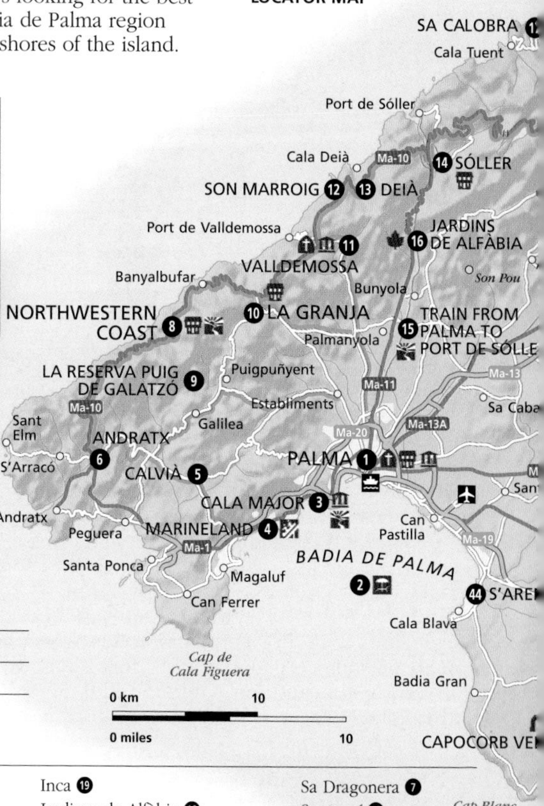

SEE ALSO

- ***Where to Stay*** pp144–50
- ***Where to Eat*** pp159–65

SIGHTS AT A GLANCE

Alcúdia 22
Algaida 43
Andratx 6
Artà 27
Badia de Palma 2
Cabrera Island National Park pp84–5 39
Cala Major 3
Cala Millor 30
Cala Rajada 29
Calvià 5
Cap de Formentor 21
Capocorb Vell 41
Capdepera 28
Colònia de Sant Jordi 38
Deià 13
Felanitx 34
Inca 19
Jardines de Alfàbia 16
La Granja pp64–5 10
La Reserva Puig de Galatzó 9
Llucmajor 40
Manacor 32
Marineland 4
Muro 24
Palma pp46–55 1
Parc Natural Mondragó 36
Parc Natural de S'Albufera 23
Petra 26
Pollença 20
Porto Cristo 31
Puig de Randa 42
S'Arenal 44
Sa Calobra 17
Sa Dragonera 7
Santanyí 35
Santuari de Lluc pp72–3 18
Ses Salines 37
Sineu 25
Sóller 14
Son Marroig 12
Valldemossa 11
Vilafranca de Bonany 33

Tours

Train from Palma to Port Sóller 15
Northwestern Coast of Mallorca pp62–3 8

For additional map symbols *see back flap*

GETTING THERE

Mallorca has air links with Menorca and Ibiza, as well as with many Spanish towns and cities. However, the majority of visitors arrive by chartered flights. Mallorca's airport is 11 km (7 miles) east of Palma. It is also possible to get here by ferry, from one of the Spanish mainland ports. A new high-speed ferry linking Valencia, Ibiza and Palma has reduced the journey time considerably. When travelling around Mallorca, you can use its efficient bus service or the one or two railway lines connecting Palma with Sóller and also with Inca, Sa Pobla and Manacor. However, the best way to explore the island is by car.

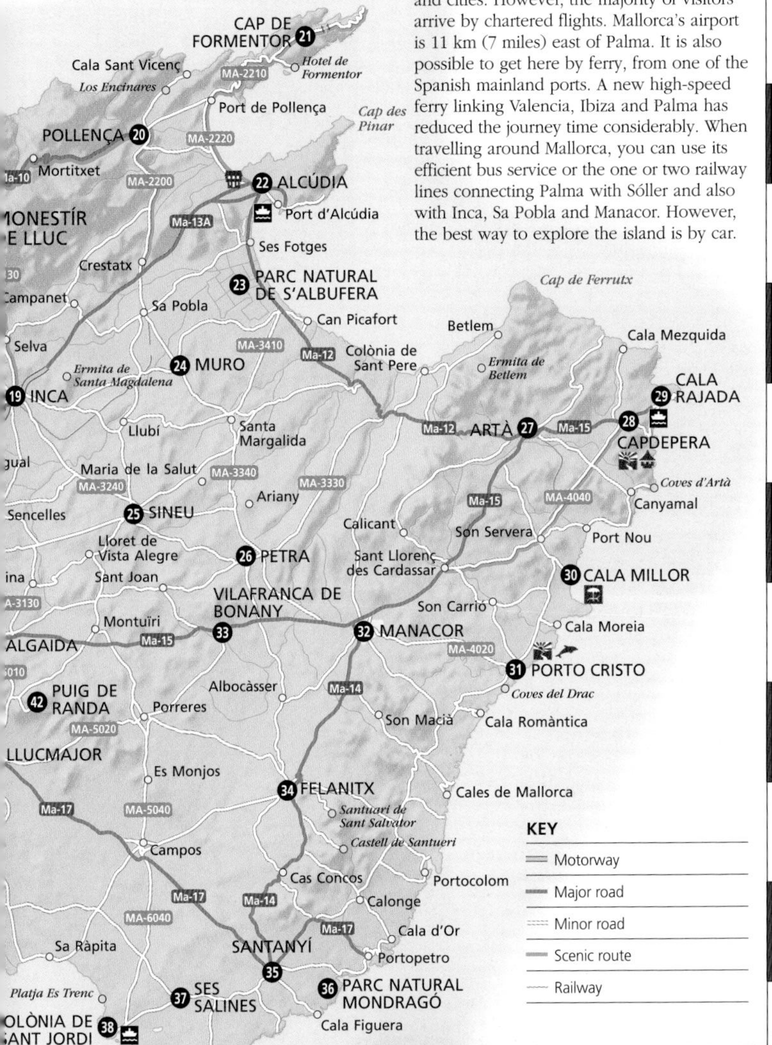

KEY

- Motorway
- Major road
- Minor road
- Scenic route
- Railway

Beach in Palma Nova on the Badia de Palma

Street-by-Street: Palma ❶

In 1983, Palma became the capital of the newly created Autonomous Community of the Balearic Islands and transformed itself from a provincial town into a metropolis. Today, it has over 300,000 inhabitants and captivates all visitors as it once captivated Jaume I, who, after conquering it in 1229 described it as the "loveliest town that I have ever seen". It is pleasant to stroll along the clean, attractive streets past renovated historic buildings. The town and harbour are full of life while bars and restaurants, busy with locals and tourists, remain open late into the night.

Caixa Forum Palma
Built in 1902, this is the most beautiful 20th-century building in Palma. Formerly the Grand Hotel it now houses a cultural centre.

★ Palau de l'Almudaina
This former royal residence was the home of Jaume II and was built after 1309, on the site of an Arab fortress.

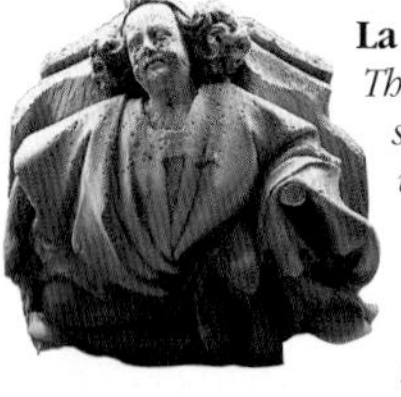

La Llotja
The elevation of this small Gothic building, which once housed the stock exchange, is decorated with magnificent sculptures.

CARRER UNIÓ

PLAÇA REI JOAN CARLES

PASSEIG D'ES BORN

AVINGUDA D'ANTONI MAURA

KEY

 Suggested route

★ Cathedral
The Gothic cathedral, standing near the shore and towering over the town, is built of golden sandstone excavated in Santanyí.

Parc de la Mar

0 m 100

0 yards 100

For hotels and restaurants in this region see pp144–50 and pp159–65

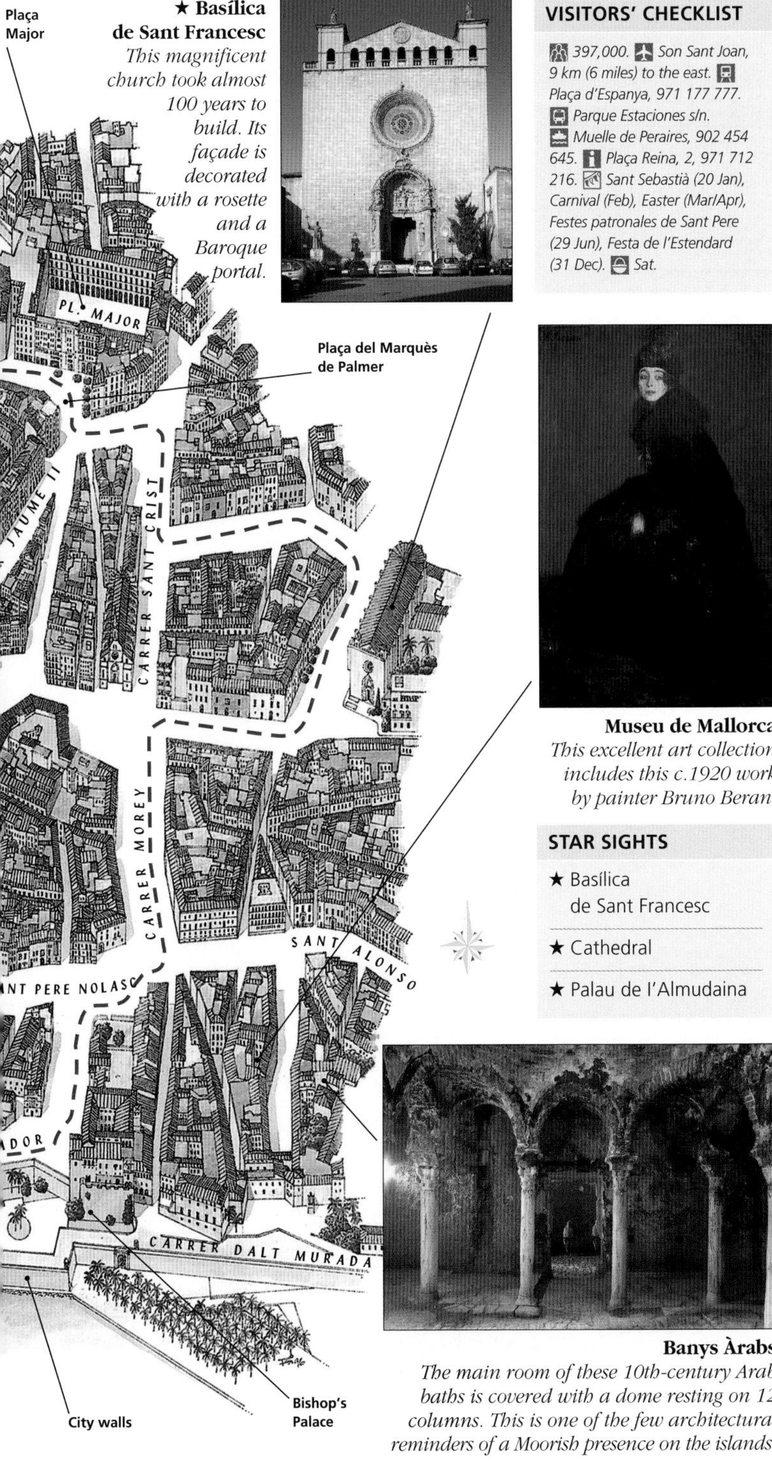

★ Basílica de Sant Francesc
This magnificent church took almost 100 years to build. Its façade is decorated with a rosette and a Baroque portal.

Museu de Mallorca
This excellent art collection includes this c.1920 work by painter Bruno Beran.

Banys Àrabs
The main room of these 10th-century Arab baths is covered with a dome resting on 12 columns. This is one of the few architectural reminders of a Moorish presence on the islands.

VISITORS' CHECKLIST

397,000. Son Sant Joan, 9 km (6 miles) to the east. Plaça d'Espanya, 971 177 777. Parque Estaciones s/n. Muelle de Peraires, 902 454 645. Plaça Reina, 2, 971 712 216. Sant Sebastià (20 Jan), Carnival (Feb), Easter (Mar/Apr), Festes patronales de Sant Pere (29 Jun), Festa de l'Estendard (31 Dec). Sat.

STAR SIGHTS

- ★ Basílica de Sant Francesc
- ★ Cathedral
- ★ Palau de l'Almudaina

Horsedrawn cabs in Palau de l'Almudaina

Exploring Palma

Of all the Balearic towns, Palma is the richest in historic sights. Christian kings, Arab rulers and Jewish merchants have all left their mark on the Balearic capital and it is a genuine pleasure to stroll through its narrow streets and quiet courtyards.

Cathedral (La Seu)

Plaça Almoïna, s/n.
Tel *971 723 130.*

After the capture of Palma by Jaume I, the town's main mosque was used as its cathedral. Work on the present cathedral *(see pp50–51)*, known in Catalan as La Seu, began in 1230, immediately after the fall of Palma. The main work lasted for almost 400 years and resulted in a monumental Gothic church.

It has three entrances, each framed with a portal. The most beautiful of these is the 14th-century Portal de Mirador, overlooking the Bay of Palma to the south. It is topped with a pediment depicting the Last Supper. Built above the Gothic Portal de l'Almoina is a fortified belfry. The main Portal Major (Great Door), facing the Almudaina palace, has a Neo-Gothic finish and is the least successful of the three.

The splendid interior features 14 slender octagonal pillars supporting the vault. The 44-metre (145-ft) central nave is one of the highest in Europe. The eastern rose window, measuring over 12 m (40 ft) in diameter, is made of 1,200 pieces of stained glass.

The cathedral features stalls made of walnut, an interesting stone pulpit and 14 chapels, including Nostra Senyora de la Corona, with statues of allegorical angels.

In the oldest part of the cathedral, hidden behind the altar, is the Trinity Chapel, containing the tombs of Jaume II and Jaume III (not open to visitors). In the early 20th century, Antoni Gaudí removed the Baroque altar and put in its place an alabaster table, with an illuminated canopy symbolizing the crown of thorns.

Palau de l'Almudaina

Carrer de Palau Real. ***Tel*** *971 214 134.*

"Almudaina" means "citadel" in Arabic. This royal residence of Jaume II was built after 1309, using the walls of an Arab fortress. The Gothic palace includes Moorish-style arches and carved wooden ceilings. It is King Juan Carlos's official Palma residence. The museum here includes the Santa Ana chapel with a Romanesque portal and a Gothic drawing room, which is sometimes used for official receptions.

Parc de la Mar

The Parc de la Mar was established in the 1960s in the area between the southern section of the city walls and Ronda Litoral. Its designers, Josep Lluís Sert and Joan Miró *(see p58)*, built the park on several levels and its central points include a man-made lake in which you can see a reflection of the cathedral, and a giant mural by Miró. Nearby **Ses Voltes** is an exhibition space, used for art exhibitions and concerts.

La Llotja

Plaça Llotja.

This late-Gothic building (a former stock exchange) was erected between 1426–56 after plans by Guillem Sagrera – the designer of La Seu's Portal del Mirador. The vault rests on slender spiral pillars, the walls are pierced by tall windows. The entrance from the square, framed by a portal, is adorned with a pediment featuring a statue of the Guardian Angel. La Llotja's interior is open only for special exhibitions.

A section of the giant mural by Joan Miró, Parc de la Mar

Consolat de Mar

Passeig de Sagrera.

This elegant Renaissance-Baroque building, erected in 1614–26, is the seat of the Balearic Islands' government.

The façade features a magnificent covered arcade. The interior has a fine coffered ceiling (1664–9). The Consolat building joins with La Llotja via **Porta Vella del Moll** – a former harbour gate, brought here in the late 19th century.

Passeig d'es Born

This is one of Palma's most beautiful corners. In Arab times it featured a moat that guarded access to the walls. Now this wide avenue, which gets its name from the 17th-century jousting tournaments held here, is Palma's main promenade and it forms the axis of the entire city.

At the southern end is **Plaça de la Reina**. The entrance on this side is guarded by stone sphinxes. At the north end is **Plaça del Rei Joan Carles I**, with a stone obelisk resting on bronze turtles standing at its centre. The avenue's most noteworthy house is the **Palau Solleric** residence (No. 27). It was built in 1763 as the home of a merchant who traded in cattle and olive oil and has a beautiful Baroque courtyard. Now a cultural centre, it also has a gallery, café and bookshop.

East frontage of Passeig d'es Born

Avinguda Unió and Plaça Weyler

This lively area is full of shops and there are also numerous cafés in the squares and streets leading off Avinguda Unió In **Plaça Mercat** two identical buildings stand side by side. These fine examples of *Modernista* architecture were built by a wealthy banker, Josep Casasayas, in 1908.

The real gem of the district's architecture, however, is the **Caixa Forum Palma** in Plaça Weyler. The former Grand Hotel was given its present name after the Fundació La Caixa savings bank financed its restoration. It was reopened in 1993 by King Juan Carlos and Queen Sofia. Built in 1903, this early example of Catalan architecture is the work of Lluís Domènech i Montaner. As an outstanding masterpiece of the *Modernista* style, it has been included on the UNESCO World Heritage list and houses, among other things, a restaurant and exhibition rooms (including a permanent collection of paintings by the important *Modernista* artist Hermengildo Anglada-Camarasa).

Almost opposite Fundació La Caixa is the **Forn d'es Teatre** (theatre bakery). This is a small, eye catching patisserie where you can buy deliciously flaky spiral pastries *(ensaimadas)*. Adjacent to the bakery is the **Teatre Principal** (1860). This is one of the most important ballet, opera and theatre venues in town.

Entrance to Forn d'es Teatre

KEY

Street-by-street map pp46–47

HTS AT A GLANCE

- guda Unió and Plaça Weyler ③
- s Àrabs ⑫
- íca de Sant Francesc ⑮
- a Olesa ⑬
- edral (La Seu) ⑧
- Walls ⑨
- solat de Mar ⑤
- otja ⑥
- de l'Almudaina ⑦
- Palau Episcopal and Museu Diocesà ⑪
- Parc de la Mar ⑩
- Passeig des Born ④
- Plaça del Marqués de Palmer ②
- Plaça Major ①
- Plaça Sant Jeroni ⑯
- Santa Eulàlia ⑭
- The Templar Chapel ⑰

Cathedral - La Seu

Palma's cathedral, La Seu, is the most precious architectural treasure of the Balearic Islands and is regarded as one of Spain's most outstanding Gothic structures. Begun by Jaume II on the site of the city's main mosque seven years after the conquest of 1299, the work took some 300 years. In the first half of the 15th century, the building works were supervised by the prominent Mallorcan sculptor and architect Guillem Sagrera. Partly destroyed during the 1851 earthquake, the cathedral was subsequently repaired by Juan Bautista Peyronnet. In the early 20th century, its interior was modernized by Antoni Gaudí. An integral part of the cathedral is its museum, which stores precious works of sacral art.

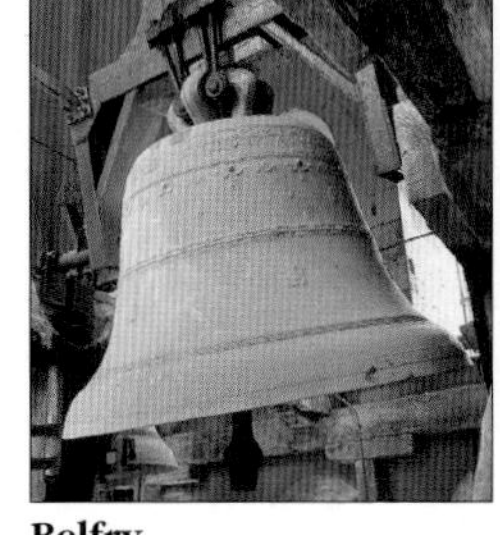

Belfry
The mighty belfry was built in 1389. The biggest of its nine bells is called Eloi.

Palma Cathedral
Towering over the former harbour in Palma, the cathedral looks most beautiful when viewed from the sea, or at night, when it is illuminated.

STAR SIGHTS

★ Baldachin (canopy)

★ Giant Rose Window

Cathedral Museum
One of the masterpieces on display in the Old Chapter House, now housing the museum, is the reliquary containing wood from the Holy Cross, encrusted with jewels.

The great organs, built in 1795, stand within a Neo-Gothic enclosure; they were restored in 1993 by Gabriel Blancafort.

★ Giant Rose Window
The largest of the seven rose windows, measuring 12 m (40 ft) in diameter, is filled with 1,200 pieces of stained glass.

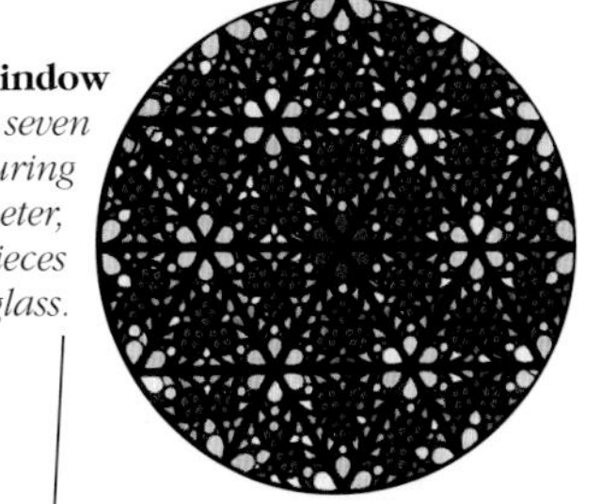

VISITORS' CHECKLIST

Plaça Almoïna s/n. ***Tel*** *971 723 130.* *10am–3:15pm Mon–Fri (Apr, May, Oct: to 5:15pm; Jun–Sep: 6:15pm); 10am–2:15pm Sat.* *pub hols.* *9am Mon–Sat; 7pm Sat; 9am, 10:30am, noon, 1pm, 7pm Sun & pub hols.*

The Capella Reial (presbytery) was remodelled by Gaudí during 1904–14.

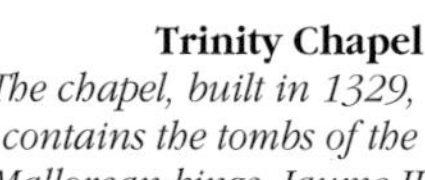

Trinity Chapel
The chapel, built in 1329, contains the tombs of the Mallorcan kings, Jaume II and Jaume III.

Bishop's Throne
Made in 1346, of white marble, the Bishop's Throne stands on a dais, in a niche.

The Barceló Chapel was designed by contemporary painter Miquel Barceló (b.1957) and boasts a large ceramic mural and stained glass windows.

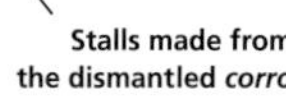

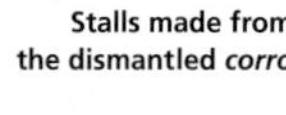

Stalls made from the dismantled *corro*

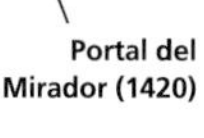

Portal del Mirador (1420)

Central Nave
Nineteen metres (62 ft) wide and 44 m (145 ft) high, the central nave, with its vault supported by 14 pillars, is one of the world's biggest.

★ Baldachin *(1912)*
Antoni Gaudí's ceremonial canopy with lights and a multi-coloured crucifix is suspended above the main altar.

Museu de Mallorca

The best museum in the Balearic Islands can be found close to La Seu, in Palau Ayamans, a residence built around 1630. The palace was erected on the foundations of an Arab house (12th–13th century), which is still visible in the underground rooms of the museum. Opened in 1968, the museum houses a superb collection of works of art associated with Mallorcan history. The collection comprises several thousand exhibits and includes prehistoric artifacts found during archaeological excavations, stone fragments of fallen buildings, priceless Moorish ceramics and jewellery, and medieval and Baroque paintings.

★ Lar Augustal
From Son Corro Sanctuary in Costixt, this 1st century AD bronze statue of a Roman domestic deity was an object of daily worship.

Paris i Helena (c.1665)
Italian painting is represented by this Baroque work by Mattia Preti, whose extensive legacy can also be seen in Rome and Malta.

★ Almohad Treasure
Items of Arab jewellery are among the museum's most precious exhibits. They are kept in the treasury room, behind bullet-proof glass.

Ground floor

Entrance

KEY

- Vaults
- Ground floor
- 1st floor
- 3rd floor

GALLERY GUIDE

The museum's collection is arranged on four floors, in chronological order. The oldest relics, including archaeological finds, are kept in the underground vault. The most recent art, including 19th- and 20th-century paintings, is exhibited on the top floor. The second floor is occupied by offices.

Urna Turó
Dating between the 3rd century BC and first century AD, this vase from Turó de Ses Abelles in Calvià imitates the ceramics of the Iberian peninsula.

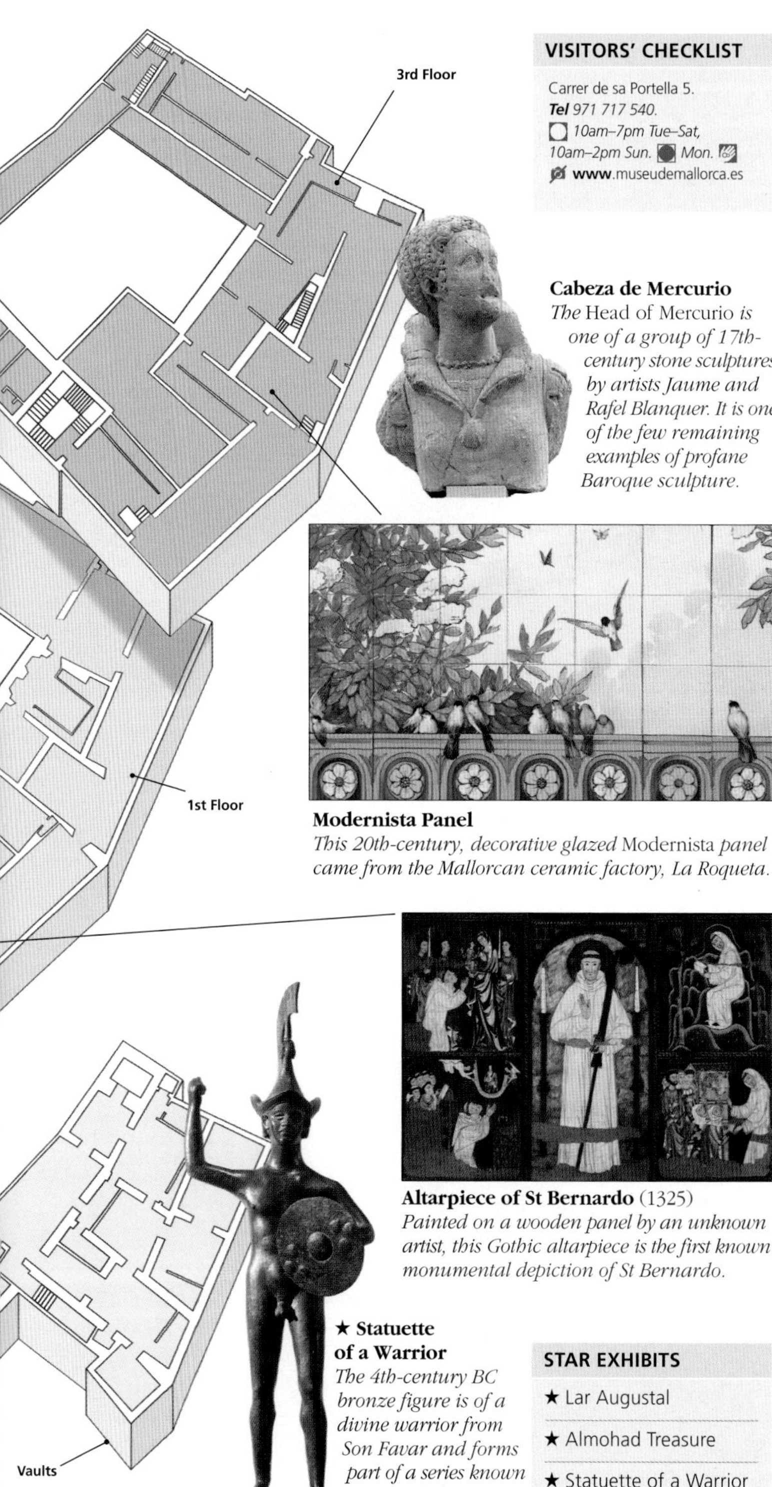

VISITORS' CHECKLIST

Carrer de sa Portella 5.
Tel *971 717 540.*
10am–7pm Tue–Sat, 10am–2pm Sun. *Mon.*
www.museudemallorca.es

Cabeza de Mercurio
The Head of Mercurio *is one of a group of 17th-century stone sculptures by artists Jaume and Rafel Blanquer. It is one of the few remaining examples of profane Baroque sculpture.*

Modernista Panel
This 20th-century, decorative glazed Modernista *panel came from the Mallorcan ceramic factory, La Roqueta.*

Altarpiece of St Bernardo (1325)
Painted on a wooden panel by an unknown artist, this Gothic altarpiece is the first known monumental depiction of St Bernardo.

★ Statuette of a Warrior
The 4th-century BC bronze figure is of a divine warrior from Son Favar and forms part of a series known as Mars Balearicus.

STAR EXHIBITS

★ Lar Augustal

★ Almohad Treasure

★ Statuette of a Warrior

Plaça del Marquès de Palmer

This square lies at the end of Carrer Colom – a shopping street running from Plaça Cort, the site of the Ajuntament (Town Hall). It features a five-storey *Modernista* apartment building, Can Rei (20th century). Equally interesting is the nearby building, L'Aguila.

Plaça Major

This pedestrianized 19th-century square has a number of souvenir shops and lively cafés. Many of the square's restaurants have outdoor tables under its arcades.

The centre of the square is given over to stalls that sell a wide variety of handicrafts. There's also a stage that is frequently used by musicians and jugglers who entertain visitors to the city.

The porticoed square was laid out in 1823 following the demolition of the headquarters of the Inquisition. The new square became the main food market until the 1950s. A large underground shopping centre and car park have since been added.

Santa Eulàlia

Plaça Santa Eulàlia. *7:30am–1pm & 5:30–8pm Mon–Fri, 8am–1pm & 6–8pm Sat–Sun.*

The vast Gothic church standing at the end of Carrer Morey was built on the site of a mosque in the 13th century on the orders of Jaume II. It was completed in just 25 years. Renovations in the 19th century involved adding the belfry and remodelling the central nave. The aisle chapels feature magnificent original Gothic paintings.

The most precious relic in the church is the crucifix kept in Capella de Sant Crist. Jaume I is supposed to have carried this when he conquered Mallorca in 1229.

Another dramatic event is associated with this church. In 1435, it was the site of a mass baptism of Jews, who converted to Christianity in order to escape being burned at the stake.

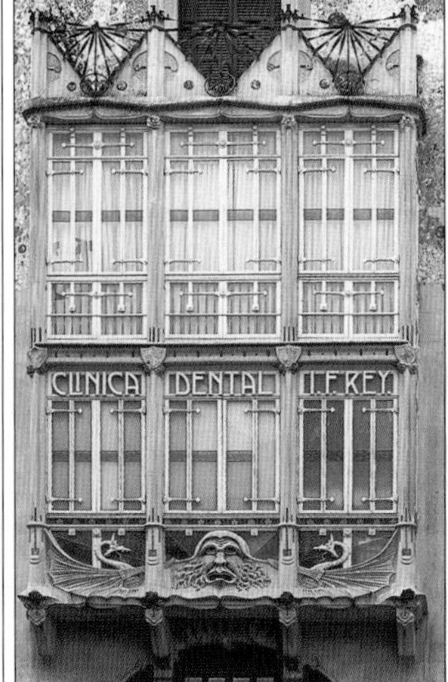

***Modernista*-style oriel window of Can Rei, at Plaça del Marquès de Palmer**

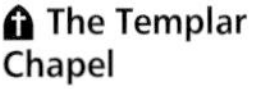

The Templar Chapel

Plaça Pes de la Palma. *9:30am–1pm & 3:30–7pm Mon–Fri, 9:30am–1pm Sat.*

The Knights Templar was a 12th-century religious and military order, founded to support the Crusades. Later it turned to banking and became so rich that it made enemies of both the ecclesiastical and secular authorities. In 1312, the pope disbanded the order and seized its assets. The Templars' Palma base was given to a rival order, the Hospitallers of St John, who remained here until the early 19th century, when the order was itself dissolved.

Access to the former fortress monastery is through a fortified 13th-century gate. The dim nave, once Gothic in style, was remodelled in the 19th century. Divided into three parts, it is covered with rib vaulting. The entrance chapels, with slender columns supporting their vaults, are decorated with geometric and plant motifs.

Plaça Sant Jeroni

Standing in a small square, with a central fountain, is the church of **Sant Jeroni**. Its elaborate doorway is all swirls and grinning gargoyles, while the church's tympanum depicts the tale of Sant Jeroni and his trials in the desert. A hermit who lived mostly in Bethlehem, this holy man translated the Bible from Hebrew into Latin. Inside the church is *Sant Jeroni*, a late 15th-century altarpiece by Pere Terrencs. There is also a vast organ, though this is rarely heard as the church is often closed.

Casa Olesa

Carrer Morey, 25.

Built in the mid-16th century, this Renaissance residence is one of Palma's most beautiful. The house is private but you can admire its courtyard through the wrought-iron gate.

Plaça Mayor, the main town square, with live entertainment

For hotels and restaurants in this region see pp144–50 and pp159–65

Monastery courtyard of Basilica de Sant Francesc

Basilíca de Sant Francesc

Plaça Sant Francesc. *9:30am–12:30pm & 3:30–6pm Mon–Sat, 9:30am–12:30pm Sun.*

The building of the Gothic church and Franciscan monastery started in 1281 and lasted 100 years. During the Middle Ages, this was Palma's most fashionable church and to be buried here was a major status symbol. Aristocratic families competed with each other by building ever more ostentatious sarcophagi in which to place their dead.

The church was remodelled in the 17th century after being damaged by lightning. Its severe façade, with giant rose window, was embellished around 1680 with a Baroque doorway, decorated with stone statues and the Triumphant Virgin Mary in the tympanum. Next to the Madonna is the carved figure of the famous medieval mystic Ramón Llull *(see p87)*, who is buried in the church.

The dark interior (its Gothic windows have been partially bricked up) contains many fine works of art, which are mainly Baroque in style. Particularly eye-catching (if you can see in the dimness) are the vast altarpiece, dating from 1739, and the organ. The delightful Gothic cloisters, planted with orange and lemon trees, offer light relief.

Standing in front of the basilica is a statue of Junipero Serra *(see p77)*, a Franciscan monk and native of Mallorca, who was sent to California in 1768 and founded Los Angeles and San Francisco.

Banys Àrabs

Carrer Can Serra 7. ***Tel*** *971 721 549.* *9am–8pm daily.*

The brick 10th-century *hammam* (bath house) is one of the few architectural reminders of a Moorish presence on the islands. A small horseshoe-arched chamber, with a dome supported by irregular columns and what would once have been under-floor heating, it has survived in its original form. There's not a lot to see but the pleasant garden has tables, where you can sit and rest.

Palau Episcopal and Museu Diocesà

Carrer Mirador 5. *Apr–Oct: 10am–1pm & 3–6pm Mon–Thu; Nov–Mar: 10am–1:30pm & 3–6pm Mon–Thu, 10am–1pm Fri.* *Sat, Sun.*

Just behind the cathedral, the Palau Episcopal (Bishop's Palace) is mostly 17th century, though work began in 1238, initiated by Bishop Ramon de Torell. The palace, which is built around a large courtyard, adjoins the city walls. Its façade was completed in 1616.

Two rooms of the palace have been given over to the modest **Museu Diocesà** (Diocese Museum). The little museum has on display items from various churches in Mallorca as well as a selection of majolica tiles. Particularly noteworthy are: a picture of St George slaying the dragon in front of Palma's city gate, painted in 1468–70 by Pere Nisart; Bishop Galiana's panel depicting the life of St Paul (who is portrayed holding a sword); the Gothic pulpit in a Mudéjar (Spanish-Moorish) style; and the jasper sarcophagus of Jaume II, which stood in the cathedral until 1904.

Sundial from Palau Episcopal

City Walls

The Renaissance city walls were built on the site of earlier medieval walls. This recently restored section once included a gallery running along the top, from where the city's defenders could fire at besieging enemies. Progress in artillery design meant that the fortifications became lower and thicker. Work on remodelling the walls began in the mid-16th century, but the bastions were only completed in the early 19th century. Today, Palma's city walls feature a walkway that provides a wide view over Badia de Palma, the cathedral and the old town.

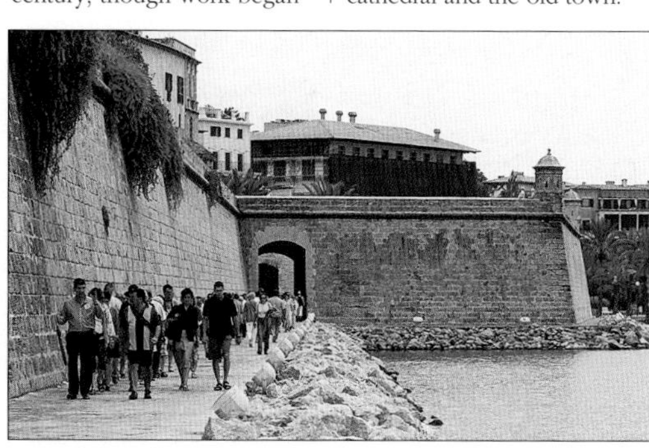

Restored city walls in Palma's old town

Painting by Pérez Villata from Museu d'Art Espanyol Contemporani

Further Afield
If you want to relax away from the hubbub of the crowded streets in Palma's old town, take a trip to the outskirts of the city. A stroll along the **harbour front**, or a trip to **Castell de Bellver**, with its lovely view of the city, is always a treat.

Carrer Sant Miquel
A narrow street that runs north from Plaça Major to Plaça Conquista, Carrer Sant Miquel is closed to traffic and is one of Palma's main shopping streets. Here, you can buy almost anything, though souvenir shops are a rarity. Here, too, you will find the Spanish Museum of Modern Art *(see below)* and, a little further on, the church of Sant Miquel. Nearby, in Plaça Olivar, stands the large iron structure of the market hall that was built in the early 20th century.

Rose window on the façade of Sant Miquel

Museu d'Art Espanyol Contemporani
Carrer Sant Miquel 11. ***Tel*** *971 713 515.* *10am–6:30pm Mon–Fri, 10am–1:30pm Sat.*

The museum occupies a Renaissance building that was remodelled in the early 20th century by Guillem Reynes i Font in the *Modernista* style. Purchased in 1916 by Juan March, the building was the first headquarters of Banca March.

The museum's exhibition occupies the first and second floors and features works by contemporary Spanish artists including Pablo Picasso, Joan Miró and Salvador Dali.

Most of the 50 or so exhibited works are paintings and sculptures by less well known artists, who nevertheless played an important role in the shaping of Spanish modern art. The museum, which also stages temporary exhibitions, is part of Fundación Juan March, a major cultural foundation.

Sant Miquel
Carrer de Sant Miquel 21. ***Tel*** *971 715 455.* *8am–1:30pm & 5–7:30pm Mon–Sat, 10am–noon & 6–7:30pm Sun.*

This 16th-century church is one of the most popular in town. It was built on the site of a mosque in which the first victory mass was said after the conquest of Mallorca by Jaume I. The Baroque altarpiece with a picture of St Michael is the work of the Spanish religious painter, Francesc Herrera.

La Rambla
Palma's biggest flower market can be found in this shadowy avenue, lined with plane trees. Towards the lower section of the boulevard are two statues of Roman emperors, erected by the Francoists in honour of Mussolini. At La Rambla's northern end stands the vast building of **La Misericordia**, remodelled in the mid-19th century in a Neo-Classical style. It houses, among other things, a conservatoire. Next to it is a botanical garden.

Plaça d'Espanya
This vast square, containing an equestrian statue of Jaume I, is Palma's main transport hub. The railway stations run services to Sóller and Inca. Most of the town's buses stop here or in the local side streets and many link up with Palma's suburbs and the nearby tourist resorts.

Poble Espanyol
Poble Espanyol, s/n. ***Tel*** *971 737 075.* *Dec–Mar: 9am–6pm daily; Apr–Oct: 9am–7pm daily.*

"Miniature Spain" is located a short way west of Palma's old town. It was built in the 1960s on the orders of the Spanish dictator General Franco. Here you can see 20 or so mini-versions of outstanding examples of Spanish architecture. They include Granada's Alhambra Palace, El Greco's house in Toledo and Barcelona's Palau de la Generalitat. There's also a craft workshop, restaurant, bar and a souvenir shop.

Copy of Alhambra in Poble Espanyol

For hotels and restaurants in this region see pp144–50 and pp159–65

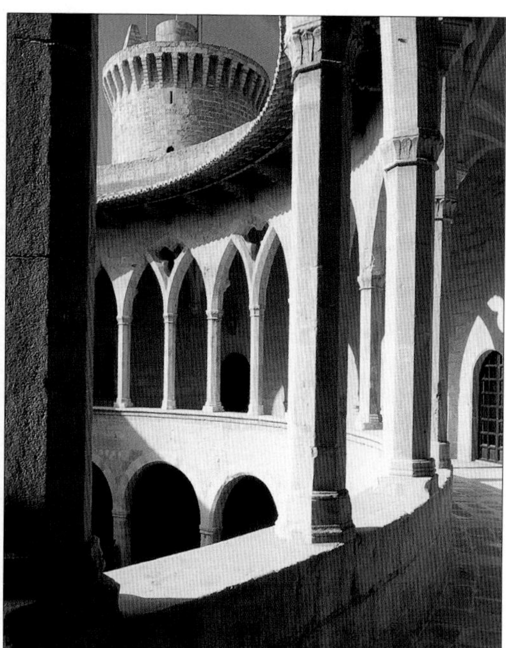
Arcades surrounding Castell de Bellver's courtyard

Opposite the entrance to Poble Espanyol stands the monumental **Palau de Congressos**. The congress centre features, among other things, the Roman Theatre and the Imperial Hall.

Castell de Bellver
C/Camilo José Cela s/n. ***Tel** 971 730 657. to Plaça Gomila. Oct–Mar: 8am–8pm Mon–Sat, 10am–5pm Sun & public hols; Apr–Sep: 8am–9pm Mon–Sat, 10am–7pm Sun & public hols.*
About 2 km (1 mile) west of Palma's cathedral, on a pine-clad hill, near the entrance to the harbour, stands one of Europe's most beautiful Gothic castles. Though it has, alas, been over-restored, the Castell de Bellver affords spectacular views of the city and bay. Built as a summer residence for Jaume II by Pere Selvà in the early 14th century when Mallorca was an independent kingdom, it was later turned into a prison and remained as such until 1915.

The castle, circular in shape, has an inner courtyard that is surrounded by two-tier arcades. Three cylindrical towers are partly sunk into the wall. The free-standing Torre de Homenaje is joined to the main building by an arch and was designed to be the final stronghold. The castle's flat roof was built to collect rainwater into an underground cistern. The entire complex is surrounded by a moat and ground fortifications.

Fishing boats in Palma harbour

A part of the castle has been turned into a museum. It has an exhibition of archaeological finds and Roman sculpture collected in the 18th century by Antonio Despuig – a historian and cardinal who left his collection to the city.

Museu Kreković
Carrer de Ciutat de Querétaro 3. ***Tel** 971 249 409. mid-Jan–mid-Dec: 9:30am–1pm & 3–6pm Mon–Fri, 9:30am–1pm Sat. mid-Dec–mid-Jan.*
The museum of the Croatian painter Kristian Kreković (1901–85) opened in 1981. It includes not only works by the artist but also paintings and handicrafts from Spain and Latin America.

Harbour Front
Palma's harbour, overlooked by the cathedral, bustles with life, as magnificent yachts come and go. Here, at the wharf, you can see fishermen at work. The nearby **Reial Club Nautic** has an excellent restaurant that often plays host to Spanish royalty.

Further on, opposite the **Auditorio** in Passeig Marítim, is a jetty for pleasure boats from where you can take a trip around the harbour. Beyond **Club del Mar**, to the south, is the ferry terminal providing regular services to the other islands of the archipelago and mainland Spain. Nearby, is a naval base. You can see most of the harbour on foot. Alternatively, hire a bicycle or horse-drawn cab. Routes end at the 15th-century **Torre Paraires** or by the lighthouse in **Potro Pi.**

Environs
Five km (3 miles) to the north lies the district of **Establiments**. Its historic sights include an old windmill that now houses a restaurant. Music lovers may be interested to know that it was here, in villa "Son Vent", on the outskirts of town, that Frédéric Chopin and George Sand stopped while on their way to Valldemossa.

Rough waters of the Badia de Palma

Badia de Palma ❷

The Bay of Palma is bounded by Cap de Cala Figuera to the west and Cap Enderrocat to the east. During the tourist boom, in the 1960–70s, the bay became surrounded by miles of high-rise hotels and hemmed in by hundreds of restaurants, bars, nightclubs and shops. Today, the eastern part of this beautiful bay is popular with German visitors, while the British tend to congregate to the west.

Platja de Palma, stretching from S'Arenal to C'an Pastilla, is one of the best beaches on the islands if you can ignore the sprawl fringing the shore. The western side is more varied, featuring pine-clad hills, sloping down to the water's edge. The beaches are smaller here, situated in picturesque coves. Along the coast are the popular resorts of Bendinat, Portals Nous, Palma Nova and Magaluf.

Cala Major ❸

Carretera Andrax 33, Illetes.

The resort area, situated to the west of Palma, is known for its **Fundació Pilar i Joan Miró**. Miró lived and worked on the island for 40 years. After his death in 1983, the artist's wife converted the house and former studio into an art centre. This modern edifice, nicknamed the "Alabaster Fortress" by the Spanish press, is the work of Rafael Moneo, a leading Spanish architect. The new building houses a permanent exhibition of Miró's paintings, drawings and sculptures, as well as a library, auditorium and a shop where you can buy items decorated with the artist's colourful designs. The Foundation owns some 140 paintings, 300 graphics and over 100 drawings by Miró.

A sculpture by Miró

Standing nearby is the **Marivent Palace,** a carefully guarded holiday residence of the Spanish royal family. The main street is lined with *Modernista* villas, which remain from the days when this was a smart resort, visited by the rich and powerful. The **Nixe Hotel** is a throwback to those days.

Fundació Pilar I Joan Miró
C/Joan de Seridakis 29. ***Tel*** *971 701 420.* *10am–7pm Tue–Sat (summer); 10am–6pm Tue–Sat, 10am– 3pm Sun (winter).*

Environs

Some 8 km (5 miles) west of Palma stands the 13th-century **Castell de Bendinat**. Remodelled in the 18th century, the castle is surrounded by pine woods and its imposing walls and towers are decorated with a Baroque frieze. Today, the castle houses a conference centre and is not open to the public. Five kilometres (3 miles) northwest of Palma are the **Coves de Genova**. Discovered in 1906, the caves have some fine formations of stalactites and stalagmites.

Palma Nova is famous for its picturesque, though crowded, beaches and lively nightlife. Nearby **Magaluf** is a busy resort with a variety of high-rise hotels and numerous restaurants and English-style pubs where you can order a full English breakfast or fish and chips.

Coves de Genova
Carrer de Barranc 45.
Tel *971 402 387.* *10am–1pm & 4–7pm Tue–Sun.*

JOAN MIRO (1893–1983)

One of the best-known artists of the 20th century, Miró was a Catalan through and through. Initially influenced by Fauvism, and later by Dadaism and Surrealism, he developed his own style, marked by lyricism and lively colouring. After arriving in Mallorca he became interested in graphics, ceramics and sculpture, scoring significant successes in every art form. His works can be seen in his studio on the outskirts of Palma, where he lived and worked from 1956. He died in Palma in 1983.

Joan Miró, one of modern art's most influential figures

For hotels and restaurants in this region see pp144–50 and pp159–65

Marineland ❹

Marineland is the only amusement park in the Balearic Islands where you can see performing dolphins and sea lions. This mini-zoo also houses a number of aquaria containing sharks and exotic fish. As well as the sea life, there is a good aviary and you can also see exotic animals such as crocodiles and snakes. This is great fun for families with young children.

VISITORS' CHECKLIST

C/Gracillaso de la Vega 9, Costa d'en Blanes.
Tel *971 675 125.*
Mar–Nov: 9:30am–6pm (last entry: 4:45pm). (Note: no food or drink can be taken in).
www.marineland.es

Entrance
Even on cloudy days there is always a queue at the front gates, with people eager to see the trained animal shows.

★ Sea Lions
The performing sea lions are well cared for at this fun park.

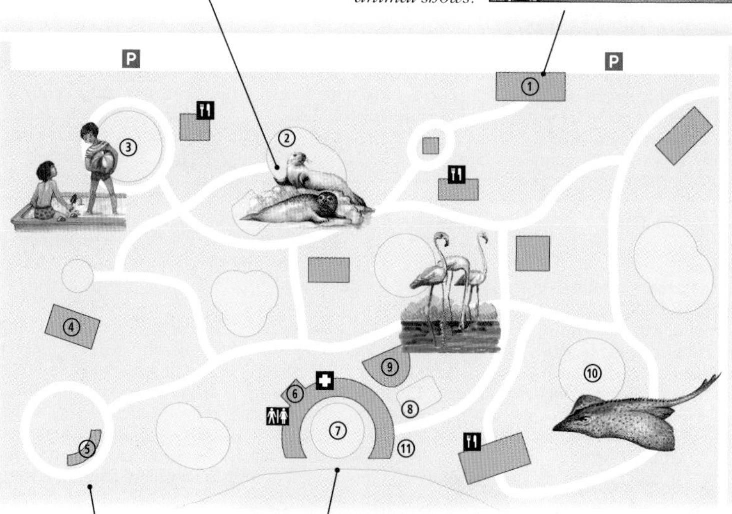

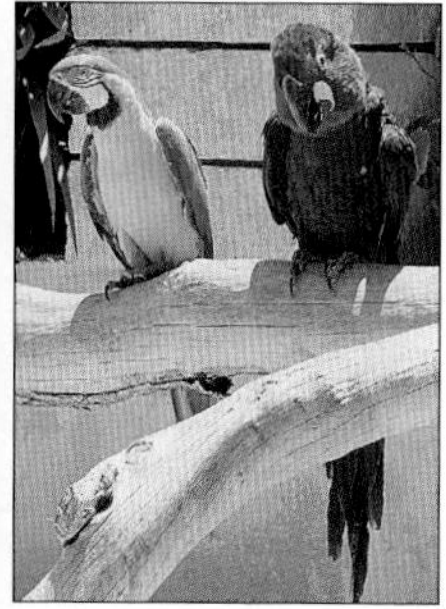

Parrots
Parrots can be seen in several places in the park, but shows are staged at a single location.

★ Dolphins
The dolphin shows always attract large crowds of appreciative spectators.

STAR ATTRACTIONS

- ★ Dolphins
- ★ Sea Lions

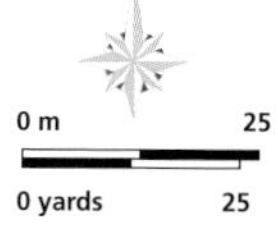

KEY

- Entrance ①
- Sea lions and seals ②
- Playground ③
- Sharks ④
- Parrot shows ⑤
- Mediterranean fish aquarium ⑥
- Dolphins ⑦
- Penguins ⑧
- Terrarium ⑨
- Ray fish ⑩
- Museum ⑪

Calvià 5

C/Julià Bujosa Sans, batle 1, 971 139 109. Sant Jaume (24 Jun). Mon. **www**.calvia.com

This quiet little town in the foothills of the Serra de Tramuntana mountains is the administrative centre of Calvià Province, which includes the resorts from Ses Illetes to Santa Ponça.

Standing on a hill in the centre of Calvià is the church of **Sant Joan Baptista**; its forecourt provides a fine view over the surrounding farms and olive groves. The original church was built here in 1245; the present structure dates from the late 19th century. The ceramic tiles lining the walls of the neighbouring public library provide a crash course in the town's history.

Few tourists make it to Calvià, where life proceeds quietly, according to a long established rhythm. Bars and restaurants serve authentic Mallorcan cuisine.

Environs

Santa Ponça is a small port, situated 7 km (4 miles) south-west of Calvià. Nearby are golf courses, good beaches and opulent residences. It was here that Jaume I landed in 1229, freeing Mallorca from Arab domination. The event is marked by the Creu de la Conquesta.

Neo-Gothic façade of Calvià's church

Typical Mallorcan fishing boats in Port d'Andratx

Andratx 6

Sant Pere (29 Jun), La Virgen del Carmen (16 Aug). Wed.

Andratx has ancient origins and was known as Andrachium by the Romans. It lies in a valley of olive and almond groves, at the foot of the Puig de Galatzó (1,028 m/3,400 ft). The local architecture is typical of the inland settlements that used to defend the island against raids by pirates. Old ochre-colour houses with colourful shutters blend well with the narrow cobblestone streets. The main historic sight is the fortified church of **Santa María**, towering over the town. It was built in the 13th century and remodelled in the early 18th century. The main tourist attraction, however, is the local market, which is held on Wednesday mornings.

Church tympanum in Andratx

Environs

Some 5 km (3 miles) southwest of Andratx is **Port d'Andratx**. The sheltered bay provides a mooring ground for upmarket yachts. As recently as the 1960s, this was just a small fishing village, which later transformed itself into a swanky resort with luxurious residences built within the woodland setting on the slopes of the La Mola cape, and affording beautiful views of the harbour. The coastal boulevard offers the best place for viewing the magnificent sunsets.

About 5 km (3 miles) east of Port d'Andratx, in **Camp de Mar**, is a vast beach and lovely bathing spot with large hotels situated close to the sea. Neighbouring **Peguera** has many inexpensive hotels. Its pleasant and safe beach is particularly favoured by families with small children and by older visitors. **Cap Andritxol**, between Peguera and Camp de Mar, is a small peninsula with an observation tower at its tip dating back to 1580. It is an excellent destination for walks and offers hikers the chance to see some rare animals and many species of native flora. **Cala Fornells**, a short way from Peguera, is a small, picturesque village and beautiful cove. Surrounded by pine trees, it has great views of the bay. It is also a good place for swimming.

A particularly scenic road runs northwards, from Andratx to Estellencs. The **Mirador de Ricardo Roca viewpoint** and Es Grau restaurant provide good stopping points for a rest en route *(see pp62–3)*.

The delightful hillside village of **S'Arracó** lies 3 km (2 miles) west of Andratx, on the road leading to Sant Elm. The local church has a marble statue of Nostra Senyora de Sa Trapa, brought to the Trappist monastery near Sant Elm in the 18th century.

Sa Dragonera ❼

A narrow rocky island, Sa Dragonera lies at an angle to the coast, about one kilometre (half a mile) from Sant Elm. It has been a nature reserve since 1988 and is home to a wide variety of birdlife and wild flowers.

According to legend, the island is visited nightly by dragons. However, its name has more to do with its shape than its popularity with mythical beasts.

This wild island is just 4 km (2 miles) long and 700 m (765 yards) wide. A rocky path runs between its two headlands, both marked by lighthouses. Apart from the lighthouse keepers, the only inhabitants of the island are wild goats and birds – the island supports cormorants, Cory's shearwater and many birds of prey including the largest colony anywhere of Eleonora's falcon.

Sa Dragonera can be reached by a ferry from Sant Elm (May–Sep), which disembarks to allow you several hours to wander and explore the island. Cruises around the island leave from Sant Elm and Port d'Andratx.

Environs

Sant Elm (San Telmo) is a quiet resort with a fine sandy beach, a wide selection of cafés and restaurants and beautiful scenery. About 4 km (2 miles) northeast of Sant Elm is an abandoned monastery. **Sa Trapa** has a mill displaying some preserved agricultural equipment. A commemorative stone stands as a warning against getting too close to the edge of the precipice, which affords a fantastic view over the island of Sa Dragonera.

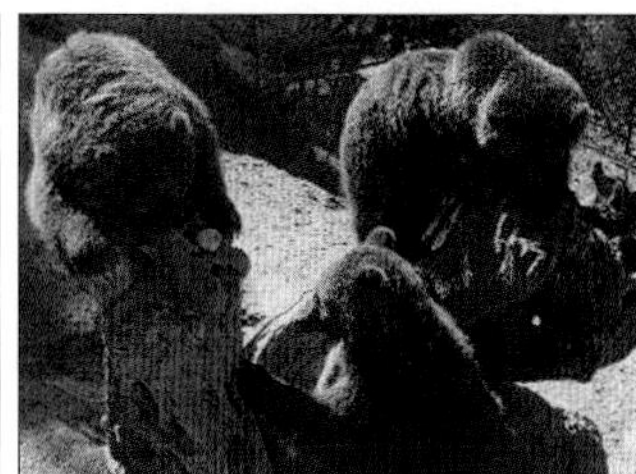

Bears in La Reserva Puig de Galatzó

Northwestern Coast of Mallorca ❽

See pp62–3.

La Reserva Puig de Galatzó ❾

18 km (11 miles) north of Palma, 4 km (2 miles) west of Puigpuñyent. ***Tel*** *971 616 622.* *10am–7pm daily (summer), 10am–6pm daily (winter).* **www**.lareserva aventur.com

This private nature reserve is situated on the eastern slope of the mighty Puig de Galatzó peak, in the southern region of the Serra de Tramuntana. Here, in an area of 250 sq km (100 sq miles), you can sample some of the splendours of nature, as the area features springs and streams, dozens of scenic waterfalls and caves, as well as a variety of interesting rock formations.

Specially designated pathways lead through the park. Notice boards explain the local flora, the origins of its unusually shaped rocks and the habits of local birds. There is much else of interest, too, including bears, a falcon show, a 1,000-year-old olive tree, *carboneros* (huts belonging to charcoal burners) and the Cova des Moro – Moor's Cave. Real adventures, such as rock climbing, abseiling and archery, are also on offer.

Sign of La Reserva Puig de Galatzó

Environs

Set amid lemon groves, 2 km (1 mile) northeast, is the quiet little farming village of **Puigpuñyent**, which has a 17th-century church.

Galilea, situated a little way south of La Reserva, is a favourite haunt for artists from all over Europe. It affords a magnificent view of the southwestern coast of Mallorca. The founder of the local church of the Immaculate Conception was Captain Antonio Barceló, a man with a fierce reputation who, in the 18th century, defended Mallorca against pirates. In nearby El Capdella the same captain Barceló founded the church of Virgen del Carmen.

Sa Dragonera, Dragon Island, viewed from Sant Elm

Northwestern Coast of Mallorca ❽

The northern slopes of the Serra de Tramuntana provide some magnificent views and a wonderful sense of isolation. Andratx and Valldemossa have a number of interesting historic sights but it is the scenery of the rugged coastline, which manages to be both sinister and beautiful, that is most impressive. The route is dramatic, traversing tunnels and gorges, but it is not difficult, except for the approach to Port d'es Canonge and Port de Valldemossa. It can be covered in a single day. If you are fit, you could even cycle.

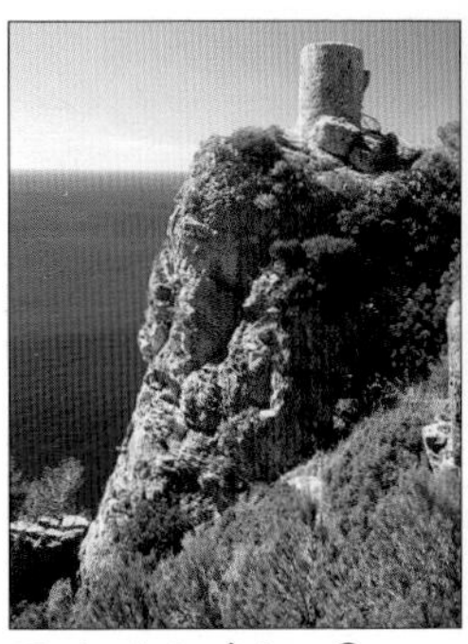

Mirador de Ses Ànimes ④
The former defence tower, standing on a steep rock, now serves as a viewpoint. The entrance to the tower is narrow and the top terrace is accessible only by stepladder.

Estellencs ③
A small town with old stone houses, an interesting, mostly 18th-century, church and a handful of souvenir shops. The route follows the main street.

Mirador de Ricardo Roca ②
This viewpoint is situated on the terrace of the Es Grau restaurant. It affords a spectacular view of the northwestern coastline.

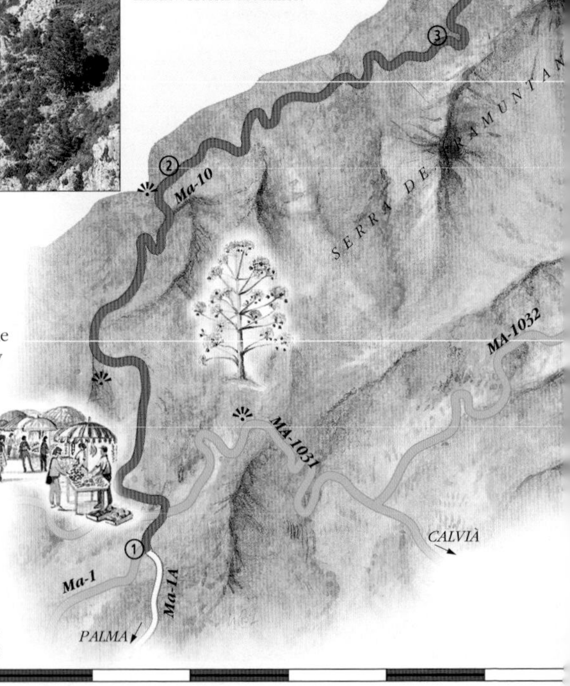

Andratx ①
A charming little town with attractive houses and cobbled streets. The market is held on Wednesday and is a time when the usually empty streets teem with life.

SERRA DE TRAMUNTANA
Ma-10
MA-1032
MA-1031
CALVIÀ
Ma-1
Ma-1A
PALMA

0 km 2
0 miles 2

For hotels and restaurants in this region see pp144–50 and pp159–65

Banyalbufar ⑤
Founded by the Arabs, this small town is surrounded by terraced fields descending to the sea. Until the late 19th century, the district was famous for its vineyards.

TIPS FOR DRIVERS

Length: *50 km (31 miles).*
Stopping-off points: *Most places along the route have a bar or restaurant; the restaurant at Mirador de Ricardo Roca is superb. Accommodation can be found in Andratx and Valldemossa.*
Further information: *Valdemossa, Jardin de la Cartuja.*
Tel *971 612 019.*

La Granja ⑦
Once a country estate, La Granja now houses one of the island's most interesting museums. It stages shows of regional dance, crafts and local wine-tastings.

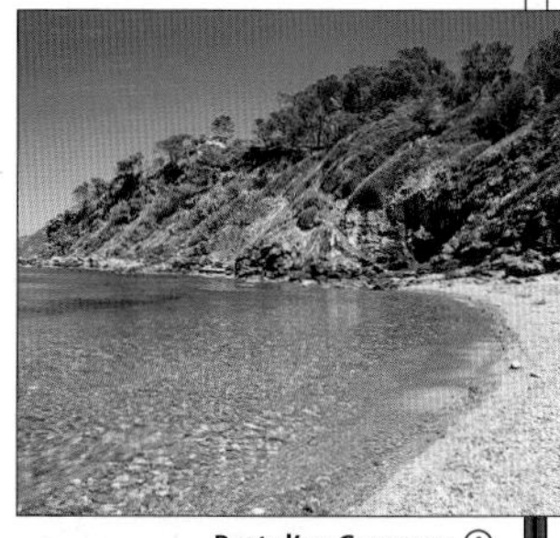

Port d'es Canonge ⑥
The road leading to this small fishing port and beach is narrow and winding, but the beauty of the spot makes it worth the trouble. Fishermen's huts and a restaurant are by the beach.

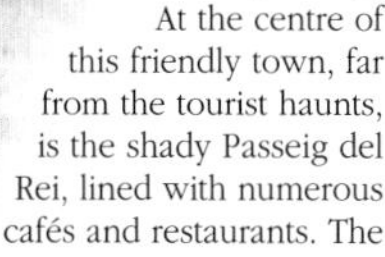

Esporles ⑧
At the centre of this friendly town, far from the tourist haunts, is the shady Passeig del Rei, lined with numerous cafés and restaurants. The nearby church was built in the early 16th century.

Valldemossa ⑩
Frédéric Chopin wintered here in 1838. It is worth taking a stroll through the town's narrow alleys, after visiting the monastery and the royal palace.

Port de Valldemossa ⑨
A small, shingly beach and a few good fish restaurants are the main reasons to follow the winding road from Valldemossa to this pretty hamlet. It offers peace and idyllic scenery, and is visited by only a handful of holidaymakers.

KEY

- Suggested route
- Other road
- Scenic route
- Viewpoint

La Granja ⑩

This country house *(finca)* lies in a wooded valley, near Esporles. From the 13th to the 15th centuries it belonged to an order of Cistercian monks, and after this to the Fortuny family. The estate has survived almost unchanged since the 18th century and is now a museum of folklore, full of antique furniture, ceramics and other artifacts. Mouth-watering hams hang in the antique kitchen, peacocks stroll around the beautiful garden and the local restaurant serves delicious Mallorcan cuisine. In the mornings it is quieter, and you can still see displays of folk dancing and local crafts.

Dye-house
This formed part of the domestic quarters, most of which were situated in basements and cellars.

Park
The estate, situated in a valley, is surrounded by a park to the south and west. Its landscaping includes streams and waterfalls; the house is almost completely hidden by a dense growth of trees.

Library
Situated next to the Renaissance bedroom, the library also served as the master's study.

Courtyard
The house is arranged around a courtyard. Don't miss the classic car that is parked in an open garage. The courtyard has a wide entrance gate to the east.

STAR FEATURES

★ Garden

★ Salon

For hotels and restaurants in this region see pp144–50 and pp159–65

★ Salon
The formal rooms are situated on the north side. Next to the salon are the games room and a small theatre. From here, French windows open onto the garden.

VISITORS' CHECKLIST

2 km (1 mile) west from Esporles.
Tel *971 610 032.*
10am–7pm daily (summer), 10am–6pm (winter).
Folklore shows: *Wed & Fri 3:30–5:15pm.*
www.lagranja.net

★ Garden
At the centre of the garden is a small fountain; the escarpment hides a grotto.

Restaurant

Corridor
Windows overlook the courtyard. On its east side is a row of smaller rooms, where you can see, among other things, an exhibition of model locomotives.

Gate to the park

Main entrance, where the shop and café are located.

Folk dancing
The twice-weekly folklore dances at La Granja, the "Ball de Botâ" or "Ball de Pagâ", spring from an ancient tradition: young female workers would lead young men in an improvised dance celebrating a good oil and cereal harvest.

Enchanting little alleys of Valldemossa, beckoning strollers

Valldemossa ⓫

1,750. Jardin de la Cartuja, 971 612 019. Sun. Santa Catalina Thomàs (28 Jul), Sant Bartomeu (24 Aug).
www.valldemossa.com

The historical records of Valldemossa go back to the 14th century, when the asthmatic King Sancho built this palace in the mountains to make the most of the clean air. In 1399, the palace was handed over to the Carthusian monks, who remodelled it as a monastery. The **Real Cartuja de Jesús de Nazaret** (Royal Carthusian Monastery of Jesus of Nazareth) was abandoned in 1835 when the monks were dispossessed.

The composer Frédéric Chopin rented a former monk's cell here in 1838 with his lover George Sand, the feminist French writer, and the monastery is now the town's main tourist attraction. In front of the entrance, in Plaça de la Cartuja de Valldemossa, is a monument to Chopin.

The monastery includes a chapel with a ceiling decorated with late-Baroque paintings by Miguel Bayeu, a relative of Goya's. Behind the chapel are rows of shady arcades. The prior's cell, despite its name, consists of several spacious rooms with access to a private garden offering a magnificent view of the valley below. The rooms house an exhibition of religious artifacts. The adjacent cells contain mementos of Chopin and George Sand.

The 17th-century monastery pharmacy contains a variety of ceramic and glass jars with wonderfully detailed descriptions of their contents (look out for the jar containing "powdered beasts' claws").

The monastery also houses the excellent **Museu Municipal Art Contemporani**, which has a small collection of works by distinguished Spanish artists including Antoni Tàpies, Joan Miró and Juli Ramis – a modernist painter and native of Mallorca. There is also a cycle of illustrations by Pablo Picasso, *Burial of Count Orgaz*, inspired by the famous El Greco painting.

On leaving the arcades you can proceed to the **Palau del Rei Sanç** – the Palace of King Sancho. This is the oldest fortified part of the monastery. The main point of interest is the wooden drawbridge connecting the two chambers over the palace's entrance. Once used as a political prison, the palace now serves as a venue for displays of folk dancing and recitals of Chopin's music.

Valldemossa itself is charming and always bustling. Most visitors are keen to see the places associated with Chopin, but a stroll along the town's narrow cobbled alleys is definitely worthwhile.

The modest house at c/Rectoría 5 is where the saintly nun Catalina Thomàs was born to a peasant family. The house has been converted into a richly decorated chapel, with the statue of the saint standing in front, holding a jug with flowing water. Nearby is the 15th-century church of Sant Bartomeu, now, unfortunately, partly destroyed.

Real Cartuja de Jesús de Nazaret
Plaça de Cartuja de Valldemossa.
Tel *971 612 106. Sun.*

Environs

Port de Valldemossa lies some 6 km (4 miles) north of Valldemossa. This is a small fishing village scenically poised on the shores of a narrow bay and surrounded by rugged cliffs. It is reached by a narrow, hairpin road. The local beach, although small and pebbly, is enchanting and occupies a beautiful location. The demanding journey is rewarded by a number of local restaurants specializing in seafood.

SANTA CATALINA THOMAS (1531–74)

Catalina Thomàs is the only Mallorcan saint. At the age of 23, she joined an Augustinian order. Known for her humility, she declined the position of Mother Superior, saying that she did not wish to govern but to serve God. She is buried in the chapel of Santa María Magdalena convent in Palma, where she spent many years of her life. She was canonized in 1930.

Tile with the image of the Saint, on one of Valldemossa's houses

For hotels and restaurants in this region see pp144–50 and pp159–65

Frédéric Chopin and George Sand

The great Polish composer Chopin spent four months in Valldemossa's 14th-century monastery *(see opposite)* during the winter of 1838–39. Chopin was accompanied by Aurora Dupin, better known as the French novelist George Sand, and her children. Their arrival here was partly to escape the prying eyes of Parisian society and partly on account of the composer's health. Chopin suffered from tuberculosis, though the weather was so bad during his stay that it made him worse. The short visit to the town by this unusual couple, described by Sand in *A Winter in Mallorca,* has contributed to the popularity of Valldemossa, despite the fact that Sand labelled the locals as "savages".

Chopin monument in Valldemossa

Garden in front of cell No. 2, *in which Chopin's scores and George Sand's manuscripts are held. To this day there is a dispute over which cell Chopin occupied (No. 2 or No. 4). The garden terrace affords a fine view.*

Portrait of George Sand
A French writer and journalist, Sand was a highly unconventional figure. She was morally way ahead of her time – she wore trousers, smoked cigars and "lived in sin".

Manuscript of Prelude No. 24, opus 28, *one of the many works composed by Chopin during his short visit to Mallorca, even though his piano only arrived three weeks before he left the island.*

A fresh red rose *is always placed on the upright piano in cell No. 2. The composer's favourite* Pleyel *piano was brought from Paris and now stands in cell No. 4.*

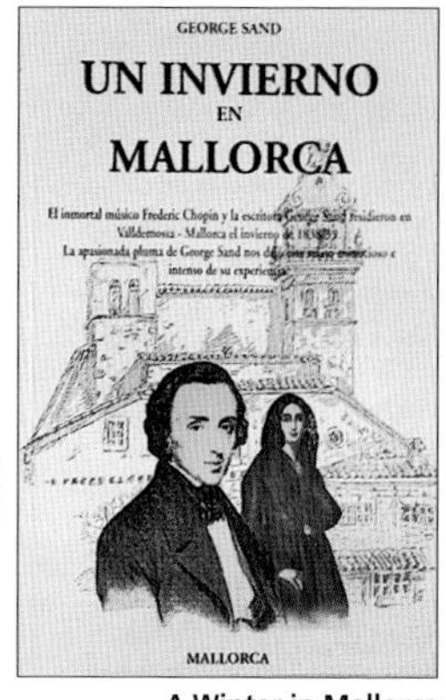

A Winter in Mallorca
George Sand's description of her visit to Mallorca with Chopin has enjoyed lasting popularity.

Rotunda in the garden of Son Marroig

Son Marroig ⓬

3 km (2 miles) northeast of Deià
9:30am–8pm (summer); 9:30am–6pm (winter). Sun.
www.sonmarroig.com

This late-medieval mansion, perched high above the seashore, was remodelled in the 19th century to become the residence of the Habsburg Archduke Ludwig Salvator. The Austrian aristocrat was fabulously rich and came to Mallorca hoping to escape from the strict morality of the Viennese court. He fell in love with the island, settled here and gave himself over to exploring and promoting the Balearic Islands.

The house is now a museum, dedicated to his life and work and including some of his pen drawings and manuscripts. It is surrounded by a terrace and graced by a rotunda of white marble. From here, the Archduke enjoyed fine views over the wooded shore to the narrow promontory of **Sa Foradada** where he used to moor his yacht *Nixe*. It takes less than an hour's walk to get there.

Environs

A short way southwest of Son Marroig is the **Monestír de Miramar**. The house was built in 1276 for Ramón Llull but was acquired by Ludwig Salvator in 1827. The Archduke entertained Princess Sisi here during her visit to Mallorca.

Monestír de Miramar
Tel 971 616 073.
10am–4:30pm.
Mon–Sat.

Deià ⓭

700. Sant Joan Baptista (24 Jun). www.deia.info

This lovely mountain town lies at the spot where the mighty Puig d'es Teix meets the sea. Deià is mostly associated with the English novelist and poet Robert Graves *(see opposite)*. Graves settled here in 1929 and for the next 56 years lived and worked here, making the place popular with other artists, including Picasso and the writer Anaïs Nin.

Towering over the town is the modest church of **Sant Joan Baptista** (1754–60). The adjacent building houses the **parish museum** with a collection of religious objects. Deià also has an interesting **Museu Arqueológic** founded by the American archaeologist William Waldren, displaying the prehistory of Mallorca.

Hotel La Residencia, in the grounds of a former estate, has attracted many famous guests including Princess Diana and Sir Bob Geldof.

LUDWIG SALVATOR

The Habsburg Archduke Ludwig Salvator was born in 1847. He first visited Mallorca at the age of 19 and became captivated by the island. He settled here permanently, learned the local dialect and created a scandal by marrying a local carpenter's daughter. He was tireless in exploring and promoting Mallorca, producing a seven-volume work devoted to the island's history, archaeology, folklore and topography. It is thanks to him that a 10-km (6-mile) long stretch of the coast that he owned has survived intact. In 1910, he was awarded honorary citizenship of Mallorca. He died in 1915.

Museu Arqueológic
Es Clo Deià. **Tel** 971 639 001.
5–7pm Tue, Thu, Sun.

Environs

A winding road leads to **Cala de Deià**, a pretty cove with a shingle beach and clear water.

Hotel La Residencia viewed from the church hill

For hotels and restaurants in this region see pp144–50 and pp159–65

Modernista building of Banco de Sóller, one of Sóller's landmarks

ROBERT GRAVES (1895–1985)

Robert Graves was an English novelist, poet and classical scholar. Severely wounded on the Somme during World War I, his frank autobiography, *Goodbye to All That*, earned him enough money to move to Mallorca where he set up home, accompanied by his muse and mistress, the poet Laura Riding. Here, he wrote two tremendously successful historic novels: *I, Claudius* and *Claudius the God*, which made him world famous. The outbreak of the Spanish Civil War interrupted his stay but he returned to the island in 1946. He died in 1985 and is buried in the local church of Sant Joan Baptista beneath a simple gravestone.

Robert Graves' tombstone in Deià's cemetery

Sóller ⓮

Plaça Constitució 1. **Tel** *971 638 008.* *Sat.* *Festes de Moros i Cristians (2nd Sun in May).* **www**.sollernet.com

Situated in a valley, Sóller is sheltered by the Serra de Alfàbia mountain massif and overshadowed by the lofty Puig Major (1,445 m/4,740 ft). Its name reputedly derives from the Arabic word *suliar*, meaning "golden bowl" – the valley is famous for its many orange groves.

Arabs, who settled here in the late 8th century, built canals and irrigation ditches and the town grew rich thanks to its plentiful supply of oranges and the vineyards and olive groves, planted on the slopes of the Serra de Tramuntana. In exchange for its oranges and wine, it imported goods from France and links between the town and France remain strong.

Plaça Constitució is a lively square and the centre of Sóller. Mature trees, fountains and lively cafés give the place its unique atmosphere. Notable buildings include the *Modernista* castle-like **Banco de Sóller**, which is the work of Joan Rubió i Bellver, a disciple of Antoni Gaudí, and the Neo-Gothic church of **Sant Bartomeu**, also designed by Rubió. Particularly eye-catching is the vast rosette window on the church façade, carved in stone, and the Baroque sculptures contrasting with the dark interior.

To the north of the square stands **Museu Casa de Cultura**, occupying a renovated building in Calle Sa Mar. Here, you can recapture the atmosphere of old Sóller as you stroll through rooms decorated with antique furnishings, a courtyard and an old kitchen with amusing majolica plates.

Museu Balear de Ciències Naturals (Balearic Museum of Natural Science), on the outskirts of Sóller, was opened in 1992 in a late 19th-century mansion house. Its exhibits include a collection of Mallorcan fossils and rocks and specimens of the local flora. The adjacent **Jardí Botànic** contains plants native to the Balearic Islands.

The town's **vintage electric train**, nicknamed the "Red Arrow", which runs between Palma and Sóller, provides a superb ride through the mountains. From the Sóller terminus you can hop aboard a **vintage tram**, which takes you on to Port de Sóller *(see p70)*.

Fountain in Plaça Constitució in Sóller

Museu Casa de Cultura
C/Sa Mar 9. **Tel** *971 634 663.* *11am–1pm & 5–8pm Tue–Fri.*

Museu Balear de Ciències Naturals and Jardí Botànic
Ctra Palma–Port de Sóller. **Tel** *971 634 064.* *10am–6pm Mon–Sat, 10am–2pm Sun.*

Environs Port de Sóller, situated 5 km (3 miles) from Sóller, is a pleasant although crowded resort with numerous seafood restaurants next to the harbour and by the beach. Here, you can enjoy a boat trip along the coast, or go for a hike to the nearby lighthouse.

Punta Grosa lighthouse, near Port de Sóller

Train from Palma to Port de Sóller ⓯

The most enjoyable way to travel from Palma to Sóller is aboard the "Red Arrow", an electric narrow-gauge railway line, which opened in 1912. After passing through farmland, the 27-km (17-mile) route winds its way through the steep peaks and valleys of the Serra de Tramuntana. The line is justifiably regarded as one of the most attractive in Europe, and the narrow-gauge rolling stock, musty carriages and clanking engine only add to the experience.

Sóller ④
After a one-hour ride the train reaches Sóller. From here a vintage tram running through the busy town centre takes you to Port de Sóller.

Mirador Pujol d'en Banja ③
Two special tourist trains, leaving Palma daily at 10:50am and noon, stop briefly at this viewpoint to provide a splendid view of Sóller, the surrounding mountains and the coastline.

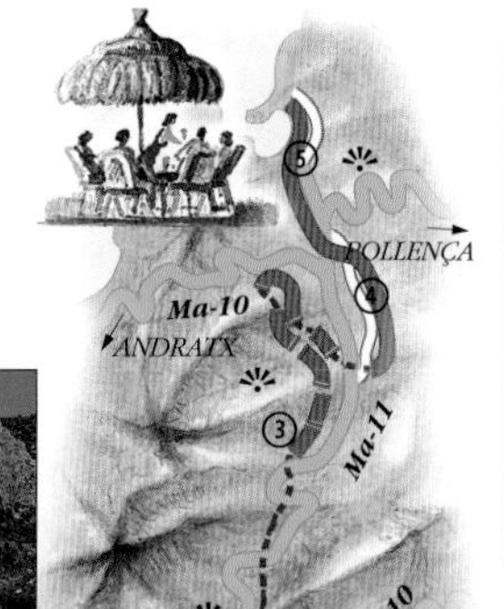

Port de Sóller ⑤
The journey from Sóller to Port de Sóller takes 15 minutes. The tram route runs along the beach and ends at the harbour. Trams run much more frequently than the train.

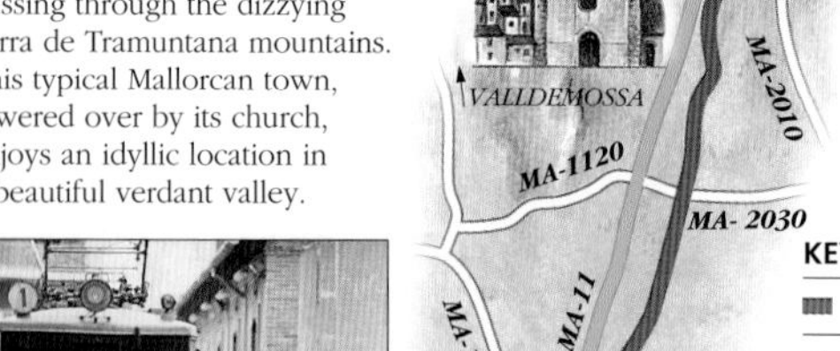

Bunyola ②
This is the last stop before passing through the dizzying Serra de Tramuntana mountains. This typical Mallorcan town, towered over by its church, enjoys an idyllic location in a beautiful verdant valley.

0 km 2
0 miles 2

KEY

- Suggested route
- Route through the tunnel
- Motorway
- Scenic route
- Other road
- Viewpoint

Palma ①
A trip aboard this vintage electric train is a real delight. The line was originally built to transport fruit to Palma from Sóller at a time when the journey by road took an entire day.

TIPS FOR PASSENGERS

Length: *27 km (17 miles).*
Stopping-off points: *Sóller has many cafés and restaurants.*
Information: *Plaça d'Espanya 2, Palma (971 752 051); C/ Castanyer 7, Sóller (971 630 301); or contact www.trendesoller.com*

Jardines de Alfàbia ⑯

14 km (9 miles) north of Palma. *Tel 971 613 123. Apr–Oct: 9:30am–6:30pm Mon–Fri, 9:30am–1pm Sat; Nov–Mar: 9:30am–5:30pm Mon–Fri, 9:30am–1pm Sat.*

Most visitors come to see the magnificent Moorish gardens of this old manor house, set amid lemon groves. Footpaths shaded by pergolas criss-cross streams and take you past murmuring fountains, ivy-clad walls and beds of splendid roses. The house is approached via a long stately avenue of plane trees.

Following the conquest of the island by Jaume I, the estate was given to the Moorish governor Benhabet. Benhabet had been the governor of Pollença but supported the king by provisioning the Catalan army during the invasion. For this help, Jaume I gave Benhabet this land and he set about planning an estate in the Moorish style. After his death the castle became the residence of the Mallorcan kings. The origin of the estate's name goes back to the days of Arab rule, when it was called *Al-Fabi* ("Jug of olives").

The house itself, with its courtyard surrounded by domestic buildings and shaded by a giant plane tree, is actually modest though attractive. Most notable is the 14th-century oak throne made for Jaume IV. The gatehouse features a lovely Mudéjar (Spanish-Moorish) style vault, with an inscription praising Allah.

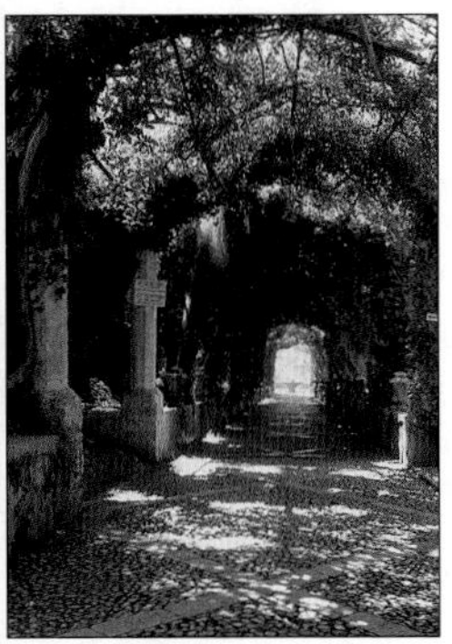

Sun shining through a pergola in Alfàbia gardens

Beach at the end of Torrent de Pareis canyon, near Sa Calobra

Sa Calobra ⑰

30 km (19 miles) NE of Fornalutx.

This tiny hamlet occupies a beautiful cove surrounded by high cliffs. A busy tourist centre, its main attraction is the **Torrent de Pareis** (River of the Twins) canyon, which is reached by a coastal walkway, leading partly through a tunnel.

It is also possible to reach this impressive canyon from **Escorca**, a hamlet on the way from Sóller to Pollença. This route is extremely difficult, however, and requires rock-climbing skills, ropes and wetsuits! It takes about six hours to cover it. During the winter and spring or after heavy rainfall it is virtually impassable as the bottom of the canyon, known as the "Great Canyon of Mallorca", fills with torrential waters. Once upon a time Sa Calobra was accessible only by boat. Now there is a twisting road leading to it, which in view of its breakneck descents and bends has been nicknamed *Nus de la Corbata* ("Knotted neck-tie"). Two kilometres (1 mile) before Sa Calobra you can take a left turn to the popular resort of **Cala Tuent**. Set against the northern slopes of Puig Major, the quiet village has a modest gravel and sand beach. The Es Vergeret restaurant has a large selection of fish dishes – its terrace affords a fine view of the rocky coast.

SERRA DE TRAMUNTANA

The northern coast of Mallorca is dominated by the Serra de Tramuntana (Mountains of the North Wind), which run from Sa Dragonera in the west to Formentor in the east. The highest peak of this 90-km (55-mile) stretch is Puig Major (1,445 m/4,740 ft), though part of this is used by the military and closed to visitors. The steep slopes are covered with sweet smelling wild rosemary and are home to goats, sheep and rare birds. The best way to enjoy this area is on foot and a number of maps are easily available that list walking routes through all or part of the mountain range. Alternatively, you can explore the mountains by car, although great care should be taken on the narrow and twisting roads and frequent hairpin bends that descend through steep cliffs to the sea.

Steep mountain slopes west of Monestír de Lluc

For hotels and restaurants in this region see pp144–50 and pp159–65

Santuari de Lluc ⓲

The sanctuary at Lluc is the spiritual centre of Mallorca and has been a place of pilgrimage for over 800 years. The main point of interest is the little statue of the Virgin *(La Moreneta de Lluc)*, which, so the story goes, was found in a cave by an Arab shepherd boy who had converted to Christianity. The image was initially moved to the church but it kept returning to the same spot. A chapel was built to house this miraculous object and this has since been decorated with precious stones. Thousands of pilgrims now arrive here every year to pay homage.

Statue of Joaquim Rosselló i Ferrà
Father Rosselló, who arrived in Lluc in 1891, was the founder of the Sacred Heart Missionary Congregation and the spiritual reviver of the sanctuary.

Church
The original Renaissance-Baroque church was built during 1622–84 and was designed by Jaume Blanquer. Much of the complex dates from the 18th and 19th centuries.

Statue of Bishop Campins
A patron of the sanctuary, Bishop Pere-Joan Campins commissioned Antoni Gaudí and Guillem Reynés to renovate the basilica and build its Way of the Cross.

STAR SIGHTS

- ★ Els Porxets
- ★ La Moreneta de Lluc
- ★ Museu de Lluc

★ Museu de Lluc
Opened in 1952, the museum houses local handicraft, such as siurells *(whistles) and majolica, as well as works of art, paintings, coins and archaeological finds.*

School Grounds
The buildings behind the church belong to the Els Blavets, a school choir founded in 1531. The name derives from the choir's blue cassocks.

VISITORS' CHECKLIST

From Palma. *11:30am & 7:30pm Mon–Sat; 11am, 12:30pm, 5pm & 7pm Sun.* **Museum *Tel*** *971 871 525.* *10am–1:30pm & 2:30–5:15pm daily.* **Botanical Garden** *10am–1pm & 3–6pm daily.* **Fonda Restaurant *Tel*** *971 517 022.* *1–3:30pm & 7:30–9:30pm Wed–Mon.* *Mon pm.* *Cami dels Misteris del Rosari (Mar/Apr).* **www.**lluc.net

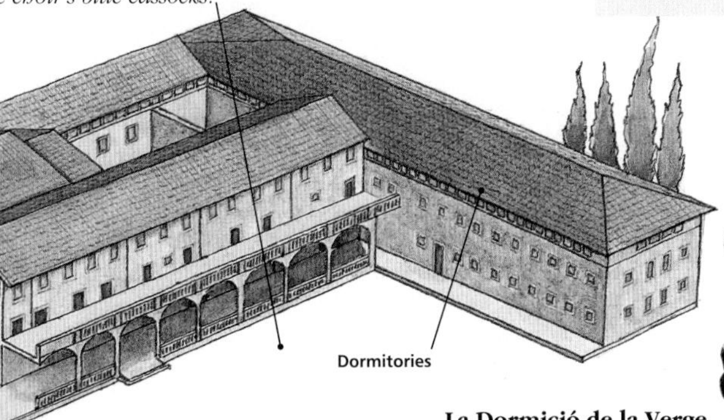

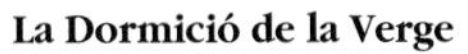

La Dormició de la Verge
The first of the seven steles carved by Miquell Cosquell and Pere Merçol (1399), once standing along the road between Caimari and the sanctuary, now stands in Plaza dels Pelegrins.

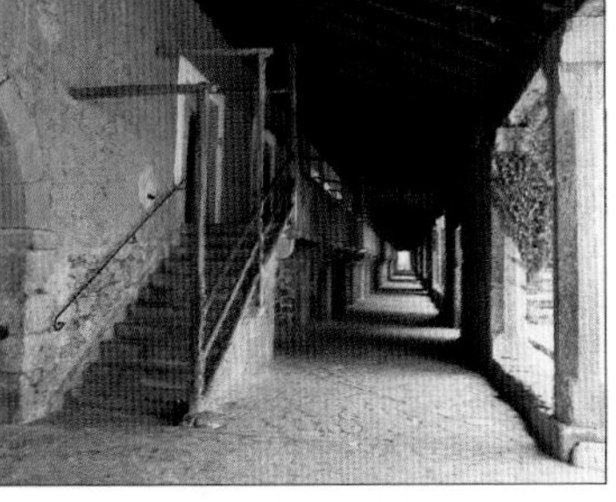

★ Els Porxets
The 16th-century building was extended in the early 18th century. It consists of pilgrim quarters on the first floor and stables on the ground floor.

★ La Moreneta de Lluc
The tiny statue of La Moreneta *("the little dark One") is just 62 cm (24 in) high. It stands in a niche inside the Royal Chapel, built during 1707–24, at the back of the main altar.*

Plaza dels Pelegrins
The drive leading to the monastery is surrounded by greenery and lined with bars, cafés and souvenir shops. It provides a magnificent view of the Serra de Tramuntana.

Inca ⓳

23,000. Thu.
Dijous Bo (3rd Thu in Nov).

Inca, the last stop on the train journey from Palma, is the third largest town on the island. A modern industrial place, visitors come here nevertheless, attracted by the cheap leather goods in Avinguda General Luque and Gran Via de Colon. Thursday, market day, is Inca's busiest time. The stalls lining the streets and squares stretch over several districts of town. Here you can buy almost anything – souvenirs, household goods, flowers and food. Inca is also known for its traditional Mallorcan cuisine, including *caracoles* (snails) and for its wine cellars converted into restaurants *(cellers)*.

Environs

About 2 km (1 mile) past the town, heading towards Alcúdia, is a right turn in the road that leads to the top of **Puig d'Inca** (296 m/970 ft), with a small sanctuary, **Ermita de Santa Magdalena**. For nearly 800 years on the first Sunday after Easter crowds of pilgrims have congregated here. There is a good view from the top over the surrounding fields and mountains. Near the road to Alcúdia are the **Coves de Campanet**, a complex of small but beautiful caves surrounded by tropical gardens. The neighbouring small town of **Sa Pobla** holds one of the best Sunday markets on the island.

Coves de Campanet
Ctra. Palma–Alcúdia, 39 km (24 miles). ***Tel*** *971 516 130.*
from 10am daily.

Steps of the Way of the Cross, leading to El Calvari, in Pollença

Pollença ⓴

Claustro de Santo Domingo, 971 535 077. Sun.
Sant Antoni (17 Jan), Los Moros y los Cristianos (2 Aug).

Founded by the Romans in the foothills of the Serra de Tramuntana, Pollença has retained much of its old-world charm with narrow, twisting streets, some good restaurants and a lively Sunday market. The remains left by the town's founders include **Pont Romà**, a bridge spanning the banks of the Torrente de Sant Jordi river, at the north end of town.

After 1229, the Knights Templar began the building of the parish church of **Nostra Senyora dels Angels**. Remodelled in the 17th century, the church façade has a fine rosette window, while its dark interior is decorated with paintings and a vast altar that is several storeys high.

The pride of the town is the beautiful **Via Crucis** (Way of the Cross). It leads to the **El Calvari chapel** standing on top of the hills and housing a Gothic statue of Christ. Climbing the seemingly endless set of steps (365 in all), you pass the Stations of the Cross. The chapel may also be reached by walking along the streets. The statue of Christ is carried down to the parish church in a moving torchlight procession every Good Friday, during the *Davallament* (the Crucifixion).

The building of the former **Convent de Sant Domingo** (Dominican monastery) now houses the **Museu Municipal** with its collection of Gothic sacred art, archaeological

Colourful stall with souvenirs at Inca's Thursday market

finds and a small collection of modern paintings.

To soak up the sleepy atmosphere of Pollença, head for **Plaça Major**, where the locals gather in the cafés and bars.

Museu Municipal
Carrer Santo Domingo. ***Tel*** *971 530 437.* *Tue, Thu & Sun.*

Environs

The family-friendly resort of **Port de Pollença**, situated 6 km (4 miles) to the east beside a pleasant bay, has a long, sandy beach. Just southeast of Pollença a steep narrow road, then a footpath, climbs 330 m (1,000 ft) to **Puig de Maria**, where a 17th-century hermitage has a rustic restaurant and bar, and simple rooms to let with wonderful views.

Cap de Formentor 21

6 km (4 miles) from Port de Pollença.

The Formentor Peninsula, at the northern end of the Serra de Tramuntana, is a 20-km (12-mile) long headland of steep cliffs, that is in some places 400 m (1,300 ft) high. The footpath from the road leads to the **Mirador des Colomer** from which you can enjoy spectacular views of the sea and the **El Colomer** rock. There is also a beautiful view of the 16th-century watch tower, **Talaia d'Albercutx**, standing much higher than the viewpoint. Further on, the road passes through the Mont Fumat tunnel and runs among rocky hills, covered with vegetation, up to the **lighthouse** rising to 260 m (850 ft). On a clear day you can see Menorca and its capital, Ciutadella. The rugged cliffs provide nesting sites for thrushes and rock doves, also falcons, swallows and martins.

A spur from the main road leads to the lovely public beach of **Cala Pi de la Posada**, which is served by bus from Port de Pollença and gets very crowded in summer. The road ends at one of the oldest, most luxurious resorts on the island – the Hotel Formentor. Opened in 1929, it is noted for its opulence and fashionable clientele *(see p148)*.

Inside the Gothic church of Sant Jaume in Alcúdia

Alcúdia 22

Ctra d'Artà 68, 971 892 615. *Tue–Sun.* *Romeria de la Victòria (2 Jul).*

The delightful town of Alcúdia, surrounded by 14th-century walls, lies at the base of the peninsula separating Pollença Bay from Alcúdia Bay. Originally, this was a Phoenician settlement. Having conquered the island, the Romans built a town here, called Pollentia, which from the 2nd century was the capital of the island. In 456, it was destroyed by the Vandals. Around the year 800, Moors built their fortress here, naming it *Al-Kudia* (On the Hill). After the Reconquest, Alcúdia prospered as a trading centre well into the 19th century.

Town hall window in Alcúdia

The beautifully restored town is entered through the vast **Porta de Moll** gate. The Gothic church of **Sant Jaume** at the centre is 13th-century. Near the church are a few **remains of Roman houses**. Adjacent to these is **Museu Monogràfic**, which displays objects from Roman times.

On the outskirts of town, along the road to Port d'Alcúdia, is the **Oratori de Santa Anna**. Built in the early 13th century, it is one of the oldest Mallorcan sanctuaries. Nearby are the remains of a first-century BC **Roman theatre** – this is the smallest Roman theatre to have survived in Spain.

Museu Monogràfic
Carrer de Sant Jaume 30. ***Tel*** *971 547 004.* *10am–4pm Tue–Fri, 10:30am–1pm Sat & Sun.*

Environs

Port d'Alcúdia, 2 km (1 mile) south of the town, is the most popular tourist destination on Mallorca's northeast shores. It has a lovely sandy beach, a marina and a harbour as well as hotels, restaurants and clubs.

The road to Es Mal Pas brings you to **Cap des Pinar** where, in 1599, Philip II erected a watchtower, Torre Major. A branch road leads to the **Ermita de la Victòria**. It has a revered 15th-century wooden statue of Victoria, Alcúdia's patron saint.

Lighthouse on Cap de Formentor

The marshes of Parc Natural de S'Albufera, crisscrossed with canals

Parc Natural de S'Albufera ㉓

9am–7pm daily (to 4pm Oct–Mar); Reception Centre: 9am–4pm daily.

The wetland south of Port d'Alcúdia, occupying the shores of Lake Grande up to C'an Picafort, was once a swamp. Most of it was drained in the 1860s, but a portion remains, which in 1985 become the Parc Natural de S'Albufera. The marshes can be explored on foot, following the marked trails. A major conservation project, this is an excellent place for observing over 200 species of birds including grey and purple herons, summer osprey and Eleonora's falcon. The park reception is in **Sa Roca** where you can obtain a free map and a list of some of the park's birds.

Muro ㉔

13 km (8 miles) east of Inca. *Sun.* *Revelta de Sant Antoni Abat (17–18 Jan).* **www**.ajmuro.net

The agricultural town of Muro is a pleasant, sleepy place, situated at the centre of the plain, surrounded by cultivated fields. It is full of old mansions built by rich landowners, which give the town its unique charm. Each year on 17 and 18 January, Muro is the scene of the *Revelta i Beneides de Sant Antoni Abat* – a big fiesta on the eve of St Antoni's day. The town's inhabitants and visitors gather around bonfires, drinking wine and eating sausages and *espinagades* – delicious pies made with eels caught in the S'Albufera marshes.

The town is dominated by the church of **Sant Joan Baptista**, remodelled around 1530. This large structure, built in the Catalan Gothic style, features colourful stained glass windows and a beautiful rosette on the façade. The interior includes Baroque furnishings and a vast main altarpiece. Adjacent to the church is a huge, seven-storey belfry that once served as a watchtower. The view from the top can be stunning and encompasses all of the surrounding area.

The **Convent des Mínims** and the church of **Santa Ana** are in Plaça de José Antonio Primo de Rivera, once the venue for bullfights. Nearby is the **Museu de Mallorca, Seccio Etnològic**, which is situated in an old mansion house. Here, you can see a collection of local furniture, folk costumes, agricultural tools and a series of workshops including a blacksmith's and a cobbler's. The museum also has a collection of *siurells* – whistles.

Baroque cartouche from the museum in Muro

Museu de Mallorca, Seccio Etnològic
Carrer Major 15.
Tel *971 717 540.* *10am–3pm Tue, Wed, Fri–Sun; 10am–2pm Thu.*

Environs

Some 11 km (7 miles) east of Muro, on Badia d'Alcúdia, adjacent to the Parc Natural de S'Albufera, is the sandy beach of **Platya de Muro** with its stone-pines growing amid the dunes. About 3 km (2 miles) north is **Sa Pobla**, which has a lovely 17th-century Baroque church and two museums: Museu d'Art Contemporani and Museu de la Jugeta, which has a collection of toys from the 19th and 20th centuries. The town's main square, Plaça Constitució, hosts a busy Sunday market, selling mainly agricultural produce. **Santa Margalida**, situated 5km (3 miles) southeast, has a history reaching back to Roman times. The views of the mountains and plain are outstanding from here.

Multi-storey alterpiece in Muro's Sant Joan Baptista

Sineu ㉕

30 km (19 miles) northeast of Palma. *3,200.* *Wed.* *Fira Maig (24 Apr).*

Sineu is one of the most interesting agricultural towns of the central Es Pla plain and has a rich history. Attracted by its strategic position, at the very heart of the island, Jaume II built his **palace** here. King Sancho came here to benefit from the fresh air and declared the town the centre of Mallorca. Later, Jaume III slept here the

For hotels and restaurants in this region see pp144–50 and pp159–65

night before the battle of Llucmajor, in which he was killed fighting the army of Pedro of Aragón. Today, the palace is occupied by an order of nuns that is known as the *monges del palau* (sisters of the palace).

Adjacent to the former royal residence stands the biggest parish church on the island, **Nostra Senyora dels Àngels**. This Gothic structure was built in 1248 and remodelled in the 16th century. In front of the church, in Plaça de Sant Marcos, stands a statue of a winged angel – the symbol of St Mark the Apostle, the patron saint of the town.

In the neighbouring Sa Plaça square are two excellent restaurants serving traditional Mallorcan cuisine: the Celler Ca'n Font and the Celler Es Grop.

At one time, the Inca-Artà railway line passed through the town. Now, the former station building, dating from 1879, houses the **S'Estació Art Gallery**. Wednesday's market is one of the biggest agricultural fairs in Mallorca and sells local produce and livestock.

Stained glass church window in Sineu

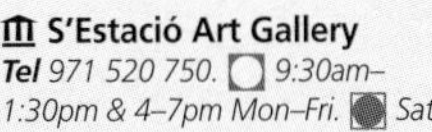

S'Estació Art Gallery
Tel *971 520 750. 9:30am–1:30pm & 4–7pm Mon–Fri. Sat.*

Environs
About 4 km (2 miles) north, near the road to Llubia, are the ruins of a Talayotic structure.

Monumental church in Petra, towering over the neighbourhood

Petra ㉖

50 km (31 miles) east of Palma. *Wed. Santa Pràxedes (21 Jul), Festa de Bunyols (30 Oct).* **www**.ajpetra.net

This small town is the birthplace of Junipero Serra. Aged 54, the Franciscan monk travelled to America and Mexico and after a series of arduous journeys on foot, founded missions in California. The old houses lining the labyrinth of narrow alleys have changed little since Serra's time here. The town makes the most of its famous son and all places associated with Junipero Serra are well marked. These include **Casa Natal Fray Junipero Serra**, a humble building in Carrer Barracar Alt where Serra was born. Next to this is a small but interesting **museum**, opened in 1955. The exhibition is devoted to his life and work and includes wooden models of the nine American missions established by Serra as well as a range of memorabilia. At the end of the street in which the Serra family house stands, on the outskirts of town, is the 17th-century monastery of **Sant Bernat**, which has a statue of Serra standing in front of it. The Majolica panels down a side street next to the monastery are a gift from grateful Californians and pay tribute to the famous monk's many achievements.

Museu y Casa Natal Fray Junipero Serra
C/Barracar Alt 6–8. ***Tel*** *971 561 149. by appointment only.*

Environs
Some 7 km (4 miles) west lies the small town of **Sant Joan**. Its 13th-century parish church, remodelled in the 15th and 18th centuries, acquired its present form in the 1930s. If there is time, head for the Santuari de la Mare de Déu de la Consolació, standing on the outskirts of town. Built during the Reconquest period and restored in 1966, it is now a place of pilgrimage.

Ariany, 4 km (2 miles) to the north, is a small agricultural town. Famous during the days of Jaume I, it became the region's capital in 1982. Its houses are dwarfed by the high tower of the Neo-Romanesque church.

JUNIPERO SERRA

Junipero Serra was born in Petra in 1713 and played an important role in the history of the Spanish colonization of North America. In 1749, he left on a mission to Mexico, and later travelled to California, where he established nine missions and sought to convert the native Indians to Christianity. Some of Serra's missions prospered after his death and became the cities of San Diego, Santa Barbara, Los Angeles and San Francisco. He died in 1784 and was beatified in 1988.

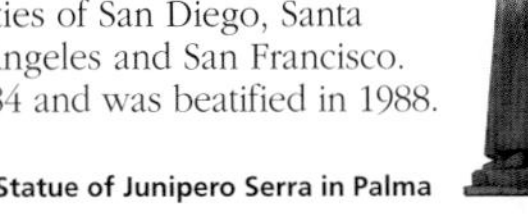

Statue of Junipero Serra in Palma

The medieval fortress of Capdepera

Artà ㉗

Wed. San Antonio (12–13 Jun), Sa Fira (2nd Sun in Sep).

This hilltop town was built on the site of an Arab stronghold; its name is derived from the Arabic word *jertan* ("garden"). Much of its medieval walls and fortifications have survived to this day.

The town's most interesting structure is the hilltop **Santuari de Sant Salvador**. It can be reached from the mid 13th-century parish church of **Transfiguració del Senyor** via steps (actually a Way of the Cross) shaded by a line of cypresses.

Madonna from the Artà chapel

The chapel and its surrounding walls were built during 1825–32. It contains a revered 17th-century statue of the Virgin with Child. The courtyard affords a lovely view of the town's rooftops.

Environs
Ses Païsses, a short way to the south, is a 3,000-year-old Bronze Age settlement. The remains include fragments of the defence walls and a huge watchtower. Some of the stone blocks weigh about eight tons. The archaeological findings from this site can be seen in Artà's regional museum.
The **Ermita de Betlem**, about 7 km (4 miles) to the north, is built on a hill. Established in 1805, the tiny church has a number of primitive frescoes.

Capdepera ㉘

Wed. Fiesta Nostra Senyora d'Esperança (18 Dec).

Towering above the town is a castle. It was built in the 14th century to defend the coast against pirates. At the highest point of the castle stands the Gothic church of **Nostra Senyora d'Esperança**. The outside stairs lead to a flat roof from which there is a nice view of the town's terracotta roofscape.

Castell de Capdepera
Tel *971 818 746. 9am–7:30pm daily (Nov–Mar: to 4:30pm).*

Environs
The **Coves d'Artà**, regarded as one of Mallorca's wonders, are situated some 6 km (4 miles) to the south. Two thousand Arabs were found hiding here by Jaume I during the Reconquest. In the 19th century, the caves were studied by a French geologist and became popular with tourists – Jules Verne is said to have written *Journey to the Centre of the Earth* after visiting them *(see opposite)*.

Coves d'Artà
Canyamel k. Capdepery.
Tel *971 841 293.*
Apr–Oct: 10am–6:30pm; Nov–Mar: 10am–5pm. 1 Jan, 25 Dec.

Cala Rajada ㉙

Plaça dels Pins, 971 563 033.

A small seaside resort and bay, Cala Rajada is famous for its beautiful beach shaded by a stone-pine forest. The rocky coast surrounding it is regarded as one of the most attractive in this part of Mallorca. You would hardly guess it but until recently this was just a small fishing village – only the old jetty, which is now used by pleasure boats and sailing yachts, remains.

Above the Cala Gat bay stands **Palau Joan March**, a stately home named after its owner, a rich tobacco merchant, banker and patron of the arts. Unfortunately, both this palace and its lovely gardens are now closed to the public.

Palau Joan March
C/Joan March.
to the public.

Environs
From Cala Rajada it is worth taking a 2-km (1-mile) walk to **Cap de Capdepera**, the easternmost headland of Mallorca. The nearby **Platja de Canyamel** is a new resort with lovely sandy beaches. There is also a local golf course and the former watchtower Torre de Canyamel now houses a restaurant specializing in tasty Mallorcan cuisine.

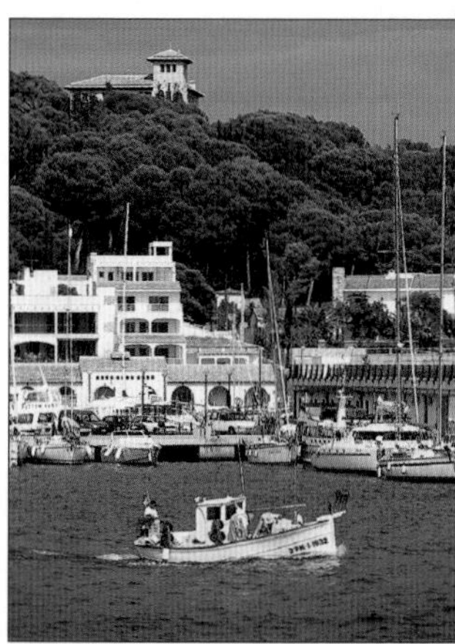
Fishing boat leaving Cala Rajada's harbour

Mallorca's Caves

Mallorca is famous for its caves, which are carved out of the island's limestone rocks. Many were known by the locals for hundreds of years and they once provided shelter for the early settlers, or served as hiding places from marauding pirates, dens for smugglers or religious sanctuaries. In the 19th century Archduke Ludwig Salvator began to take an interest in them and recruited a French geologist, Edouard Martel, to study them. In 1896 Martel rediscovered the Coves d'Artà. He was amazed by their size (some are the size of a cathedral) and the large number of stalactites and stalagmites.

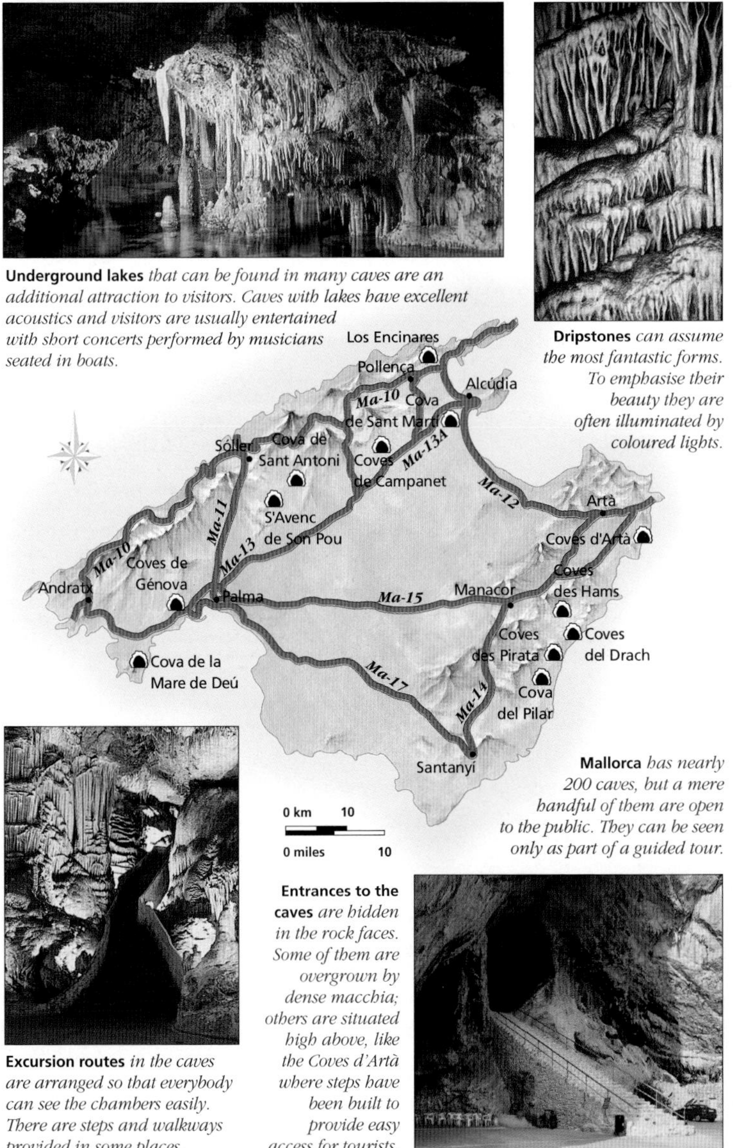

Underground lakes *that can be found in many caves are an additional attraction to visitors. Caves with lakes have excellent acoustics and visitors are usually entertained with short concerts performed by musicians seated in boats.*

Dripstones *can assume the most fantastic forms. To emphasise their beauty they are often illuminated by coloured lights.*

Mallorca *has nearly 200 caves, but a mere handful of them are open to the public. They can be seen only as part of a guided tour.*

Excursion routes *in the caves are arranged so that everybody can see the chambers easily. There are steps and walkways provided in some places.*

Entrances to the caves *are hidden in the rock faces. Some of them are overgrown by dense macchia; others are situated high above, like the Coves d'Artà where steps have been built to provide easy access for tourists.*

Sandy beach of Cala Millor, one of Mallorca's most popular spots

Cala Millor 30

Avenida Joan Servera Camps s/n, 971 585 864.

Cala Millor is one of the most popular resorts on the east coast of Mallorca. The first hotels began to appear here as early as the 1930s, but the real tourist invasion did not start until the 1980s. Similar to neighbouring Cala Bona and Sa Coma, Cala Millor has many beautiful beaches; the main one is 1.8 km (1 mile) long and is quite magnificent. As you would expect, the resort has plenty of bars, restaurants and clubs.

Environs

At the **Safari-Zoo**, a wildlife park 2 km (1 mile) to the south, you can explore by car, miniature road train or as part of a guided coach tour. Some 4 km (2 miles) northwest is **Son Servera**. Not the prettiest of Mallorcan agricultural towns, its prime feature is the church, which was begun in 1905 by Joan Rubió, a disciple of Antoni Gaudí, and which remains unfinished to this day.

Porto Cristo 31

C/Bordils 53A, 971 815 103.

The ancient fishing port of Porto Cristo is situated at the end of a long bay, where the El Rivet flows into the sea. Today it is a pleasant family resort but as early as the 13th century this was a seaport for the inland town of Manacor. As the best sheltered harbour on the eastern coast of Mallorca it was also an important naval base. During the Spanish Civil War, Republicans landed here with the intention of taking over the island from General Franco's forces. Despite initial successes, the attack was repelled.

Aquarium decoration in Porto Cristo

Porto Cristo is one of the few places on the eastern coast of Mallorca where you can find last-minute hotel accommodation during the high season. Among its attractions are the sandy beach and an **aquarium** with fish from all over the world.

Environs

Some 2 km (1 mile) south of Porto Cristo are the **Coves del Drac**. The "Dragon's Caves" are one of Mallorca's treasures. Although they have been known for centuries, they were unexplored until 1896. They feature an attractive array of dripstones, as well as one of the world's largest underground lakes, 177 m (580 ft) long, 40 m (131 ft) wide and over 30 m (98 ft) deep. A ride by boat under the stalactite vault is an unforgettable experience.

The **Coves d'es Hams**, 2 km (1 mile) to the east, derive their name from the hook-shaped stalactites *(hams)* found here. Boatloads of floating musicians on the underground lake produce an unusual musical ambience.

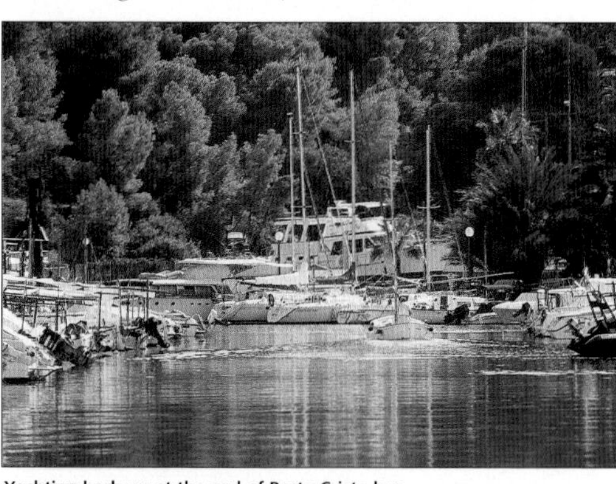

Yachting harbour at the end of Porto Cristo bay

Coves del Drac
Tel *971 820 753. Apr–Oct: 10am–5pm daily; Nov–Mar: 10:45am–noon & 2–3:30pm.* www.cuevasdrach.com

Coves d'es Hams
Tel *971 820 988. daily.* www.cuevas-hams.com

For hotels and restaurants in this region see pp144–50 and pp159–65

Manacor 32

Pl. Ramon Llull s/n, 971 847 241. 8am–3pm Mon–Fri.

Manacor is Mallorca's second largest town and boasts a centuries-long tradition of handicraft. It produces furniture and ceramics, including the famous Mallorcan black porcelain, but it is most famous for its simulated pearls. The town is also known for the local speciality – *sobrasada de cerdo negro* – spicy sausage, and sweets called *sospiros* (sighs).

Places worth visiting in Manacor include the church of **Nostra Senyora dels Dolors** in Plaça del Rector Rubi, built in the late 19th century on the site of a former mosque. Its lofty clock tower, resembling a minaret, is a town landmark. The most notable features of the church's interior are the vast wooden door and a figure of the crucified Christ, dressed in white robes, with long flowing hair.

Numerous shops in town sell simulated pearls, which have been produced here since 1890. In order to see them being made, you can visit **Perlas Majorica**, a factory offering free tours. Here, glass beads are covered with consecutive layers of a compound made of fish scale mixed with resin, dried, polished to a high shine and set in silver or gold.

Perlas Majorica
Avinguda Majórica 48.
Tel *971 550 200. 9am–7pm Mon–Fri, 10am–1pm Sat & Sun.*

Opulent interior of the Gothic church in Manacor

Music room in the stately home of Els Calderers

Environs
Sant Llorenç des Cardassar is 9 km (6 miles) to the north-east. The local church has two figures of the Madonna. The first is a wooden statue dating from the 12th or 13th century. The second, carved in stone, was made in the 15th century, probably in France.

Colourful fruit and vegetable stall in Vilafranca de Bonany

Vilafranca de Bonany 33

Wed. Festa de Meló (Sep).

The agricultural town of Vilafranca de Bonany lies on the road to Manacor. It is known for its colourful market stalls set along the highway. These sell peppers, sun-dried tomatoes and garlic, as well as fruit and vegetables grown in the local gardens. Also on offer are tiny doughnuts called *bunyelos*. The only historic building in town is the **Santa Barbara church** (1731–8).

Environs
About 2 km (1 mile) northeast, on top of Puig de Bonany (317 m/1,040 ft) is the **Ermita de Bonany** sanctuary. The monastery's stone cross was erected for Junipero Serra, who left from here in 1749 on a mission to California *(see p77)*. The sanctuary is 17th-century and was built as an act of thanksgiving for a good harvest – *bon any* or "good year". The modern church dates from 1925 and is entered via an imposing gate, decorated on top with ceramic tiles featuring portraits of St Paul and St Anthony. From the church forecourt you can see a splendid panorama of the central plains of Es Pla.

One kilometre (half a mile) northwest of Vilafranca de Bonany is **Els Calderers** – a landed estate established in the 17th century by the Veri family. The stately home is surrounded by fields and farm buildings. Today, parts of the estate are open to the public; these include the private chapel, the granary and the large kitchen. The rooms contain original furniture and are decorated with paintings, family photographs and *objets d'art*, all of which maintain the atmosphere of the former residence. The fire burning in the fireplace and the open piano give visitors the impression that the owners have only just stepped out.

Els Calderers
Tel *971 526 069.*
10am–6pm daily.
www.elscalderers.com

Felanitx 34

Avinguda Cala Marsals 15, Porto Colom, 971 826 084. Sun. Fiesta San Joan Pelós (24 Jun).

From a distance, the busy little town of Felanitx looks as though it is surrounded by a wall with many turrets. As you approach, it becomes apparent that these are windmills built on the outskirts of town. Felanitx is the birthplace of the outstanding medieval architect Guillem Sagrera (1380–1456) and the highly original 20th-century painter Miquel Barceló.

This small agricultural town has a fine **13th-century church**. Sant Miquel's magnificent Renaissance-Baroque façade, approached by steep stairs, hides a building erected in 1248. It is also worth visiting Felanitx to taste the locally produced *sobrasada de porc negre* – spicy pork sausage, and to buy some of the ceramics made here.

Environs

About 5 km (3 miles) southeast, on top of the 400-m (1,312-ft) high hill, are the ruins of Castell de Santueri, an Arab castle remodelled in the 14th century by the kings of Aragón. The view from the ruins is a magnificent panorama of the surrounding area. The Santuari de Sant Salvator stands 4 km (2 miles) east of Felanitx, on top of Puig de Sant Salvador, the highest mountain of the Serres de Llevant.

Huge façade of Felanitx's main church

Giant cactus in the Botanicactus garden, near Santanyí

Founded in the 14th century, and remodelled in the 18th century, the sanctuary is an important place of pilgrimage. The view includes the southeastern coast of Mallorca.

Santanyí 35

Perico Pomar 10, 971 657 463.

This old town is full of stone houses built from the local honey-coloured sandstone. The same sandstone was used in the building of the cathedral in Palma and Castell Bellver.

One of the old town gates, **Sa Porta**, in Plaça Port is a reminder of medieval times when the town was an important fortress defending southeastern Mallorca, and surrounded by several walls. Towering over the town is the vast church of **Sant Andreu**. The interior of this 18th-century church features a huge Rococo organ brought here from a Dominican monastery in Palma.

Environs

North of town, on top of the Puig Gros hill stands a 16th-century chapel with a beautiful picture of the Madonna. The **Santuari de Consolació** is accessed via stone steps, which have been climbed for centuries by footsore and weary pilgrims. Some 5 km (3 miles) east of Santanyí is **Cala Figuera**, with an unspoilt fishing harbour situated in a bay that resembles a fjord. The adjacent and equally picturesque **Cala Santanyí** bay is situated at the end of a rocky canyon with steep banks, overgrown with trees. Here, rising from the sea, is the **Es Pontas rock**. Six kilometres (4 miles) east is the **Botanicactus**, a garden which has nearly 400 species of cacti.

Rocky coastline in the Parc Natural Mondragó

Parc Natural Mondragó 36

8 km (5 miles) east of Santanyí. ***Tel*** *971 181 022. 8:30am–1:30pm Mon–Fri, 10am–1pm Sat & Sun.*

This relatively small, unspoilt area has wonderful footpaths and pretty country lanes and is an ideal destination for walking trips. The routes are marked and are generally easy going. The coastline itself is rugged, but it is still possible to find small, sandy coves, the best of which are Mondragó, S'Amarador and Caló des Burgit. In the pine forest, which covers most of the park, there are small ponds and dunes.

For hotels and restaurants in this region see pp144–50 and pp159–65

Ses Salines 37

Dr Barraquer 5, 971 656 073.

Ses Salines is a modest little town that is sometimes overlooked by visitors. It owes its origin, wealth and name to the nearby salt works. The **Salines de Llevant** are large salt lakes and marshes. This area is inhabited by numerous species of birds such as the spotted crane, marsh harrier, kestrel, warbler and hoopoe. During the migration season the marshes are visited by flocks of plover, avocet, tattler, godwit and osprey. There are many paths through the marshes, making them an excellent area for walking and cycling trips, particularly for bird-watchers.

Environs

Cap de Ses Salines is 3 km (2 miles) south of Ses Salines. This is the southernmost promontory of Mallorca. The view from the lighthouse is magnificent and encompasses the entire south coast of the island as well as Cabrera Island.

Banys de Sant Joan de sa Font Santa lies 4 km (2 miles) northeast of Ses Salines. The local hot springs, with water temperatures rising as high as 38°C (100°F), have been known since the 15th century when they were used to treat a variety of conditions, including leprosy. The local chapel dates from this period. The present bathhouse was built in 1845. Today, the waters are still believed to be beneficial and are used to treat rheumatism and a variety of respiratory ailments.

Campos, probably founded by the Romans, is situated 12 km (7 miles) from Ses Salines. The town, rarely visited by tourists, is full of historic remains. The Neo-Classical church of Sant Julià (1858–73) features a painting, *Sant Crist de la Paciència*, by the 17th-century Spanish master Bartolomé Esteban Murillo; the Gothic retable is the work of Gabriel Mògera. The church has a small parish museum. The former Torre de Can Cos, which once guarded the town against pirate attacks, became incorporated into the present town hall in 1649. Markets are held here every Thursday and Saturday.

Some 10 km (6 miles) to the north of Ses Salines is **Ermita de Sant Blas**, which has a recently restored 13th-century chapel.

Lighthouse at the Cap de Ses Salines headland

Colònia de Sant Jordi 38

52 km (32 miles) east of Palma.

Dr Barraquer 5, Ses Salines, 971 656 073.

The town of Colònia de Sant Jordi lies on the southern end of the island. It has a handful of modest hotels, a few restaurants, a pretty beach and an interesting harbour.

Sa Ràpita beach, a favourite with windsurfers

Many people come here with the sole purpose of catching a boat to nearby Cabrera Island *(see pp84–5)*, which, according to Pliny, was the birthplace of the famous Carthaginian leader, Hannibal. The pleasure boats to Cabrera Island sail daily from May until mid-October.

The town's other main attraction is the nearby salt lake, *Salines de S'Avall*, from which huge quantities of salt were once extracted – the main source of the town's wealth.

Excursions to Cabrera
C/Explanada del Port.
Tel *971 649 034.*

Environs

One of Mallorca's most beautiful beaches is 7 km (4 miles) to the north, in **Es Trenc**, which can also be reached via a shorter route along the coast. This small but constantly developing resort is very popular with visitors to the southern coast of Mallorca. The 4-km (2-mile) stretch of beach can easily accommodate the large numbers of holidaymakers, and is not generally too busy.

Sa Ràpita is a small place near S'Estanyol de Migjorn. The local beach provides good conditions for windsurfing. In summer, the marina is also a popular place. The only historic remains are of the defence tower, which once guarded the coast against pirates. Equally beautiful beaches can be found to the south of Colònia de Sant Jordi. When they get too busy, try **Platja des ses Roquetes**.

Beach and harbour in Sa Ràpita, near Colònia de Sant Jordi

Cabrera Island National Park ㊴

Native species of peony

Cabrera ("goat island") lies just 18 km (11 miles) from mainland Mallorca. A rocky, bare place and virtually uninhabited, it nevertheless has a rich history. It served as a prison camp during the Napoleonic War and was used as a base by Barbary pirates. Since 1991, Cabrera Island, together with an archipelago of 157 sq km (60 sq miles), has been designated a national park. This protection extends not only to rare species of plants, but also includes the surrounding marine life.

Es Castell
The 14th-century castle is one of the few reminders of the island's past. A small museum close to the jetty includes a history of the island.

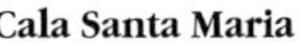

Cala Santa Maria
In the course of a few hours, you can see the shore areas surrounding the bay. Exploring the interior requires permission from the park staff.

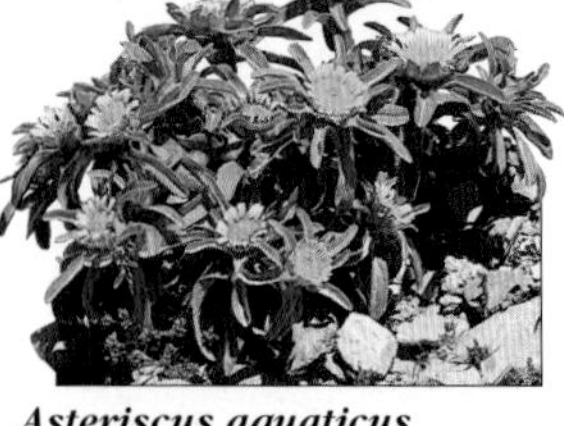

Asteriscus aquaticus
Though this plant is found on all the islands of the archipelago, Cabrera is home to some rare native plant species.

A memorial was built for the French soldiers abandoned on Cabrera by the Spanish during the Napoleonic Wars. Of the 9,000 prisoners, only 4,000 survived.

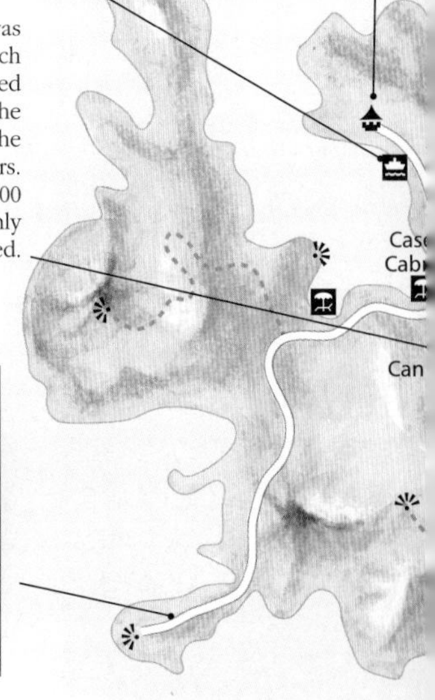

Cap de N'Ensiola
At the island's southwest tip is a lighthouse that can be reached via a winding road. Permission for this must be obtained from the park's office in Palma.

For hotels and restaurants in this region see pp144–50 and pp159–65

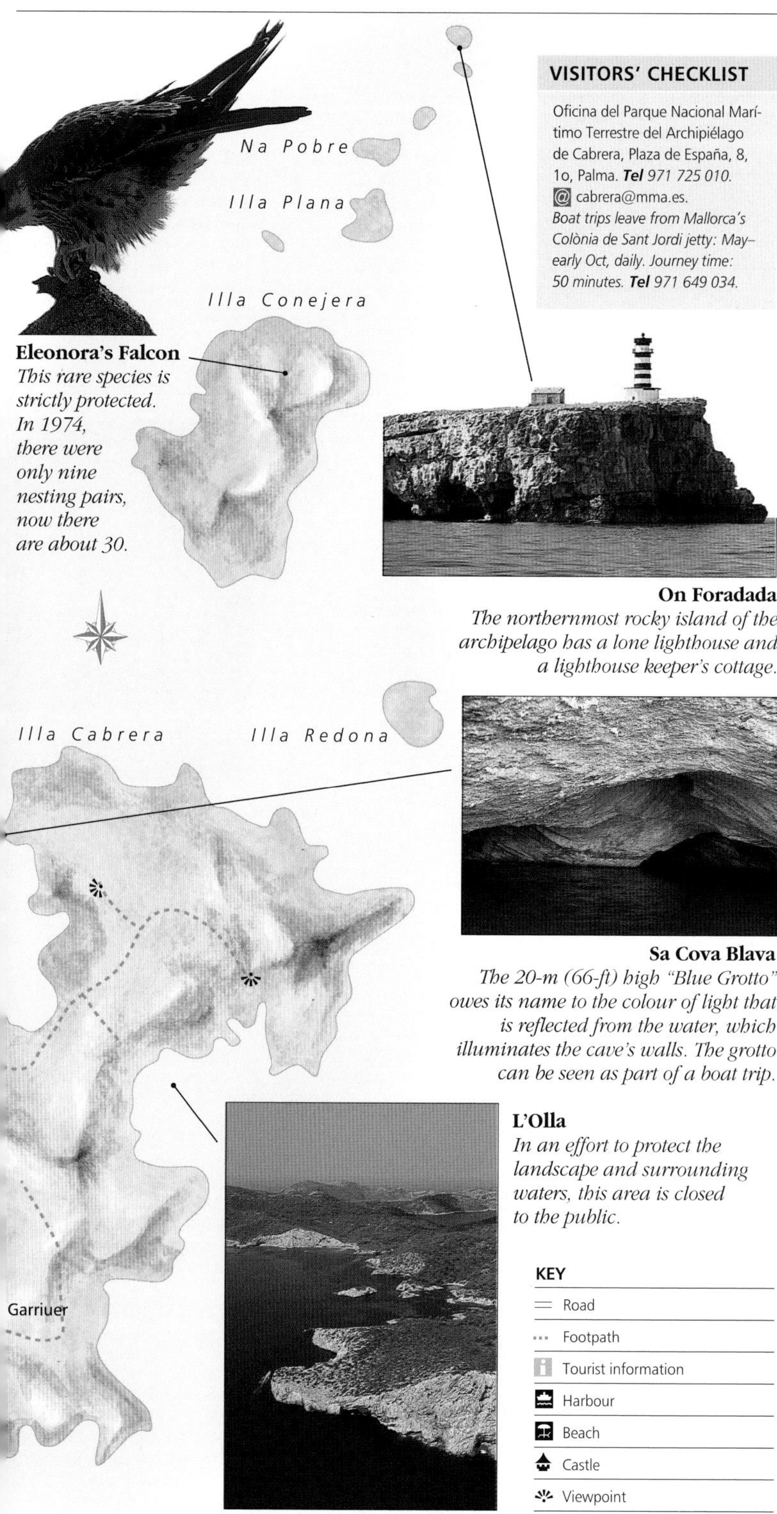

Eleonora's Falcon
This rare species is strictly protected. In 1974, there were only nine nesting pairs, now there are about 30.

On Foradada
The northernmost rocky island of the archipelago has a lone lighthouse and a lighthouse keeper's cottage.

Sa Cova Blava
The 20-m (66-ft) high "Blue Grotto" owes its name to the colour of light that is reflected from the water, which illuminates the cave's walls. The grotto can be seen as part of a boat trip.

L'Olla
In an effort to protect the landscape and surrounding waters, this area is closed to the public.

VISITORS' CHECKLIST

Oficina del Parque Nacional Marítimo Terrestre del Archipiélago de Cabrera, Plaza de España, 8, 1o, Palma. ***Tel*** *971 725 010.* cabrera@mma.es.
Boat trips leave from Mallorca's Colònia de Sant Jordi jetty: May–early Oct, daily. Journey time: 50 minutes. ***Tel*** *971 649 034.*

KEY

- Road
- Footpath
- Tourist information
- Harbour
- Beach
- Castle
- Viewpoint

Sunday market in Llucmajor

Llucmajor 40

Ayuntamiento: Plaça d'España 12, 971 662 600.
Tue, Fri. **www**.llucmajor.org

Formerly the main town of the southern region, Llucmajor has long been associated with Mallorca's shoemaking industry and had a thriving market in medieval times. It was just outside Llucmajor's walls, in 1349, that Pedro IV of Aragón killed the last king of Mallorca, Jaume III. The monument standing at the end of Passeig de Jaume III commemorates the event.

The **town hall**, built in 1882, is in the main square. Nearby is the 18th-century church of **San Miquel**, built over a 14th-century church. The most prized historic building in town is the Franciscan **Església Conventual de Sant Bonaventura**. This 17th-century church contains many precious historic objects, including an impressive altarpiece (1597) painted by Gaspar Oms.

Capocorb Vell 41

Tel *971 180 155.*
10am–5pm Fri–Wed.

Mallorca has fewer prehistoric remains than Menorca, but this Talayotic settlement on a rocky plateau on the southern coast of the island is well worth visiting. The settlement was probably established around 1000 BC. Originally, it consisted of five *talayots* (stone structures resembling towers, covered with a wooden roof) and 28 smaller dwellings. It is worth taking a closer look at the remains of the Cyclopean walls, reaching 4 m (13 ft) in places, which would have served as protection for this ancient village. Not much is known about the inhabitants of the settlement, and the function of some of the rooms is unclear. The narrow underground chamber, for instance, is too small to be used for living quarters and may have served as a ritual site. A free leaflet, in English, provides more information on these fascinating remains and is available at the site entrance.

The megaliths scattered through this quiet area, amid fields and fruit trees, were declared a cultural heritage site as early as 1931. Apart from a restaurant and a small bar, there are few other traces of modern civilization here.

Environs

Some 5 km (3 miles) southeast of Capocorb Vell, lies **Cala Pi**. This is a small cove with an enticing sand beach. Several luxurious villas have sprung up around here, well hidden behind pine trees. During the high season, many yachts drop anchor here. The area is dominated by a watchtower (1659), which provides views of the entire Badia de Palma. About 7 km (4 miles) to the south is **Cap Blanc**, which has a lighthouse. From here there is also a splendid view over the coast towards Cabrera Island. A large section of the peninsula is used for military purposes and it is therefore important not to stray from the route that leads to the lighthouse.

Ruins of the prehistoric settlement in Capocorb Vell

Tree-shaded courtyard of the church at Puig de Randa

Puig de Randa 42

8 km (5 miles) northeast of Llucmajor. *971 660 994.*

In the middle of the fertile plains of Es Pla rises the distinctive Puig de Randa hill (549 m/1,800 ft), which provides stunning views of the whole of Mallorca. Ramón Llull *(see opposite)* founded a hermitage on top of this hill in the 13th century and it was here that he trained missionaries bound for Africa and Asia. Nothing remains of the original building but Llull's legacy has ensured that the site is an important place for Catholics.

The monastery (the oldest part of which dates from 1668) is a popular destination for pilgrimages, particularly those associated with the blessing of the crops – *Benedición de los Frutos* – on the 4th Sunday after Easter.

Tucked under a steep cliff face, **Santuari de Nostra**

Senyora de Gràcia is the first of the religious buildings you come to. The interior of the chapel is decorated with beautiful majolica tiles. A little further up the hill is the 16th-century **Santuari de Sant Honorat**. This hermitage houses a courtyard that is filled with ancient trees. The passage to the church is decorated with tiles depicting the sanctuary's history.

The culmination of the pilgrimage is the **Santuari de Nostra Senyora de Cura**, which is on the site where Llull once lived. The gate in the wall surrounding the monastery is 17th-century and opens onto a courtyard built of typical golden Mallorcan sandstone. The monastery, much of which is fairly modern, houses a library and a study centre. The stained-glass windows of the church depict the most important moments of Llull's life.

Algaida ㊸

Fri. Sant Honorat (16 Jan), Sant Jaume (25 Jul).

Most people pass through the outskirts of this small town on their way to Puig de Randa. If you like churches, however, it is worth stopping here in order to visit the Gothic church of **Sant Pere i Sant Pau**, with its ornamental gargoyles.

Environs

The odd-looking castle on the road from Palma to Manacor dates from the 1960s and houses **Ca'n Gordiola**, a glassworks, museum and shop. Here, you can see skilled glass-blowers producing the pale blue and green glass that has been produced on the island for hundreds of years. On the first floor is a museum exhibiting items collected by several generations of the Gordiola family.

Ceramic sign of Ca'n Gordiola, advertised outside a Palma shop

Some 9 km (6 miles) to the east is **Montuïri**. The town, built on a hill, is famous for its agricultural produce. Nineteen of the original 24 windmills still stand as testimony to the town's former glory. Just outside Montuïri, on the road that leads to Pina, is one of the best preserved Mallorcan Talayotic remains – **Son Fornés**. This prehistoric settlement has two *talayots* and includes nine dwellings, which were used up until Roman times.

S'Arenal ㊹

Pça Rein Ma Cristina s/n. ***Tel*** *971 440 414.*

A little to the east of Palma, S'Arenal offers several kilometres of sandy beaches. A tree-lined boulevard runs along the shore, with bars, restaurants, nightclubs and shops. A series of stainless-steel beach bars stretches along the coast. These *balnearios* are numbered: No. 1 is near the harbour, No. 15 is by the Ca'n Pastilla marina (a miniature "tourist train" travels to the marina). In peak season, the resort's narrow alleys throb with life, day and night. S'Arenal's harbour provides mooring places for yachts. On the outskirts of town is **Aqualand El Arenal**, a children's paradise of pools, water slides and playgrounds.

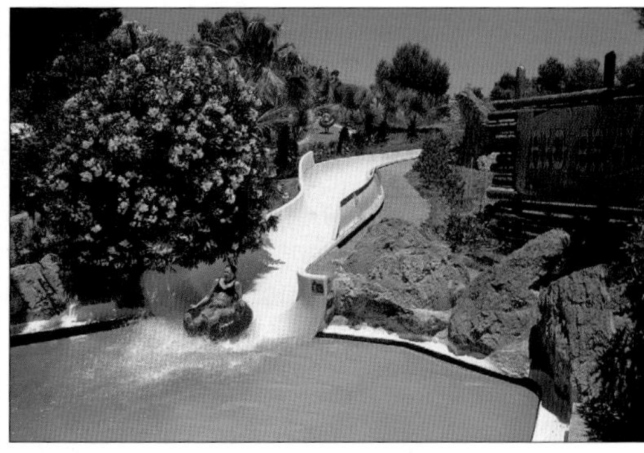

One of several water slides in Aqualand El Arenal

Aqualand El Arenal
S'Arenal. ***Tel*** *971 440 000.*
May & Jun 10am–5pm daily; Jul & Aug: 10am–6pm daily.

RAMON LLULL

This prominent Mallorcan was born in Palma to a noble family around 1232. During his youth he lived life to excess. Quite why he changed his ways is not known though legends abound. One story has it that he abandoned court life after seeing a vision of the crucified Christ. At the age of 30 he became a monk and devoted the rest of his days to the Catholic faith. He became a religious scholar, founded a missionary school and wrote over 260 works of theology, philosophy, physics, chemistry and warfare. During the final 30 years of his life he travelled around the world. He is believed to have been stoned to death in Algeria in 1315.

Statue of Ramón Llull in Palma

Mallorca's Beaches

Mallorca has nearly 80 beaches. The best are around Badia de Palma and to the north and northeast of the island. These are great for swimming and sunbathing and are very popular during the peak season. Some of the island's best beaches have been incorporated into larger resorts and include restaurants, fun parks, watersports and beachside bars. It is still possible to find more secluded beaches and coves, however, though these tend to have fewer facilities and may be difficult to reach.

Ses Illetes ⑥

This small beach, barely 120 m (390 ft) long, is off the beaten track. Despite that, and the lack of facilities, it remains popular.

Palma Nova ④

One of the best beaches on the Badia de Palma. Nearby buildings are hidden among dense greenery; the Serra de Tramuntana hills can be seen in the distance. It is a good base for family holidays.

Portals Nous ⑤

This beach, typical of the Balearic Islands, is on a long narrow cove. The thrills and spills of Marineland are nearby (see p59).

Magaluf ③

Magaluf's beach has long been popular with visitors, and the town – one of the oldest resorts in Mallorca – is full of restaurants, bars and clubs. Another attraction is the nearby Aqualand Magaluf (shown).

Ma-1
Ma-19
Costa d'en Blanes
Ma-19

Cala Portals Vells ②

An untouched small beach. The bay attracts those who seek peace, but at peak times it can be crowded even here.

El Mago ①

This small beach on the bay is favoured by nudists. This is one of three nudist beaches in this part of the bay.

KEY

- Motorway/highway
- Major road
- Scenic route
- Other road

Cala Major ⑦

This small bay is lined with houses and hotels. The golden beach is hardly secluded but it is one of the nicest in this area.

Ca'n Pastilla ⑨

A miniature train runs from here to S'Arenal. The local beach is similar to Platja de Palma, with umbrellas and deckchairs for hire. It also has a playground for children.

Palma ⑧

Inhabitants of the Balearic Islands' capital make the most of C'an Pere Antoni beach, or other beaches along the Badia de Palma.

Platja de Palma ⑩

At the height of the holiday season this 5-km (3-mile) long beach becomes exceptionally crowded. Behind the row of cafés and bars next to the beach are hotels, apartments and clubs.

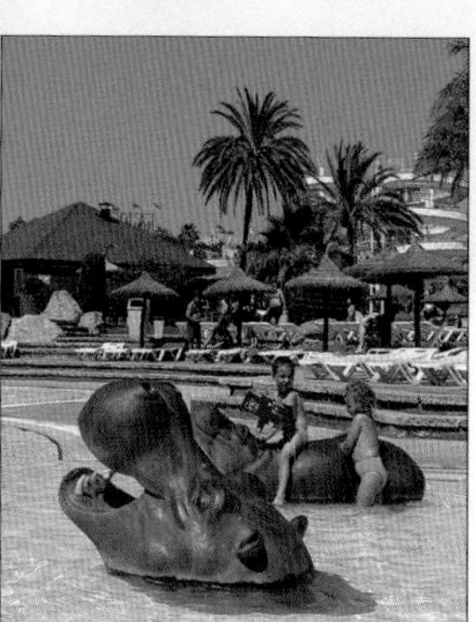

S'Arenal ⑪

S'Arenal lies at the eastern end of Platja de Palma, and is the most popular resort along this part of the coast. Its main attraction, apart from the beach, is Aqualand El Arenal fun park with its pools and rides.

40

MENORCA

Menorca is the second largest of the Balearic Islands and has low-key, family-friendly resorts and nearly as many beaches as Mallorca and Ibiza combined. Situated furthest from the mainland, it is one of the quieter islands and has escaped most of the side-effects of package holidays. Its small towns and villages appear to be havens of tranquillity, even at the peak of the season.

Travelling across Menorca, the variations in landscape are perhaps less obvious than those of Mallorca. The changes are more gradual, as red-soil and sandstone farmlands become pine-clad ravines, and small, sheltered coves alternate with steep, rocky shores.

Most of the Balearic Islands' megalithic monuments from the Talayotic period are found on this island, including a good number of the cone-shaped towers *(talayots)* which give the period its name. As with the other islands, Menorca has had its share of visiting conquerors, including the Greeks, the Romans and, during medieval times, the Arabs who defended the island until 1287. During the 18th century, the island was ruled by the English and French in turn, before becoming a Republican stronghold during the Spanish Civil War.

Locally-bred black horse in Ciutadella

The two oldest and largest towns in Menorca are Maó and Ciutadella; both are full of historic buildings. The island's capital, Maó (often referred to by its Spanish name of Mahón), is the best natural harbour in this part of the Mediterranean. Ciutadella, Menorca's former capital, is situated on the northwestern end of the island and also has a natural harbour. When travelling around Menorca you can appreciate the charm of the island's unhurried lifestyle. Its inhabitants are attached to their traditions and customs – for instance, unlike the rest of Spain, they prefer local gin to wine. Fiesta celebrations are particularly lively.

Colourful traditional folk dancers in Maó accompanied by live music

◁ A narrow alley in Poblat de Pescadors in Binibeca

Exploring Menorca

Menorca is sometimes referred to by the locals, jokingly, as "the bit between Maó and Ciutadella". The island mainly attracts those looking for peace and relaxation such as older visitors and families with young children, who wish to avoid the late-night clubs and bars found elsewhere. The island, proclaimed a biosphere reserve by UNESCO, is also a favourite with nature lovers. King Juan Carlos drops anchor in Fornells harbour from time to time, when he gets tired of the busy Mallorcan scene. In Fornells you can savour *caldereta de llagosta* – a delicious lobster stew for which the island is famous. Those who enjoy historic monuments can also find much of interest. The vast numbers of Talayotic structures, and the palaces and churches of Ciutadella and Maó are all worth visiting. One way to explore the island is on horseback.

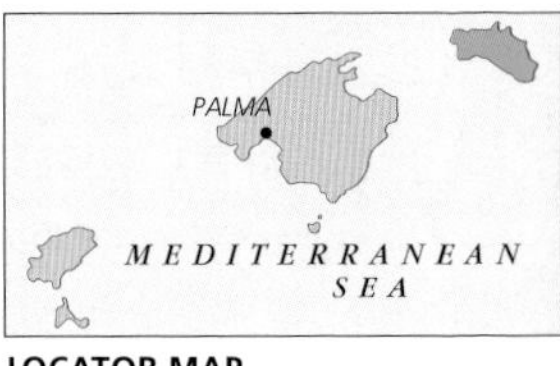

LOCATOR MAP

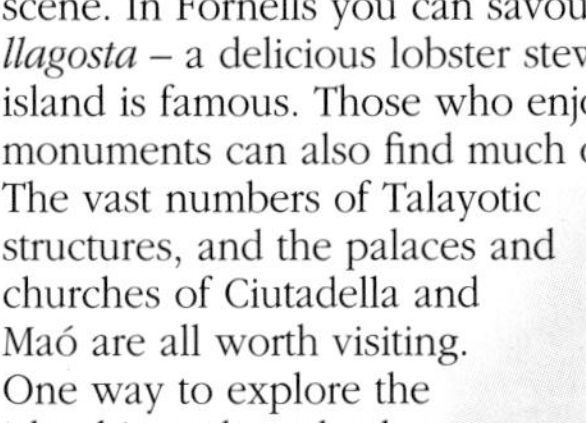

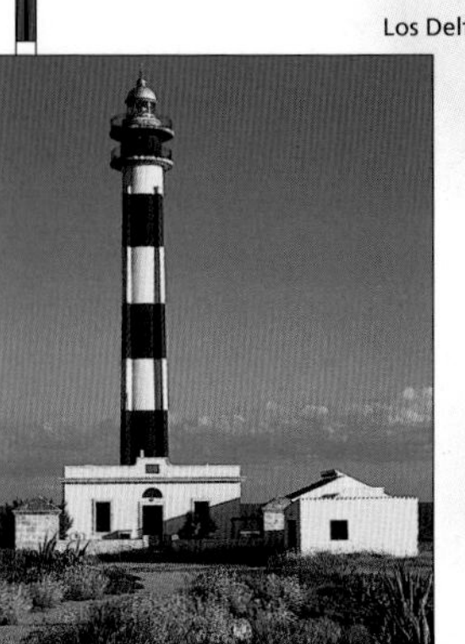

Lighthouse at Cap d'Artrutx

SIGHTS AT A GLANCE

Alaior 8
Binibeca Vell 5
Cala en Porter 7
Cales Coves 6
Cap de Cavalleria 11
Ciutadella pp108–9 16
Es Castell 3
Es Grau 2
Es Mercadal 9
Es Migjorn Gran 12
Ferreries 13
Fornells 10
Maó pp94–5 1
Sant Lluís 4
Santa Galdana 14

Tours

Western Coast of Menorca 15

GETTING THERE

The best way to travel to Menorca is by air. During the high season there are flights from many European countries and other regions of Spain. The most reliable way to travel out of season is via Palma or Barcelona. The airport is near Maó and has good transport links with major towns on the island. You can also travel to Menorca by ferry from Palma or Barcelona. The main road on the island connects Maó with Ciutadella. Minor roads branch from it, running towards the northern and southern coasts. There are no problems reaching large towns and resorts, but some small, attractive places maybe difficult to get to. It is best to travel around the island by hire car, as some of the smaller towns and villages have no bus service.

For additional map symbols *see back flap*

Beach and boats at anchor in Cala Binibeca

Taula and *talayot* in Trepucó, Menorca's most famous megalithic settlement

SEE ALSO

- ***Where to Stay*** pp150–52
- ***Where to Eat*** pp165–8

Maó ❶

In some respects, Maó (or Mahón in Spanish) is like a small, provincial town. A pretty place, it has a population of almost 30,000 and lies on the steep, southern shore of a bay that is one of the best natural harbours in the world. The remains of the old city walls, several beautiful churches, colourful Spanish mansions and Georgian town houses make it a fascinating place to explore. At the same time, it is the island's capital and is a city of culture – its Teatre Principal was the first opera house in Spain when it opened in 1829.

Muse in front of Teatre Principal

Exploring Maó

When exploring Maó, it is best to start from Plaça d'Espanya. Here, and around the neighbouring squares, are the town's main historic buildings. The whole district is dominated by the vast Baroque church of **Santa Maria**. For most people, however, the real pleasure is in strolling along the narrow alleys of old Maó and soaking up its unique atmosphere. Some of Maó's streets have restricted car access, turning them into virtual pedestrian precincts. Stopping for a rest in one of the numerous cafés is an experience to savour.

Església del Carme

Plaça Carme

This imposing Baroque church began life as a Carmelite convent in 1751. In 1835, the convent was confiscated by the state and the building was substantially restored in 1941 after being damaged during the Spanish Civil War. The vast interior of the former church, one of the biggest in Maó, is preserved in a Rococo style,

Colourful houses built on the high escarpment in Plaça Espanya

but despite its opulence it gives an impression of emptiness.

The complex, mostly closed to visitors, occupies the vast quarter between Plaça Carme and Plaça de la Miranda. The square behind the monastery offers a beautiful view over Cala Sergo.

Mercat

Plaça Carme. *9am–9pm Mon–Sat.*

Maó's famous town market (Mercat) takes place in a series of renovated monastery buildings next to Església del Carme. The cool cloister has been turned into a picturesque fruit and vegetable market, where *queso Mahón*, one of Spain's most delicious cheeses, is much in evidence. Here, you can also buy meat and other food products, as well as souvenirs. The rows of market stalls set under the figures of the saints and other religious symbols provide a strange contrast.

Narrow alleys leading away from Maó's old centre

Museu Hernández Mora

Claustre del Carme, Plaça de la Miranda. ***Tel*** *971 350 597.*

The Menorcan historian Hernández Mora (1902–84) donated his collection of antique furniture, sea charts, paintings, engravings and other works of art to the town. The exhibits provide a fascinating slice of Menorcan history during the 18th and 19th centuries, when the French and English ruled the island in turn.

Plaça Espanya

Plaça Espanya is the central square of old Maó. A busy **fish market** occupies a circular bastion on the north side of the square and offers countless varieties of fish, squid, shellfish and other seafood. From here steps lead down to Maó's waterfront.

Teatre Principal

Costa Deià 40.

Tel *971 355 603, 971 355 776.*

Maó's theatre opened in 1829, and beats the Liceu in Barcelona and Teatro Real in Madrid, to be Spain's first opera house. Built by the Italian singer and architect, Giovanni Palagi, it was often chosen by the big Spanish opera companies to premiere their Spanish tours. Today, it is used mainly as a cinema but it also hosts some concerts and cultural events including an annual musical festival at the end of March.

Santa Maria

Plaça Constitució.

7:30pm Mon–Sat; 8am, 10.30am, noon, 8.30pm Sun.

This church standing near the town hall was begun in 1287 on the site of a mosque, after the defeat of the Moors by

For hotels and restaurants in this region see pp150–52 and pp165–8

Façade of the town hall opposite Església de Santa Maria

Alfonso III. It was rebuilt in a Neo-Classical style in the 18th century and remodelled several times after that, although the large, gloomy interior has retained much of its Catalan Gothic austerity and is almost devoid of any ornamentation, with only the transept and the vaults featuring rich Baroque decorations. The most striking features of the interior are the Rococo main altarpiece and the vast organ, built in 1806 by the Swiss maker Johann Kyburz and imported from Barcelona with the help of the British. It is a mighty piece with four keyboards and 3,120 pipes. Look out for the figures of trumpet-blowing angels.

Ajuntament

Plaça Constitució.

The town hall was built in 1613 and its façade *(left)* was remodelled in 1789, giving it a typically Spanish appearance. It features an ornamental clock, presented to the town by Richard Kane, the first British governor of Menorca. Inside, the walls are lined with portraits of local notables, French and Spanish governors and, still hanging to this day, portraits of the British monarch George III alongside Queen Charlotte.

Harbour

The best way to arrive in Maó is by sea so that you catch your first sight of its magnificent natural harbour from the prow of a ship. Several centuries ago the famous Genoese admiral, Andrea Doria concluded that June, July, August and Mahón were the best ports in the Mediterranean, by which he meant that outside the safe sailing season of the summer months, it was prudent to seek shelter here.

Today, the tranquil atmosphere of the harbour makes it difficult to imagine a time when this was once a vast British naval base. Tours of the harbour in a glass bottomed boat leave regularly from Maó and Es Castell.

VISITORS' CHECKLIST

29,000. 5 km (3 miles) southwest, 971 157 000. Plaça Esplanada 40, 971 363 790. Tue & Sat. Procesión marinera de la Verge del Carme (mid-Jul), Verge de Gràcia (7–9 Sep).

Maó, perched on steep slopes, seen from the harbour

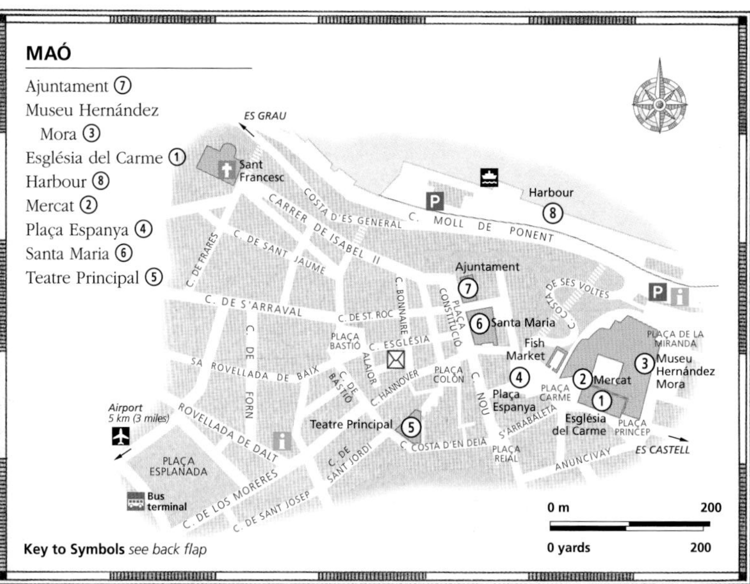

Further Afield

Venturing outside Maó's centre involves a pleasant stroll along narrow avenues lined with quaint houses, and passing all the main historic sights of the town. The most interesting include the magnificent chapel of the Immaculate Conception in the church of **Sant Francesc**, built in an ornamental Spanish Baroque style. The **Museu de Menorca** is also well worth a visit if only for its extensive range of items from the Talayotic period. Another interesting place to see is the **gin distillery**.

For a longer hike, Maó is a good starting point for a walk along the coast – head north to **Cala Llonga**, or south right up to **Port de Malborough**.

Some of the Xoriguer distillery's ancient gin-making equipment

Xoriguer Distillery

Andén de Poniente 91. *Tel 971 362 197.*

Gin production on the island is a legacy of the British occupation, although its local brands taste rather different to the ones currently produced in Britain. You can acquaint yourself with the gin distillation process by visiting the Xoriguer distillery, close to the harbour steps, which was founded in the 18th century.

As well as juniper, which is imported from the Pyrenees, gin contains a number of other aromatic herbs. Menorcan gin is sold only in Menorca and in a handful of restaurants in Mallorca.

The distillery also produces various liqueurs, including the *hierbas* that are believed by some to have therapeutic properties. All these drinks can be tasted on site, and of course bought in the shop.

Gobierno Militar, one of the most magnificent buildings in Maó

Sant Francesc

Plaça de Monestir. *6:30pm daily, 10am, 7:30pm Sun.*

The church of Sant Francesc with its light-coloured Baroque façade (1719–92), stands at the end of **Carrer Isabel II**.

The church's imposing interior has a vast, dark nave with a soaring Gothic altar at the end of it.

The church's most outstanding feature is its octagonal chapel of the Immaculate Conception built in a fanciful Spanish Baroque style and decorated with stucco garlands of vine and roses. This is the most beautiful example of Baroque ornamentation in Menorca. Its creator is believed to be the famous painter, sculptor and architect, Francesco Herrara.

Ornament from Sant Francesc

Adjoining the south side of Sant Francesc is the monumental structure of the monastery, with an arcaded courtyard. Currently it houses the Museu de Menorca.

Museu de Menorca

Avda Dr Guàrdia s/n. ***Tel** 971 350 955. Apr–Oct: 10am–2pm & 6–8pm Tue–Sat, 10am–2pm Sun; Nov–Mar: 9:30am–2pm Tue–Fri, 10am–2pm Sat & Sun. public hols.*

This museum occupies the former cloisters of a Franciscan monastery. The collection includes works of art and archaeological relics. Many of the exhibits date from prehistoric times, and there is an extensive selection from the Talayotic period, as well as Roman, Byzantine and Arabic artifacts. Among the most interesting exhibits are a bronze statuette of a bull, Punic jewellery and some huge amphorae.

Gobierno Militar

Carrer Isabel II.

The Military Governor's House and army headquarters are housed in one of Maó's most beautiful buildings. The palace was built in 1768, during the second British occupation. The building is still used by the army and can therefore be seen only from the outside, though the arcaded courtyard is well worth a peek.

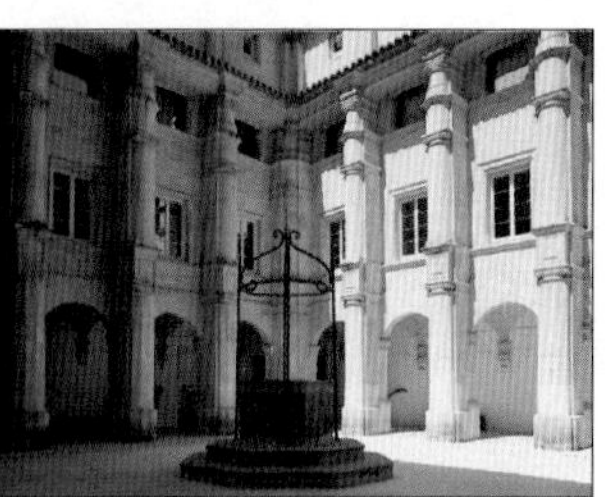

Courtyard of the former Franciscan monastery

Plaça Bastió

This small, irregular-shaped square has limited vehicle access, and serves as a good place for children to let off steam. Visitors who are fatigued by sightseeing often stop here for a rest.

At the north corner of the square stands

For hotels and restaurants in this region see pp150–52 and pp165–8

the medieval **Portal de Sant Roc** that is named after Saint Roch, a 14th-century hermit who was believed to be able to ward off the plague. Flanked by bulky twin turrets and a connecting arch, it is one of the few remaining fragments of Maó's medieval walls and was once the exit point from the city onto the road leading to Alaior. The fortifications did not stop Barbarossa from plundering the town, which he took in 1535, destroying most of the city's defences.

Portal de Sant Roc, viewed from the street leading to the town hall

Plaça Esplanada

Plaça Esplanada, with its flower beds shaded by pine trees, is the biggest square in the city and was once used as a military parade ground. Now, it provides a popular meeting place for the locals, especially at the weekends. The ice-cream sellers and swings make it equally popular with local children. There is a market on Tuesday and Saturday mornings.

The square is flanked on three sides by low buildings, many of them housing bars, cafés and restaurants. The western section of the square features a huge Civil War memorial erected during the days of Franco. At the back of the square are army barracks built during the first British occupation of the island and now used by the Spanish Army.

Buses on their way to other island towns stop near here.

MAYONNAISE

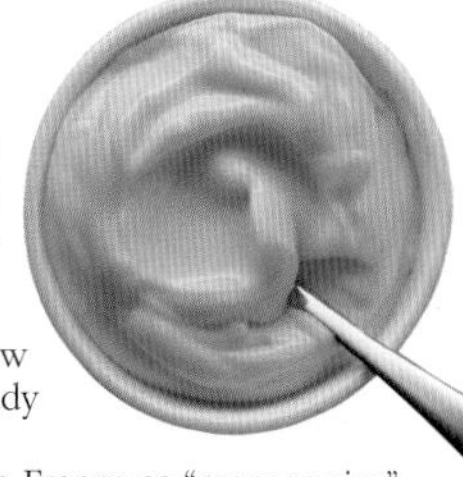

Following his victory over the British, Louis-François-Armand de Vignerot du Plessis, a cousin of Cardinal Richelieu, stopped at a local inn where he was served a tasty sauce. On his return to Paris, he introduced the sauce to the royal court, where the new garnish was an instant hit. Already known on the islands as "salsa mahonesa", it became known in France as "mayonnaise".

Ateneu Científic Literari i Artístic de Maó

Rovellada de Dalt 25.
***Tel** 971 360 553.*

Menorca's Centre of Culture and Science can be visited by appointment only. It has a collection of local ceramics, natural history exhibits (shells, birds etc.), maps and charts, a library and permanent exhibitions of works by Spanish artists Pasqual Calbó, Màrius Verdaguer and Juan Vives Llull.

Sant Antoni

Carrer de Vassollo.
8pm Mon–Sat, 10:30am Sun.

The 17th-century church of St Anthony was closed after it was pillaged during the Civil War. Following its restoration, it is once again used as a place of worship and provides a venue for cultural events.

Es Freginal

The park is a green oasis in the middle of town. During high season is serves as a venue for nightly cultural events. It also provides a stage for musicians taking part in the annual jazz festival.

Environs

About 2 km (1 mile) east of Maó, on the opposite side of the bay, are two swanky suburbs – **Sant Antoni** and **Cala Llonga**. A short distance further, at the end of the headland, stands the vast **La Mola** fortress, guarding the entrance to the harbour. During the days of Franco it was used as a jail for political prisoners.

Near Sant Antoni is the stately home of **Golden Farm** – a beautiful example of Menorcan Palladian architecture. Admiral Nelson is reputed to have first met his mistress Lady Hamilton here, although this is unlikely. Inside is a collection of mementos associated with the couple and an extensive library. The house is not open to the public.

Es Mutar, 9 km (6 miles) to the northeast, is a charming village of white houses standing at the foot of a rocky crag, on the shores of a bay. Neighbouring **Sa Mesquida** lies further along this rocky shoreline. The village is dominated by a well-preserved watchtower.

Plaça Esplanada, where locals come to relax

Lush shores of S'Albufera's Es Grau

Es Grau ❷

6 km (4 miles) north of Maó.

This small fishing village, fringed by dunes and pine forests, lies on the bay with a wide, sandy, horseshoe-shaped beach. Its safe shallow water is perfect for families with young children. At the weekend, the place becomes busier with day-trippers from Maó. From here you can take a cruise boat to nearby **Illa d'En Colom**, which has some nice beaches, the best of them being S'Arsenal des Moro.

West of Es Grau is the fresh water lagoon, S'Albufera, the largest stretch of marshland on the island. The **Parc Natural S'Albufera**, where hunting and fishing are prohibited, is a UNESCO biosphere reserve and a magnificent area for hiking or bird watching.

Es Castell ❸

2 km (1 mile) southeast of Maó.

Es Castell, once known as Villa Carlos, is a former military outpost. Originally called Georgetown, it was established in 1771 by the British and named for George III. The Georgian houses surrounding Plaça d'Esplanada serve as reminders of the British presence. One of the barrack buildings, **Cuartel de la Cala Corp**, houses a small museum with a collection of weapons and uniforms. Another sight is the parish church of **Nostra Senyora del Roser**.

Museo Militar de Menorca
Plaça Esplanada 19.
Tel *971 362 100.* *11am–1pm Mon & Thu.*

Environs
Illa Pinto was the site of the main British Navy base on the island, built in the 18th century. The local chapel is dedicated to Virgen del Camen, the patron saint of fishermen and the Spanish Navy.

Illa del Rei is where Alfonso III landed in 1287 during the Reconquest. **Illa Plana**, the smallest island on the bay, has the remains of a quarantine centre built in 1490 for those arriving at the island. **Illa Llazaret**, the largest of the islands, situated at the entrance to the bay, was once a peninsula, until it was cut off from the mainland by the St George Canal in the early 1900s. On the nearby headland are the remains of **Fort San Felip**, a 16th-century fortress that once guarded the southern entrance to Maó's harbour. In its day, the fortress was one of the most highly advanced systems of defence in Europe and could house an entire garrison of soldiers underground. It was destroyed by the Spanish in 1782 and now only its ruins remain. On the opposite side of the bay, near the village of Sant Esteve, is **Fort Malborough**. Built by the British to back up Fort San Felip, it has since been restored and now houses a museum and has a number of displays (some with loud sound effects) on Menorca's military history.

French honeysuckle

Sant Lluís ❹

5 km (3 miles) south of Maó.

This quaint little town, consisting of a square, a church and a few dozen whitewashed houses, was built by the French during the Seven Years War (1756–63), as a quarters for Breton sailors. The French coat of arms on the church façade stands as a reminder of those days.

A windmill, **Moli de Dalt**, at the town's entrance was built in 1762. Today, it is the only working windmill on the island and serves as the town's symbol. Next to it is a small museum with a collection of farm implements. The road into town bypasses the centre and heads towards the resorts of S'Algar, Cala d'Alcaufar, Punta Prima, Biniancolla, Binibeca Vell and Cap d'en Font.

Environs
Trepucó is a prehistoric site with a well-preserved *taula*. In the seaside villages of **S'Algar** and **Cala d'Alcaufar**, hotels stand side by side with fishermen's cottages. **Punta Prima** is the largest local resort. From here you have the view of the uninhabited island of **Illa de l'Aire**, with its lighthouse. West of town is a guard tower built by the Spaniards in the 18th century.

Colourful houses and apartments in Es Castell

For hotels and restaurants in this region see pp150–52 and pp165–8

Prehistoric Menorca

Menorca is exceptionally rich in megalithic structures. Most of the remains date from the Talayotic period – a civilization that flourished between 2000 and 1000 BC. The period derives its name from the *talayots* (from *atalaya*, the Arabic word for a watch-tower), the stone structures that are dotted around the island, mostly in former settlements. There are various theories as to what their original purpose was – they may have been used as defensive towers, burial sites or storehouses.

Huge talayot **in the Trepucó settlement**

TYPES OF STRUCTURES

The ancient stone structures scattered throughout Menorca (and to a lesser extent found in Mallorca) fall into three main categories: *taulas*, *talayots* and *navetas*.

Taulas *(table) consists of two slabs of rock, one placed on top of the other in a "T" formation. Some are up to 4.5 m (15 ft) high. Suggestions as to their original function range from a sacrificial altar to a roof support.*

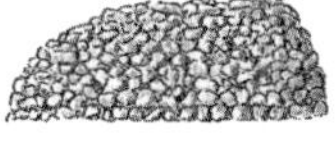

Talayots *are circular or square buildings. Their purpose is a mystery – they may have been tombs, guard-houses, meeting places or even dwellings.*

Navetas, *shaped like an upturned boat or a pyramid, were probably built as a sepulchre or a dwelling. At least 10 of them remain in Menorca.*

Spectacular 3-m (10-ft) high *taula* at Talati de Dalt settlement

MEGALITHIC SITES

Menorca has an estimated 1,600 megalithic sites. Talayotic remains can be seen all over the island, usually in rural areas, but they are more highly concentrated on the plains of the more fertile south.

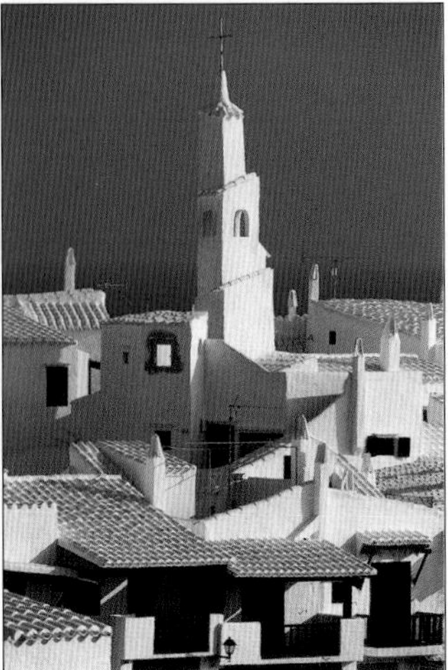

White houses and steeple in Binibeca Vell

Binibeca Vell 5

9 km (6 miles) south of Maó.

Binibeca Vell stands out amid the similarity of many of Menorca's southern seaside resorts. Also known as *Poblat de Pescadors* ("Fishermen's Village"), it was built as a resort development in 1972 to resemble a traditional Menorcan coastal fishing village. It has whitewashed, two-storey houses, wooden balconies and a maze of streets that are so narrow you can touch the buildings on both sides with outstretched arms. The blaze of white walls, small patios and lush gardens enhance the Mediterranean atmosphere with a touch of eastern influence. The "village" even has a church steeple, though no church. Nearby are a number of pleasant coves and beaches, including **Cala Binibeca**, **Cala Binisafúller** and the smallest beach in Menorca – **Es Caló Blanc**.

Environs

The nearby resorts lack any distinguishing features, apart from the beaches and their associated attractions, so it is worth taking a trip to the village of **Sant Climent**, which has a small market and lovely 19th-century church. Sant Climent also has a venue, the Restaurant-bar Casino, which puts on jazz concerts twice a week. These concerts are popular, as long as you can hear the music above the noise from the nearby international airport. Nearby **Torelló**, right on the edge of the airport, has a *talayot* with aircraft warning lights!

Cales Coves 6

11 km (7 miles) west of Maó.
Sant Clement.

This complex of prehistoric caves is best seen from the sea. Carved in the cliffs above a picturesque bay, the caves date from the Neolithic era. During the Talayotic period, the caves were used solely as burial chambers. Later they became the site of pagan rituals. On the shore are the remains of a Roman harbour (some of the "newest" caves have Roman inscriptions). Nearby is a small beach.

Cala en Porter 7

15 km (9 miles) west of Maó.

The seaside resort of Cala en Porter is one of Menorca's oldest holiday towns and is a sprawl of virtually identical holiday villas. Nevertheless, it provides good tourist facilities, including one of the loveliest beaches on the island, which is accessible via winding stairs and suitable for children. Its most unusual attraction is **Cova d'en Xoroi**, a huge cave, situated halfway down a steep cliff, which consists of several large chambers and tunnels. It has now been turned into a nightclub.

Cova d'en Xoroi
Tel *971 377 236.*
Apr–May: 11am–9pm daily; Jun–Oct: 11am–11pm daily.

Environs

About 15 km (9 miles) north-west is the resort of **Son Bou**, with the ruins of an early Christian basilica (5th–6th century AD). The cliffs hide a number of caves that have been cut into them.

Alaior 8

Sant Llorenç (2nd Sat & Sun in Aug). **www**.alaior.org

This market town, situated on a hill along the road from Maó to Ciutadella, is famous for its production of exquisite Menorcan cheeses.

Cala en Porter, one of the loveliest beaches in Menorca

For hotels and restaurants in this region see pp150–52 and pp165–8

Restaurant set in an old windmill in Es Mercadal

This is the dairy capital of Menorca (the island is also famous for its ice cream), with the biggest factories producing the famous *queso Mahón*, a white, half-fat cheese made of pasteurised cow's milk with added sheep's milk that gives it its distinctive flavour.

Besides buying cheese, you could also visit the fortified Baroque parish church of **Santa Eulàlia** (1674–90). The Munt de l'Angel **watchtower** stands on a hill behind the church and provides a beautiful view of the area. The huge fiesta celebrated on the day of St Lawrence includes riding shows, parades and horse races through the streets of the town.

Environs

Torralba d'en Salord, one of Mallorca's biggest Talayotic settlements, is situated along the road to Cala en Porter, about 3 km (2 miles) from Alaior. The local *taula* is one of the best-preserved and the tallest on the island. The rectangular temple has also survived in good condition. A bronze statuette of a bull discovered on this site can now be seen in the Museu de Menorca, in Maó *(see p96)*.

Some 5 km (3 miles) to the south is **Torre d'en Gaumés**, another settlement dating from the Talayotic period, which has a range of buildings including three *talayots*.

Es Mercadal ❾

 *Sun.*

Sant Martí (3rd Sun in Jul).

Es Mercadal lies at the very heart of Menorca, along the Maó–Ciutadella road. Founded in the 14th century, the town has been largely overlooked by tourism and earns its keep through farming and a number of local industries. The town itself is charming, with trailing bougainvillea and the pretty 18th-century parish church of **Sant Martí**. Es Mercadal is known for its excellent Menorcan cuisine and you may like to stop for a snack or meal in one of its pleasant small cafés or in Can Aguedet, at c/Lepanto 3, a restaurant that is very popular with the locals.

Detail from the façade of Alaior church

Environs

Some 3 km (2 miles) east, the convent of **Santuarii de Toro** was built in 1670 on the steep hill of Monte Toro, which at 350 m (1,148 ft) is the highest point in Menorca. Occupied by the nuns of a Franciscan order, it is regarded as the spiritual centre of Menorca and an ancient centre of pilgrimage.

Inside this 17th-century church is a statue of the Black Madonna – Verge del Toro – set within the main altarpiece, which depicts the Virgin Mary in a golden crown, holding the infant Jesus in her arms.

According to local tradition, the statue of the Virgin Mary has been worshipped here since the 13th century. These days, pilgrims visit Monte Toro, particularly on the first Sunday in May, to participate in the *Festa de la Verge del Toro*. Following mass in the church, the pilgrims then descend the stairs leading to Es Mercadal on their knees.

The old fortress has a military surveillance station. Nearby stands a huge stone statue of Christ, commemorating the Spaniards killed during the colonial war in Morocco.

Some 6 km (4 miles) north-east, are **Hort de Llucaitx** – an amusement park where you can go horseriding, and **Son Parc** – the only golf course on the island.

CALDERETA DE LLAGOSTA

This delicious lobster stew is the speciality of the northern regions on Menorca. Fresh lobsters are brought in every morning by local fishermen. The best stews are served in Fornells, which is famous for its seafood. The dish is extremely expensive but absolutely delicious. One popular way to enjoy it is to eat the gravy with bread, treating it as a soup, and have the lobster with mayonnaise as a main course.

Tempting lobster stew

BAR CASA DEL MAR
B.A.R.

Harbour and yacht marina in Fornells

Fornells ⑩

Fiesta de San Diego de Alcalá (13 Nov).

A picturesque fishing village, Fornells is situated 10 km (6 miles) north of Es Mercadal. During the summer season luxury yachts moor side by side with the fishing boats. The place has some excellent seafood restaurants. The local speciality is *caldereta de llagosta* *(see p101)* and it is thought to be so good here that King Juan Carlos frequently sails over in his yacht from Mallorca just to eat in one of the waterfront restaurants. Once Fornells was a major port and you can still see the remains of fortifications built as a defence against Arab and Turkish pirates. At the entrance to the harbour is a huge round watchtower. The village has no beach, but offers excellent facilities for diving, sailing and windsurfing.

In high season there are cruises to the small island of **Illa Ravells**, with its ruins of an old English fort. Boat trips can also be taken to **Illa dels Porros** and to the cape of **Na Guillemassa**, which has some interesting caves.

Environs
West of Fornells is **Cala Tirant** with a red sand beach. On the east coast of the bay are luxury villas surrounded by masses of colourful flowers, shrubs and cacti. The view from here extends to Cap de Cavalleria.

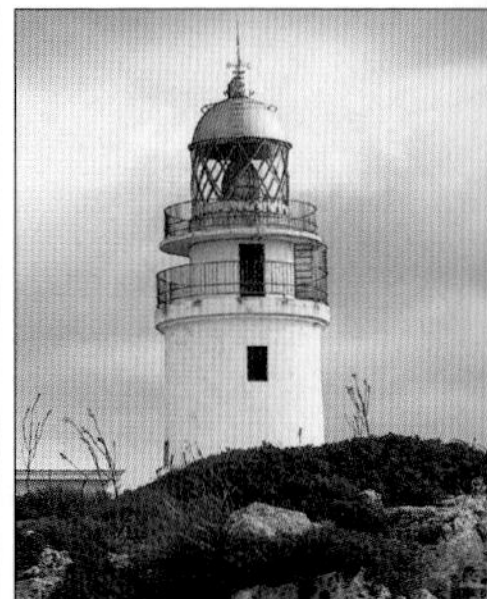
Cap de Cavalleria lighthouse rising above the rocks

Cap de Cavalleria ⑪

Cap De Cavalleria is situated 13 km (8 miles) to the north of Es Mercadal. This is the northernmost point of

Menorca's Beaches

Menorca has fewer easily accessible beaches than Mallorca or Ibiza. The best ones are to be found at the eastern end of the south coast. These are small, sandy beaches, tucked away in coves. There is an increasing number of beaches being developed west of Santa Galdana, and the local resorts of Son Xoriguer and Cala en Bosch are gaining popularity. Beaches on the northeastern coast are also popular.

Els Canutells ②
A golden beach lies at the end of a narrow bay that cuts deep into the land. Small beaches on the eastern part of the bay are also good places for swimming.

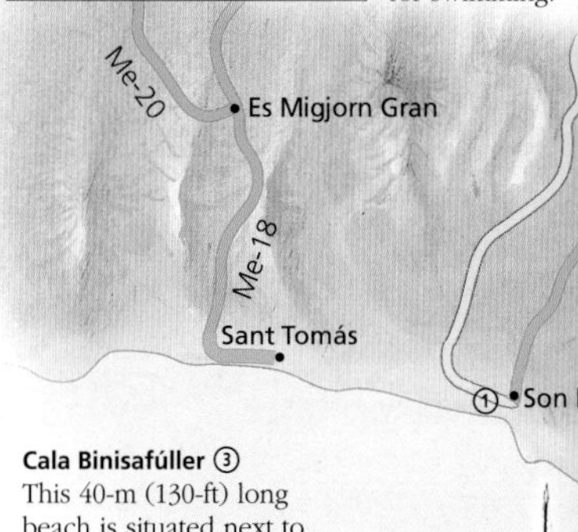

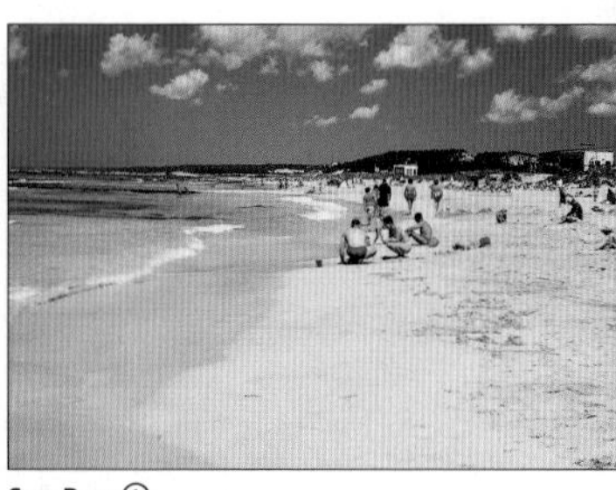

Son Bou ①
Some 3 km (2 miles) long, Son Bou is the longest beach in Menorca. At its eastern end are the ruins of an early-Christian basilica.

Cala Binisafúller ③
This 40-m (130-ft) long beach is situated next to the road between Cap d'En Font and Punta Prima. It is mainly used by holidaymakers staying at the nearby apartments and bungalows.

◁ Marina and the old town of Ciutadella, illuminated by the rising sun

Menorca and of all the Balearic islands: a tall, rocky headland swept by the northern wind – the "tramontana" – and washed over by the rolling waves of the sea. The steep cliffs provide nesting grounds for peregrine, sea eagle and kite. The road leading to Cap de Cavalleria runs through lovely picturesque areas, however it is necessary to stop several times on the way to open and shut the numerous farm gates.

At the western end of the peninsula are the remains of **Sanitja**, a Phoenician settlement mentioned by Pliny, which you can visit on a boat trip from Fornells. The Romans built a port on this site, called Sanisera. Nearby is a museum with a modest exhibition of Talayotic and Roman relics. More worthwhile is a trip to the **Torre de Sanitja**, a watchtower built by the British in the late 18th century in order to guard the entrance to this natural harbour. Further west is a stretch of barely accessible, unspoilt beaches. The most beautiful of these are **Cala del Pilar**, **La Vall d'Alagiarens** and **Cala Pregonda**.

Magnificent beach in Sant Tomàs near Es Migjorn Gran

Es Migjorn Gran ⓬

11 km (7 miles) south of Es Mercadal. Wed. San Cristobal de Ses Corregudes (Jul–Aug).

A small, tranquil village set among fertile fields, Es Migjorn Gran has a sleepy, provincial flavour. From here you can take a 5-km (3-mile) walk to the sea shore. The road leads through the **Barranc de Binigaus** canyon filled with fragrant wild herbs and flowers. You could stop on the way to see the limestone walls and caves, including the biggest of them – **Cova des Coloms**.

Environs

Some 11 km (7 miles) south of Es Migjorn Gran is the resort of **Sant Tomàs**. A dozen or so hotels line its main street, but there are no all-night clubs, and few restaurants. However, the place does have a great beach.

Cala Binibeca ④
This wide beach is near Binibeca Vell. The beach and the surrounding area have hardly been developed. A restaurant is by the car park.

Cala Alcaufar ⑥
The beach runs along the bay, on the south-east coast. The northern shore of the bay is densely built up.

Punta Prima ⑤
This southernmost beach of Menorca is one of the most popular on the island. The beach overlooks the rocky island of Illa de l'Aire.

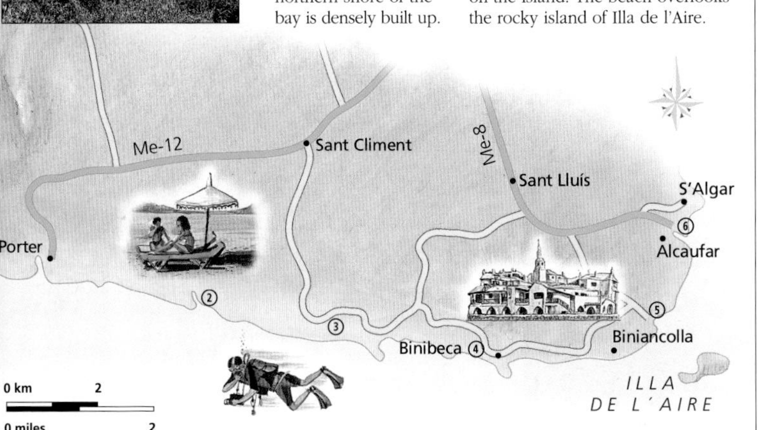

Beach on Santa Galdana bay

Ferreries ⓭

C/Sant Bartomeu. **Tel** 971 363 790 (Maó). 10am–1pm & 6–9pm Sat. Sant Bartomeu (23–25 Aug). **www**.ferreries.org

Ferreries is situated at the foot of the S'Enclusa hill. At 142 m (466 ft) above sea level, this picturesque little town is the highest settlement in Menorca. Its name derives from the many blacksmiths *(ferreries)* who once worked around here. At the heart of the village is the **Plaça d'Espanya**. Here, at a weekly Saturday market, you can buy leather goods as well as produce brought in by local farmers, including vegetables, fruit, cheese and honey. In Plaça l'Església is the parish church of **Sant Bartomeu** (1705) and the town hall. It is also worth stepping into the **Museu de la Natura de Menorca**, to see a selection of the island's natural wonders.

Carrer Fred, close to the main square in Ferreries

Museu de la Natura de Menorca
C/Mallorca 2. **Tel** 971 350 762 or 971 374 505. 9:30am–noon & 6–9pm Tue–Sat; 10am–1pm & 6–9pm Sun. **www**.gobmenorca.com/cnatura

Environs
About 6 km (4 miles) north of Ferreries are the ruins of **Santa Agueda** castle. Not much remains of this Moorish stronghold, but the view from the top of the second highest mountain in Menorca justifies the effort of the 260-m (853-ft) climb.

The strategic advantages of the hill were well known to the Romans who, in the 2nd century, chose it as the site for their first fortress. The Moors adapted the site to build a summer residence for the Menorcan governor and improved the surrounding fortifications. The fort was the last stronghold to surrender during the Reconquest.

Festa de los Roselles in Ferreries

Ferreries is the centre of the leather industry. Along the road to Maó are several shops selling Menorcan sandals.

Santa Galdana ⓮

5 km (3 miles) south of Ferreries.

The only way to get to Santa Galdana is by car from Ferreries or on foot, along the d'Algendar canyon. Situated on a beautiful bay, the town's popularity is growing, and a number of high-rise hotels have begun to pop up. Most of the other buildings are villas, set among the trees. The main tourist attraction is the beach with its white sand and turquoise water, sheltered from the wind by high cliffs and a pine forest.

It is worth taking a walk west from here to the charming **Marcella cove**. The adjacent **Macarelleta cove** has a nudist beach. Both beaches are well established and can be accessed by steps carved into the rock.

Further west is **Cala en Turqueta**, probably the most beautiful bay on this part of the coast. Another beach, situated in a charming cove east of Santa Galdana, is **Cala Mitjana**, which is a lovely spot, though it can get busy in summer.

GIN IN MENORCA

One legacy of the 100-year rule of Menorca by the British is the tradition of producing and drinking gin, which was a popular drink with the many British sailors stationed here. Unlike the rest of Spain, where wine is the most popular tipple, Menorcans have taken to gin in a big way. The production process can be seen in the 18th-century Xoriguer distillery, next to the landing stage in Maó *(see p96)*. The gin produced by the Xoriguer distillery is the most popular brand on the island and is sold in *canecas* – ceramic bottles reminiscent of the clay jugs that were once used by British sailors.

Gin from the distillery in Maó

Western Coast of Menorca ⓯

The region between Ciutadella and Cap d'Artutx is excellent for exploring. Whether walking, cycling or driving, you can enjoy the best of the island, including a nature reserve near Son Xoriguer, the Son Olivaret megalithic remains and the churches and museums of Ciutadella, the former capital of Menorca. Parts of this unspoilt region can even be explored on horseback.

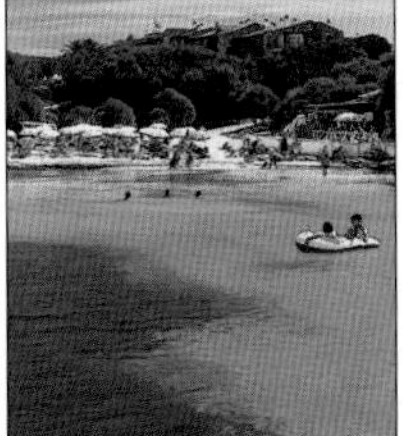

Sa Caleta ⑤
Near the beach, at the entrance of Cala Santadria bay is a former defence tower, Es Castellar.

Cala Blanca ④
This small beach is tucked away between bungalows, villas and a cluster of narrow streets. Visited mainly by locals, it is uncrowded and has safe swimming.

Son Olivaret ③
The two sets of megalithic structures – Son Olivaret Nou and Son Olivaret Vell – include both *talayots* and *taulas*.

Cala en Bosch ②
This harbour, situated in a sheltered bay, has a landing stage for pleasure boats. Next to the harbour there is a shopping centre.

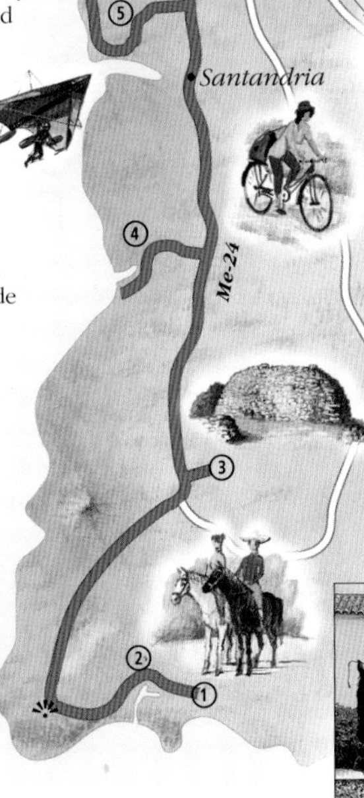

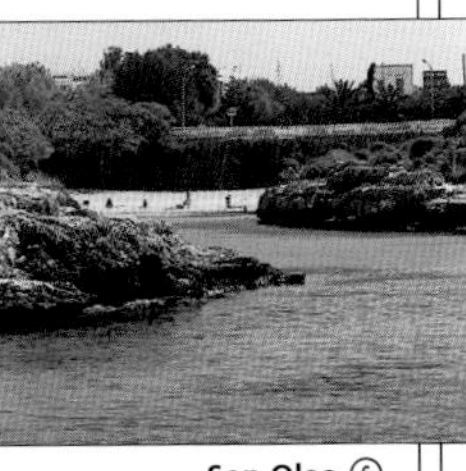

Son Oleo ⑥
On the outskirts of Ciutadella is a small beach, lying at the end of a long narrow bay. It is fairly quiet and used mainly by the locals.

Ciutadella ⑦
Take at least one day to explore the former capital of Menorca. From here you can make trips north to Cala en Blanes or to Cala Morell.

Son Xoriguer ①
Son Xoriguer is also the starting point for trips on horseback to the neighbouring reserve. The route leads past two beaches and then along the seashore.

TIPS FOR TOURISTS

Length: *16 km (10 miles).*
Stopping-off points: *Stop off for refreshments at one of the restaurants in Cala en Bosch or Ciutadella. A good place for swimming is Cala Blanca, halfway along the route.*

KEY

- Suggested route
- Other road
- Viewpoint

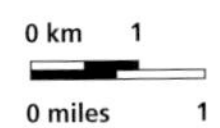

Ciutadella 16

A picturesque town with narrow, winding streets, handsome palaces and a busy harbour, Ciutadella has always competed with Maó. In the days of Arab rule it was the island's capital and in 1558 it was invaded by the Turks who killed many of its inhabitants and carted off some 3,500 more to slave markets in Istanbul. Of its buildings, only the cathedral remained. Those who survived were determined to rebuild Ciutadella. Most of the Menorcan aristocracy continued to make it their home, even after Maó became the capital.

Cross from Santa Clara's façade

Plaça d'es Born, the town's principal square

Exploring Ciutadella

Though there are few traces of Arab rule, Ciutadella has much to offer in the way of architecture. Numerous opulent palaces and Gothic and Baroque churches reveal just how successful the restoration of Ciutadella in the 17th and 18th centuries was. The main square in town is Plaça d'es Born, a characterful area close to the Gothic cathedral. The Museu Diocesà, housing sacred art objects that document the cultural and religious life of the island, is well worth a visit.

Plaça d'es Born

This is a former Arab military drill ground and was rebuilt in a Neo-Renaissance style in the 19th century. It is considered to be one of Spain's most beautiful squares. At its centre stands an **obelisk** marking *Any de la Desgràcia* – the "Year of Calamity", when Turkish corsairs invaded Ciutadella. The square is lined with historic buildings, including the **town hall**, a former palace of the Moorish governor, as well as the late 19th-century **Teatre Municipal d'es Born** and 19th-century palaces with Italian-style façades. The most imposing of these is the early 19th-century **Palau de Torre-Saura**. The adjacent **Palau Salort**, dating from the same period, is Ciutadella's only aristocratic residence that is open to visitors. The opulent Hall of Mirrors and the majestic painted ceiling in the ballroom make this handsome house well worth visiting. The square is also worth seeking out for its restaurants and open-air cafés and bars.

Neo-Gothic canopy above the cathedral altar

Catedral

Plaça de la Catedral.

Work on the cathedral began towards the end of the 13th century on the site of a mosque. Although it suffered fire damage, it escaped much of the destruction during the Turkish raid but was heavily remodelled after 1558. During the Civil War the workers' militia destroyed most of its furnishings.

One of the oldest parts of the cathedral is the Gothic south entrance that bears stone carvings of weird creatures and the heraldic crests of the Menorcan knights and nobility. The main Neo-Classic entrance dates from the early 19th century. The dominant feature of the interior is the Neo-Gothic canopy hanging over the main altar.

Capella del Roser

C/del Roser.

The façade of this small church includes a beautiful 17th-century Spanish Baroque-style doorway. Destroyed during the Civil War, the church was rebuilt and is now used as a municipal exhibition hall.

Cafés spilling onto the pavements at Plaça Nova

For hotels and restaurants in this region see pp150–52 and pp165–8

Can Saura and Palau Martorell

C/de Santissim.

These two adjacent palaces were built in the 17th century. Their distinctive façades reflect the character of the town's noble mansions built during that period.

Museu Diocesà de Menorca

C/Seminari 7. ***Tel** 971 481 297.*

10:30am–1:30pm Tue–Sat.

The Diocese Museum occupies a former Augustinian convent and cloister. Its collection of prehistoric and modern artifacts includes a miniature statuette of a bull and a bronze casting of a mermaid. It also has a collection of Catalonian paintings, and some sacred objects made of precious metals, including chalices and communion cups. Next to the monastery is the Baroque **Església de Socors**.

Ses Voltes' arches line the walkway leading to the cathedral

Sant Crist

Near the bank building that was formerly the house of Menorcan aristocrat, Joan Miquel Saura, stands the Baroque Capella del Sant Crist, built in 1667. Its fanciful façade is decorated with stone carvings of fruit garlands and masks. The statue of Christ above the high altar is said to have dripped with sweat in 1661 and became the object of a folk cult. Standing near the chapel is a column topped with a bronze figure of the Lamb of God, the work of local artist Matias Quetglas.

VISITORS' CHECKLIST

*28,500. Plaça de la Catedral 5. **Tel** 971 382 693.*

Fri & Sat.

Festa Sant Joan (23–24 Jun).

www.ciutadella.org

Plaça Nova

This small square is the site of the town's most popular cafés and bars. Ses Voltes, an arcarded walkway which runs from here to the cathedral, is one of the main streets of the old town. The Moorish vaulted arches that line the street hide a good selection of patisseries and souvenir shops.

Plaça Llibertat

This charming square situated at the rear of the former Augustinian monastery is well known to all who shop for food. Its two covered markets, selling fresh meat, fish, fruit and vegetables, are popular with the locals.

Arcades of the covered market in Plaça Llibertat

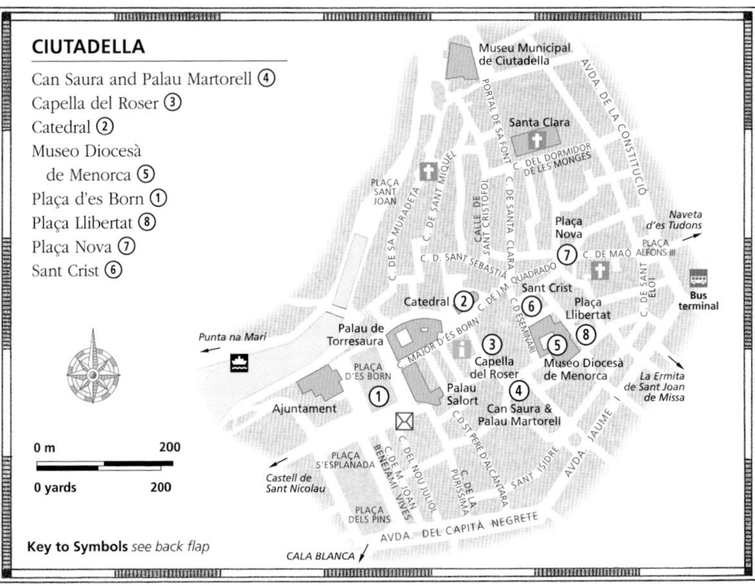

Further Afield

The old town boundaries are defined by the wide avenues of Avda. del Capità Negrete, Avda. del Jaume I and Avda. de la Constitució. Outside these limits there are a few interesting sights, including the **Castell de Sant Nicolau**, the remains of the city fortifications and the harbour. A stroll along the north coast of the bay will take you to **Punta na Mari**. Ciutadella, situated on Menorca's west coast, makes a good base from which to explore the area. From here you can get to **Cala Morell** in the north, or **Cap d'Artrutx** 10 km (6 miles) to the south.

Statue of a horse, the star of the Festa Sant Joan

Santa Clara

C/Santa Clara. *10:15am Sun.*

The original church and convent of Santa Clara was founded in 1287 by Alfonso III. Destroyed during the Turkish raid in 1558, it was rebuilt in the 17th century only to be destroyed again during the Spanish Civil War. A community of nuns still lives here. The wood carving depicting the *Adoration of Shepherds*, seen in the convent, was stolen by the Turks and taken to Istanbul but subsequently recovered.

Museu Municipal de Ciutadella, Bastió de sa Font

Plaça de sa Font s/n. ***Tel*** *971 380 297.* *10am–2pm Tue–Sat.* **www**.ciutadella.org/museu

The museum occupies the bastion of the former town fortifications built in 1677. This is the only preserved fragment of the town's fortifications. Founded in 1995, the Museo Municipal has a good collection of Talayotic, Roman and Muslim artifacts, most of which are kept in a large, vaulted room. There are crafted beakers and tumblers, ceramic bowls and jugs, bronze weapons and jewellery (with a distinct Phoenician influence). There is also an odd collection of human skulls, showing the damage caused by the practice of trepanning.

Plaça Alfons III

This modest square is on the outskirts of the old town, by Avda. de la Constitució. Several cafés and restaurants shelter under the trees. The square can be seen from some distance and you can't miss the old windmill, now housing a tourist office. This is a good place to sit or pick up a souvenir.

Plaça de s'Esplanada and Plaça dels Pins

These two adjacent green squares are the lungs amid the historic buildings of Ciutadella. The many bars and restaurants provide pleasant places in which to relax and the peace is broken only by the screech of brakes from the nearby bus garage. In the evening there are jazz concerts here.

An alley leading to Santa Clara

Windmill and tourist office in Plaça Alfons III

La Ermita de Sant Joan de Missa

Carrer de Comte Cifuentes.

The chapel situated southeast of the town centre is an important venue for the Festa Sant Joan celebrations. Vespers are sung here on the evening of 23 June. The nearby road, which leads to Marcarella, Marcarelleta and Cala en Turqueta beaches, is transformed into a racecourse during the two days of celebrations *(see box)*.

Harbour

Moll Comercial.

Ciutadella's shallow harbour was the main reason the British moved the island's capital to Maó. Today, the harbour has been dredged and can accommodate large ferries linking Ciutadella to Barcelona, as well as the many yachts and fishing boats that moor here. Having descended from Plaça d'es Born to the ferry terminal, it is worth taking a walk along the bay to soak up some of the harbourside activity. Early in the morning you can see fishermen returning with their catch, the first bars opening and the town waking up to a new day.

From **Punta na Mari**, at the entrance to the bay, you can see Castell de Sant Nicolau. On the other side of the harbour bay, about 500 m (1,640 ft) further on, is **Cala des Degollador**'s tiny beach. The beaches of **Platja Petita** and **Sa Platja Gran** are several hundred metres further on.

A phenomenon peculiar to Ciutadella bay is the mysterious *rissaga* wave. No one is able to predict when this event will take place, but it can cause flooding of the port to a height of several metres. The last big *rissaga* occurred in 1984 and left the harbour under 2 m (7 ft) of water.

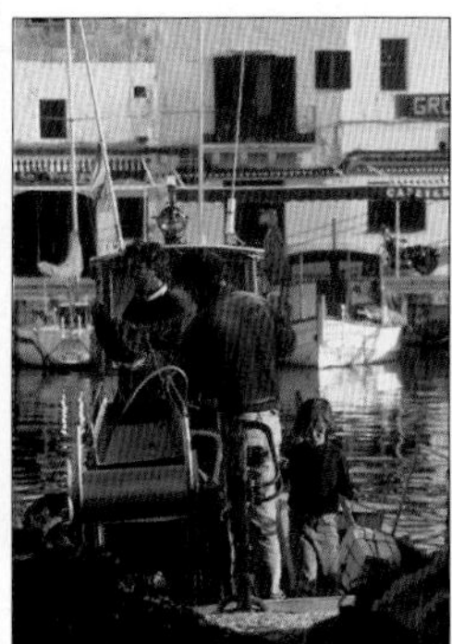

Fishermen in the harbour preparing their nets

Castell de Sant Nicolau

Plaça Almirall Farragut.

The 17th-century Castell de Sant Nicolau was built as a watchtower to protect the harbour. You can still enter the stronghold via a drawbridge and in the evening the castle remains open to provide a vantage point for the spectacular sunsets over the harbour. It also serves as a venue for temporary exhibitions.

Standing near the castle is the statue of a four-star admiral of the United States Navy, David Farragut, hero of the American Civil War and son of an immigrant from Menorca. The admiral is depicted in his uniform with epaulettes, holding a telescope. When he returned to Menorca in 1867, he was awarded honorary citizenship and a huge crowd turned out to greet him.

Environs

Naveta d'es Tudons, 5 km (3 miles) east of town, is Menorca's best preserved prehistoric ruin. The Bronze Age structure, built of stone blocks, is 7 m (23 ft) high and 14 m (46 ft) long and was used as a burial chamber. When it was excavated, in the 1950s, more than 50 bodies were discovered. In **Torre Llafuda**, about 3 km (2 miles) away, amid the shade of olive groves, stands one cracked *taula* and a well-preserved *talayot*. The pleasant setting and the surrounding fertile farmland make this a good place to stop and relax. Travel southeast of Ciutadella and you find a number of beautiful beaches hidden in small coves. These include **Cala des Talader**, dominated by a stone watchtower. Along the road leading to **Son Saura** is Son Catlar, Menorca's biggest prehistoric settlement. Its wall is several metres high and built of enormous stone blocks. Inside, amid the sea of ruins you can distinguish one *taula* and five *talayots*.

A short way to the north are two large resorts – **Cala en Blanes** and **Los Delfines** (which has a small aquapark). Eight kilometres (5 miles) northeast is the tourist village of **Cala Morell**. The man-made prehistoric caves are dug into rocks and were used for burials in the late Bronze and Iron Ages. They are now open to the public.

Aqua Center

Urb los Delfines.

Tel *971 388 251. May–Oct: 10:30am–6:30pm daily.*

FESTA DE SANT JOAN

This midsummer festival (23–24 June) has provided the citizens of Ciutadella with an opportunity to go wild since the 14th century. St John's Day begins with mass in the cathedral but fireworks, jousting and the carrying of a live sheep through the streets are also part of the fun. For most, the highlight of the day is the *caixers* (horsemen). Representing the medieval social classes, they ride among the noisy crowds.

Prancing horse in the streets of Ciutadella

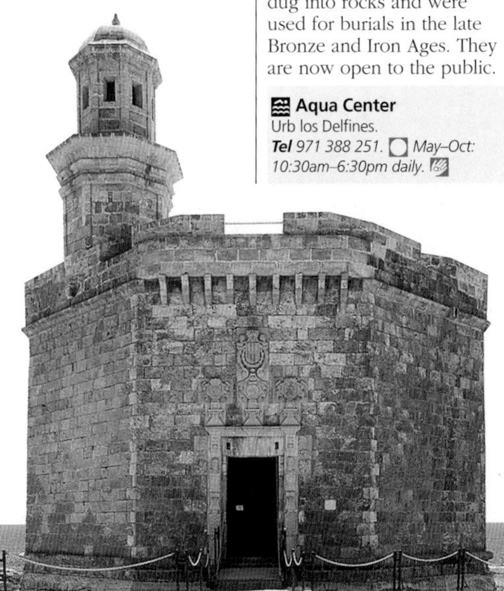

Castell de Sant Nicolau guarding the entrance to the harbour

IBIZA

Despite its reputation as a party island, Ibiza has maintained much of its rural charm. Fields of almonds and figs, olive groves, the relentless munching of the flocks of sheep – all are part of modern-day Ibiza. Yet there is no denying that the island is a magnet for clubbers, who flock here every summer attracted by the music, lovely beaches, lively nightlife and extraordinary tolerance of the locals.

The closest of the Balearic Islands to mainland Spain, Ibiza is intersected by a modest range of mountains and surrounded by scores of islets and protruding rocks. Its 200-km (125-mile) long coastline is extremely varied with small coves hiding beautiful beaches and mysterious caves.

Together with Formentera and a number of outlying islets, Ibiza belongs to the group of islands dubbed by the Greeks as the Pitiusas or "pine tree islands". Besides the Greeks, Ibiza's visitors included the Phoenicians, the Carthaginians and the Romans. The last big invasion took place in the 1960s when the island was "discovered" by hippies, and subsequently began to appear in all the European holiday brochures. Tourism took a firm and rapid hold on the economy and during the 1990s Ibiza gained entry into the *Guinness Book of Records* as the entertainment island of the world. Thousands of visitors fill the resorts, and big-name nightclubs offer a wealth of DJs and dancing. Ibiza sets the new trends in fashion – what is worn here will subsequently become a "must" in the rest of Europe.

Peasant woman in traditional costume

Away from the clubs, the north of the island is a rural patchwork of almond, olive and fig groves. The most distinctive features of the southern region are the vast salt lakes where sea salt is extracted to this day. Dalt Vila, the old part of Eivissa, is one of the best preserved medieval towns in Europe, despite its influx of pleasure seekers. For many locals time still moves at a gentle pace on the island.

An alley in Sa Penya, in the old district of Eivissa.

◁ **Sunset seen from the beach in Cala Benirràs**

Exploring Ibiza

Ibiza has much to offer holidaymakers. It is the Mediterranean's club capital and the majority of visitors come here to enjoy the delights of over 50 local beaches in sheltered coves, as well as to revel in the nightclubs of Eivissa and Sant Antoni. Everyone should visit Dalt Vila, Eivissa's old town, for its Gothic cathedral and to see and be seen in one of the many swanky restaurants and chic bars. Those in search of tranquillity can head for the island's interior where the hilly countryside is peppered with old stone cottages. For the energetic, the rugged coastline to the northwest provides excellent walking.

LOCATOR MAP

Platja d'en Bossa near Sant Jordi

Cap d'Aubarca
SANTA AGNES DE CORONA 7
Cap Nunó
PM812
Illa Sa Conillera
SANT ANTONI DE PORTMANY 6
C731
Cala Bassa
Cala d'en Bou
Illa de s'Esparta
Cala Conta
Port d'es Torrent
PM803
Cala Tarida
Sant Agustí des Vedra
Cala Molí
5
Cala Vedella
SANT JOSÉP DE SA TALAIA 4
Sa Talaiassa 475m
WEST COAST OF IBIZA
Cova Santa
Cala d'Hort
Es Cubells
Illa es Vedrà
Cala d'Es Cubells
Sant Francesc de S'Est
SES SALINES 3
Cap Llentrisca
La Cana

0 km 5
0 miles 5

SEE ALSO

• ***Where to Stay*** pp153–4

• ***Where to Eat*** pp168–70

For additional map symbols *see back flap*

GETTING THERE

Ibiza has fewer scheduled flights than Mallorca. Most visitors arrive by charter flight. During the holiday weekends, Ibiza's airport becomes one of the busiest on the planet. The planes landing here are mainly from the UK, bringing tourists for a week or two of partying. Barcelona and Madrid also have frequent flights to the island. Ferries from Eivissa and Sant Antoni de Portmany harbours sail for Mallorca and Formentera, as well as to Barcelona and Dénia.

Cala d'en Ferrer seen from the top of Sant Miquel, near Na Xamena

SIGHTS AT A GLANCE

Eivissa pp116–19 ❶
Els Amunts ❽
Jesús ⓭
Portinatx ❿
Sant Antoni de Portmany ❻
Sant Joan de Labritja ❾
Sant Jordi de Ses Salines ❷
Sant Josép de sa Talaia ❹
Sant Vicent de Sa Cala ⓫
Santa Agnès de Corona ❼
Santa Eulària des Riu ⓬
Ses Salines ❸

Tours

West Coast of Ibiza pp126–7 ❺

KEY

Major road
Minor road
Scenic route
△ Summit

Plaça des Parque below Dalt Vila in Eivissa

Street by Street: Eivissa ❶

Eivissa's coat of arms

Attracted by the hilltop site and sheltered harbour, the Phoenicians founded Eivissa in the mid-7th century BC. The Puig de Molins necropolis dates from those days. Dalt Vila (Upper Town) is the oldest remaining part of Eivissa and since 1999 has been a UNESCO World Heritage site. Strengthened by fortifications begun by the Emperor Charles V, it once guarded the entrance to the bay. Sa Penya, at the end of the harbour under Dalt Vila, was once the fishermen's quarter and is still one of the more colourful parts of town. La Marina, stretching out along the waterfront, is the place to go for night-time entertainment.

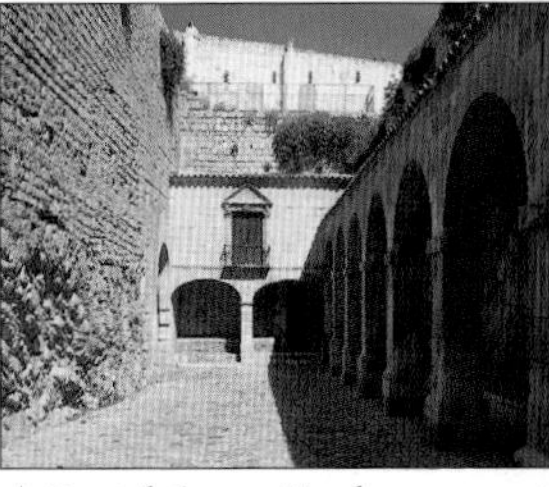
★ Portal de ses Taules
A broad paved drive leads from Sa Penya to Portal de ses Taules – the main town gate.

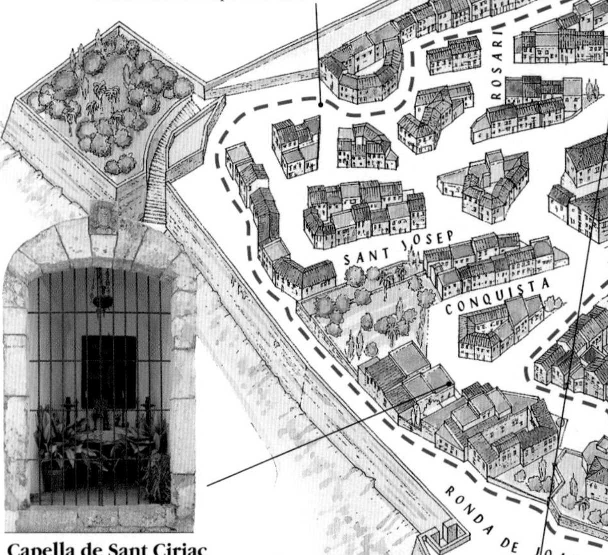

Museu d'Art Contemporani

Plaça del Sol's shady square looks out over the harbour and is full of shops and cafés.

Capella de Sant Ciriac
A mass is celebrated here each year in August to mark the capture of the town by Jaume I in 1235.

Plaça de la Vila
The main square of Dalt Vila is lined with shops, restaurants and cafés to tempt passing visitors.

KEY

– – – Suggested route

For hotels and restaurants in this region see pp153–4 and pp168–70

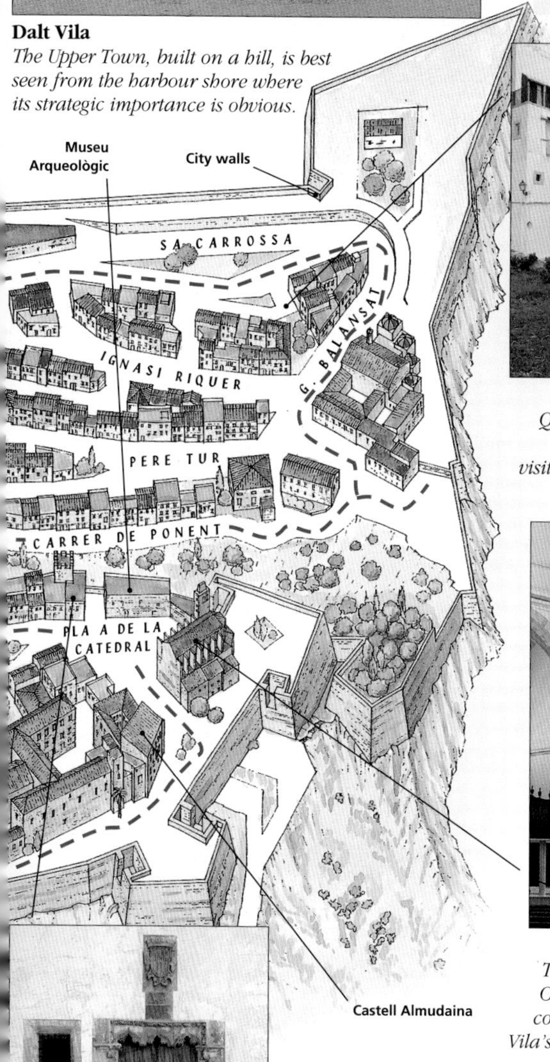

VISITORS' CHECKLIST

47,000. Es Codolar, 8 km (5 miles) to the southwest. ***Tel*** *971 809 000. C/Antoni Riquer 2, 971 301 900. Mon–Sat (summer). Sant Cristòbal (10 Jul), Nostra Senyora de les Neus (5 Aug), Sant Salvador (6 Aug), Sant Ciriac (8 Aug).*

Dalt Vila
The Upper Town, built on a hill, is best seen from the harbour shore where its strategic importance is obvious.

Museu Arqueològic

City walls

Sa Carrossa
Quiet by day, Sa Carrossa is popular with Eivissa's gay visitors and is a hip night-time hangout in the summer.

★ Cathedral
The cathedral, dedicated to Our Lady of the Snows, was completed in 1592. It is Dalt Vila's most impressive building.

Castell Almudaina

Reial Curia
The modest house of the former Royal Tribunal of Justice, standing near the cathedral, has a fine Gothic doorway.

STAR SIGHTS

- ★ Cathedral
- ★ Portal de ses Taules

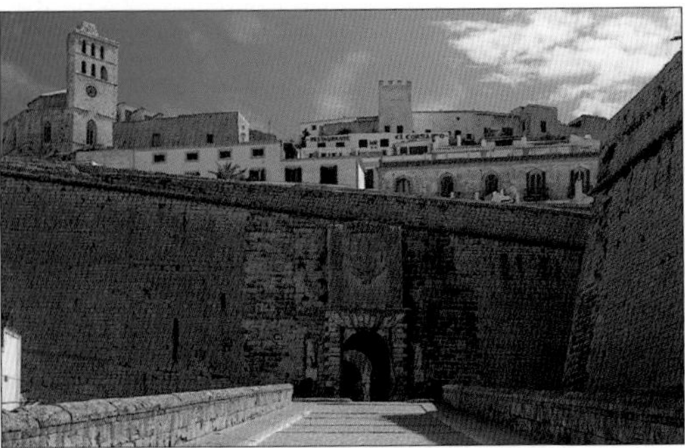
Vast city walls surrounding Dalt Vila

Exploring Eivissa

Eivissa is the largest and most beautiful town on the island. To avoid the crowds, visit early in the morning. For a romantic stroll, visit after dark when it is a bit cooler. In Sa Penya and Sa Marina, the harbour district, you can take a break and see evidence of present-day Eivissa. The place is full of bars, restaurants, clubs and market stalls. As night falls, the streets outside Dalt Vila become one huge dance floor.

Cathedral

Plaça de la Catedral.

The Cathedral Church of Santa María de las Nieves (Our Lady of the Snows) stands at the highest point in Dalt Vila, near the severely dilapidated medieval castle (Castell).

Ibiza's consecutive rulers used this place as the site for their temples in Punic times. In AD 283, on the orders of the Roman Emperor Marcus Aurelius, a temple was built here and dedicated to the god Mercury. Following the conquest of the island by the Catalans, work began to build a Christian church, which was completed in 1592. The only remains of the original Gothic structure are the tower and the vestry portal. In the 18th century, the cathedral was remodelled in a heavy Baroque style. The vestry houses a small museum with a collection of beautifully embroidered chasubles (priestly garments), as well as Gothic and Baroque paintings. On the first floor is a collection of altar pieces in silver and gold plate.

Fortifications

The present city walls surrounding Dalt Vila were erected in the 16th century during the reign of Felipe II, according to plans by the Italian architect Giovanni Battista Calvi. In 1585, with the completion of the impressive Portal de ses Taules (decorated with the coat of arms of Felipe II and replicas of ancient Roman statues), the city's defences were in place.

The view from the northern bastion of Santa Llucia encompasses the new town, the harbour docks and the nearby island of Formentera.

Museu Arqueològic

Plaça de la Catedral 3. ***Tel*** *971 301 231.* *Apr–Oct: 10am–2pm, 6–8pm Tue–Sat, 10am–2pm Sun; Nov–Mar: 9am–3pm Tue–Sat, 10am–2pm Sun.*

The archaeological museum houses a collection of prehistoric artifacts and relics dating from the times of the island's Carthaginian, Roman and Moorish rulers. On display are tombstones, statuettes and coins, as well as glass and ceramic objects. The museum building is itself impressive, and was the home of Ibiza's government for 300 years.

Museu d'Art Contemporani

C/Ronda Narcis Puget. ***Tel*** *971 302 723.* *10am–1:30pm, 4–6pm Tue–Fri, 10am–1pm Sat & Sun.* *public holidays.*

The Modern Art Museum in Portal de ses Taules consists of two underground galleries of the former arsenal, built within the city walls. The museum was founded in 1969 and includes several hundred works by artists living in Ibiza. Some works are for sale, but prices can be rather steep.

Replica Roman statue at Portal de ses Taules

Plaça de Espanya

The **Ajuntament** (town hall) dominates this square and occupies a building that was once a Dominican monastery and a school for the town's poor. Adjacent to it is the church of Santo Domingo *(see p119)* with its later Baroque façade (entrance from Carrer Balansat). The local *chiringuito* bar, open 24 hours, serves a variety of Balearic snacks and specialities. Carrer Pere Tur features several splendid 18th-century mansions. Among them is **Casa Riquer**, once home to Antonio Riquer, the most famous buccaneer in Ibiza.

Fresh fruit at a stall in Es Mercat Vell

Sa Torre bastion guarding the harbour

Santo Domingo

Carrer Balansat.

Below the city walls is the late 16th-century church of Santo Domingo, commonly known as El Convent.

It is worth visiting this to see the lovely paintings covering the vaulted ceilings, and the ceramic tiles lining the walls and floors. The Capella del Roser has an interesting Baroque altar.

Es Mercat Vell

Plaça de la Constitució.

The old market building lies north of Portal de ses Taules. The hall, resembling an ancient Greek temple, was built in 1873. Every morning it is packed with vendors selling fresh fruit and vegetables. A short distance further on is the **Sa Peixateria** fish market.

Sa Penya

The Sa Penya district, situated between Dalt Vila and the harbour, was once inhabited mainly by fishermen and has always been a fairly "picturesque" part of town. Even today, it does not enjoy a good reputation and when venturing here you should take extra care of your wallet and any valuables you might have. During high season, the streets get very crowded. The place is full of cafés, bars and clubs. Life in Sa Penya only starts in earnest after dark.

Sa Marina

Like Sa Penya, Sa Marina was originally a working class district and sprang up as overcrowding in Dalt Vila forced many people to live outside the city walls. Now the area around the harbour provides ferry links to mainland Spain and is packed with restaurants, cafés, bars and shops. Its narrow alleys are full of stalls selling clothes and souvenirs. Many of these offer items reminiscent of the days when the island was a favourite with hippies.

Sa Torre

A small military defence tower stands at the end of Carrer Garijo. The bastion was restored in 1994 and is a relic of the fortifications that once guarded the entrance to the harbour. Today, it affords a view over the entire bay and the harbour and on to Formentera.

Monument als Corsaris

Passeig des Moll.

In the early 19th century, the inhabitants of Ibiza, tormented by constant pirate raids, enrolled the help of Antoni Riquer, a buccaneer who fought battles with the pirate ships that brazenly attacked the passing merchant vessels.

His struggles with Novelli, a buccaneer in the pay of the British who commanded the large brig *Felicity*, became the stuff of legend. Despite being hugely outgunned by Novelli, Riquer sank the enemy vessel after a fierce battle, for which the grateful Ibizans erected this monument. It is believed to be the world's only monument that is dedicated to a pirate.

Teatro Pereyra

C/Conde Rosselón 3.

Built in 1898, this was the first theatre in Ibiza. Now this Neo-Classical building houses a cinema. It is worth dropping in to the adjacent café Teatro Pereyra one evening, when the live music only adds to the unique atmosphere of this place.

Passeig de Vara de Rey

Eivissa's main street is named after General Joachim Vara de Rey, a Spanish general who perished in Cuba during the Spanish–America war in 1898. The street's many bars and restaurants are very popular in the evenings.

Puig des Molins

Via Romana 31. ***Tel*** *971 301 771.*

10am–2pm, 6–8pm Tue–Sat, 10am–2pm Sun.

Many of the objects associated with Punic culture on display in the Museu Arqueològic were unearthed from this ancient burial site. The "Hill of the Windmills" was one of the Mediterranean's top burial sites and the remains of the nobility would have been brought here from all over the Carthaginian empire. Ibiza, being free of snakes and scorpions, was attractive to the Carthaginians whose religion specified a burial site free of poisonous creatures.

Neon sign of Teatro Pereyra café

Environs

There are several beaches near Eivissa served by local buses. **Playa de Talamanca** is not large, but is nearest to the town. On the opposite side of the capital, at its southern end, is **Platja de ses Figueretes. Es Cavallet**, a short way down the coast, is very popular, especially with gay visitors. **Ses Salines**' beach, a little further on, is favoured by many people staying in Eivissa and has regular bus links to the city.

Monument to General Vara de Rey

Nightlife in Ibiza

In the early 1960s, Ibiza became a popular haunt of hippies who were drawn to this isolated Spanish outpost by the beauty of the scenery and the relaxed way of life. They brought with them valuable foreign cash and the local bars, shops and businesses started to prosper. At times, though, even the islanders' legendary tolerance was strained and in 1968 the loud music, drugs and sex on the beach resulted in the deportation of 41 people. Where hippies led, however, the rest have followed and Ibiza is today the club capital of the world.

Foam party, popular in the clubs of Ibiza

BIRTH OF CLUB CULTURE

The pioneers of clubland were Pacha and Amnesia, which opened in the early 1970s. The Ku club, currently known as Privilege, joined the scene shortly afterwards. Banking on the popularity of the party scene at the time, they offered their own more stylish and restrained version. Gradually, word spread and the clubs became fashionable with the rich and the famous.

The 1980s and 1990s heralded the emergence of DJs who decamped to Ibiza for the summer and forged a new type of dance music. Some became stars in their own right, performing to crowds of 3,000 or more. From then on, the club scene in Ibiza gained its own momentum and it is now a major part of the island's economy.

CLUBS

There are seven major clubs on the island, each capable of accommodating several thousand people. The biggest of them, **Privilege**, can host parties for up to 10,000 guests. Every night they offer new attractions, including parties in foam, Brazilian nights, ghost nights and "Flower Power" balls. In addition, the clubs make their premises available to other promoters that operate on the continent. The biggest and best known of these is Manumission. Admission charges are high and may be anything up to €50. Drinks are also expensive.

Smaller clubs are cheaper. They do not offer such elaborate entertainment, but have their own unique charm. They tempt their guests in with free drinks and various fun gimmicks. In the Sa Penya and La Marina districts of Eivissa, revellers often end up partying on the streets. During high season, special night bus services run between Eivissa and Sant Antoni, where most of the clubs are concentrated.

Scantily clad podium dancer – a big feature of many Ibiza clubs

CLUBBERS

People of all ages can be found in Ibiza's many clubs because there are no age limits, although young people prevail. Many come to party, others are drawn by sheer curiosity. For some, the Ibiza club scene is simply a way of life. The clubs are most frenetic during summer weekends, when they are invaded by clubbers from all over Europe. The rule is to visit several clubs each night. As is usual at such hectic events, there may be an occasional petty theft or scuffle. You may also come across drug dealers and con artists offering various goods at bargain prices to drunken passers-by. Nevertheless, generally speaking, the clubs have tight security and are safe places.

Neon sign of a club in Eivissa

Coloured lights and laser beams at El Divino

MUSIC AND DANCING

Dancing in the local clubs is led by some of the world's top DJs. They include Fat Boy Slim, Paul van Dyk, Mark Spoon, Carl Cox and John Digweed, to mention but a few. These DJs dictate which music will later find its way into the clubs of London, Paris and Berlin. Each year they try to surprise their fans with something new. As the party season ends in Ibiza, most of the seven top clubs and their associated DJs go on worldwide tours, promoting their latest music. Individual clubs also produce CDs of last season's hits.

Although many kinds of music can be heard in Ibiza, the clubs have become famous for their summer anthems and for a unique Balearic Beat that is a fusion of electronic music with Latin and funk rhythms. Much of it is based on drum machines pounding out four beats to the bar but Ibiza is known for its eclectic tastes and has produced a more subtle sound often branded as "chillout".

Gaudy poster advertising Space

No one style of dancing prevails in the clubs and you will often see a free-form frenzy. Many people just copy the podium dancers.

CLOTHES

It is not necessary for people to wear any special clothes to be admitted to an Ibizan club, the exception being theme parties, when you are expected to wear appropriate costume and come dressed as a "Flower Child" or astronaut for example.

Clubbers who are playing in foam or jets of water tend to be scantily dressed. Regular clubbers are usually fashionably dressed, with clothes that are often provocative and sexy. As with the music, club fashions change every year.

DJ Sonique at the decks in Es Paradis Terranal

BEFORE AND AFTER

Most clubbers do not wait until midnight to begin partying. After a day spent relaxing on the beach, many people start their evening in cafés, bars and pubs. The first to open their doors are the small clubs. By the time **El Divino** or **Amnesia** open their doors, the party on the island is already in full swing. Even at dawn, it is common to still see people dancing in the streets of Eivissa. Some beaches have daytime dance cafés and clubs, such as Bora-Bora opposite the flamboyant **Space** club on Platja d'en Bossa (Space hosts a party that begins at 8am!).

Dancing crowds at Amnesia enjoy a sudden deluge of foam

THE BEST CLUBS IN IBIZA

Amnesia, Sant Rafael. ***Tel*** *971 198 041.* **www**.amnesia.es

Blu, Navarra 27, Figueretes. ***Tel*** *971 305 361.*

Eden, c/Salvador Espriu s/n, Sant Antoni. ***Tel*** *971 803 240.* **www**.edenibiza.com

El Divino, Puerto Eivissa Nueva s/n, Eivissa. ***Tel*** *971 318 338.* **www**.eldivino-ibiza.com

Es Paradis Terrenal, C/Salvador Espriu s/n, Sant Antoni. ***Tel*** *971 346 600.* **www**.esparadis.com

KM5, Ctra Sant Josep. ***Tel*** *971 396 349.* **www**.km5-lounge.com

Manumission **www**.manumission.com

Martina, C/Murtra 5 (Platja d'en Bossa). **www**.martinaibiza.com

Pachá, Avinguda Ocho de Agosto s/n, Eivissa. ***Tel*** *971 313 600.* **www**.pacha.com

Privilege, Sant Rafael. ***Tel*** *971 198 160.* **www**.privilegeibiza.com

Pussycat, Passeo Marítimo I, Sant Antoni de Portmany. ***Tel*** *971 346 167.* **www**.pussycat-ibiza.com

Space, Platja d'en Bossa. ***Tel*** *971 396 793.* **www**.space-ibiza.com

Summum, Edificio Cala Blanca, Sant Antoni de Portmany. ***Tel*** *971 343 997.*

Sant Jordi de Ses Salines ❷

4 km (2 miles) southwest of Eivissa.
Sat.

The small village of Sant Jordi de Ses Salines lies along the road leading from Eivissa to the airport. It was established in the 15th century, but there is not much evidence left of its ancient pedigree. The most important local sight is the modest white church of **Sant Jordi** that stands surrounded by a high wall. A quirky Saturday market takes place here from 8am and has a good mix of cheap jewellery, clothes and second-hand books.

Environs

A little further on is **Platja d'en Bossa**. The local beach is popular with young people, especially the southern end where a dynamic club scene has developed. Much of this is based around Space, a huge club that opened in 1988 *(see pp120–21)*. Close to this is Bora-Bora, a club-bar where parties spill out onto the sand.

Children have not been forgotten here. Behind the beach is a large water park, Aguamar, with numerous pools and slides.

A short way south of Sant Jordi is a hippodrome where you can bet on trotting races, popular throughout the Balearic Islands.

Aguamar
Platja d'en Bossa. ***Tel*** *971 396 790.*
May–Oct: 10am–6pm daily.

Ses Salines, a haven for many species of bird

Ses Salines ❸

10 km (6 miles) southwest of Eivissa.

Situated at the southern end of Ibiza are the saline lowlands – Ses Salines. These natural salt pans are extremely important for the local wildlife and were known as the "Salt Gardens" in Phoenician times.

They are sheltered to the north by the Serra Grossa hills that rise up to 160 m (520 ft) in some places; to the south they are flanked by the wooded areas of Faló and Corbari. In 1992, the area was given special protection as a nature reserve.

For centuries, the revenue from the local salt production provided a large chunk of the island's income. Until quite recently, the place was served by a narrow-gauge railway carrying salt to La Canal – a small port at the southern end of the peninsula. Salt production still continues here, though not on such a grand scale – some 70,000 tonnes of the stuff are exported each year.

Built between the salt lakes is the village of **Sant Francesc de S'Estany**, where some salt workers still live. It has a small picturesque church. The asphalt road that passes the church leads to a 16th-century watchtower, **Torre de sa Salt Rossa**, 2 km (1 mile) away. From here there is a fine view over nearby Illa Sal Rossa island, the wide beaches of Figueretes lying to the south of the capital and Dalt Vila in Eivissa.

Ses Salines' beach, **Platja de Salines**, is one of the island's most fashionable spots. One section of this beautiful, long sandy beach has been set apart for nudists.

Slides in Aguamar, near Sant Jordi

Sant Josep de sa Talaia ❹

21,000. *C/Pedro Escanellas 33–9, 971 343 363.*
Sant Josép (19 Mar).

The small town of Sant Josep de sa Talaia, 13 km (9 miles) west of Eivissa, is the municipal capital of the southwestern region and is off the beaten track. Its pace of life is slow. It is worth visiting the local traditional tavern, Bernat Vinya, where men gather to play cards and chat over a glass of wine. The only historic relic to visit is the **church**, built in the typical island style.

Environs

The town lies at the foot of Ibiza's highest mountain, **Sa Talaiassa** (475 m/1,558 ft). Keen walkers can make the two-hour hike to the peak along a well-marked trail that starts in Sant Josép. From the top there is a magnificent panorama of the district, including the rocky islet of **Es Vedrà**. In order to take a closer look at Es Vedrà you need to drive along the coast up to the sandy bay of **Cala d'Hort**, with its pleasant sandy beach and several terraced restaurants.

According to legend, Es Vedrà was once the home of the sirens who lured Odysseus. Sailors and divers experience a strange magnetic anomaly here, and some believe the island to have been a landing site for aliens. This lofty rock, now inhabited only by birds and flocks of wild goats and sheep, makes an extraordinary impression. Occasionally, in calm weather, it even blows off a plume of steam.

Some 5 km (3 miles) from Sant Josép, situated to the right of the road that leads to Eivissa, is **Cova Santa**. The main attractions of this cave, which is the largest in Ibiza, are its huge stalactites, some of which are a dozen or so metres long.

West Coast of Ibiza ❺

See pp126–7.

Sant Antoni de Portmany ❻

21,000. Passeig de Ses Font s/n, 971 343 363. Sant Antoni (17 Jan), Sant Bartolome (24 Aug).

The second largest town in Ibiza was known as Portus Magnus by the Romans. The large bay that provided a natural harbour for ships now boasts yacht marinas and a ferry terminal. Once upon a time this was a small fishing village until it was transformed in the 1960s into a busy, commercialized summer resort with scores of hotels. Regular bus services run from here to Eivissa and Santa Eulària des Riu.

Fountain in Passeig de ses Fonts in Sant Antoni de Portmany

Amid the sea of high-rise hotel buildings stands the 14th-century church of **Sant Antoni Abat**. This fortified parish church, now standing in Plaça de Església, was built on a hill, away from the harbour, and served as a shelter for the local population during pirate raids. Originally, there were defensive guns positioned on the church roof.

The bustling fishing harbour is popular with visitors. A palm-fringed promenade runs along the bay. At one end is a large flower bed with sculptures made in Sant Rafael, including the ingenious *Columbus' Egg*. The famous entertainment district between Carrer de Mar and Carrer Ample comes to life only after dark. The local clubs, including Es Paradis and Eden, are among the island's best *(see pp120–21)*.

***Columbus' Egg* in Sant Antoni**

Of the nearby beaches, **Cala Bassa** and the blue-flag **Cala Conta** are probably the best. **Port d'es Torrent** is also popular, especially with families *(see p127)*.

Santa Agnes de Corona ❼

8 km (5 miles) northeast of Sant Antoni de Portmany.

Santa Agnes de Corona has maintained its old-world atmosphere. There is not much here apart from a small quaint church, a shop and a bar where you can quench your thirst and enjoy a plate of *tapas*. You can take a walk from here to the nearby summit of **Es Camp Vell** and on to the neighbouring village of **Sant Mateu d'Aubarca**.

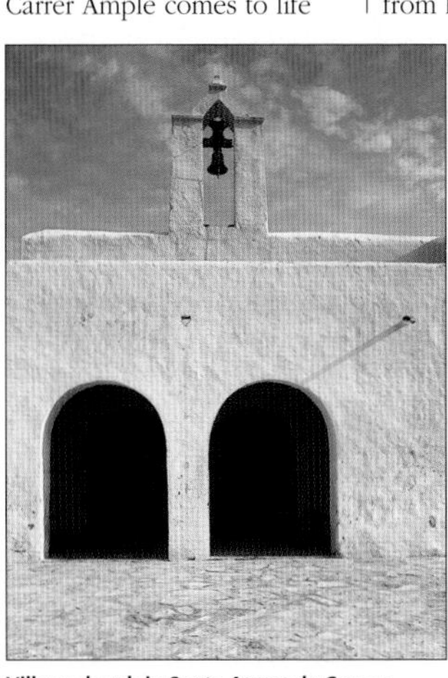

Village church in Santa Agnes de Corona

Environs

Southwest of Santa Agnes de Corona is an original early-Christian chapel of **Santa Agnes**, discovered in 1907 in a grotto. Local legend says that a sailor was saved from drowning by St Agnes during a fierce storm, and built a chapel to her on the spot where he was washed up by the waves. On St Agnes's Day, local people make a pilgrimage to this site.

West Coast of Ibiza ❻

The main attraction of Ibiza's west coast is its magnificent beaches, many of which are tucked away in small coves and offer family-friendly facilities and safe bathing. Some of the resorts have become built up in recent years but the west coast remains one of the island's most beautiful areas with a romantic coastline, pristine waters and remote mountains clad in pine trees. The mysterious islet of Es Vedrà *(see p123)*, just off the coast, is a remarkable sight and featured in the film *South Pacific* as Bali Ha'i. The route suggested here cuts across the Serra de Sant Josép in the south and bypasses the highest peak on the island, Sa Talaiassa (475 m/1,558 ft).

Illa Sa Conillera

Illa de s´Esparta

Cala Molí ⑥
This small resort is flanked by steep cliffs and consists of modest villas and pensions surrounded by green pine trees. Its beach *(right)* is regarded as one of the most beautiful on the island.

Cala Vedella ⑤
This little resort is slowly becoming fashionable. Situated at the mouth of a narrow inlet, it has a wonderful beach and plenty of low-rise hotels and apartments. The resort is unlikely to be spoilt as there is no room for large hotels.

Mirador des Savinar ③
The best way to reach nearby Torre de Pirata, a former watchtower and now a viewpoint, is on foot. A drive over the bumpy road may damage your car. The point provides the best view of Es Vedrà.

Cala d'Hort ④
This is the southernmost resort on the western coast. Many visitors come to this beach, far from the main resorts and towns, to admire the view of Es Vedrà, others to enjoy the exquisite local *paella.*

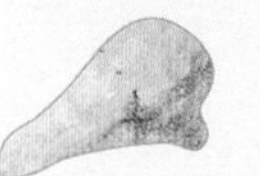

Illa Vedranell

Illa Es Vedrà

Cap Llentrisca ②
The rough track leading along the craggy cliffs is fairly difficult, but from here you can see the entire south coast of the island.

0 km 2
0 miles

◁ **Es Vedrà, a forbidding and mysterious rock rising from the sea**

Cala Tarida ⑦
Another beautiful cove, Cala Tarida has golden beaches and a number of family-friendly hotels. Until recently a quiet corner of the island, it is beginning to get busy, especially during high season.

TIPS FOR DRIVERS

Length: *About 20 km (12 miles).*
Stopping-off points: *All resorts have bars and restaurants. Overnight accommodation may be difficult to find during peak season.*
Additional information: *There are no petrol stations along the entire route. The nearest one is in Sant Josép de sa Talaia. Some places can be reached by bus.*

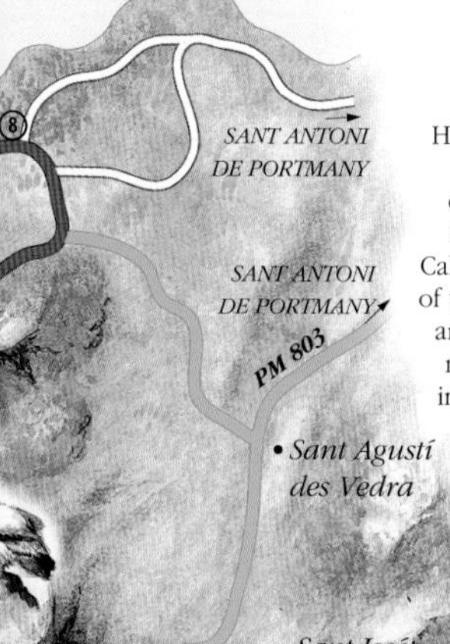

Port d'es Torrent ⑧
Here you can join an organized canoe trip to Illa Sa Conillera and Cala Bassa. Several of the nearby villas are owned by the rich and famous, including Claudia Schiffer.

Cala Bassa ⑨
One of the most beautiful and popular beaches in the region of Sant Antoni de Portmany; it can be reached by bus. Numerous cruising boats visit the local harbour.

Es Cubells ①
This village has a beautifully simple church and a modest restaurant. It offers a magnificent view over Cala d'Es Cubells. On a clear day you can see Formentera from here.

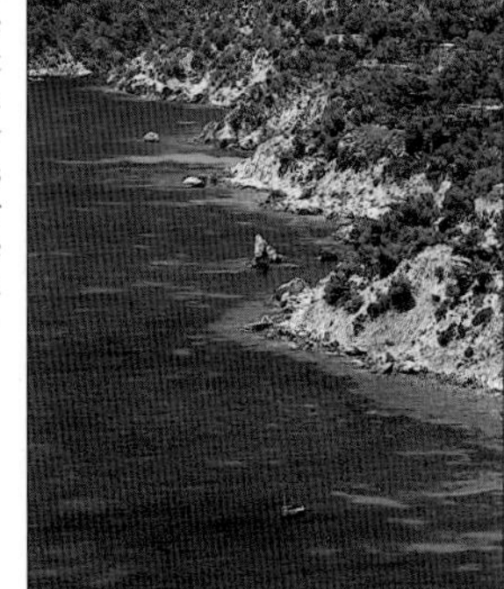

KEY

- Suggested route
- Other road
- Scenic road
- Viewpoint

Animals grazing around St Mateu d'Aubarca

Els Amunts 8

Ibiza's spectacular mountain range, Els Amunts, is situated in the northern part of the island and stretches from Sant Antoni de Portmany in the west to Sant Vicent de Sa Cala in the northeast.

Rarely visited by tourists, the region has maintained its unspoiled charm. Pinewood hills are interspersed with fertile valleys full of olive, almond and fig groves, as well as the occasional vineyard. The shore rises steeply and the roads leading to the water's edge are narrow, unmade and rugged, presenting a challenge even to four-wheel-drive vehicles. The area is a hiker's paradise; walking around you are likely to meet only the local shepherds.

Except for the small resorts, such as Port de Sant Miquel, Portinatx or Cala Sant Vincent, the inland towns, including Sant Joan de Labritja and Santa Agnes de Corona *(see p123)*, have maintained their traditional, rural character. A good example of this is the little village of **Sant Mateu d'Aubarca**, where you can see flocks of sheep and goats grazing in the orchards.

Near Sant Llorenç lies the fortified settlement of Balàfia. Believed to be the island's only surviving Moorish hamlet, the whitewashed interlocking houses with flat roofs and amber coloured watchtowers once acted as fortresses during pirate attacks.

Sant Joan de Labritja 9

16 km (10 miles) north of Eivissa. *Sant Joan (24 Jun), Santa Maria (5 Aug).*

This quiet little town in the north of the island of Ibiza lies in the shadow of the Es Fornás mountain (410 m/1,345 ft). The only buildings of note in town are the **Ajuntament** (town hall) and a small 18th-century **church**. The local cafés and restaurants are well worth visiting. Sant Joan was popular with hippies in the 1960s and you can stock up on beads, Roman sandals and magically endowed crystals at the New Age Bazaar.

Environs

About 7 km (4 miles) west of town is the small village of **Sant Miquel de Balansat**. It has an impressive 16th-century fortress-church that provided shelter during the frequent raids by pirates, who once ventured deep into the island's interior in search of loot and slaves. Every Thursday at 6pm, there is a music and dance show performed by a local folklore group in front of the church. Dressed in traditional costumes, they entertain people with lively dances to tunes played on traditional instruments including drums, local flutes *(xeremia)* and triangles *(espasi)*.

Port de Sant Miquel is 4 km (2 miles) north of Sant Miquel. It has a fishing harbour and a handful of hotels. The resort is popular with families and has facilities for water sports as well as a diving centre. Nearby, on top of a hill, stands one of the island's most exclusive hotels – Hacienda Na Xamena. The top of the 200-m (656-ft) high cliff provides a magnificent view over the surging waves below.

To the north of the town is the **Cova de Can Marça**. This cave, which was used by tobacco and liquor smugglers, is one of the most beautiful of its kind on the island, and is on a par with the caves found in Mallorca. There is an entrance fee which buys you a sound and light show and a 40-minute guided tour.

East of Port de Sant Miquel is **Cala de Benirràs**. It gets very busy in the evenings, when visitors arrive to admire one of the most beautiful sunsets on the island. At other times it is relatively quiet. On Thursday nights it becomes a venue for hippy concerts and dances.

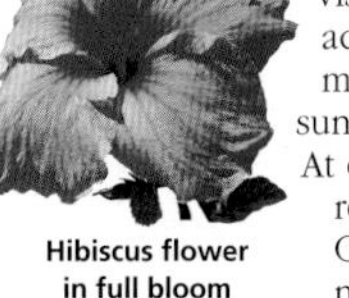

Hibiscus flower in full bloom

Cova de Can Marça
Port de Sant Miquel. *daily.*

Portinatx 10

8 km (5 miles) north of Sant Joan de Labratija.

The northernmost holiday village of Ibiza was built as a family resort. It consists solely of hotels, apartments,

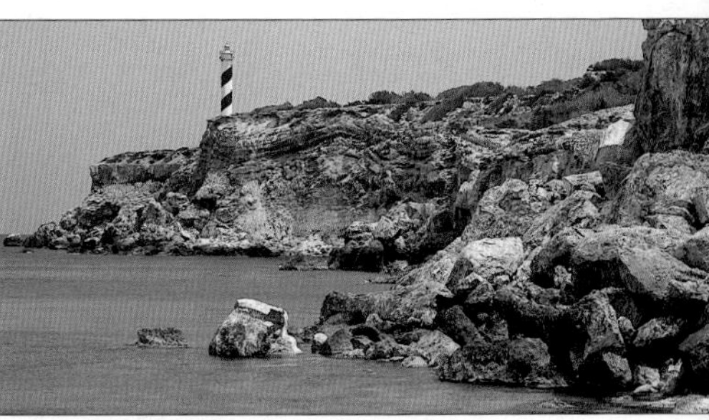

Lighthouse on Punta de Sa Galera, near Portinatx

For hotels and restaurants in this region see pp153–4 and pp168–70

Coastal boulevard in Cala de Sant Vincent

souvenir shops, restaurants and numerous cafés.

It is an attractive, quiet place with four beaches – Sa Torre, S'Arenal Petit, S'Arenal Gran and Es Portitxol – separated from each other by rocky protusions. It can become busy during high season, but instead of baking on a beach you may prefer to go water skiing or take a trip in a glass-bottomed boat to admire the life lurking beneath the clear waters.

Environs

Nearby, just 4 km (2 miles) west of Portinatx, is **Cala Xarraca**, a beautiful beach with views along the north coast. The beach provided the setting for the film *South Pacific*.

Sant Vicent de Sa Cala ⓫

13 km (5 miles) east of Sant Joan de Labratija.

Sant Vicent de Sa Cala lies along the main road leading from Sant Joan de Labratija to the east coast of Ibiza. Running to the south of it is the range of the Serra de Mala Costa mountains. The only local historic building is the modest 19th-century **parish church**, open only during service hours.

Sant Vicent de Sa Cala is nevertheless worth visiting for a different reason. The passage of time seems almost to have ground to a halt here. The locals live in old, whitewashed houses overgrown with flowering plants. They work on the land using age-old methods and tools. They have neither telephones nor any other modern conveniences. The island authorities set up the **Camp d'Aprenatge** here, where pupils from local schools learn about the old ways of rural life and about Ibiza's natural environment.

Environs

About 3 km (2 miles) east of town is **Cala de Sant Vicent**. This beautiful cove has become a modern resort, with quiet hotels and good restaurants. Visitors love the beach with its clean water and rugged scenery, surrounded by green pine forests.

From here, signposts point towards the famous **Cova d'es Culleram**, discovered in 1907, which was a temple to the goddess Tanoit during the days of the Carthaginian rulers. The caves are closed but the finds unearthed here can be seen in the Museu Arqueològic at Dalt Vila, in Eivissa *(see p118)*.

Another interesting destination for a walk is **Punta Grossa** – a headland situated a little way to the east, which has a lighthouse. The view from here includes the Illa de Tagomago and the eastern cost of the island. **Tagomago** island lies 6 km (4 miles) southeast of Cala de Sant Vicent. It is uninhabited and has no regular ferry links with the main island but it is often visited by cruise boats and yachts. The clear waters around the island are popular with scuba divers.

HIPPIES

Hippies began arriving in Ibiza in the 1960s, attracted by the beaches, the people and the unhurried lifestyle. It soon became the "in" place and tour operators were quick to catch on. Most of the hippies moved on long ago but the hippy style has found its way into the island's culture. A small number of hippy families still live on the island; one community is near Balàfia.

Hippy stall selling jewellery

Fortified church at the top of Puig de Missa in Santa Eulària

Santa Eulària des Riu ⓬

30,000. C/Riquer Wallis 4, 971 330 728. Santa Eulària (12 Feb).

Ibiza's third largest town stands on the banks of the island's only river, the Riu de Santa Eulària. The town's main shopping street is Passeig Generalissim. This **Ramblas** connects the main street with the coastal promenade. During the day, the palm trees provide welcome shade. At night there are many lively clubs, restaurants and cafés to enjoy.

You can escape the town by by walking up nearby **Puig de Missa** (67 m/219 ft). At the top is a 16th-century **fortified church**, regarded by many as the loveliest and best-preserved example of its kind in Ibiza. This whitewashed building, once used by the town's inhabitants as a shelter from pirates, is surrounded by a handful of picturesque local houses and a small cemetery. The adjacent flat-roofed building houses the modest **Museu Etnològic**. Just a short walk away is the **Museu Barrau**, which has a collection of paintings, furniture and drawings by the Spanish Impressionist Laureá Barrau.

Museu Etnològic
Puig de Missa. ***Tel*** *971 332 845.* *10am–2pm & 5:30–8pm Tue–Sat, 4–6pm Sun.*

Museu Barrau
Puig de Missa. ***Tel*** *971 330 072.* *10am–2pm Tue–Sat.*

Environs

Es Canar, a popular resort 4 km (2 miles) north of Santa Eulària des Riu, lies on the shore of a pine-fringed bay with a beautiful beach. The local hippy market (May–Oct: Wed) is the best known and biggest in Ibiza. Held in the grounds of the Punta Arabi club, it attracts large crowds. Here, you can buy jewellery and unusual clothes and T-shirts though much of the stuff on sale is not made locally. Nearby are two large camp sites and a couple of beaches – **Cala Nova** and **Cala Llenya**. During the summer there is a daily boat trip to Formentera.

Anita's Bar in **Sant Carles de Peralta**, a little town 8 km (5 miles) northeast of Santa Eulària, was the cradle of the island's hippy culture and still remains popular. Two kilometres (1 mile) south of Sant Carles is a hippy bazaar, Las Dalias. On Saturdays and Sundays, the colourful stalls display everything from beads and bangles to bongos and intricate water pipes. There is also a café-bar here.

Town hall in Plaça de Espanya

About 5 km (3 miles) south of Santa Eulària is **Cala Llonga**. This is one of the most popular resorts on the southeastern shores of the island. Its beautiful sandy beach makes it an ideal place for families with young children.

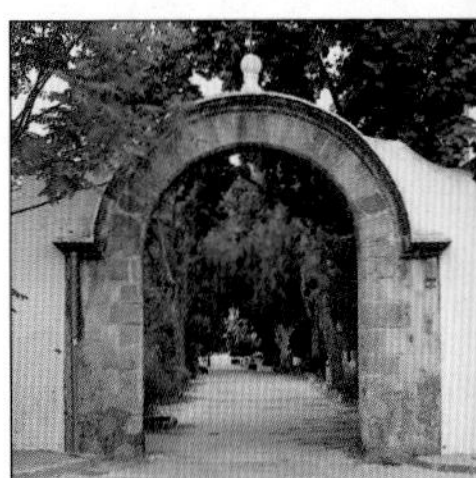

Arcaded entrance to a church garden in Jesús

Jesús ⓭

2 km (1 mile) north of Eivissa.

This modest village is situated near Eivissa, on the road to Santa Eulària. The church of **Nostra Mare de Déu de Jesús** has a unique early 16th-century Gothic-Renaissance altar of the Virgen de los Angeles. Painted by the Valencian artists Pere de Cabanes and Rodrigo de Osona, it illustrates scenes from the life of the Virgin Mary, Christ and the Apostles. There are a couple of cafés opposite the church.

Environs

A short way to the south and within walking distance of Eivissa is **Talamanca**. Its main attractions, beside the 2-km (1-mile) sandy beach, are the Aqualandia water park and some good fish restaurants.

For hotels and restaurants in this region see pp153–4 and pp168–70

Ibiza's Beaches

Apart from the clubs, Ibiza's main attraction is its beaches. There are over 50 of them, adding up to over 50 km (30 miles) of stunning coastline. Many of the most popular ones are on the southeast coast, between Santa Eulària des Riu and Cala de Sant Vicent, and have excellent facilities. It is still possible to find a quieter spot. The delightful Cala d'en Serra, for instance, near Portinatx, has a *chiringuito* ("refreshment shack") and little else.

Cala es Figueral ①
A long, sandy beach with small, rocky islets near the shore. The northern portion is used as a nudist beach.

Cala de Boix ②
Surrounded by green hills, this beach remains relatively deserted even during high season. It is situated near Punta Prima, offering a view of Illa de Tagomago.

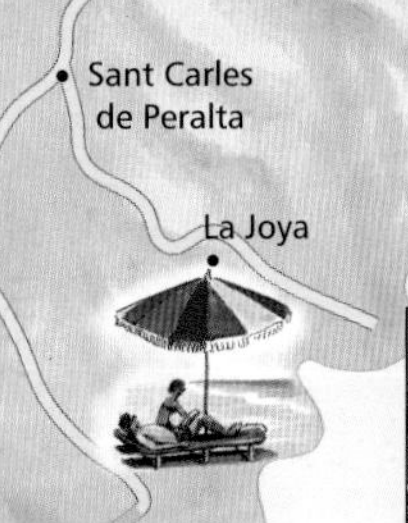

Platja des Canar ③
This popular resort has a small beach, situated near the pleasure boat harbour. The surrounding area is full of shops, bars and restaurants.

Platja des Niu Blau ④
This pine-fringed beach in a cove with shallow water is a particular favourite of families.

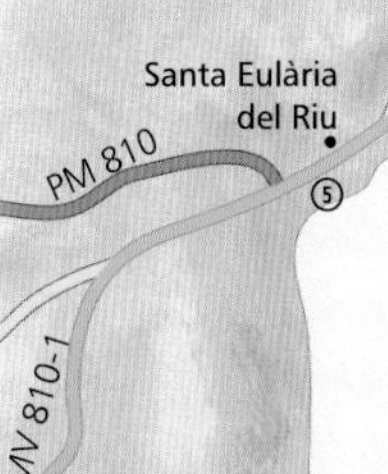

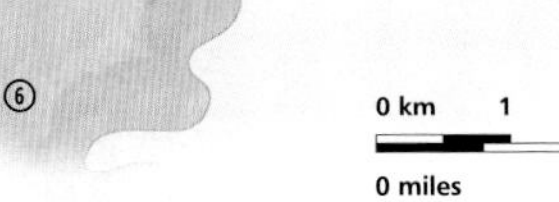

Cala Llonga ⑥
Situated between Puig de ses Torretes and Punta Roja, on a 300-m (1,000-ft) wide bay, Cala Llonga is a friendly resort and attracts hundreds of holidaymakers.

Platja del Pinos ⑤
The beach, close to Santa Eulària, is situated at the mouth of the seasonal Riu de Santa Eulària that dries up in the summer.

FORMENTERA

The tiny island of Formentera, 4 km (2 miles) south of Ibiza, is just 85 sq km (32 sq miles) in area, including its two satellite islets, Espardell and Espalmador. A sense of peace and tranquillity pervades the island. The beaches are secluded, the grassy farmland is serene and the tiny clusters of whitewashed houses that make up the island's villages are positively slumberous.

It is the very lack of high-profile tourist facilities that attracts visitors. Its beaches are some of the emptiest and cleanest to be found anywhere in Spain, high-rise hotels are nowhere to be seen and the main means of transport on the island are bicycles and scooters – the tourist office will encourage you to cycle rather than hire a car.

Scooter – the basic means of transport on the island

The Greeks called it Snake Island (although snakes are rarely seen), but never settled here. The more practical Romans left settlers on the island to grow cereals and other crops, and named it *Frumenteria* (Wheat Island), giving rise to its present name.

Following the fall of the Roman Empire, the island became a refuge for outlaws and pirates. For two centuries it was ruled by the Arabs. Throughout the Middle Ages, Formentera remained practically deserted. The second major wave of settlers arrived in the late 17th century. It was at that time that several defensive watchtowers were built, although only a handful of them survive today.

Ever since that time, Formentera has managed to maintain its unique character as a virgin island. The quiet farmsteads and villages appear to have remained unaffected by modern living and the loveliest corners of the island are only reached by rough, unpaved roads. For the peace loving visitor, it is a tranquil idyll. Even so, the island's economy is entirely dependent upon its summer visitors, most of whom come for day trips. Each summer the island's population doubles but there are still plenty of quiet spots to be found.

A popular beach party in Es Pujols – a rare sight on Formentera

◁ Northern coast of Formentera, seen from the Es Mirador restaurant

Exploring Formentera

With few hotels and plenty of seclusion on offer, Formentera is a paradise for those seeking a quiet holiday, free from distractions. The coastline is stunning, with crystal-clear turquoise waters and pristine beaches. The nightlife is calm and unhurried in the bars and restaurants of Sant Francesc – the island's tiny capital. Es Pujols is the main resort. It, too, is small scale but it is a lively, fun place to be with some good bars and a couple of laid-back clubs. For a little gentle sightseeing, the island has a handful of ancient defensive towers, pretty village churches and some prehistoric ruins in Ca Na Costa.

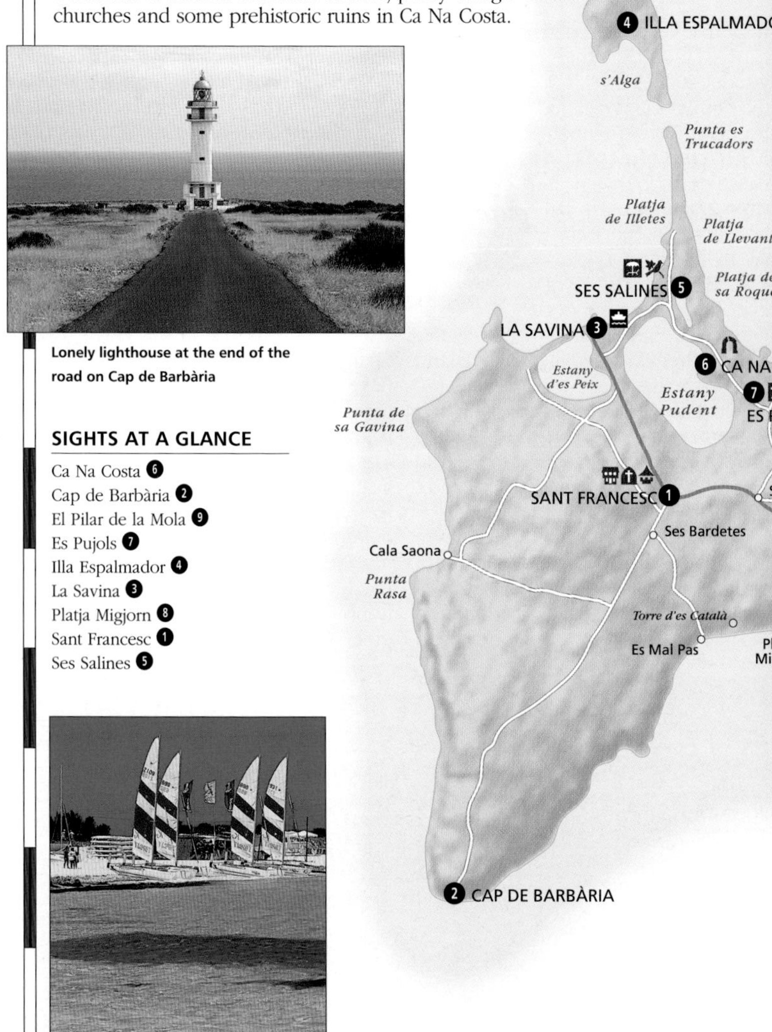

Lonely lighthouse at the end of the road on Cap de Barbària

SIGHTS AT A GLANCE

Ca Na Costa 6
Cap de Barbària 2
El Pilar de la Mola 9
Es Pujols 7
Illa Espalmador 4
La Savina 3
Platja Migjorn 8
Sant Francesc 1
Ses Salines 5

Catamarans with sails aloft on the beach in Es Pujols

For additional map symbols *see back flap*

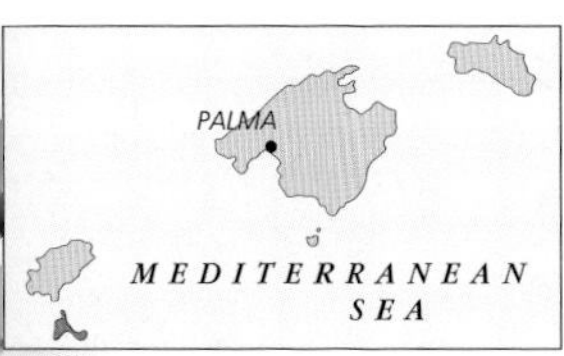

LOCATOR MAP

Platja Migjorn, the longest beach on Formentera

Quiet beach in Cala Saona, used by the guests of the only hotel

GETTING THERE

There is no airport on Formentera, but the island has good sea links with Ibiza. Most services run between La Savina and Eivissa. The voyage takes about one hour (fast ferries take 25 minutes) although journey times can vary. Sant Antoni and Santa Eulària des Riu also have ferry links with Formentera. Buses from La Savina harbour go to various parts of the island, but the best way to travel is by scooter or bicycle. The main road cuts across the island, connecting La Savina to Punta de sa Ruda. There are also good roads leading to Es Pujols, Cala Saona and Cap de Barbària.

KEY

- Major road
- Minor road

SEE ALSO

• ***Where to Stay*** p155

• ***Where to Eat*** p171

Plaça de la Constitució in Sant Francesc

Sant Francesc ❶

9,000. Port de la Savina, 971 302 057. Sant Francesc Xavier (3 Dec).

Formentera's tiny capital is a mere 3 km (2 miles) from La Savina harbour and contains most of the island's historic buildings. In Plaça de la Constitució is an imposing **fortified church** dating from 1729, which was used by the many of the island's inhabitants as a shelter from the frequent pirate raids that ravaged the island. Now it houses the local government offices and a post office. Nearby is the **Museu Etnòlogic**. Carrer de Jaume I and its adjacent streets are full of market stalls selling clothes and souvenirs. Among them, you can find hippy stalls offering jewellery.

The oldest building in town is the 14th-century **Capilla de sa Tanca Vell**, a stone structure with no windows and covered with a barrel roof, which was also often used as a refuge from pirates. Also worth visiting is the local restaurant, Es Pla, situated along the road to Cala Saona, which is famous for its Indian cuisine and large selection of beers.

Environs

Some 3 km (2 miles) to the east is **Sant Ferran**. This modest village with a lovely church was once the centre of alternative culture, taken over by large numbers of hippies. The legendary Fonda Pepe bar and the library, run by an American called Bob, were hippy meeting places in the 1960s. It is worth going there for a drink, just to savour the hazy atmosphere of "flower power" nostalgia.

Not far from Sant Ferran is **Cova d'en Xeroni**, a limestone cave, discovered by accident in 1975. The cave has been illuminated with 1970s disco lights, which only adds to the charm of the guided tour.

Cova d'en Xeroni
Ctra. Sant Ferran–La Mola, 6 km (4 miles). *May–Oct: 10am–1:30pm & 2:30–8pm daily.*

Cap de Barbària ❷

8 km (5 miles) southwest of Sant Francesc.

A bumpy road leads from Sant Francesc southwards, across an area of wild desert, to the distant Barbària headland. This is the southernmost point of Formentera and it features an 18th-century defence watchtower, **Torre des Garroveret**, as well as a lighthouse warning passing ships of the numerous rocks that jut from the sea at the island's tip. Nearby are the unearthed remains of a fortified megalithic settlement. The area is also rich in sculptures built of stones placed one by one by passing visitors. The most typical and eye-catching features of this windswept desert are pine trees twisted into weird shapes by the wind, and rocks eroded by centuries of wind and water.

Torre des Garroveret in Cap de Barbària

Environs

Travelling from Sant Francesc, you pass the little road leading to **Cala Saona**. Here, positioned in a small cove, are a beautiful sandy beach, a handful of restaurants and a solitary hotel.

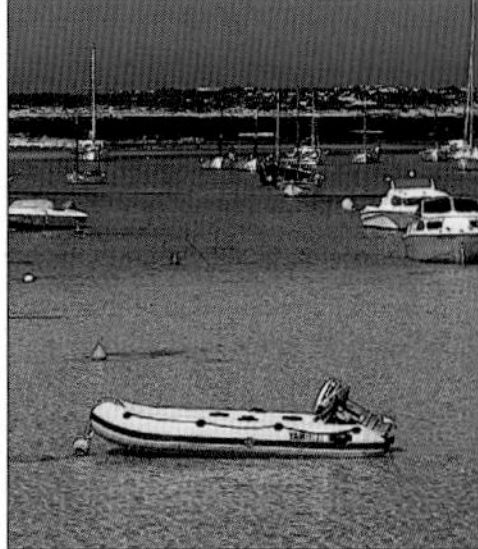

Moored boats in the Estany d'es Peix lake

La Savina ❸

3 km (2 miles) north of Sant Francesc.

The only harbour in Formentera providing ferry links with Ibiza is situated in the northern part of the island. Apart from when visitors are spilling on or off the ferries, La Savina is a fairly sleepy, unassuming place. Nevertheless, it is possible to find several shops and super markets here as well as car, scooter and bicycle hire. Buses to Sant Francesc, El Pujols and other villages depart from stops behind the ticket offices. There is also a taxi stand here. In view of the small distances involved, cab rides are not very expensive.

La Savina adjoins the protected salt water lagoons of **Estany Pudent** and **Estany d'es Peix**. The latter has a fishing harbour that is always full of boats seeking shelter in the shallow, calm waters of the lagoon; drying nets can be seen hanging along the shore.

For hotels and restaurants in this region see p155 and p171

The southern coast of Illa Espalmador as seen from Formentera

Illa Espalmador ❹

This small, 3-km (2-mile) long island is situated between Formentera and Ibiza. There is no regular ferry service however during high season the island is visited by pleasure boats sailing from La Savina.

The tiny island is popular with day trippers from Ibiza who flock here for the chance to sunbathe on the shores of **s'Alga**, a large natural harbour situated at the southern end of the island. This is also a favourite spot for yachts cruising the archipelago. A short walk north of the beach is a **sulphurous mud pool** where you can indulge in a bath of warm, sticky ooze (get there early to avoid the rush). The island's only monument is the **Torre de sa Guardiola**, an 18th-century defence tower that has recently been restored.

At low tide, some people attempt to walk across the sound to Formentera, although this is prohibited by the notice boards displayed at the tip of the **Es Trucadors** peninsula – the only traces of man's presence on this spit of white sand are the fragments of boats, nets and buoys washed ashore by the sea.

Ses Salines ❺

3 km (2 miles) north of Es Pujols.

The flat, salty marshes found along the road leading from La Savina to Es Pujols are famous for their birdlife. The most common species include the heron and the fen-duck. During the summer season, the grounds are also visited by flamingoes. Until recently it was commercially viable to produce salt here, but in 1955 the area was declared a listed zone in view of its ecological importance. Now the area including Ses Salines, Estany Pudent and the Punta de sa Pedera headland to the west of La Savina island forms a nature reserve.

Situated to the north of Ses Salines are **Platja Illetes** and **Platja Llevant**, which are considered to be among the loveliest beaches the Balearic Islands have to offer. The adjacent 200-year-old salt-mill now houses a restaurant.

Salt was valued for centuries, not only as a condiment but also as legal tender. Even today it is still being produced in the traditional way in many places throughout the Balearic Islands. Sea water floods the shallow lagoons and then evaporates when heated by the sun, leaving behind pure salt. This creates a specific environment on which salt-loving flora and fauna thrive. Salty shrimps are the favourite food of many birds, including the black-winged stilt.

Ca Na Costa ❻

1.5 km (1 mile) north of Es Pujols.

Situated close to the Es Pujols resort is the megalithic burial chamber of Ca Na Costa (1800–1600 BC), a circle of seven vertical limestone blocks. The simplicity of the stone ring belies its historical importance as it is the only structure of its kind in the Balearic Islands and the most precious historic relic on Formentera. It is also the only evidence of prehistoric human habitation remaining on the island.

The excavations were begun in 1974 and unearthed a number of objects, including ceramic and bronze vessels and axes, which are now on display in Eivissa's Museu Arqueològic *(see p118)*.

Ses Salines seen from the Es Moli de Sal restaurant

Popular beach in Es Pujols

Es Pujols 7

7 km (4 miles) northeast of Sant Francesc. *Virgen del Carmen (16 Jul).*

The small resort of Es Pujols is the island of Formentera's main holiday centre. It is a low-key, relaxed kind of place with a small marina at the eastern end of the town. Some of the island's best beaches are within easy walking distance and the nightlife in the bars, restaurants and clubs, for otherwise sleepy Formentera at least, is quite lively.

Environs

A short way east of Es Pujols, standing on a peninsula, is a 17th-century watch tower – **Torre de Punta Prima**; next to it is one of the best hotels on the island – the luxury Punta Prima Club. A little further along the coast, among the rocks, is **Cova de ses Fumades Negres**.

Platja Migjorn 8

This lovely beach is a 5-km (3-mile) long stretch of fine sand, with pale-turquoise waters. It is fringed by pine forests and is the longest beach on the island. At its eastern end is the **Torre d'es Català**; at its western end are the **Cova d'es Ram** caves. The holiday village of **Maryland** in the east and **Es Ca Marí** in the west have numerous hotels and apartments tucked away in the woods. The central section of the beach is the most pleasant and secluded. A handful of bars and restaurants are set back from the beach and are more easily accessible by car. The most popular of them, the Blue Bar, doubles up as a low-key nightclub.

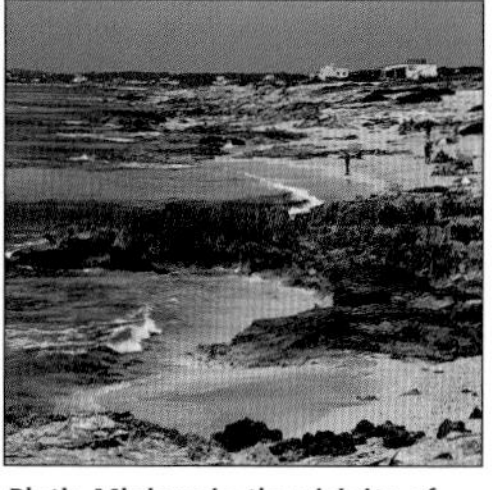

Platja Migjorn in the vicinity of Es Arenals

El Pilar de la Mola 9

11 km (7 miles) southeast of Sant Ferran.

Situated at the heart of the La Mola plateau, El Pilar de la Mola is a fairly sleepy little place and makes a good stopping off point on a trip to Formentera's 19th-century lighthouse, **Faro de la Mola** *(see below)*.

El Pilar de la Mola's most interesting historic building is the whitewashed church of **Nostra Senyora del Pilar**, built in 1784. The town is best known for its craftsmen, whose workshops are open to visitors. At the popular Sunday market you can buy jewellery, good quality leather goods and excellent local cheese (which goes perfectly with a glass of the local dry red wine).

Environs

Es Caló is a small fishing village on the north coast of the island. Unusually, it has no harbour and the boats have to be pulled ashore on special rails. When travelling from here towards La Mola it is essential to stop at the **El Mirador** bar, which offers a magnificent panoramic view of Formentera. Some 2 km (1 mile) north of El Pilar de la Mola, rises the 133-m (436-ft) high Ferrer hill. A little further on, to the west, is the **Cova d'es Fum**, a large cave where the locals hid their treasures during a Viking raid in 1118. Unfortunately for them, the Viking pirates discovered the hiding place and, having smoked them out, slaughtered the defenders and made off with the loot.

Travelling 3 km (2 miles) east, you arrive at **Punta de sa Ruda** – a rocky crag that drops steeply towards the crashing sea, over 100 m (320 ft) below. The views of the island from here are stunning. The Faro de la Mola lighthouse, built in 1861, is situated at the edge of the crag and was the inspiration for "the lighthouse at the end of the world" in Jules Verne's *Journey Around the Solar System.* A statue of the French writer stands close by.

The village church in El Pilar de la Mola

Formentera's Beaches

In terms of beauty, the beaches of Formentera can easily rival those of Ibiza. The unspoiled natural environment, magnificent sand and clean waters attract an increasing number of visitors. Most have no hotels or clubs nearby and only a few feature bars or restaurants, which for many people only adds to their charm. The roads leading to some of the beaches (even the popular ones) can be quite rough and, as a consequence, they are never as busy as elsewhere on the Balearic Islands.

Platja de Illetes ①
The most popular beach in Formentera. Stretching to the north of it is the Es Trucadors peninsula.

Platja de Llevant ②
This beach, occupying the eastern side of the peninsula, is much quieter than Platja de Illetes. Its northern end is a favourite spot for nudists.

Platja de sa Roqueta ③
Situated next to the only hotel in this area, you can walk along the shore to Es Pujols or Platja de Llevant from here.

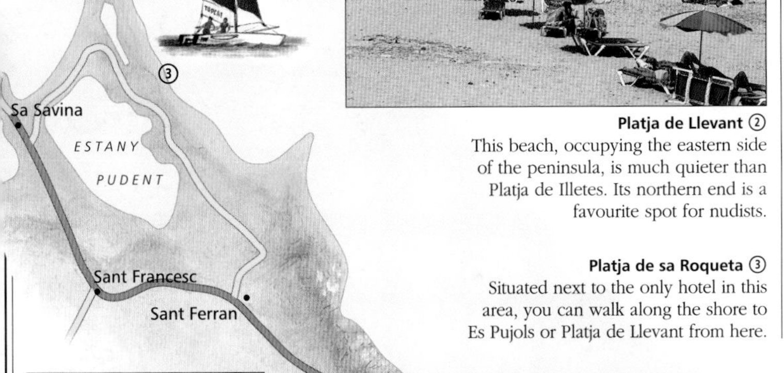

Sa Savina
ESTANY PUDENT
Sant Francesc
Sant Ferran
PM 820
El Pilar de la Mola

Platja de Tramuntana ④
A number of small beaches are tucked among the rocks. This spot is popular with nudists and anyone who wants to escape the bustling atmosphere of Illetes and Platja Migjorn.

Es Caló de Sant Augusti ⑤
Several beaches are situated to the west of town. They can be reached via the footbridges that cross the thicket covering the dunes.

0 km 2
0 miles 2

TRAVELLERS' NEEDS

WHERE TO STAY

The Balearic Islands are one of Europe's most popular holiday destinations. Their magnificent climate, fine beaches and close proximity to mainland Europe mean that visitors arrive in their thousands between June and September. Unsurprisingly, a large number of hotels have been developed to cater for the demand. Until recently, this has meant that much of the accommodation on offer has been fairly basic and it can be hard to find better accommodation at affordable prices. The hotels still include mostly two- and three-star places, but the local authorities are raising the standard of service. Many hotels close down during low season. Mallorca has the best-developed hotel facilities. Formentera has the fewest hotels.

Logo of Amic Hotels chain

The exclusive La Residencia in Deià, Mallorca

HOTELS

Most hotels on the Balearic Islands are situated along the coast, around the old town centres and harbours, and are usually within easy reach of the beaches. There are more hotel beds in the Balearics than in the whole of Greece. Even so, at the height of the season it can be difficult to get a room unless you have booked with a tour operator, as most of the rooms are snapped up well in advance. The most popular resorts are so densely packed that finding a quiet hotel with a sea view is virtually impossible. As an alternative, some historic buildings such as palaces have been turned into luxury hotels. These offer a higher standard and bags of old-world charm but at a premium price.

Many hotel developments are located in remote spots. Most provide a range of attractions. These include evening entertainment as well as recreation facilities such as tennis courts, swimming pools and gymnasiums. It is certainly advisable to check in advance to find out whether these facilities are included in the basic price.

FINCAS

As elsewhere, rural hotels and apartments are becoming popular on the Balearic Islands, especially with those seeking quiet, out-of-the-way places. This type of holiday is offered by *fincas*. *Fincas* are hotels that occupy former country mansions or farmhouses, predominantly in the island's interior. Mostly found in Mallorca, they are not necessarily a cheap option but can provide a degree of authenticity not found elsewhere. Rooms are mostly furnished with period furniture, which accentuates the character of the place.

Some *fincas* are very high-class, and cater for the wealthy. Others are in ordinary country houses and may be surrounded by holiday bungalows and apartments. When choosing to stay in a *finca* you should bear in mind that they are typically far from the beaches and town nightlife. All tourist information offices have lists of organizations offering this type of service. Details can also be found on the Internet.

Traditional bungalows on Ibiza

CAMP SITES

Those who enjoy camping or caravanning will have difficulties in the Balearics. There are few camp sites and those that do exist are generally situated in unattractive locations. Before travelling, check the facilities on the island you intend to visit. Camping on unauthorised sites is allowed with some limitations. You are not allowed to pitch a tent in town, on military grounds, tourist sites or within 1 km (half a mile) of an official camp site.

◁ Soaking up the sun on Cala Millor's beach, Mallorca

The elegant Formentor, a favourite of the rich and famous

CONVENTS AND MONASTERIES

The Balearic Islands do not have the equivalent of the state-run parador hotels that you find elsewhere in Spain but as well as the *fincas* it is also possible to find accommodation in convents and monasteries. This is mainly true of Mallorca, where the most popular hotel of this type is the Santuari de Lluc. These inexpensive rooms are intended for people who are prepared to put up with a certain lack of luxury (it is a monastery after all). However, they are very popular with visitors and you may have problems finding a room during the high season, despite the fact that they are away from the big resorts.

PRICES

The price you will have to pay for a hotel room depends on the season. Although the main holiday season coincides with the summer months, prices only peak during the month of August. This is a general rule that applies despite the fact that tariffs vary considerably from one island to the next. Out of the tour operators' peak season, rates are generally much lower. When enquiring about prices, you should remember that hotels can quote their tariffs in a variety of ways. Some are per room, others per person per night. Always check what is included in the price. In many cases breakfast has to be paid for separately.

Most of the Balearic Islands' hotels and apartments are block-booked in advance by travel agents and tour operators. Booking this way can prove much cheaper than trying to book directly with the hotel. You should also bear in mind that not all hotels accept credit cards. Many smaller places may insist that you pay in cash.

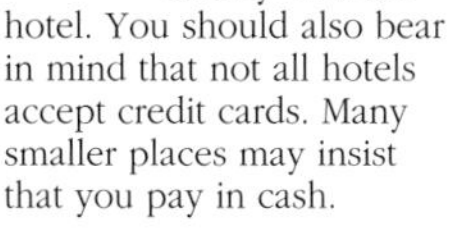

Handprints at the El Palacio Hotel

BOOKING

Accommodation may be booked in writing or via the Internet, as many hotels have their own websites. Obviously, you can also book over the telephone, but it is always preferable to have a piece of paper to confirm your reservation. It is relatively easy to find accommodation off-season, even at short notice. Problems can arise with the more popular hotels. If you are planning a visit during the peak season, you should book well in advance.

Some hotels may require a deposit or even full payment at the time of booking, in which case you should take your receipt with you. Despite the set price lists, it can be worthwhile to haggle over the price, particularly out of season.

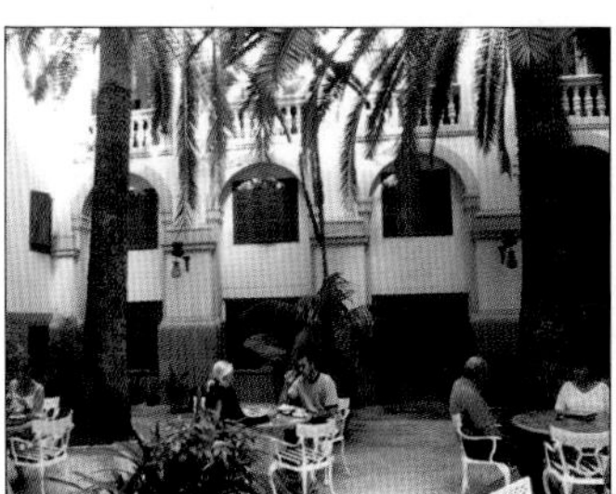

The charming patio of the Hotel Born, Palma

DIRECTORY

GENERAL ACCOMMODATION

www.hotelsearch.com
www.ibiza-hotels.com
www.interhotel.com
www.mallorcahotelguide.com
www.tourspain.es
www.visitmenorca.com

HOTEL CHAINS

www.amic-hotels-mallorca.com
www.barcelo.com
www.iberostar.com
www.insotel.com
www.riu.com
www.solmelia.es

FINCAS

Asociación de Agroturismo Balear
Avda. Gabrìel Alomar i Villalonga 8A, 2nd floor, Palma.
Tel *971 721 508.*
Fax *971 717 317.*
www.agroturismo-balear.com
www.baleares.com/fincas
www.fincasmenorca.com
www.mallorcaonline.com
www.rusticrent.com
www.weeking.com

CAMP SITES

Federación Española de Empresarios de Campings
C/Valderribas 48, Esc 3, 1° C, 28007 Madrid.
Tel *914 481 234.*
Fax *914 481 267.*
www.fedcamping.com

www.campingsonline.com
www.infocamping.com
www.interhike.com/spain/baleares.html

Choosing a Hotel

The hotels in this guide have been selected across a wide price range for their good value, facilities and location. The listings highlight some of the factors that may influence your choice. Entries are listed by island, beginning with Mallorca. For information on restaurants in the area, see pages 159–171.

PRICE CATEGORIES
For a standard double room per night, including tax and service charges.

€ Under €80
€€ €80–€120
€€€ €120–€150
€€€€ €150–€225
€€€€€ Over €225

MALLORCA

ALARÓ L'Hermitage €€€€

Ctra Alaró–Bunyola s/n, 07349 **Tel** *971 180 303* **Fax** *971 180 411* **Rooms** *24*

This former religious property is now a small hotel near the Alfabia mountains. Rooms are antique in style, some with fireplaces, all with access to the gardens. The restaurant is in an old olive mill, with terrace, and the gardens hold two swimming pools. The hotel also offers art courses, and massage and beauty therapies. **www.hermitage-hotel.com**

ALARO Stil S'Olivaret €€€€

Carretera Alaró–Orient, km 3, 07340 **Tel** *971 510 889* **Fax** *971 510 719* **Rooms** *27*

Parts of this former olive estate house date back to Muslim times, from the early 11th century, others to the Reconquest. The buildings now comprise 24 rooms and three suites, mixing antique decor with contemporary fittings. There is also a lounge and sauna, as well as external sports options. **www.stilhotels.com**

ALCÚDIA Marte €

Avenida Tucán s/n, 07410 **Tel** *971 891 600* **Rooms** *282*

The smallest of three purpose-built complexes in the Mac mega-hotel, Marte is a short distance from the beach and the town centre. Standard rooms have two queen-size beds, balcony and en-suite bathrooms; family suites have two bedrooms (one with bunk beds) and balcony. All the usual resort hotel facilities are also available. **www.mac-hotels.com**

ALCÚDIA Condes de Alcúdia €€

Avda de la Platja s/n, 07410 **Tel** *971 545 492* **Fax** *971 546 609* **Rooms** *238*

A high-rise hotel for family holidays: all rooms are for two adults and two children. As well as a vast pool, there's a wet bar and solarium, Internet room, café, restaurant and two bars. Watersports and archery are among the sports on offer, and there is a full programme of day and night entertainments. **www.hotelesglobales.com**

ALCÚDIA Cas Ferrer Nou Hotelet €€€

Carrer Pou Nou 1, 07400 **Tel** *971 897 542* **Fax** *971 897 549* **Rooms** *6*

This cosmopolitan boutique hotel has six unique *habitaciones* (three rooms, three suites) that mix natural decorative elements with an avant-garde taste. The Sappho Room has a private terrace complete with a double bed for sleeping under the stars, while three of the rooms come with their own Jacuzzi. **www.nouhotelet.com**

ALCÚDIA Ciudad Blanca €€€€

Juan Carlos I 43, 07408 **Tel** *971 890 085* **Fax** *971 890 048* **Rooms** *303*

This aparthotel is spread out among several complexes, all set in large gardens with fun pools, kiddy pool, whirlpool and extensive sun terraces. Accommodation is in three types: single studio, studio and family apartment. All have full self-catering facilities and balconies. A wide range of sports and guided hiking tours is on offer. **www.iberostar.com**

ALGAIDA Finca Raims €€€

Carrer Ribera 24, 07210 **Tel** *971 665 157* **Fax** *971 665 799* **Rooms** *5*

This high-ceilinged building was once the Raims family's *bodega* (the family chapel still stands by the entrance); in 1999 the winery architecture was adapted to five very special suites (named after grapes), with sitting rooms and all modern facilities. There are gardens, a pool and a palm-shaded inner courtyard restaurant. **www.finca-raims.com**

ALGAIDA Possessio Binicomprat €€€

Finca de Binicomprat s/n, 07210 **Tel** *971 125 028* **Fax** *971 663 773* **Rooms** *4*

This large rural establishment is surrounded by pine and oak forests and working vineyards. Each of the four suites has a sitting room, kitchen and terrace, with TV, modem and fireplace. Outdoor areas include gardens, a large terrace and a pool. The restaurant is partly alfresco and supplied from the surrounding farmlands. **www.fincabinicomprat.com**

ANDRATX Mon Port €€

Cal d'Egos, Finca la Noria, 07157 **Tel** *971 238 623* **Fax** *971 238 624* **Rooms** *111*

This impressive building of warm local stone conceals all mod cons behind a façade that blends seamlessly into the landscape overlooking Andratx port. Rooms are airy, with terraces giving on to the central open area, and suites are large, with sitting rooms and Jacuzzis. Mon Port also boasts a state-of-the-art spa and gym. **www.hotelmonport.com**

Key to Symbols *see back cover flap*

ANDRATX Son Esteve  €€€

Cami c'as Vidals 42, 07157 ***Tel*** *971 235 272* ***Fax*** *971 235 412* ***Rooms*** *7*

Away from the coast, in rolling wooded countryside, this *agroturism* has seven comfortable, rustic-style rooms, all heated and with en-suite facilities, TV and minibar. There is also an outdoor pool and a solarium. Guests can explore the area by horse. **www.sonesteve.com**

ANDRATX La Pergola €€€€

Avda S'Almudaina, 16, 07157 ***Tel*** *971 671 550* ***Fax*** *971 674 318* ***Rooms*** *92*

This popular two-storey aparthotel is built around pools and gardens, and offers ample facilities for family holidays, including a gym, solarium and tennis court. La Pergola also offers amenities such as a restaurant, bar, laundry, conference rooms and even medical services. **www.la-pergola.com**

ANDRATX Villa Italia €€€€€

Camino Sant Carles 13, 07157 ***Tel*** *971 674 011* ***Fax*** *971 673 350* ***Rooms*** *16*

A Florentine-style mansion built in the 1920s by an Italian millionaire, Villa Italia has been restored to house this luxurious hotel. Inside there are stucco ceilings and marble floors, and the huge gardens – with fountains, tiles and Italianate balustrades – offer great sea views. A restaurant and a spa complete the picture. **www.hotelvillaitalia.com**

ARTÀ Son Cardaix €€

Ctra Palma–Artà, km 63, 07570 ***Tel*** *971 829 138* ***Fax*** *971 829 254* ***Rooms*** *9*

This 15th-century *finca* has been sensitively renovated to incorporate the features of the original *casa señorial* (gentleman's home) into a 21st-century hotel. Eight of the nine suites have sitting rooms; four have fireplaces for colder days. The extensive grounds (with pool) are witness to Son Cardaix's original grandeur. **www.soncardaix.com**

ARTÀ Can Moragues €€€

C/Pou Nou 12 ***Tel*** *971 829 509* ***Fax*** *971 829 530* ***Rooms*** *8*

This pleasant 18th-century town mansion fitted with discreetly modern facilities is a haven in the middle of this busy town. Rooms are light and airy, with lots of bare stone and glass, and avant-garde, minimalist decor. The garden features an orange-shaded terrace and pool; the interior, a solarium and sauna. **www.canmoragues.com**

BANYALBUFAR Sa Baronia €

C/Baronia 16, 07191 ***Tel*** *971 618 146* ***Fax*** *971 148 738* ***Rooms*** *39*

On the island's unspoilt northwest coast, this family-run hotel was built as an extension to a 17th-century baronial tower. The extension itself is rather unattractive, but the warm welcome and the tranquillity of the area make up for it. Sa Baronia has all the facilities of a resort hotel in a spectacular mountain setting with fine views. **www.hbaronia.com**

BINISSALEM Finca Can Davero €€€

Ctra Binissalem–Biniali, km 2.6, 07350 ***Tel*** *637 475 720* ***Fax*** *971 870 582* ***Rooms*** *10*

Hidden in mature gardens of olive and fruit trees, with a castellated tower above the pool, this *finca* has ten suites, all with sitting rooms, balconies or terraces, and all mod cons. The three-storey Torre suite has its own roof terrace, too. There is a separate pavilion for meetings or study. Outdoor activities can be arranged. **www.candavero.com**

BINISSALEM Scott's Hotel €€€€

Plaza de la Iglesia 12, 07350 ***Tel*** *971 870 100* ***Fax*** *971 870 267* ***Rooms*** *17*

Mallorca's first boutique hotel is this elegantly decorated 18th-century townhouse in the wine-producing town of Binissalem. The owners have given thought to every detail, right down to the handmade beds. Facilities include a restaurant, bar, lounge, library, pool, Jacuzzi and gardens. Try the excellent bistro for dinner. **www.scottshotel.com**

CALA MAJOR Nixe Palace €

Avenida Joan Miró 269, 07015 ***Tel*** *971 700 888* ***Fax*** *971 403 171* ***Rooms*** *133*

One of the original luxury hotels in Palma, the Nixe offers spacious rooms overlooking a palm-shaded terrace, outdoor pool and beach. In addition to Internet and Wi-Fi access, the hotel has an indoor pool and spa with gym and thermal springs. **www.hotelnixepalace.com**

CALA MILLOR Castell del Mar €€€

C/Bonanza 1, 07560 ***Tel*** *971 587 535* ***Fax*** *971 585 755* ***Rooms*** *230*

Most of this large beachfront hotel's rooms have sea views, and larger family suites have sitting rooms, too. All have balconies. The large gardens have two pools (there is also one indoors), and there is an extensive range of health options: wellness centre, gym, Turkish bath and sauna. **www.cm-hotels.com**

CALVIÀ Illetas Club Playa €€

Paseo de Illetas 62, 07181 ***Tel*** *971 402 411* ***Fax*** *902 337 723* ***Rooms*** *67*

Built on a rocky stretch of coast, but with access down to two small beaches, this modern complex of one- and two-bedroom self-catering apartments also offers all the usual facilities: restaurant, bar and pool. As well as a children's club, it has a Jacuzzi, sauna, gym and gardens. Most larger apartments also have sea views. **www.roc-hotels.com**

CALVIÀ Barcelo Albatros €€€€

Paseo de Illetas 15, 07181 ***Tel*** *971 402 211* ***Fax*** *971 402 154* ***Rooms*** *119*

Built around a pleasant garden with a cluster of pools, this spacious hotel has all you need for a comfortable holiday. All rooms have terraces (mostly with sea views), with satellite TV, Wi-Fi and other hi-tech features. There are also several specially fitted suites for travellers with disabilities. Health and beauty treatments are available. **www.barcelo.com**

CALVIÀ Hospes Maricel €€€€€

Ctra d'Andratx 11, 07181 ***Tel*** *971 707 744* ***Fax*** *971 707 745* ***Rooms*** *29*

This five-star hotel has taken a grand 17th-century palace and refitted it with 21st-century luxury features, including an infinity pool. Large rooms all have king-size beds, plasma TVs, DVD players and other special features. In addition to the usual five-star amenities, there is a spa, therapy and beauty centre. **www.hospes.es**

CAMPOS Migjorn €€€€

Poligono 18, Parcela 477, 07630 ***Tel*** *971 650 668* ***Fax*** *971 651 418* ***Rooms*** *10*

An inland hotel, Migjorn mixes traditional stone architecture with contemporary design. Each apartment has a lounge as well as a bedroom, with either a balcony or terrace overlooking the extensive gardens. The hotel is set in sprawling grounds, with a large pool and a restaurant. **www.hotel-migjorn.com**

CAPDEPERA Cases de Son Barbassa €€

Ctra Cala Mesquida–Camí de Son Barbassa, 07580 ***Tel*** *971 565 776* ***Fax*** *971 566 057* ***Rooms*** *12*

Mallorca has a wealth of ancient structures now serving as boutique hotels, but no other can claim an important Talayot site, Son Barbassa, at the end of the garden. This hotel has been exquisitely furnished throughout, with a terrace, pool and restaurant, and dramatic sleeping quarters such as the Tower Suite. **www.sonbarbassa.com**

CAPDEPERA Can Simoneta €€€€€

Ctra Artà–Canyamel 8, 07580 ***Tel*** *971 816 110* ***Fax*** *971 816 111* ***Rooms*** *16*

Perched on a cliff above the Canyamel beach, with big windows opening on to the sea, this is an elegant, light and spacious hideaway featuring white walls, blond wood and glass. All rooms have sea or mountain views. A terrace bar and restaurant, large garden and pool are some of the facilities on offer. **www.cansimoneta.com**

DEIÀ D'es Puig €€€

C/d'es Puig 4, 07179 ***Tel*** *971 639 409* ***Fax*** *971 639 210* ***Rooms*** *5*

This small but elegant townhouse comprises just four rooms, some with views of the Serra Tramunta, and a suite-apartment. The leafy terrace boasts a pool and outdoor spaces for breakfast and relaxing. The top-floor suite also has a private terrace with spectacular views over the town and the surrounding countryside. **www.hoteldespuig.com**

DEIÀ Costa d'Or €€€€

Lluc–Alcari s/n, 07197 ***Tel*** *971 639 025* ***Fax*** *971 639 347* ***Rooms*** *41*

Set in a forest in the small hamlet of Lluc-Alcari, this country estate offers more amenities than most small country hotels, not least a tennis court, pool and gym. Some rooms have floor-to-ceiling sea views, while others look out over the mountains. The panoramic restaurant overlooks a pool and terrace garden area. **www.hoposa.es**

DEIÀ La Residencia €€€€€

Son Canals s/n, 07179 ***Tel*** *971 639 011* ***Fax*** *971 639 370* ***Rooms*** *64*

Two splendidly restored 16th- and 18th-century manors have been combined into this legendary hotel, a favourite hideaway of VIPs and celebrities. The rooms and suites (some with private pools) are beautifully done, with traditional Mallorcan furniture and pale linen. La Residencia also has a spa and a restaurant. **www.hotellaresidencia.com**

DEIÀ Sa Pedrissa €€€€€

Ctr De Valldemossa s/n, 07197 ***Tel*** *971 639 111* ***Fax*** *971 639 44556* ***Rooms*** *8*

This 17th-century country house overlooking the sea below Deià has been transformed into an *agroturism* hotel like few others. All rooms are discrete and feature views of land or sea, around a pool and gardens with a spectacular setting. The Sa Tafona restaurant offers new ways with classic dishes – under the stars. **www.sapedrissa.com**

FELANITX Es Passarell €€€

2ª Vuelta 117, 07200 ***Tel*** *971 183 091* ***Fax*** *971 183 336* ***Rooms*** *10*

This English-owned *finca* was built in the 19th century but recently renovated into a modern country-style hotel with a large pool and shady terrace. All apartments have full facilities, and the larger ones boast four-poster beds. A wide range of activities, including guided hikes, yoga and art and jewellery craft, is available. **www.espassarell.com**

INCA Fina Son Vivot €€

Ctra Palma–Alcúdia, km 30, C/Son Vivot, 07300 ***Tel*** *971 880 124* ***Rooms*** *4*

A working *huerta* (orchard/farm) supplies fruit, vegetables and meat to the restaurant of this magnificent country house, whose four rooms and communal areas retain the decor of centuries ago. Facilities are thoroughly modern, though, and there is a large outdoor pool in the grounds. **www.sonvivot.com**

INCA Casa de Virrey €€€

Carretera Inca–Sencelles, km 2.4, 07300 ***Tel*** *971 881 018* ***Fax*** *971 883 323* ***Rooms*** *16*

This grand 17th-century country mansion has eight rooms and eight suites, combining period detail with modern amenities. The public spaces retain original details such as marble fireplaces, and are decorated with original art and antiques. Casa de Virrey also organizes concerts and art exhibits. **www.casadelvirrey.net**

LLUC Santuari de Lluc €

Plaza des Pelegrins 1, 07315 ***Tel*** *971 871 525* ***Fax*** *971 517 096* ***Rooms*** *129*

The rooms and apartments at the spectacular Santuari de Lluc were originally modest quarters for pilgrims to the island's most important religious shrine. Accommodation is basic, but clean and comfortable (en-suite facilities, heating), but the point of staying here is the unique chance to sleep in such a remarkable setting. **www.lluc.net**

Key to Price Guide *see p144* **Key to Symbols** *see back cover flap*

LLUCMAJOR Gran Hotel Son Julia €€€€€

Crta S'Arenal s/n, 07620 ***Tel*** *971 669 700* ***Fax*** *971 669 701* ***Rooms*** *25*

This opulent 19th-century mansion has seven degrees of luxury over just 25 rooms: from a basic room with canopied bed, plasma TV and Internet connection, to the palatial Imperial, with its own sitting room, walk-in shower, Jacuzzi and mini gym. Of the three pools, one is infinity and another roofed with Moorish domed ceilings. **www.sonjulia.com**

MANACOR Finca Es Rafal Roig €€

Ctra Manacor–Ca'n Picafort, km 8.2, 07500 ***Tel*** *971 557 109* ***Fax*** *971 557 111* ***Rooms*** *5*

Parts of this country establishment date back to the 12th century. The five units, each with a terrace and kitchen, have stone walls, arched and beamed ceilings, and country-style decor. There's a large pool and terrace, but no restaurant. The *finca* is close to four golf courses, and there are watersports at nearby bays. **www.esrafalroig.com**

MANACOR Son Trobat €€€

Ctra Manacor–Sant Llorenç, km 4.8, 07530 ***Tel*** *971 569 674* ***Fax*** *971 569 874* ***Rooms*** *25*

This handsome large *finca* has 25 stone beamed or vaulted rooms. They are decorated in country style but feature modern facilities, including TV and Internet access. Son Trobat is surrounded by orange, lemon and other orchard trees, and is only a five-minute drive from some of the main golf courses on the island. **www.sontrobat.com**

MANACOR Son Amoixa Vell €€€€

Ctra Manacor–Cales de Mallorca, km 5.4, 07500 ***Tel*** *971 846 292* ***Fax*** *670 899 455* ***Rooms*** *14*

A large 16th-century *finca* sitting among olive, fig, lemon and orange groves. The original stone beamed and arched architecture has been retained, along with a pleasant country-style decor. All rooms have air conditioning and Internet access, and there is a pool and a well equipped health and beauty centre. **www.sonamoixa.com**

MONTUÏRI Es Figueral Nou €€

Carretera Montuïri–Sant Joan, km 0.7, 07230 ***Tel*** *971 646 764* ***Fax*** *971 646 747* ***Rooms*** *25*

Tiled floors, beamed ceilings and country furniture are the decor highlights of this 15th-century building, which became a *bodega* in the 1800s and is now a small hotel. The large grounds incorporate two pools, a sauna and gym. Excellent hiking and biking trails can be found in the surrounding countryside. **www.esfigueralnou.com**

MONTUÏRI Fina Sa Rota d'en Palerm €€€

Carretera Lloret–Montuïri, km 0.8, 07230 ***Tel*** *971 521 100* ***Fax*** *971 521 101* ***Rooms*** *9*

This 18th-century *casa señorial*, set in the countryside outside Montuïri, has only recently opened its small collection of rooms and two- and four-bedroom houses, all set around a central farmhouse. Larger properties have sitting rooms and shaded patios. There is a pleasant restaurant for candlelit dinners on the terrace. **www.sa-rota.com**

MURO Amapola €

Urb Las Gaviotas s/n, 07458 ***Tel*** *971 890 551* ***Fax*** *971 890 744* ***Rooms*** *156*

A six-storey hotel close to the Muro beach, with a small lake at the edge of its grounds. Rooms have balconies or terraces, satellite TV and music, and en-suite bathrooms. As well as a pool, there is also a tennis court, minigolf, table tennis and billiards. Nature excursions can be arranged. **www.grupotel.com**

MURO Playa Esperanza €€€€

Avda S'Albufera 4, 07458 ***Tel*** *971 890 568* ***Fax*** *971 890 938* ***Rooms*** *332*

This six-storey hotel opens on to the sandy Muro beach. Rooms have balconies and coastal or sea views. As well as indoor and heated outdoor pools, there is a spa, gym, tennis court, solarium and wellness centre, hairdresser, child-care service, day and night entertainments and sailing facilities. **www.esperanzahoteles.com**

PALMA Born €

C/Sant Jaume 3, 07012 ***Tel*** *971 712 942* ***Fax*** *971 718 618* ***Rooms*** *29*

The Marquis of Ferrandell's town mansion, built in the 16th century and restored in the 18th, makes a splendid hotel. Centrally situated in a quiet street at the top of Passeig d'es Born, this spacious and comfortable family hotel is built around a large and leafy patio. Rooms have period decor and modern conveniences. **www.hotelborn.com**

PALMA Dalí €€

Bartolomé Fons 8, 07015 Cala Mayor ***Tel*** *971 405 201* ***Fax*** *971 701 014* ***Rooms*** *97*

This modern three-star hotel is handy for the nearby Fundación Miró. All rooms have air conditioning and central heating for the cooler months, as well as balconies, some overlooking the busy port and the historic lighthouse. The centre of Palma is just five minutes away by car. **www.hoteldali-palmademallorca.com**

PALMA Melea Pallas Atenea €€

Paseo Marítimo 29, 07014 ***Tel*** *971 281 400* ***Fax*** *971 451 989* ***Rooms*** *361*

Looming over the marina and with the Bellver Castle on the hill behind it, the Atenea is a large international establishment aimed squarely at the business market. Rooms are large, some with views of sea, city and cathedral, and have all hi-tech connections. The hotel is also specially adapted for disabled visitors. **www.solmelia.com**

PALMA Zurburán €€

Josep Villalonga 16, 07014 ***Tel*** *971 221 771* ***Fax*** *971 453 602* ***Rooms*** *40*

Situated in a quiet residential area to the west of the city centre, close to the Castell de Bellver and Passeig Marítim seafront, this smart hotel has modernist decor in its tranquil public spaces and rooms. Key features include a cafeteria and restaurant, rooftop terrace, Internet and Wi-Fi facilities, and private parking. **www.sercotelhoteles.es**

PALMA Catalonia Majorica €€€

Garita 3, 07015 **Tel** *971 400 261* **Fax** *971 405 906* **Rooms** *168*

This hotel overlooking the Passeig Marítim and bay has expanded to accommodate large conference and business facilities. It has outdoor and indoor pools, a gym, Jacuzzi and solarium, and an all-day restaurant. Most rooms have balconies with views, full amenities and 24-hour service. **www.hoteles-catalonia.com**

PALMA Jaime III €€€

Paseo de Mallorca 14b, 07011 **Tel** *971 725 943* **Fax** *971 725 946* **Rooms** *88*

With full business facilities, the sleek Jaime III offers boutique hotel style to professional travellers and tourists alike. Rooms have satellite TV, Internet and Wi-Fi links, and the hotel spa offers massages, sauna, Turkish baths, Jacuzzi and fitness machines. Centrally located near the cathedral with an all-day restaurant. **www.hotelhmjaimeiii.com**

PALMA San Lorenzo €€€€

San Lorenzo 14, 07012 **Tel** *971 728 200* **Fax** *971 711 901* **Rooms** *9*

This luxurious hotel could be Palma's best-kept secret. Rooms have balconies and are sumptuously decorated, and there is also a small rooftop pool and terrace. Although minutes away from the city centre, San Lorenzo feels a long way from the city hubbub. Some rooms have open fires for cooler nights. **www.hotelsanlorenzo.com**

POLLENÇA Desbrull €€

Marqués Desbrull 7, 07460 **Tel** *971 535 065* **Fax** *971 535 226* **Rooms** *5*

This renovated townhouse offers boutique hotel-style comfort, mixing period architecture with avant-garde decor. The five suites all have contemporary fitted baths and state-of-the-art technology, while the bar, restaurant and lounge feature artworks by leading island artists (some of which are for sale). **www.desbrull.com**

POLLENÇA Posada de Lluc €€€€

Roser Vell 11, 07460 **Tel** *971 535 220* **Fax** *971 535 222* **Rooms** *8*

With a history dating back to the 15th century, when it was donated to the nearby Santuari de Lluc as a travellers' rest (*posada*) for pilgrims and scholars, this hotel has a rich past. The building's original, ample, dimensions have been maintained, and rooms feature original stone walls and beamed ceilings. **www.posadalluc.com**

POLLENÇA Son Sant Jordi €€€€

Calle Sant Jordi 29, 07460 **Tel** *971 530 389* **Fax** *971 535 109* **Rooms** *8*

Four-poster or canopied beds, beamed ceilings and stone floors are features of this renovated townhouse. The decor is rustic or classical, but complemented by modern facilities, including satellite TV and RDSL phone lines. The gardens offer an outdoor pool and a small sauna, and there is a terrace restaurant for alfresco dining. **www.sosantjordi.com**

POLLENÇA Formentor €€€€€

Playa de Formentor s/n, 07470 **Tel** *971 899 101* **Fax** *971 865 155* **Rooms** *127*

Writers, opera singers, film stars and even the Dalai Lama have signed the visitors' book of this luxury hotel on the island's northwest tip. No longer the celebrity haunt it once was, the Formentor still remains an elegant retreat. Amenities include pool, gym, gardens and three restaurants. The beach is on the doorstep. **www.hotelformentor.net**

POLLENÇA Son Brull €€€€€

Ctra Palma–Pollença s/n, 07460 **Tel** *971 535 353* **Fax** *971 531 068* **Rooms** *23*

Avant-garde design meets classic rural style in this large country mansion surrounded by mature gardens. Suites and rooms all have the latest technology (including Bang & Olufsen home entertainment system), its restaurant specializes in Mallorcan *nueva cocina*, and there is a full range of sporting activities available, as well as a spa. **www.sonbrull.com**

PORTO CRISTO Son Josep de Baix €€

Ctra Porto Colom, km 8.4, 07680 **Tel** *636 410 979* **Fax** *971 650 472* **Rooms** *4*

This small, remote *agroturismo* probably calls for independent transport, but it promises a rare experience when you get there. Three rustic but modern apartments for two to four people, with arched stone ceilings, stone walls and stylish decor and fittings, sit in open countryside near the wild beaches below Manacor. **www.sonjosepdebaix.com**

PORTO CRISTO Felip €€€

Burdils 41, 07680 **Tel** *971 820 750* **Fax** *971 820 594* **Rooms** *96*

The Felip has stood on the seafront opposite the Club Nautico for more than 100 years. It now occupies two four-storey buildings, with a terrace, pool and gardens. All rooms have air conditioning, Internet connection, modern bathrooms and balconies; some enjoy lovely sea views. **www.thbhotels.com**

PORTO CRISTO Son Mas €€€€€

Carretera Porto Cristo–Porto Colom, 07680 **Tel** *971 558 755* **Fax** *971 558 756* **Rooms** *16*

At various points in its 400-year history, this building was a fort, a farm and a wheat mill. Parts of it still survive in an elegant modern hotel surrounded by olive, orange, almond and fig trees. Rooms have attractive timbered or vaulted ceilings. As well as an infinity pool, there is a gym, plus biking and hiking options nearby. **www.sonmas.com**

RANDA Es Recó de Randa €€€

C/Font 21, 07629 **Tel** *971 660 997* **Fax** *971 66 25 58* **Rooms** *14*

A restaurant-with-rooms in a quiet village at the foot of the Puig de Randa mountain, this is a great base for visiting the religious sites nearby. Many of the rustically decorated rooms offer breathtaking views of the mountains and citrus groves. The standout feature is the curved pool with views of the surrounding countryside. **www.esrecoderanda.com**

Key to Price Guide *see p144* **Key to Symbols** *see back cover flap*

SANTANYÍ Pinos Playa €€

Costa d'en Nofre 15, 07659 **Tel** *971 165 000* **Fax** *971 165 003* **Rooms** *104*

One of two resort developments at this otherwise quiet beach, Pinos Playa is split between two buildings. All rooms have balconies, some with sea views, and Wi-Fi connection. Studios and apartments also have kitchens, dining rooms, and balconies or terraces. The site is rather remote, but there is a full range of transport links. **www.pinosplaya.com**

SANTANYÍ Cala Santanyí €€€

Sa Costa des Etics, 07660 **Tel** *971 165 505* **Fax** *971 165 509* **Rooms** *24*

This small beach hotel surrounded by pines has balconies with beach views in all rooms, which come with lounge areas and, in the suites, self-catering facilities. All rooms have Wi-Fi connection. As well as restaurant, bar and pool, the hotel also has a new spa and wellness centre with Jacuzzi, sauna and gym. **www.hotelcalasantanyi.com**

SANTANYÍ Colonia San Jordi Club €€€

Camino de los Estanques s/n, 07638 **Tel** *971 656 577* **Fax** *971 655 712* **Rooms** *192*

Accommodation at this complex is spread out among six low-rise developments, surrounded by gardens and close to the Es Trenc beach. All rooms have full amenities, and family studios come with sitting rooms. As well as a range of restaurants and bars, the hotel has three pools, exercise facilities, sports and entertainments. **www.blau-hotels.com**

SANTANYÍ Finca Sa Carrotja €€€

Sa Carrotja 7, 07640 **Tel** *971 649 053* **Fax** *971 649 162* **Rooms** *6*

The handsome stone building housing this 16th-century farmhouse has six air-conditioned suites. The large gardens include a heated pool and terrace, and give on to fields that supply organic produce for pre-arranged meals (special diets are catered for, too). The hotel also has free bike hire for explorers. **www.sacarrotja.com**

SES SALINES Es Turó €€€€

Carretera Campos – Sa Colònia de Sant Jordi, km 5.2, 07640 **Tel** *971 649 531* **Fax** *971 649 548* **Rooms** *10*

Find rural calm and tasteful comfort in this stone-built hotel surrounded by almond and olive groves. The spacious suites are decorated in traditional style. The hotel has a pool and a lounge with a stone fire for cooler nights. The terrace restaurant has views of Cabrera Island in the distance. Good hiking trails are nearby. **www.esturo.com**

S'HORTA Sa Pletassa €€€€

Caminoviejo S'Horta, Cala Marçal, 07669 **Tel** *971 837 069* **Fax** *971 729 572* **Rooms** *11*

An inland traditional stone country house surrounded by beautiful gardens. All rooms are unique, some have wooden beams and beds covered with a canopy – all have modern facilities. Nearby, two small cottages that house two to four people are available for rent. The hotel has free Wi-Fi, and golf facilities are in close proximity. **www.sapletassa.com**

SINEU Son Cleda €€

Plaça es Fossar 7, 07510 **Tel** *971 521 038* **Fax** *971 520 142* **Rooms** *8*

The second boutique hotel to open in the charming town of Sineu is located in a renovated 16th-century townhouse decorated to blend in with the warm local stone. All rooms have satellite TV and Internet connection, and the interior patio and terrace restaurant are both pleasant suntraps. **www.hotelsoncleda.com**

SINEU Leon de Sineu €€€

Carrer dels Bous 129, 07510 **Tel** *971 520 211* **Fax** *971 855 058* **Rooms** *8*

The first boutique hotel in Sineu is a sympathetic modernization of a 15th-century town mansion. In addition to a popular restaurant and bar, there are mature gardens and a small pool. The family-run Leon de Sineu prides itself on its fresh, healthy food and can accommodate special dietary requirements. **www.hotel-leondesineu.com**

SÓLLER Hostal Brisas €

Camino de Muleta 15, 07108 **Tel** *971 631 352* **Rooms** *46*

This simple seaside hotel was built in the 1960s in traditional style. Rooms are basic but more than adequate, and the best have views of the sea from private terraces. The Brisas is perfectly located for a relaxed beach holiday, just a few steps from the beach, and has a simple café-bar that serves local dishes. **www.hotel-brisas.com**

SÓLLER La Vila €€

Plaça Constitució 14, 07100 **Tel** *634 641* **Fax** *638 745* **Rooms** *8*

Dating from 1904, the height of Spanish *modernista* style, this small townhouse hotel has retained some spectacular period details. All rooms have balconies or French windows, and there is a leafy private garden and terrace. Rooms are large, with state-of-the-art en-suite facilities. **www.lavilahotel.com**

SÓLLER Finca Can Coll €€€

Cami de Can Coll 1, 07100 **Tel** *633 244* **Fax** *631 905* **Rooms** *9*

This small *finca*, or farmhouse, in the Sóller valley has just nine rooms, each furnished in traditional Mallorcan rustic style and with views of the countryside. With various lounges, honesty bar, dinners by arrangement, leafy terraces, outdoor pool and gardens, the atmosphere is relaxed, and there is a big log fire for cooler nights. **www.cancoll.com**

SÓLLER L'Avenida €€€€

Gran Via 9, 07100 **Tel** *634 075* **Fax** *633 597* **Rooms** *8*

An opulent 19th-century mansion boasting a startling Neo-Classical pool and terrace, L'Avenida mixes period design with modernist decor to striking effect. The rooms and suites all have contemporary bathrooms, and in addition to the usual hi-tech connections, the hotel also has a video library for in-room DVD facilities. **www.avenida-hotel.com**

SÓLLER Finca Ca N'Ai €€€€€

Camí de Son Sales 50, 07100 ***Tel*** *971 632 494* ***Fax*** *971 631 899* ***Rooms*** *11*

This enchanting hotel has been converted from a 300-year-old Mallorcan mansion surrounded by orange groves. The large suites, all with modern facilities, are furnished in an earth-toned rustic style, and set in and around the central manor house. The service has a personal touch, and the cooking is excellent. Open mid-Feb–Oct. **www.canai.com**

SÓLLER Gran €€€€€

Romaguera 18, 07100 ***Tel*** *638 686* ***Fax*** *631 476* ***Rooms*** *204*

The imposing 19th-century façade lives up to this hotel's name, as do the modernized facilities behind it. Rooms are big, with a range of five-star luxuries, and most have views of either the town or the surrounding countryside. As well as a panoramic rooftop pool and terrace, the hotel has a spa and gym complex. **www.granhotelsoller.com**

VALLDEMOSSA Cases de C'as Garriguer €€

Ctra Valldemossa a Andratx, km. 2.5, 07170 ***Tel*** *971 612 300* ***Fax*** *971 612 583* ***Rooms*** *10*

This courtyarded stone building, once the guard's house (*garriguer*) of the ancient Son Olesa country estate, has now been converted into a peaceful rural hotel. The spacious bedrooms are furnished with antiques and have wooden-beamed ceilings. Most have private terraces, with spellbinding views of the hills. **www.vistamarhotel.es**

VALLDEMOSSA Mirabo €€€€

Ctra Valldemossa, km 15, 07170 ***Tel*** *661 285 215* ***Fax*** *971 612 531* ***Rooms*** *8*

This 500-year-old property in the hills overlooking Valldemossa has been transformed into a small luxury hotel, with ultramodern design set against rough-hewn stone. Only the number of rooms detracts from the impression that the Mirabo might be an artist's country home. That, and the glorious infinity pool. **www.mirabo.es**

VALLDEMOSSA Valldemossa €€€€€

Ctra Vieja de Valldemossa s/n, 07170 ***Tel*** *971 612 626* ***Fax*** *971 612 625* ***Rooms*** *12*

Two impressive19th-century stone mansions have been combined in this imposing hotel that mixes traditional design with modernist decor. Three double rooms and nine junior suites (named after famous visitors) have TV, DVD and modem, and share a communal pool and solarium. Some suites have their own pool. **www.valldemossahotel.com**

VILAFRANCA DE BONANY Sa Franquesa Vella €€

Ctra Petra–Felanitx, km 8.3, 07250 ***Tel*** *971 834 452* ***Fax*** *971 560 682* ***Rooms*** *9*

This 15th-century building sits on a small hill above farmland (which still supplies produce to the hotel kitchen). The apartments have modern facilities, kitchens and individual terraces, and there is a pool with views. As well as hiking and biking, activities include harvesting and egg collecting – for supper. **www.safranquesavellamallorca.com**

MENORCA

ALAIOR Jardin de Menorca €€

Urbanización Torresolí s/n, 07712 ***Tel*** *971 378 040* ***Fax*** *971 378 050* ***Rooms*** *144*

This relatively small complex consists of a series of low-rise apartment buildings set in large gardens with three linked pools at the centre. Accommodation is spacious, modern and upscale. There is also an indoor pool, gym, spa therapies, badminton and squash courts, and several restaurants. **www.grupohg.com**

ALAIOR Sa Barerra €€€€

Cala'n Porter s/n, 07712 ***Tel*** *971 377 126* ***Fax*** *971 377 251* ***Rooms*** *26*

This is a stylish independent hotel with a strong Moroccan flavour to its design. All rooms have plasma-screen TVs and balconies overlooking the grounds or the sea. The large pool has a view of the seasonal "torrent" that runs into the bay. The hotel is unable to accommodate under-12s. **www.hotel-menorca.net**

ALAIOR Sol Milanos Pinguinos €€€€

Playa de Son Bou, 07730 ***Tel*** *971 371 200* ***Fax*** *971 372 032* ***Rooms*** *517*

This vast hotel on one of Menorca's longest beaches is best described by its theme: *The Flintstones*. Most rooms have a sea view, and all have air conditioning, TV and bar. The hotel has three restaurants (two of them themed), a large pool with children's area, gardens and beach-based watersports, including a diving centre. **www.solmelia.com**

CIUTADELLA Hostal Sa Prensa €

Plaça de Madrid s/n, 07760 ***Tel*** *971 382 698* ***Rooms*** *7*

This is probably the best of the cheaper hotels in Ciutadella, which has a shortage of good budget accommodation. Book early to get one of the four bedrooms with terraces and great views of the port; the other three rooms are plainer and overlook nondescript apartments. A café-bar downstairs serves breakfast. Closed 15 Dec–15 Jan.

CIUTADELLA Agroturismo Biniatram €€

Ctra Cala Morell s/n, 07760 ***Tel*** *971 383 113* ***Fax*** *971 482 827* ***Rooms*** *8*

This small rustic *finca* has eight suites, each accommodating between two and four people, all with self-catering facilities and either balconies or terraces in comfortably modernized farm buildings. Rooms are light and airy, and there is a large pool in the grounds. Restaurants and the beach are within walking distance. **www.biniatram.com**

Key to Price Guide *see p144* **Key to Symbols** *see back cover flap*

CIUTADELLA Hostal Ciutadella €€

C/San Eloy 10, 07760 ***Tel*** *971 383 462* ***Fax*** *971 484 858* ***Rooms*** *17*

Just around the corner from the Plaça de Alfons III, this simple, modern hotel offers good value, no-frills lodging. The rooms are plainly furnished and spotless, and cooled with ceiling fans in summer. Simple meals are served in the family-friendly café-bar on the ground floor.

CIUTADELLA Hotel Portl Ciutadella €€

Passeig Marítim 36, 07760 ***Tel*** *971 482 520* ***Fax*** *971 380 419* ***Rooms*** *94*

Overlooking an estuary on the bay, this low-rise hotel has larger and more modern rooms than many of its counterparts, but no gardens other than a large central one dominated by a large pool. All rooms have full facilities, TV and broadband connection. The hotel also has a restaurant, bar, gym, and health and beauty centre. **www.sethotels.es**

CIUTADELLA Hesperia Patricia €€€€

Paseo San Nicolas 90–92, 07760 ***Tel*** *971 385 511* ***Fax*** *971 481 120* ***Rooms*** *44*

This modern, cream-coloured chain hotel with white bay windows near the harbour is a comfortable option with all amenities, but without a pool or grounds to make it a long-term holiday base. Its business facilities attract the working traveller, but the location and efficient staff make it a good bet for tourists, too. **www.hesperia.es**

CIUTADELLA Hotel Sant Ignasi €€€€€

Carretera Cala Morell, 07769 ***Tel*** *971 385 575* ***Fax*** *971 480 537* ***Rooms*** *16*

A grand country mansion built in 1777 as part of a farm estate, the Sant Ignasi was modernized in the 18th century and opened as a hotel in 1998. The grounds are vast, with gardens, a large pool and vineyards that supply wine and cava to the hotel's noted restaurant, Es Lloc. Rooms are big and decorated with antiques. **www.santignasi.com**

ES CASTELL Agamemnon €€€

C/Agamenón 16, 07720 ***Tel*** *971 362 150* ***Fax*** *971 362 154* ***Rooms*** *75*

Sitting on a low bluff above the bay at Es Castell, with marvellous views from all rooms and most public areas, the Agamemnon occupies a prime position. All rooms have generously sized terraces. A large pool dominates the gardens, and the hotel also has its own dock for a range of water-based activities. **www.sethotels.es**

ES CASTELL Son Granot €€€€€

Carretera de Sant Felip s/n, 07720 ***Tel*** *971 355 771* ***Fax*** *971 355 555*

Built as an officer's home by the British in the 18th century, this was a wreck when its Spanish owners bought and restored it as a hotel. The grandeur remains in its hilltop position, entrance staircase and interiors, which mix period detail with modern design. A variety of sports and cultural activities is on offer. **www.songranot.com**

ES MERCADAL Hostal Jeni €€

Mirada del Toro 81, 0740 ***Tel*** *971 375 059* ***Fax*** *971 375 114* ***Rooms*** *24*

Painted bright orange on a street corner in the town centre, this surprisingly spacious hotel has more than its humble façade might suggest, not least a large terrace with pool at the rear. Recently renovated, its rooms have air conditioning and town views. The hotel also has a restaurant specializing in traditional island cuisine. **www.hostaljeni.com**

ES MIGJORN GRAN Lord Nelson €€

Playa de Santo Tomás, 07749 ***Tel*** *971 370 125* ***Rooms*** *177*

Close to Santo Tomás beach, and surrounded by gardens, this aparthotel has beach or coast views from the sizeable balconies of each apartment. As well as self-catering facilities, there is a restaurant and two bars, two pools and a variety of activities, including volleyball, aerobics and even language lessons. **www.hotelesglobales.com**

ES MIGJORN GRAN Santo Tomas €€€€

Playa de Santo Tomás, 07749 ***Tel*** *971 370 025* ***Fax*** *971 370 204* ***Rooms*** *85*

Set in its own private gardens just above the beach of Santo Tomás, this three-storey hotel has sea or coast views from its rooms, all with a wide terrace or balcony. There's a large pool, gym, Jacuzzi, spa and beauty centre, terrace restaurant and bar with sea views. Wild, unspoiled beaches are just a walk away. **www.sethotels.es**

ES MIGJORN GRAN Sol Menorca €€€€

Playa de Santo Tomás s/n, 07749 ***Tel*** *971 370 050* ***Fax*** *971 370 348* ***Rooms*** *188*

This low-rise hotel is located above two small beaches on the south coast, so all rooms enjoy either morning or afternoon sun. It is small enough to be quiet, but large enough to have a full range of services, plus restaurant, pool and gym. A plus for some: the hotel makes a point of dissuading those with young children. **www.solmelia.com**

FERRERIES Los Delfines €€

Urb Los Delfines s/n, 07750 ***Tel*** *971 388 150* ***Rooms*** *104*

Built around a central plaza, this complex of low-rise apartments resembles a small Mediterranean village square. Self-catering apartments accommodate two to four people. There is also a restaurant, bar and a large pool. A variety of sports and entertainments is available, and the beach is a short walk away. **www.hotelesglobales.com**

FERRERIES Sol Gavilanes €€€€

Cala Galdana, 07750 ***Tel*** *971 154 545* ***Fax*** *971 154 546* ***Rooms*** *346*

Night or day, this 12-storey mammoth on the Galdana beach looks like an ocean cruise liner. All 11 suites and most of the rooms have a sea view. There are three restaurants, a large bar and two pools set in gardens surrounded by pine trees. The wide range of activities includes a gym, spa, diving and human chess. **www.solmelia.com**

FERRERIES RTM Audax Spar €€€€€

Urb Serpentona s/n, 07750 ***Tel*** *971 154 646* ***Fax*** *971 154 647* ***Rooms*** *244*

A dedicated spa hotel, the Audax has a range of options for health and beauty treatments or simple relaxation. Rooms have balconies with views and a choice of pillows; some have their own Jacuzzi. As well as a cleverly designed rooftop pool, there is an indoor pool, gym and numerous other health, fitness and beauty facilities. **www.rtmhotels.com**

FORNELLS Cala Fornells €€€

Cala Fornells, Paguera, 07160 ***Tel*** *971 686 950* ***Fax*** *971 687 525* ***Rooms*** *94*

Opened in 1947 by the Peña Gayà family, now in their third generation as its owners, this occupies a privileged spot on a low rocky bluff above two tiny coves. Sea views can be enjoyed from virtually all rooms. There are two pools, a restaurant, bar terrace, gym, sauna and Jacuzzi. Each April the hotel hosts a regatta. **www.calafornells.com**

FORNELLS Hesperia Villamil €€€€

Bulevar de Peguera 66, 07160 ***Tel*** *971 686 050* ***Fax*** *971 686 815* ***Rooms*** *125*

Set amid pine woods on the beach, this hotel's rooms have balconies with either sea or mountain views (the latter are cheaper). While the hotel opens on to the beach, it also has a large swimming pool surrounded by a terrace, as well as a spa, gym and tennis court. **www.hesperia-villamil.es**

MAÓ Hostal Jumé €

C/Concepció 6, 07701 ***Tel*** *971 363 266* ***Fax*** *971 364 878* ***Rooms*** *35*

Run by a charming elderly couple, this pension offers functional rooms (all with en-suite facilities) with no frills at low prices. It is conveniently central (close to the port and the market), and the owners go out of their way to make their guests comfortable. There is a simple, old-fashioned café-bar serving breakfast and local dishes.

MAÓ Hostal La Isla €

Santa Catalina 4, 07760 ***Tel*** *971 366 492* ***Rooms*** *22*

A simple and friendly family-run inn in the old part of Maó, just five minutes' walk from the centre. The rooms are spread over three floors, and each has views of the surrounding streets. Accommodation is basic but clean, with decent-sized rooms. There are no frills, although each room has air conditioning, television and en-suite facilities.

MAÓ Posada Orsi €

Infanta 19, 07702 ***Tel*** *971 364 751* ***Fax*** *971 357 394* ***Rooms*** *16*

Aimed at young budget travellers (some rooms share bath facilities), this is still a good option in Maó. Rooms are clean and very brightly furnished, plus there is a shared kitchen and a rooftop patio. The Orsi also has four en-suite rooms and a top floor apartment. It offers bike hire and Eastern therapies. **www.posadaorsi.com**

MAÓ Del Almirante €€

Ctra de's Castell s/n, 07720 ***Tel*** *971 362 700* ***Fax*** *971 362 704* ***Rooms*** *39*

Built in the 1700s in Georgian style, this mansion was the home of Admiral Collingwood, a friend of Lord Nelson. All rooms have balconies with views either of the port or the town. Some are in a modern annexe overlooking the swimming pool. The hotel also has a garden with a tennis court, and a Wi-Fi zone. **www.hoteldelalmirante.net**

MAÓ Port Mahon €€€

C/Fort de l'Eau13, 07701 ***Tel*** *971 362 600* ***Fax*** *971 351 050* ***Rooms*** *82*

Housed in a red-and-white colonial-style building, this hotel – probably the most luxurious in the city – overlooks the harbour. Rooms are large, with all services and a central Wi-Fi zone. Some have Neo-Classical stone balconies with sea views. The hotel grounds include wide terraces and a swimming pool surrounded by lawns. **www.sethotels.es**

MAÓ Casa Alberti €€€€

C/Isabel II 9, 07701 ***Tel*** *971 354 210* ***Fax*** *971 354 219* ***Rooms*** *6*

Originally built in 1740 and recently renovated, this large mansion, painted the local raspberry pink, is a true work of art. The rooms mix classical architecture with minimalist design. The winding, whitewashed staircase leads to a glorious roof terrace with good views of the sea. Guests share a modernist *comedor*. **www.casalberti.com**

MAÓ RTM Capri €€€€€

C/San Esteban 8, 07703 ***Tel*** *971 361 400* ***Fax*** *971 350 853* ***Rooms*** *75 & 7 apartments*

This town centre hotel offers a high level of comfort, with large rooms fitted with all mod cons, balconies and a choice of pillows. Some rooms also have Jacuzzis. The hotel has an ingenious roof pool that is open or covered depending on the weather, and an extensive range of gym, therapy and beauty services. **www.rtmhotels.com**

SANT LLUIS Alcaufar Vell €€€€

Ctra de Cala Alcalfar, km 7.3, 07713 ***Tel*** *971 151 874* ***Fax*** *971 151 492* ***Rooms*** *1*

This grand country house dates back to the 14th century, although the current property is a Neo-Classical *casa señorial* of more recent vintage. Rooms are styled in a mix of country and antique. There are gardens and a pool, and a working *finca* that supplies breakfast and dinner, which can be enjoyed either indoors or alfresco. **www.alcaufarvell.com**

SANT LLUIS Biniarroca €€€€

Cami Vell 57, 07710 ***Tel*** *971 150 059* ***Fax*** *971 151 250* ***Rooms*** *18*

More a life project for the owners than a business, this is an artists' home turned into a garden-cum-hotel, the former inspired by Italian estate gardens, the latter by Menorcan rural home comforts. A variety of rooms and suites open on to a garden and pool, and there is a terrace restaurant for candlelit dinners. **www.biniarroca.com**

Key to Price Guide *see p144* **Key to Symbols** *see back cover flap*

IBIZA

CALA MOLÍ Hostal Cala Molí €€

San José s/n, 07830 **Tel** *971 806 002* **Fax** *971 806 150* **Rooms** *8*

Ibizan rustic comfort that will not cost a fortune. The rooms are whitewashed and simply furnished, with private balconies. They all face a pretty, tree-shaded terrace, and there is a swimming pool if you cannot make the walk to the nearby beach. The cheerful staff will give you tips on what to see in the surrounding area. **www.calamoli.com**

EIVISSA Casa de Huéspedes Vara de Rey €€

C/Vara de Rey 7, 07800 **Tel** *971 301 376* **Rooms** *11*

In the heart of the whitewashed maze of Ibiza's Old Town, this intimate little pension offers quirkily decorated rooms painted by young local artists. All rooms are bright and clean, with views of the town; none has private facilities, but this means bargain prices, making this inn ideal for travellers on a budget. Open Mar–Nov. **www.hibiza.com**

EIVISSA Hostal La Marina €€

C/Barcelona 7, 07800 **Tel** *971 310 172* **Fax** *971 314 894* **Rooms** *25*

A classic on the seafront, this hotel is located in a modernized 19th-century building that retains some charming original details. Rooms are brightly painted in Mediterranean colours, and the best ones have lovely sea views. In high season, La Marina is a little overpriced, but at other times it offers a good deal. **www.hostal-lamarina.com**

EIVISSA Los Molinos €€€€

Ramón Muntaner 60, 07800 **Tel** *971 302 250* **Fax** *971 302 250* **Rooms** *168*

Located directly on the seafront, this hotel offers beautiful views from most of its guestrooms. The large rooms are well equipped with all modern comforts and despite being a short walk from the busy nightlife nearby, Los Molinos is a quiet and peaceful place to stay. Beautiful pool area and gardens. **www.thbhotels.com**

EIVISSA Marítimo €€€€

Ramon Muntaner 48, 07800 **Tel** *971 302 708* **Fax** *971 301 438* **Rooms** *82*

The Marítimo is five minutes from the town centre, right on Figueretas beach. All rooms are en-suite, with modern decor and balconies (not all have a sea view, though). The hotel has buffet and à la carte restaurants, a café, bar, gym and Jacuzzi, and it also offers bike- and car-hire facilities. **www.hotelmaritimo-isladeibiza.com**

EIVISSA Torre de Canónigo €€€€

C/Mayor 8, Dalt Vila, 07800 **Tel** *971 303 884* **Fax** *971 307 843* **Rooms** *8*

Built on the remains of the Roman city in the 12th century, this former fortification next to the cathedral has history in spades. Today its eight suites offer probably the most luxurious rooms in the Old Town, sumptuously decorated, with contemporary bath facilities, balconies and living rooms with spectacular town views. **www.elcanonigo.com**

EIVISSA Hotel Pacha €€€€€

Paseo Marítimo s/n, 07800 **Tel** *971 315 963* **Fax** *971 310 253* **Rooms** *55*

More a sci-fi movie set than a hotel, the Pacha embodies the "chill" philosophy of the club that opened it. It offers 53 gleaming, state-of-the-art modernist suites, plus two luxury rooftop suites with private balconies and Jacuzzis. With a restaurant and bar, it is a hotel straight out of Kubrick's *2001: A Space Odyssey*. **www.elhotelpacha.com**

PORTINATX Cas Mallorqui €€

Cala Portinatx s/n, 07810 **Tel** *971 320 505* **Fax** *971 320 504* **Rooms** *9*

This small family-run hotel sits on a row of boathouses at the water's edge. All rooms have balconies with sea (and sunset) views. There is a restaurant terrace and bar, and the lack of pool and other amenities is offset by the enviable position. Favoured by watersports enthusiasts, Cas Mallorqui can also arrange craft hire. **www.casmallorqui.com**

PUIG D'EN VALLS Ca n'Arabi €€€€

Puig d'en Valls s/n, 07819 **Tel** *971 313 505* **Fax** *971 313 733* **Rooms** *15*

Between the small towns of Jesús and Puig d'en Valls, this small hotel features discrete suites clustered around a large pool. All have sturdy, rustic decor and private verandahs; the larger ones have Jacuzzis, too. The property is surrounded by orange groves, with bars and restaurants a ten-minute walk away. **www.canjaume.org**

PUIG D'EN VALLS Can Jaume €€€€

Puig d'en Valls s/n, 07819 **Tel** *971 318 855* **Fax** *971 199 839* **Rooms** *12*

A short walk from its sister hotel Ca n'Arabi, Can Jaume is slightly more upmarket. Its suites and rooms have been given a pastel modernist touch by the same designer. They all have flat-screen TVs and balconies or terraces giving on to gardens and pool. Activities such as riding and diving are available nearby. **www.canjaume.org**

SAN CARLOS Can Talaias €€€

Apartado 244, San Carlos, 07850 **Tel** *971 335 742* **Fax** *971 335 032* **Rooms** *6*

This delightful oddity was the dream home of English actor Terry Thomas, who discovered it in the 1970s and fell for the sea view from its hilltop. Now run by his son and daughter-in-law, Can Talaias has six large, airy and beautifully decorated rooms, with a pool and patio restaurant sharing the view. **www.hotelcantalaias.com**

SAN JUAN Can Marti €€€

San Juan s/n, 07810 ***Tel*** *971 333 500* ***Fax*** *971 333 112* ***Rooms*** *4*

The owners of this eco *finca* quit the fields in summer to host guests at a rural retreat that proudly flaunts its lack of TV, pool, hairdryers and air con (natural ventilation is sufficient). That noted, all four suites have ADSL, CD player, modern baths and self-catering facilities. The stunning setting repays the sacrifice. Closed Oct–Mar. **www.canmarti.com**

SAN RAFAEL Can Lluc €€€€€

Can Gasparó, 07816 ***Tel*** *971 198 673* ***Fax*** *971 198 547* ***Rooms*** *12*

A luxury *finca* outside Eivissa town, this high-end *agroturismo* offers either a Jacuzzi or a hydro-shower in each designer bathroom, fireplaces in each room, and four-poster beds in the larger suites. Can Lluc has extensive gardens and a large pool, plus outdoor Jacuzzi, and there is a fleet of bicycles available for free to explore the island. **www.canlluc.com**

SANT ANTONI DE PORTMANY Osiris Ibiza €

Playa Es Puet s/n, 07820 ***Tel*** *971 341 688* ***Fax*** *971 341 685* ***Rooms*** *97*

A family-run modern hotel in the popular resort of Sant Antoni, this is a great place for families on a budget. Osiris Ibiza is close to the beach and various watersports facilities, and has its own pool with a section for young children. The rooms are large and bright and offer views of the sea or the gardens. Open May–Oct. **www.hotelosiris.com**

SANT ANTONI DE PORTMANY Pike's Hotel €€€€€

Camí de Sa Vorera s/n, 07820 ***Tel*** *971 342 222* ***Rooms*** *15*

Popular with a hip crowd (George Michael and Grace Jones have both stayed), this grand old *finca* has 15 suites, each with a variation on Moroccan and Spanish rustic design, plus all mod cons. There is a garden, a pool with wet bar, and a smart *nueva cocina* restaurant. VIP guests jump the queue at Pacha, Privilege and other clubs. **www.pikeshotel.com**

SANT JOAN DE LABRITJA Can Escandell €€€

San Juan s/n, 07810 ***Tel*** *971 333 540* ***Fax*** *971 333 052* ***Rooms*** *9*

This 200-year-old *finca* has been transformed into a small luxury hotel mixing rough-hewn rock and whitewashed walls with hi-tech fittings. All suites have CD and DVD players, fireplaces, free ADSL links and a Wi-Fi area. There is also a terrace and pool. The owners can organize sailing, fishing, diving and private boat trips. **www.canescandell.com**

SANT MIGUEL Ca's Pla €€€€

San Miguel de Balansat s/n, 07800 ***Tel*** *971 334 587* ***Fax*** *971 334 604* ***Rooms*** *16*

Sixteen rooms and suites hidden in subtropical gardens just five minutes from the sea. The style is antique-rustic, but all rooms feature modern amenities. As well as a pool and sauna, recent additions include a gym, meeting rooms and a helipad. The hotel can organize horse riding, diving, sailing, golf and car hire. **www.caspla-ibiza.com**

SANT MIGUEL Na Xamena €€€€€

San Miguel s/n, 07815 ***Tel*** *971 334 500* ***Fax*** *971 334 514* ***Rooms*** *65*

Probably the most luxurious hotel on the island, this former *finca* is set on a spectacular clifftop, with sea views from most suites. It offers two restaurants, cascade pools, spa facilities and a range of high-end suite options. The ultimate chill-out hotel. **www.hotelhacienda-ibiza.com**

SANTA AGNÈS DE CORONA Can Pujolet €€€€

Agroturismo Santa Inés Can Pujolet s/n, 07828 ***Tel*** *971 805 170* ***Fax*** *971 805 038* ***Rooms*** *10*

This secluded *finca* near the cliffs north of Santa Inés is a working ecological farm producing fruit, vegetables and wines for the family hotel's kitchen. Its suites provide rustic comfort, with satellite TVs and terraces opening on to lush gardens where olive groves hide a pool, Jacuzzi, restaurant and bar. **www.ibizarural.com**

SANTA AGNÈS DE CORONA Es Cucons €€€€€

C/Cami des Plå de Corona 110, 07828 ***Tel*** *971 805 501* ***Fax*** *971 805 510* ***Rooms*** *14*

The Cuckoos is an elegant hotel first built as a country house in 1652. Rooms and suites mix whitewashed rough-hewn walls with calming pastel decor; some have four-poster beds, and all have air conditioning and CD/DVD players. The hotel has a pool, gardens and a restaurant, and it offers massages and therapies. **www.escucons.com**

SANTA EULÀRIA DES RIU Les Terrasses €€€€€

Ctra de Santa Eulalia, km 1, 07800 ***Tel*** *971 332 643* ***Fax*** *971 338 978* ***Rooms*** *8*

This small complex has more than a touch of the Greek Islands about it, with bright white walls, pastel decor and antique furniture. Each room is individually styled, with a mix of traditional and contemporary influences. There are two pools, lush gardens and a tennis court. Dinner is prepared with produce from the garden. **www.lesterrasses.net**

SANTA GERTRUDIS Cas Gasi €€€€€

Camino Viejo de Sant Mateu s/n, 07814 ***Tel*** *971 197 700* ***Fax*** *971 197 899* ***Rooms*** *10*

Built in 1880, this large mansion does not stint on luxury. Its suites combine country house comforts with modern bathrooms, CD and DVD players, designer toiletries and bathrobes. There is a large pool in the mature gardens, and a restaurant specializing in island cuisine. *The Cherry* is a private yacht available to guests. **www.casgasi.com**

TALAMANCA Ayre Hotel Ocean Drive €€€€€

Marina Botafoch s/n, 07800 ***Tel*** *971 318 112* ***Fax*** *971 312 228* ***Rooms*** *42*

Although it opened as recently as 1998, this is an Ibiza classic, designed on the model of Art Deco hotels, with Mies van der Rohe and Le Corbusier decor. All rooms follow the design theme, and most have views. The bar, lounge and restaurant are similarly styled. Wealthier clubbers and DJs use this hotel as a hangout. **www.ayrehoteles.com**

Key to Price Guide *see p144* **Key to Symbols** *see back cover flap*

FORMENTERA

CALA SAONA Hotel Cala Saona €€€€

Platja Cala Saona s/n, 07860 ***Tel*** *971 322 030* ***Fax*** *971 322 509* ***Rooms*** *114*

This popular hotel is the only option in the secluded Playa Cala Saona, one of the prettiest of Formentera's beaches. It offers all the facilities of a large hotel in a quiet pine forest setting. All rooms have a balcony or terrace (not all with sea views), and there is a bar, a tennis court and gardens with a children's area. Open Apr–Oct. **www.hotelcalasaona.com**

ES CALÓ Hostal Entre Pinos €€

Ctra La Mola, km 12.3, 07820 ***Tel*** *971 327 019* ***Fax*** *971 327 018* ***Rooms*** *54*

A recently renovated family-run hotel among pine woods and close to the beaches of Es Caló and Arenal. Slightly more upmarket than its neighbours, it offers air conditioning, central heating, TV and minibars in the suites; standard rooms have fewer amenities. There is also a terrace bar, large pool and garden. **www.hostalentrepinos.com**

ES PUJOLS Hostal Lago Playa €€

Playa Sa Roqueta, 07860 ***Tel*** *971 328 507* ***Fax*** *971 328 842* ***Rooms*** *26*

One of just four options in the Lago Playa complex here on the beach, and with better and more modern amenities than its Lago II extension (which has no balconies or views). All rooms have balconies or terraces, and some have sea views. The beach is just beyond the gardens. **www.lagoplaya.com**

ES PUJOLS Rosales €€€

Avda Miramar s/n, 07870 ***Tel*** *971 328 123* ***Fax*** *971 328 161* ***Rooms*** *5*

Built in 1966, the Rosales is close to the Pujols beach. All rooms have balconies, and the larger suites also have street level terraces. The hotel is wheelchair-friendly, with ramps and other facilities to enhance disabled access. There is a café bar on site and myriad other services nearby. **www.rosales-formentera.com**

ES PUJOLS Hostal Tahiti €€€€

C/Fonoll Marí s/n, 07871 ***Tel*** *971 328 122* ***Fax*** *971 328 817* ***Rooms*** *74*

All rooms in this hotel spread over three floors on the Pujols beach have air conditioning and balconies with either sea or lateral views. The larger poolside suites have kitchens, too. The family-run Tahiti also has a restaurant, bar and play pool. Watersports options are just a minute away on the beach. **www.tahiti.es**

ES PUJOLS Sa Volta €€€€

C/Miramar 94, 07871 ***Tel*** *971 328 125* ***Fax*** *971 328 228* ***Rooms*** *25*

The standard rooms at this family-run hotel close to the beach are simple but comfortable. It is worth splashing out on one of the three semi-suites, which have canopied beds and spacious private terraces. The hotel also has a car-, scooter- and bike-hire service. Open Mar–Dec. **www.savolta.com**

LA SAVINA Bellavista €€€

C/Almadrava 19, 07870 ***Tel*** *971 322 255* ***Fax*** *971 322 236* ***Rooms*** *40*

A small and comfortable family-run hotel in the centre of La Savina. All rooms are en-suite and have views of either the sea or the Estany Pudent lagoon; rooms on higher floors are quieter. The hotel houses the renowned restaurant of the same name, one of the best seafood restaurants in the area. **www.guiaformentera.com/bellavista**

PLATJA MIGJORN Insotel Club Formentera Playa €€€€€

Sant Francesc Xavier s/n, 07860 ***Tel*** *971 328 000* ***Fax*** *971 328 035* ***Rooms*** *293*

The largest hotel on the island, with accommodation in small low-rise buildings set in large gardens. The hotel is used by major travel operators and has all the facilities of the all-inclusive holiday: pool, gym, play area and a wide range of watersports. There is a dress code at dinner, and music most nights. **www.insotel.com**

PLATJA MIGJORN Riui la Mola €€€€€

Platja Migjorn, 07871 ***Tel*** *971 327 000* ***Fax*** *971 327 000* ***Rooms*** *328*

This ziggurat-style hotel has accommodation in various two- to four-storey buildings all facing the sea. Rooms are upscale, with generous bathrooms and balconies. Suites have sitting rooms, too. A large pool has a children's area, and there is also a restaurant, bar, tennis and other sports. The beach is at the edge of the gardens. **www.riu.com**

PLATJA S'ARENAL Las Dunas Playa €€

Dunas Playa – Carretera la Mola, km 11, 07860 ***Tel*** *971 328 041* ***Fax*** *971 328 052* ***Rooms*** *44*

A low-key development offering apartments for two to six people in small units spread among the sand dunes, with self-catering facilities and balcony or terrace. The central reception building has a bar and restaurant, and other facilities are located a 20-minute stroll along Platja Migjorn beach. **www.guiaformentera.com/lasdunas**

SANT FERRAN Hostal Illes Pituises €€

Avda Juan Castelló Guasch 48, 07871 ***Tel*** *971 328 189* ***Fax*** *971 328 017* ***Rooms*** *26*

This family-run hotel is situated on a main road, so ask for a rear room overlooking the pleasant terrace and gardens when booking. All rooms are en-suite, with air conditioning and either balconies or terraces. The hotel also has a bar and restaurant open for breakfast, lunch and dinner. **www.illespitiuses.com**

WHERE TO EAT

The resorts and large town centres found in the Balearic Islands offer a good selection of restaurants, able to satisfy even the most demanding of palates. While the resorts do, of course, cater for visitors who have come for the beaches rather than the food, good quality local cuisine is in plentiful supply. Restaurants serving local specialities can be easily spotted thanks to their signs: *Cuina Mallorquína*, or *Cuina Menorquína*. Those restaurants that are open all year are likely to be more authentic than seasonal establishments, though they can also be pricier. On Ibiza or Formentera, gourmets have fewer opportunities to sample traditional local cuisine, but even here there are restaurants that are well worth recommending.

Restaurant sign in Alcúdia

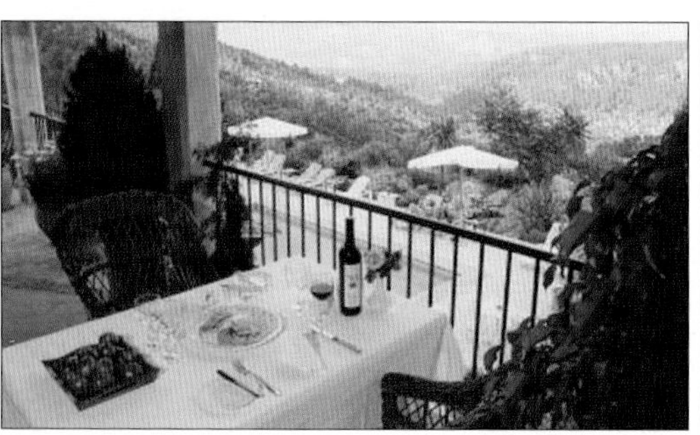

A simple *finca* restaurant in Mallorca

LOCAL CUISINE

The delicious cuisine of the Balearic Islands can be quite time-consuming to prepare but is well worth the wait. Many of the dishes are Catalan in origin. *Ensaimadas*, delicious spiral pastries that are dusted with icing sugar, are commonplace. So, too, are the spicy pork pâtés *(sobrasadas)*. Hearty soups, another essential part of any menu, are prepared in a different way on every island. Rustic 'one-pot' dishes are also popular. The best known of these is *caldereta de llagosta (see p101)*.

Although the number of restaurants offering lobster and other seafood is so great that one would expect these dishes to be inexpensive, in fact this is far from the truth. The price paid for lobster here is similar to that charged by restaurants in Paris or London. It is also worth remembering that dinner in a restaurant that specializes in local cuisine will cost more than a meal eaten in a small restaurant by the beach.

WHEN TO EAT

As with the rest of Spain, lunchtime in the Balearic Islands is usually between 1:30pm and 3pm. Some restaurants may be closed after 3pm. Many others will be full and you may have to wait a long time to be served. Outside traditional mealtimes, the menu selection can be limited. As an alternative, bars can provide a good variety of food and snacks while beachside restaurants are good for snacks at any time of the day.

Dinner on the islands usually starts after 9pm, when the temperature drops. This is when the restaurants, cafés, gardens and bars fill up. For Spaniards this is a time to meet with friends. Restaurants tend to fill up for Sunday lunch and booking is essential at this time.

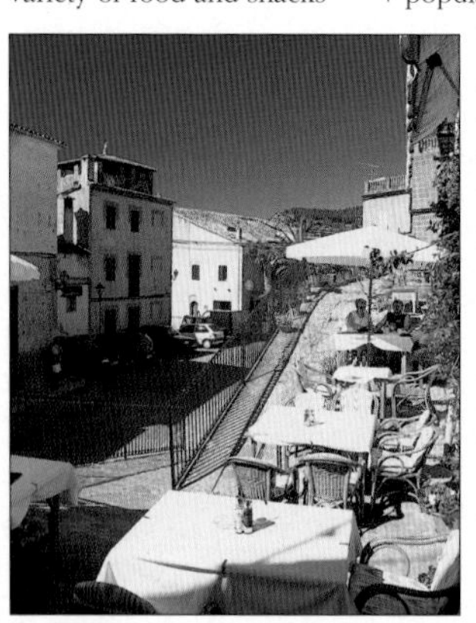

A modest restaurant in Estellencs

PLACES TO EAT

There is a boundless choice of places to eat in the Balearic Islands. This is especially true during the high season, when many restaurants are open that are closed during the other months of the year. In the cheaper bars it is worth trying *tapas* or *raciones* (snacks) as these are most likely to be freshly prepared (a *racion* is often enough for two). When venturing into a bar that is popular with the locals, you should try the set price *menú del día* (menu of the day). This is a full three-course meal, accompanied by a drink. Often these menus are very good value and may cost as little as €9.

Many of the best restaurants are far from the resorts and do little to advertise themselves to visitors. Though the menus may look the same as beachside restaurants, the prices and quality can vary enormously. Most of these can be found

Restaurant garden in Eivissa, Ibiza

away from the beaches, hidden in alleys or down narrow streets near the harbours. Some are located in small villages outside the big towns or on main roads. Lunch or dinner in one of these restaurants can turn into an expedition but it is often well worth the trip. Apart from your favourite dishes, you may also like to try the *especialidad del día* (daily special) or order a dish recommended by the chef.

Many visitors prefer to use their hotel's restaurant for breakfast and dinner, and take their lunch in bars and restaurants close to the beach. Some hotels have wonderful restaurants, others are just adequate. One point in hotel restaurants' favour is that they can offer a wide selection of food, low prices, fast service and a friendly atmosphere. Most of them serve a safe, international cuisine and you are likely to see paella, pizza, fish and chips, roast chicken and curry all on the same menu. These restaurants successfully compete with the popular fast-food chains. Restaurants that are near or on less crowded beaches tend to offer much better food, but the choice may be limited.

VEGETARIANS

The food of these islands tends to be on the heavy side and is based mainly on pork and fish, but it also has a lot to offer vegetarians. It is easy to make a meal of *tapas* consisting of vegetables such as artichokes, broad beans, aubergines, peppers, tomatoes or *tortilla española* (Spanish omelette). One of the simplest vegetarian dishes is *tumbet* (a tomato-rich vegetable stew). Local vegetarian cuisine worth recommending includes eggs *al modo de Sóller*, Sant Juan noodles and Mahón-style beans. Most restaurants, even those next to beaches, offer some vegetarian dishes. If there are none on the menu you can always ask for a vegetable or fruit salad.

Paella served in a huge dish at a beachside restaurant in Ibiza

PRICES AND TIPPING

In beachside restaurants, prices are reasonable. A lunch will cost around €15. The *menú del día* may be even cheaper. The sky is the limit on prices charged by some of the top restaurants; it all depends on your choice of menu. Some regional dishes and seafood may be expensive. The price of the latter will depend on the weight of the ordered lobster or fish.

Mallorca tends to have the highest prices, but even here you should remember that in a provincial restaurant the same meal may cost much less than in a popular resort. The final price includes service charges and tax and is therefore higher than the sum of the menu items. Normally, the tip does not exceed 10 per cent; it is usual to round up the bill.

Most restaurants welcome credit cards. Even some bars will accept this form of payment, but small sums are normally paid in cash. Some small restaurants, especially those not geared up for tourists, may not accept credit cards, however, so it is best to check in advance.

BOOKING

There are a large number of restaurants on the Balearic Islands and there should not be any problem in finding a table. Nevertheless, it is worthwhile booking a table in advance to avoid disappointment, particularly when you want to dine in a specific restaurant or one that is especially popular or some distance away.

DISABLED PERSONS

The islands' restaurants are not adapted for the needs of disabled people. They do not have wheelchair ramps and the tables inside tend to be placed close together. The most accessible are the bars and small restaurants situated along seaside promenades, with outside tables.

Enjoying a meal at the traditional restaurant La Bóveda, in Palma

The Flavours of the Balearics

This quartet of beautiful islands, strategically positioned on ancient trading routes, has been fought over for thousands of years. Each occupying force – Arabs, Catalans, French and British among them – has left its mark and the local cuisine reflects this. Mediterranean seafood, particularly spectacular lobster and crayfish, remains the most prominent local ingredient, but the islands are also known for their delicious pastries and desserts, like the feather-light *ensaimada* from Mallorca and the typical Ibizan *flaó*. Cured meats *(embutits)* and traditionally made cheeses are also local specialities.

Locally grown oranges

Seafood from the Mediterranean in a Mallorcan fish market

MALLORCA AND MENORCA

Seafood predominates in the Balearic Islands. Menorca is renowned for *caldereta de llagosta* (spiny lobster stew), once a simple fishermen's dish but now a delicacy *(see p101)*. The classic Mallorcan dish is *pa amb oli*, a slice of toasted country bread rubbed with garlic and drizzled with local olive oil. Menorca's creamy garlic sauce *all i oli* is a delicious accompaniment to meat and seafood dishes, and the island also produces fine cheese, *formatge de Maó*.

IBIZA AND FORMENTERA

Seafood also reigns supreme on Ibiza and its quieter little sister, Formentera, especially in *calders* (stews) such as *borrida de rajada* (skate with potatoes, eggs and pastis), and *guisat de peix*. Pork is the staple meat. For a picnic, try *cocarrois*, pastries filled with meat, fish or vegetables and *formatjades*, soft-cheese-filled pastries flavoured with cinnamon. Delicious local desserts include *gató* (almond cake served with ice cream) and Ibizan *flaó*, made with creamy cheese and eggs, and flavoured with mint.

Ensaimadas

Cuscussô Menorquin (bread pudding)

Flaó Ibicenco

Galletas de Alaior (aniseed biscuits)

Formatjades

Gató (almond tart)

Appetizing selection of delicious Balearic pastries

REGIONAL DISHES AND SPECIALITIES

Fish and shellfish (particularly the revered local lobster) are omnipresent in the Balearics, particularly along the coast. Try them simply grilled to fully appreciate their freshness (many seaside restaurants have their own fishing boats), but you will also find wonderful, slow-cooked stews which are bursting with flavour. The rugged inland regions provide mountain lamb and kid, along with pork, which is also used to make *embutits* including spicy Mallorcan *sobrassada* which is delicious with *pa amb oli*. The tourist industry has not killed the long-standing farming tradition on the Balearics, which produce plentiful fruit and vegetables. Mallorca makes its own robust wines, particularly around the village of Binissalem, while Menorca, thanks to the long British occupation of the island, makes its own piquant gin.

All i oli

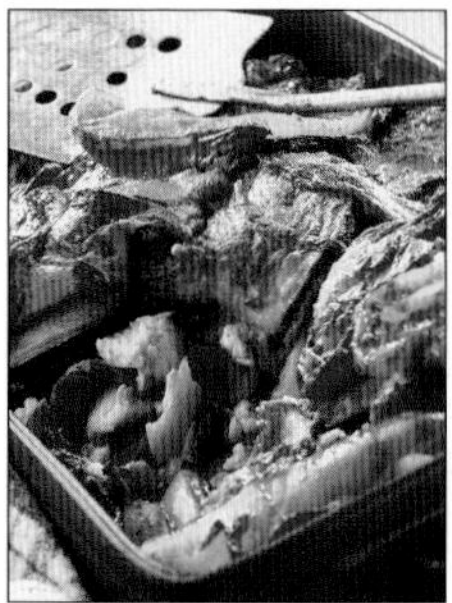

Tumbet de peix *A fish pie, made with layers of firm white fish, peppers, aubergine (eggplant) and sliced boiled egg.*

Choosing a Restaurant

The restaurants in this guide have been selected across a wide range of price categories for their good value, exceptional food and interesting location. This chart lists the restaurants by island. Within each town or city, entries are listed by price category, from the least expensive to the most expensive.

PRICE CATEGORIES
For a three-course meal for one, including half a bottle of house wine, service and tax.

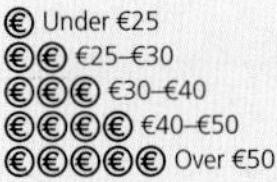

€ Under €25
€€ €25–€30
€€€ €30–€40
€€€€ €40–€50
€€€€€ Over €50

MALLORCA

ALARÓ Es Verger — €

Cami de's Castell, Castell de Alaró s/n, 07340 ***Tel*** *971 182 126*

Best reached by car or taxi, this establishment near Alaró's castle is widely held to be the best lamb restaurant in the whole of Mallorca. Like the other cuts on its rather short – and predominantly meat-based – menu, the lamb is stone-oven baked and can be matched with a sturdy country red wine. Portions are huge. Closed Mon.

ALCÚDIA Mesón Los Patos — €€€

Cami de Ca'n Blau 42, 07410 ***Tel*** *971 890 265*

The Font family, parents and offspring, have been running this restaurant on the perimeter of the Parc Natural de S'Albufera for 30 years. Named after one of the park's ducks, which is also on the menu as a house special, Los Patos prides itself on its fish dishes, too. Every Thursday, diners can enjoy eel prepared in various ways. Closed Tue.

ALCÚDIA Sa Pedrera — *Tapas* — €€€€

Ctra Sta Margalida–Alcúdia, km 1.8, 07450 ***Tel*** *971 852 732*

Part of a hotel, Sa Pedrera has a robust menu with a Galician edge, as witnessed by the fish salad. In addition to veal, lamb and several chicken dishes, the restaurant also offers rabbit – try it dressed in *aïoli*, a garlic mayonnaise sauce. Tables are on terraces and in the gardens, where guests can also use the pool. Closed Tue eve, Thu–Sun.

ALCÚDIA Jardín — €€€€€

C/Tritones s/n, 07410 ***Tel*** *971 892 391*

With a covered porch area overlooking mature subtropical gardens, Jardín offers Mallorcan *cocina nueva* in a grand setting. Fish dishes include *merluza* (hake) and salmon and prawns tartare in green mustard; meaty choices range from duck in sherry to baked suckling pig with apple. The *menú degustación* has eight tasters. Closed Jan–Mar; Mon, Tue.

BINISSALEM Can Arabi

Camí Coll d'en Simonet, 07350 ***Tel*** *971 512 211*

A classic country house restaurant with whitewashed walls, vaulted stone ceilings and an ample terrace, Can Arabi specializes in Mallorcan and Mediterranean cuisine, prepared with locally sourced organic ingredients. The menu consists mainly of grills and bakes of a wide range of game and farmed meats, with a special of boneless rabbit. Closed Mon.

BINISSALEM Singlò — €€€

Plaça Església 5, 07350 ***Tel*** *971 870 599*

A modern restaurant located in the town centre serving breakfast to late-night drinks. The kitchen delivers creative takes on Mediterranean dishes that are beautifully presented. Specialities include pork loin with sundried tomatoes and spring onion confit, and saffron monkfish on squid-ink pasta. Traditional paella and rice dishes are also available.

BUNYOLA Can Penasso — €€€

Ctra Sóller, km 14.8, 07110 ***Tel*** *971 613 212*

This large restaurant is part of a hotel, originally a *posada* on the old Palma–Sóller road. Can Penasso specializes in traditional Mallorcan food using ancient recipes. As well as rice and pasta dishes, the menu features rabbit cooked with langoustine, rape with crab, stuffed aubergines (eggplant), wood-oven-baked meats and thick stews.

BUNYOLA L'Hermitage — €€€€€

Carretera Alaró–Bunyola, 07349 ***Tel*** *971 180 303*

Located in the grounds of a hotel and former cloister, L'Hermitage provides an exquisite setting for any meal. The restaurant is in a former olive press, with a terrace outside under mature trees. Dishes are based on original monks' recipes, with a twist on turbot, duck liver and salmon with radish that belies the idea of a humble monastic diet. Closed Nov–Mar.

CALA GAMBA Club Nautico Cala Gamba — €€€

Paseig Cala Gamba s/n, 07007 ***Tel*** *971 261 045*

A highly regarded place to eat in Cala Gamba, this restaurant has a decor that is nautical in theme and large windows overlooking the craft moored in the marina. The menu is weighted towards locally caught fish, particularly sea bass in salt and the inevitable *caldereta de llagosta* (lobster stew). There is also an assortment of shellfish dishes. Closed Mon.

Key to Symbols *see back cover flap*

CALA RAJADA La Casita €€€

Calle des Farallo 6, 07590 ***Tel*** *971 563 731*

Set in a quiet area away from the bustle of the main resort, this grand old house has an interior dining room and a romantic garden for alfresco eating. Open year-round, La Casita specializes in fresh fish cooked to the chef's own recipes. It also has a full range of traditional local dishes and a *bodega* with a range of island wines. Closed lunch; mid-Nov–mid-Mar.

CALA RAJADA Ses Rotges €€€€€

C/Rafael Blanes 21, 07590 ***Tel*** *971 563 108*

This country restaurant-hotel has a splendid beamed dining room and a beautiful terrace overlooking a subtropical garden. Both the set and à la carte menus mix classic French cuisine with Mallorcan influences. Chef Gérard Tétard sources all his ingredients from the island to create a wide range of elegant dishes, not least the *menú gastronómico*. Closed Sun.

CALA SANT VICENÇ Cavall Bernat €€€€€

Calle Maressers 2, 07469 ***Tel*** *971 530 250*

At the Hotel Cala Sant Vincenç, this is a slightly formal establishment that has been included in several top tens of island restaurants. It mixes classic Mallorcan recipes with international dishes, all with a *cocina nueva* touch. Meals are served either in the wood-panelled dining room or on the hotel's terrace. Closed lunch.

CALVIÀ Ca'n Torrat €

C/Mayor 29–31, 07184 ***Tel*** *971 670 682*

Famed for its wood-fired barbecue and grill, Ca'n Torrat offers traditional local dishes such as suckling pig, roast shoulder of lamb and fried fish. You will also be able to sample the island classic *llom amb col*, a mix of sirloin and sausages stewed with onions, tomatoes, mushrooms, currants and pine nuts in a white-wine stock. Closed Tue.

CALVIÀ Can na Cucó €€

Avenida Palma 14, 07184 ***Tel*** *971 670 083*

A traditional stone house with a terrace near the seafront of Calvià, Can na Cucó is very popular with the locals and specializes in traditional Mallorcan cuisine. Recommendations include the *granada de berenjena* (aubergine/eggplant baked with cheese), the *frito mallorquín de pescado* (fried-fish mix) and locally made almond ice cream.

CAMPANET Es Mirador Monnáber €€€

Possessió Monnaber Nou, 07310 ***Tel*** *971 877 176*

Part of a grand country house hotel, with a large classical dining room and seating on the terrace and in the gardens, Monnáber has a strong line of traditional dishes with a light modernist touch. Lamb with candied apple and sea bass with saffron are just two examples. Try the local desserts, too, such as almond sponge and lemon mousse with jelly.

CAMPOS – SA RAPITA Can Pep €€€

Avinguda Miramar 30, 07639 ***Tel*** *971 640 102*

A family-run restaurant that has been on the seafront here for 20 years. The speciality is locally caught fish and seafood, much of it prepared on the grill. Among the specials are Galician-style octopus, seafood soup and paella, not to mention grouper, red mullet, sole, John Dory, lobster, oysters, clams and cockles, all from the local fish market. Closed Mon.

COLÒNIA DE SANT JORDI Pep Serra €€€

C/Enginyer Gabriel Roca 87, 07638 ***Tel*** *971 655 399*

This seafront restaurant is a favourite with islanders, particularly at weekends, when booking is advisable. It offers the customary range of fresh-caught fish and seafood, with a notable paella of langoustine. All the fish comes from the waters around the nearby island of Cabrera, where the owner fishes from his own boat. Closed Mon.

COLÒNIA DE SANT JORDI La Playa €€€€

C/Mayor 25, 07638 ***Tel*** *971 655 256*

A hotel restaurant located in a typical Majorcan house on Cala Galiota beach. The home-made dishes are based on family recipes and include paella, lobster salad and fresh fish straight off the boat, accompanied by *trampo* (Majorcan salad with peppers, tomatoes and onion). Lamb is another speciality. There is a terrace with lovely sunset views.

DEIÀ Ca'n Costa €

Ctra Valldemossa–Deià, km 2.5, 07460 ***Tel*** *971 612 263*

This rural restaurant on the Valldemossa–Deià road balances international and island fare, all cooked in rustic style and served in generous portions. Typical dishes include pork loin with local mushrooms, and thrush in a cabbage wrapping. Good range of island wines. Book ahead and ask for a terrace table to enjoy the sea views. Closed Tue; eve (winter).

DEIÀ El Olivo €€€€€

Son Canals s/n, 7179 ***Tel*** *971 639 011*

The no-less-famed restaurant of the famed La Residencia hotel *(see p146)* is set inside the former olive mill, with additional alfresco seating on a pretty terrace. It offers light lunches, a vegetarian *menú degustación*, a fantastic à la carte menu and an impeccable wine cellar. The chef's *menú degustación* is a memorable feast. Closed Oct–Mar.

DEIÀ/PORT DE SÓLLER El Guia €€

Calle Castañer 2, 07100 ***Tel*** *971 630 227*

Part of a pretty townhouse hotel in the heart of Sóller, with views of both the town and the surrounding countryside, this restaurant is very popular with local diners. Its menu is based on classic island dishes prepared using ingredients sourced from local suppliers. The *menú del día* is a bargain at just €20. Closed Dec–Feb.

Key to Price Guide *see p159* **Key to Symbols** *see back cover flap*

DEIÀ/PORT DE SÓLLER Bens d'Avall €€€

Urb. Costa Deià, Ctra Sóller–Deià s/n, 07100 ***Tel*** *971 632 381*

Superlative food in the surroundings of Deià, on a high cliff with stunning coastal views. Chef Benet Vicens Mayol, has a delicate way with *cocina nueva*, using the best local ingredients in clever combinations that will make foodies drool at the menu descriptions. Close to perfection. Closed Mon all year; Tue Jul–Aug; mid-Oct–Feb.

ESPORLES Meson la Villa €€€€

Nou de Sant Pere 5, 07190 ***Tel*** *971 610 901*

This large townhouse restaurant, close to the church and town hall building at the heart of Esporles, prides itself on being the first Castillian grill restaurant in Mallorca. Food is prepared in an old-fashioned, rustic wood-burning grill; all classic cuts are served, and guests can watch their meal being prepared. Closed Sun & lunch Jun–Aug; Wed Sep–May.

ESPORLES Sa Tafona €€€€€

Es Verger s/n, 07190 ***Tel*** *971 611 230*

Part of a modernized 16th-century country mansion hotel, this restaurant has a spectacular balcony with sweeping mountain views. The handsome building is a former olive mill, and the menu combines traditional Mallorcan cuisine with international dishes, both done in gourmet style. Sa Tafona also offers bargain weekend room-and-dinner deals.

ESTELLENCS Montimar €€

Plaza Constitució 7, 01792 ***Tel*** *971 618 576*

Montimar boasts the honour of being the favourite holiday eatery of Sam Hart, chef at hip London tapas bar Fino. Hart recommends the suckling pig and the *fri mallorquin* (sweetmeats with aubergine/eggplant and peppers), but chef-owner Guillermo Femenías Estelrich is also famed for his lamb, *tumbet* and home-made desserts. Closed Mon; Jan; Mon–Fri Nov.

ESTELLENCS Son Llarg €€

Plaza Constitució 6, 07192 ***Tel*** *971 618 564*

One of the prettiest eateries in the area, Son Llarg is housed in a beautiful old stone building by the church, with a terrace above the road and views to the sea from some tables. It specializes in traditional island fish and meat dishes. The restaurant also doubles as a gallery for island artists and stages live music concerts. Closed Tue.

FELANITX Celler Sa Sinia €€€

Calle Pescadores s/n, 07670 ***Tel*** *971 824 323*

Rated among the top three restaurants in Mallorca, Sa Sinia is famed for the seafood inventions of chef Biel Perelló. Each dish on the menu – *caldereta de llagosta* (lobster stew), *bacalao* (cod) in tomato, rape stew, turbot with capers – is his unique recipe. The same goes for his three-chocolate dessert, and the pears in wine and raspberries. Closed Mon; Nov–Jan.

FELANITX Son Terrassa €€€

Ctra Cas Concos–Felantix, km 10, 07208 ***Tel*** *971 839 551*

Part of a rural *finca* hotel, this is a characteristic rustic restaurant in the countryside around Felanitx. The owner-chefs specialize in meats and fish – in particular suckling pig, milk lamb and the daily catch – cooked over wood on a big antique *parrilla*, or grill. Fruit and vegetables come from the hotel's own farm. Closed Wed.

FELANITX Sa Llotja €€€€

C/Pescadors s/n (Porto Colom), 07670 ***Tel*** *971 825 165*

Occupying a traditional building at the port, Sa Llotja has a modern white minimalist interior. The Mediterranean cuisine is based on fresh seasonal fare, particularly fish and vegetables. Specialities include oxtail and wild mushroom risotto, tagliatelle with king prawns and lemon sauce, and monkfish and shellfish stew. Closed Mon; Nov–Dec.

FORNALUTX Es Turó ***Tapas*** €

Cami De Cas Perets s/n, 07640 ***Tel*** *971 649 531*

Es Turó sits on a low hill not far from Ses Salines and boasts views of the countryside and the sunset. This alfresco buffet-style restaurant mixes Italian and Spanish food. Its core menu revolves around pasta dishes (try the seafood cannelloni) and grilled meats, but also seafood-stuffed courgette and aubergine (eggplant). Booking recommended.

ILLETAS La Solana €€€€€

Passeig Illetas 60, 07181 ***Tel*** *971 703 235*

This romantic restaurant is part of the Virtual Beach Club which also hosts a bistro, cocktail bar and hammock area by the beach. Their motto is "fresh by day, creative by night" and lunch choices include paella, gazpacho and clams while dinner may be oven-cooked loin of sea bass on black risotto and mushrooms infused with rosemary oil. Closed Nov–Mar.

INCA Celler Ca'n Ripoll €

C/Jaume Armengol 4, 07300 ***Tel*** *971 500 024*

This restaurant is proof that this rarely visited market town hides some of the finest eateries in Mallorca. Built in 1761 as a winery, Ca'n Ripoll has a simple but excellent menu of island classics such as *tumbet* and roast milk lamb, and desserts made from local almonds. Gluten-free, vegetarian and other diets are catered for. Closed Sun Jun–Sep; Sun eve Oct–May.

INCA Celler Sa Travessa €€

Calle Murta 16, 07300 ***Tel*** *971 500 049*

Another of Inca's formidable wine cellar restaurants, Sa Travessa comes with the warning that booking is always advisable, not just on Thursdays (market day). It offers classic country cooking in atmospheric surroundings: local soups, *tumbet*, Mallorca-style *bacalao* (cod), sturdy stews, fried fish and calamares. Closed Fri; 2 wks in Jun.

INCA Celler Ca'n Amer €€€€

Calle Pau 39, 07300 ***Tel*** *971 501 261*

An unprepossessing frontage near the market hides an award-winning restaurant that represented the Balearics at Expo 92 in Seville. Dishes such as suckling pig in honey and rosemary were developed from decades of research into the origins of Mallorcan food, a mark of the care that goes into the restaurant's cuisine. Closed Sat, Sun Jun–Sep; Sun Oct–May.

JARDINES DE ALFÀBIA Ses Porxeres €€€€

Crta de Sóller 17, 07110 ***Tel*** *971 613 762*

First established in the 14th century as a *posada*, or wayside inn, this opened as a restaurant in 1983 and comes garlanded with recommendations. Menu and decor are classic Mallorcan, with the usual meats, plus quail, partridge, pheasant, boar and other game in season. Also caters to gluten-free and other specialist diets. Closed Mon; Sun eve; mid-Jun–Sep.

LA BONANOVA Samantha's €€€€

Calle Francisco Vidal Sureda 115, 07015 ***Tel*** *971 700 000*

Something of a club atmosphere pertains at this elegant *casa señorial* near Palma, particularly in the private rooms upstairs. The large dining room has a gourmet menu with subtle *cocina nueva* touches: lobster salad, salmon and bass tartare, sirloin with foie gras and calvados. There is also a light menu and a full-on *degustación* taster.

LLUCMAJOR Son Julia *Tapas* €€€€€

Crta S'Arenal a Llucmajor, 07620 ***Tel*** *971 669 700*

One of five restaurants and bars at the luxury Grand Hotel Son Julia *(see p147)*, with barrel-vaulted ceilings. Chef Isaac Gonzáles Nieto offers refined Mediterranean food with a notable Basque influence. There is also a tasing menu that changes daily. A bistro and a pool grill, with barbecue on Thursdays, complete the remarkable picture.

MANACOR C'an Mateu €€

Crta Vieja de Manacor, km 21.7, 07210 ***Tel*** *971 665 036*

Originally a 17th-century farm (the fields still supply the kitchen), this restaurant was opened in 1971 by the Ballester family, who still run it. The menu, served in a dining room or alfresco, is traditional Mallorcan, but taken up a notch with local recipes developed over the decades. Caters to gluten-free and other specialist diets. Closed Tue; mid-Jan–mid-Feb.

MANACOR La Reserva Rotana €€€€€

Camí de S'Avall, km 3, 07500 ***Tel*** *971 845 685*

Dinner on the patio of this handsome 17th-century hotel restaurant is a delightful experience. Chef Mario Fritzsche mixes classic Mallorcan dishes with international gourmet recipes, all presented with a flourish. There is also a grill serving light meals and snacks and, on some summer nights, live jazz music in the hotel grounds.

MONTUÏRI Es Moli d'en Perons €

C/Es Molinar 51, 07230 ***Tel*** *971 646 508*

Popular with locals, this simple restaurant is set in an old windmill with fantastic views. On offer are Majorcan and international dishes such as pork massala and sea bass in cava sauce. At €9, the fixed-price lunch menu is excellent value. There is also an extensive list of interesting local wines. Closed Sun; Nov.

ORIENT Dalt Muntanya €€€

Ctra Bunyola–Orient, km 10, 07349 ***Tel*** *971 615 373*

Part of a four star country hotel between Orient and Bunyola, this is a charming setting for eating indoors or out. The restaurant offers a lengthy menu promising island staples, but also rarities such as hake salad with capers, duck breast with apple and raspberries, boneless rabbit and mouth watering desserts. Closed Nov–mid-Feb.

ORIENT Mandala €€€€€

C/Nueva 1, 07349 ***Tel*** *971 615 285*

This popular restaurant in the small village of Orient is run by a French-Swiss couple whose background thoroughly informs the fare on offer. As well as conventional island favourites such as roast suckling pig, the menu also includes curries spiced with home-made chutneys and other Eastern-flavoured dishes. Closed Mon.

PALMA Celler Sa Premsa *Tapas* €

Plaza Obispo Berenguer de Palou 8, 07003 ***Tel*** *971 723 529*

Opened in a historic townhouse in 1958 and accessed via a courtyard, this popular cellar straddles traditional staples and more adventurous recipes. Culled from both the mainland and the island, the enormous menu has enough variety to feed vegetarians, too. The list of island wines is also extensive.

PALMA Juan Frau *Tapas* €€

Mercado Santa Catalina s/n, 07013 ***Tel*** *971 737 862*

Occupying a spot on one of the corners of Santa Catalina market, this informal restaurant is popular with locals and offers authentic, home-cooked Majorcan cuisine. The fare ranges from simple sandwiches and tapas to more elaborate dishes such as paella, chicken stew, *callos* (tripe) and *frit de chocos* (fried cuttlefish). Closed Sun.

PALMA La Cuchara *Tapas* €€€

Passatge Santa Catalina de Sena 4, 07002 ***Tel*** *971 710 000*

This restaurant is named after the custom of serving food with *cucharas* (spoons). The menu is vast, with a preponderance of fish and seafood, but also a wealth of veg-friendly *revueltos* (scrambled eggs) and salads, and even bacon, liver and onion. They also offer a large list of *raciones* (portions) to share.

Key to Price Guide *see p159* **Key to Symbols** *see back cover flap*

PALMA Porto Pí €€€

Calle Garita 25, 07015 ***Tel*** *971 400 087*

Said to be favoured by the Spanish royals, Porto Pí is housed in a stately old mansion near the Marivent Palace. The traditional menu includes *buey* (ox), ostrich and duck, fresh fish, including turbot in sorrel and a special dessert of baked banana, liquorice and Galliano that has its very own website. Closed Sat eve; Sun.

PALMA Caballito de Mar €€€€

Paseo Sagrera 5, 07012 ***Tel*** *971 721 074*

Close to the marina, with a large terrace and a cool designer interior, this is a Palma institution. Prime dishes include turbot in orange sauce, *zarzuela* (fish stew), bass or red bream in salt, fish of the day and oysters in season. There is a vegetarian option as well. Booking is advisable, but one floor is left unbooked for passing trade. Closed Mon Oct–May.

PALMA Casa Jacinto €€€€

Camí Tramvía 37, 07015 ***Tel*** *971 401 858*

Casa Jacinto is quite a way from the city centre, in the suburb of Genova, but it is well worth a visit. Dining is either on two spacious, modern floors or in the garden. The menu is Mallorcan and Spanish, with such options as steaks (stone-cooked T-bone), rabbit, fresh fish and some vegetarian and gluten-free dishes. Booking is advised. Closed Tue.

PALMA La Bóveda ***Tapas*** €€€€

Calle Botería 3, 07012 ***Tel*** *971 714 863*

La Bóveda is located by the cathedral. Choose from the à la carte menu – which includes roasts of chicken, fish, pork and veal, plus a decadent liqueur-flavoured sorbet for dessert – or from the tapas list, which features the notorious Galician *pimientos de padrón*, a kind of culinary dare to see which of the green bell peppers is explosively hot. Closed Sun; Feb.

PALMA Opio €€€€

Montenegro 12, 07012 ***Tel*** *971 425 450*

Part of the ultra-chic Puro hotel, a 14th-century palace decorated for the 21st century, this restaurant does not actually have a dress code, but you will feel distinctly underdressed if you arrive in beachwear. Drop-dead stylish Opio blends Spanish and Asian cuisines: langoustines, octopus and mussels, plus Japanese and Thai fusion dishes. Closed lunch.

PALMA Refectori €€€€€

Carrer de la Missió 7a, 07012 ***Tel*** *971 227 347*

This elegant, fashionable, minimalist restaurant has style in spades. Water, stone and steel are the main decor motifs; the creative cuisine is island-based (Sóller shrimps, Máo cheese, Mallorcan oil), but with a daring twist (fresh fish with olives and broth, veal in coffee sauce, chicken in cinnamon and cashews). A truly memorable experience. Closed Sat lunch; Sun.

PEGUERA La Gran Tortuga ***Tapas*** €€€€

Carretera Cala Fornells 23, 07160 ***Tel*** *971 686 023*

"The Big Turtle" has pride of place overlooking the Badia de Palma bay. The cuisine straddles hardy classics such as *caldereta de llagosta* (lobster stew) and innovative fare (pork in curried sauce). A popular dessert is a mix of bread, chocolate, oil and salt. Most tables have sea views, and gluten-free and other diets are catered for. Closed Mon.

PEGUERA La Gritta ***Tapas*** €€€€€

C/L'Espiga 9, 07160 ***Tel*** *971 686 022*

Positioned for stunning views over the sea, La Gritta has been serving up a blend of Mallorcan and international dishes for a quarter of a century. Specialities include *caldereta de llagosta* (lobster stew), salt-baked fish, home-made pastas, steak tartare and chef Antonio Salas's divine desserts. Booking is advised, especially for the terrace. Closed Dec–Jan.

PETRA Es Celler €

C/de l'Hospital 46, 07520 ***Tel*** *971 561 056*

An ancient wine cellar transformed some years ago into an authentic Mallorcan country restaurant. Es Celler has the full array of island classics: wild rice with meats, sausage stews, country soups, snails, *tumbet*, oven-roast lamb and home-made almond desserts, plus rabbit, quail, pigeon, grilled steaks and wine by the bottle or jug. Closed Mon.

PETRA Sa Plaça €€

Plaça Ramon Lull 4, 07520 ***Tel*** *971 561 646*

This stylish but unfussy village restaurant takes the traditional rustic menu a little further, with unusual dishes such as cuttlefish with meatballs, fried fish with fennel, prawns with chocolate, guinea fowl with crayfish, and chicken breast stuffed with prawns. Desserts include apple charlotte and tiramisu, and there is a good range of island wines. Closed Tue; Nov.

PORT D'ANDRATX Layn €€€€

Avenida Almirante Riera Alemany 20, 07157 ***Tel*** *971 671 855*

An ideal, if busy, spot for either lunch or dinner, Layn is right on the harbourfront and features an ample terrace with views, as well as a room inside. The daily catch, cooked with vegetables from local farms, is the core of the menu; meat dishes are also sourced locally. Desserts are mostly chocolate-based, and there is a good choice of island wines. Closed Mon.

PORT DE POLLENÇA Corb Marí €€€€

Paseo Anglada Camarassa 91, 07470 ***Tel*** *971 867 040*

On the waterfront, this emblematic rotisserie specialises in charcoal-grilled meat and seafood. Pick out the piece of meat or fish that you would like to have cooked and take a seat in the large dining room. The restaurant is set in a traditional stone building with large windows overlooking the sea and an interior terrace.

PORT DE POLLENÇA Stay €€€€€

Moll Nou s/n, 07470 ***Tel*** *971 864 013*

This restaurant boasts ultra modern, minimalist architecture and decor as well as superb views over Pollença bay. Fare is mainly fresh fish and seafood. There is also a snack menu with sandwiches, salads and a few dishes from the main menu. An excellent fixed-price day menu is available for €33.

PORTITXOL Rocamar ***Tapas*** €€€

Calle Vicario Joaquín Fuster 1, 07007 ***Tel*** *971 274 644*

At this modernist restaurant overlooking the Portitxol harbour, Spanish fish is the main theme of the menu. A variety of lobsters and other shellfish are the key dishes, along with fish- and seafood-based rice plates, as well as oysters when available. A definite cut above the average fish restaurant. Closed Mon eve.

PORTOCOLOM Sa Cuina €€

Calle Vapor de Santueri s/n, 07670 ***Tel*** *971 824 080*

This long-established family-run restaurant is located on the seafront and boasts an ample covered terrace and sea views. Sa Cuina serves fresh fish daily, with *bacalao* (cod) stew a favourite. Also on the menu are locally reared meats, such as pork fillet stuffed with spinach and plums, lamb hotpot with honey, and tongue with capers. Closed Thu; Jan.

PUERTO PORTALS El Bistro del Tristán €€€€€

Torre Capitania s/n, 07181 ***Tel*** *971 676 141*

The more modest sibling to the Michelin-starred Tristán *(see below)*, and certainly less formal, this bistro has an open terrace and seating in a garden running to the water's edge. Food is prepared with the same style as at Tristán itself, but it tends to be lighter, less complicated and more relaxed than the dress-up event meals next door. Closed Mon.

PUERTO PORTALS Tristán €€€€€

Torre Capitania s/n, 07181 ***Tel*** *971 675 547*

Said by some to be the best restaurant on Mallorca (and by the owners to be the only one offering true Italian food), Tristán has two Michelin stars. Style and prices reflect this, in an extremely elegant restaurant with a terrace (covered during bad weather) right on the edge of the marina. The food is *cocina neuva*, prepared with flair. Closed Mon; lunch.

PUIGPUNYENT The Rose €€€

C/Ciutat 3, 07194 ***Tel*** *971 614 360*

Set in an old stone house, this small, charming restaurant has a cozy dining room for the winter months and a relaxing terrace for the summer. On offer is simple but modern cuisine ranging from Italian classics to Bavarian specialities and sushi. Options include venison *pâté en croûte*, stuffed rabbit leg and chocolate lasagne. Closed Tue.

PUIGPUNYENT Oleum €€€€€

Castillo Son Net s/n, 07194 ***Tel*** *971 147 000*

The restaurant at the Son Net hotel is housed in an 18th-century olive-press building, with a lovely garden terrace. Chef Christian Rullan creates a new menu each month, but regular dishes include aubergine (eggplant) stuffed with cod, oxtail cannelloni, and fish roasted with wild herbs. Light brunch menu on Sundays. Closed Sun eve; Mon & Tue Nov–Easter.

RANDA Es Recó de Randa €€€

Font 21, 07629 ***Tel*** *971 660 997*

An old *casa señorial*, or gentleman's house, in the picturesque village of Randa, houses this small restaurant-hotel *(see p149)*. Chef Manolo Salamanca specializes in traditional Mallorcan dishes, including *bacalao* (cod) with tomatoes, lamb roasted in a wood oven and *sopa de almendras* (almond soup).

SANTA MARÍA Read's Hotel & Restaurant €€€€€

Ca'n Moragues s/n, 07320 ***Tel*** *971 140 261*

Both restaurants at this opulent country hotel boast Michelin stars. The main one, which was voted into *El Mundo*'s top ten Spanish hotel restaurants, is located in a fabulous hall and has a small but exquisite menu. The smaller eatery, Bistro 33, is less formal, with a lovely terrace. Chef Marc Fosh oversees both with flair.

SANTA PONÇA Mesón del Rey €€

Puig del Teix 7, 07180 ***Tel*** *971 690 815*

Located in the heart of Santa Ponça, this traditional restaurant is a popular choice amongst locals and serves good, authentic Majorcan and Spanish cuisine. Choices include fish stew, grilled fish and gazpacho, as well as specials such as snails in a spicy sauce on sirloin steak. Closed Nov–mid-Dec.

SENCELLES Sa Cuina de n'Aina €€

Carrer Rafal 31, 07140 ***Tel*** *971 872 992*

A pretty stone doorway hides this pleasant family-run restaurant with a lovely interior patio. Sa Cuina de n'Aina offers a different take on island food, not least with pork in white wine, ostrich fillets, pork fillet with pâté, bream, hake and seafood grills. The wine list includes wines from Inca and Binissalem, as well as mainland vintages.

SINEU Celler Son Toreo €

Son Torelló 1, 07510 ***Tel*** *971 520 138*

A historic stone townhouse converted into a restaurant with careful attention to period detail. The menu features specials such as *frito mallorquín* (fried meats), soups, suckling pig, the ratatouille-like dish *tumbet* done with pork, *lomo con col* (sausage and pork cooked with cabbage), snails in garlic sauce, and stuffed aubergines (eggplant). Closed Mon.

Key to Price Guide *see p159* **Key to Symbols** *see back cover flap*

SINEU Molí de'n Pau €€

Crta Santa Margarita 25, 07510 ***Tel*** *971 855 116*

Just outside town of Sineu, this is, as the name suggests, a former mill. The tower has remained intact, the interior has been converted into a stylish restaurant lit with halogen lamps, and the garden and terrace are perfect for eating alfresco. The menu is typical Mallorcan, with stuffed leg of lamb, fresh fish and seafood. Closed Mon.

SÓLLER Sa Cova *Tapas* €

Plaça Constitució 7, 07001 ***Tel*** *971 633 222*

Rated as one of the best tapas restaurants in Mallorca, Sa Cova is in the town square, by the railway station. As well as tapas and other snacks, this cosy small bar also cooks full meals, such as rabbit in garlic sauce, crab with snails, couscous with meats and vegetables, and vegetarian options such as stuffed aubergines (eggplant).

SÓLLER Es Faro €€€€

Cap Gros de Moleta (Port de Sóller), 07108 ***Tel*** *971 633 752*

Located on the top of a hill, the glazed and open terraces of this elegant restaurant offer splendid views of Sóller port, the sea and the mountains. On offer is the freshest local seafood with specialities including Sóller prawns, black risotto with paprika and squid, and poached sole with cava, scallops and beetroot ragoût.

SÓLLER Las Olas €€€€

Paseo Es Través s/n, 07108 ***Tel*** *971 632 515*

For 25 years, "The Waves" has been Sóller's premiere upmarket fish restaurant, with fresh fish bought from the market daily and given the restaurant's signature treatment, usually in the oven or on the grill. Many of the fish dishes have a French touch, and there's also paella, lamb and prime pork. The wine list boasts fine island vintages. Closed Tue Sep–Jun.

SÓLLER Ca's Xorc *Tapas* €€€€€

Carreta de Deià, km 56.1, 07100 ***Tel*** *971 638 280*

Like the hotel that houses it (and with which it shares spectacular views), this mixes tradition and modernity. Sit in one of three dining areas (one is the terrace). At lunchtime the bistro menu includes *Paella Ca's Xorc*; in the evenings, the chef Guillermo Moya elaborates a Majorcan-Mediterranean menu, including a six-dish tasting menu. Booking is obligatory.

SON SERVERA Pula *Tapas* €€

Ctra Son Servera–Capdepera, km 3, 07550 ***Tel*** *971 567 940*

Famous among the golfers visiting the Pula Golf Club, which uses it as a VIP area during tournaments (it overlooks the final green), Pula is the gastronomic hub of the area. Styled by leading Spanish designer Ágatha Ruiz de la Prada and said to be a favourite of King Juan Carlos, it mixes island cuisine with international gourmet dishes.

VALLDEMOSSA Arran del Cel €

C/Marqués de Vivot 10, 07170 ***Tel*** *971 612 821*

In the heart of the Tramuntana mountain range, this inviting, atmospheric restaurant serves good, unpretentious home-cooked food. Choices include paella and other local dishes that are always accompanied by Arran del Cel's famous home-made bread. Sandwiches and pizzas are also available and there is occasional live music by local bands.

VALLDEMOSSA Son Moragues €€€

Camí de Son Moragues s/n, 07170 ***Tel*** *971 616 111*

Rumoured to be the place to find Michael Douglas eating (he owns the Moorish palace in the nearby estate of the same name), this is a splendid 17th-century country house specializing in island cuisine. Try the rape and shrimp cannelloni and the fish, which is always exquisitely cooked. Stunning mountain and sea views. Closed Sun.

VALLDEMOSSA Valldemossa €€€€€

Carretera Vieja de Valldemossa, 07170 ***Tel*** *971 612 626*

This hilltop luxury hotel and restaurant occupies a spectacular 19th century country house with views over the valley below. The creative Mediterranean haute cuisine on offer includes prawn carpaccio with watercress salad and grape oil, truffle risotto and lamb with licorice, sweet potato purée and *san faina* (vegetable stew). The gourmet menu is €60.

MENORCA

ALAIOR Ca'n Jaumot *Tapas* €

C/Juan Bautista de la Salle 6, 07730 ***Tel*** *971 378 294*

Another friendly restaurant in this inland town. As well as a selection of snacks and sandwiches, there is a restaurant service in the dining room or garden, and a good wine list. On the menu, besides pizzas and tapas, is a fixed-price menu that allows you to choose from five starters and five main dishes of Menorcan food, for €13 a head. Closed Sun.

ALAIOR Sa Paissa *Tapas* €

Av Central 54, Cala en Porter, 07730 ***Tel*** *971 371 886*

This restaurant is located in a hostel of the same name in the centre of Cala en Porter. Open all day, it serves breakfast, lunch and dinner with a different menu for each mealtime. Fare includes Spanish specialities such as *panillada de pescado* (barbecued fish) and sirloin steak with prawns as well as good vegetarian options. Opt to sit on the lovely terrace.

ALAIOR Boni *Tapas* €€

Centro Commercial s/n, 07730 ***Tel*** *971 372 277*

Although this popular restaurant is located near the centre of the island, in this lively town between Maó and Ciutadella, it has its own boat, which supplies fresh fish daily. The wood grill also serves up the Boni special leg of lamb, and there are oven-cooked dishes, too. All desserts are home-made, and the staff famously friendly.

ALAIOR The Cobblers €€€

C/Sant Macari 6, 07730 ***Tel*** *971 371 400*

This busy garden restaurant and brasserie is set in a traditional wood-beamed house in the town centre. The kitchen serves up modern British food with Mediterranean influences, all accompanied by fresh local vegetables. Vegetarians are well catered for and there are occasional live music evenings.

CALA EN BOSCH Anglada €€

Es Lago de Cala en Bosch s/n, 07760 ***Tel*** *971 381 402*

This waterside restaurant has a vast menu of new Mediterranean cuisine. Starters include melon soup and Basque tuna and onion pie, while fish specialities range from hake steamed with leek to anglerfish with tarragon. With more shellfish (cockles in gin) and meat (rabbit in chocolate) dishes, there is a wealth of options.

CALA GALDANA Es Barranc €€

Urb Cala Galdana s/n, 07750 ***Tel*** *971 154 643*

This smart modern restaurant with a large canopied front terrace is pricier than its neighbours but it is considered a bargain by its many fans. The menu is lengthy, with two types of *caldereta de llagosta* (lobster stew), plus lobster in aïoli, salads, shrimp dishes, soups, tortillas and 20 different fish and meat dishes. Es Barranc also has a kids' menu.

CALES COVES Opera Due €

Urb Cales Coves s/n, 07730 ***Tel*** *971 377 375*

A fun Italian restaurant, with a choice of pizzas and fresh pasta dishes, sundry steaks and meat dishes, salads and a good selection of Spanish and Italian table wines. There are more than 20 pizzas to choose from, including oddities such as salmon pizza, and a dozen pasta options. The restaurant also has a garden, terrace and pool.

CIUTADELLA Casa Manolo €€€

Marina 117–121, 07760 ***Tel*** *971 380 003*

Day or night, reservations are strongly advised at this popular harbourfront restaurant serving a full range of local fish and seafood dishes: *caldereta* (stew), squid, oysters, clams, mussels and *gambas*, as well as grilled fish and various rice dishes. Has a good wine list, and a neat touch of fruit ice creams served in the fruit they are made from. Closed Oct–May.

CIUTADELLA Cas Ferrer de Sa Font €€€

C/Portal de sa Font 16, 07760 ***Tel*** *971 480 784*

Laid out in three rooms of an imposing 17th-century town mansion, in the heart of the old capital, Cas Ferrer has been sympathetically renovated with modern decor. It serves a small but good selection of traditional island dishes. The emphasis is on fish and stews, and the three-course *menú del día* is recommended for both quality and price.

CIUTADELLA Café Balear €€€€

Pla de Sant Joan 15, 07760 ***Tel*** *971 380 005*

Formerly a fishermen's quayside inn, this became a restaurant in the 1970s and is now one of the best fish eateries on the island. Café Balear has its own boat which sails every morning and brings back the day's menu. Fish and shellfish are cooked the traditional way, and the terrace enjoys a prime position on the quay. Closed Sun Jun–Sep; Mon Oct–May; Nov.

CIUTADELLA Ca's Quintu €€€€

Camí de Baix 8, Club Nàutic de Ciutadella, 07760 ***Tel*** *971 381 002*

One of the oldest eateries in Ciutadella and something of an institution, Ca's Quintu specializes not just in traditional Menorcan food, but in dishes specific to Ciutadella itself. That means seafood, especially shellfish, in soups, baked or fried, or in *calderetas* (stews). Booking is advised, particularly if you want a terrace table overlooking the square.

CIUTADELLA Ses Truqueries €€€€€

Camí Cala'n Blanes, km 1, 07760 ***Tel*** *971 188 384*

This renovation of an 18th-century country house is the work of father and son Ciscu and Axel Fortuny, who rebuilt it and planted the vegetable garden that supplies the kitchen. The menu veers from tradition to include hummus and goat, and there are imaginative takes on classics (lobster, lamb, suckling pig), too. Book ahead for the lovely terrace. Closed Dec–Jan.

ES CASTELL Club Nautic es Castell €€

Cala Fons s/n, 07720 ***Tel*** *971 362 542*

The nautical club at the former fortified harbour has an excellent setting and views. The menu is suitably marine: fresh fish and seafood, grilled or oven-baked, plus a variety of rice dishes and the inevitable lobster stew. They also serve *erizo* (sea urchin). Good value for money fixed-price menus for lunch and dinner.

ES CASTELL Sa Foganya €€€

Ruiz i Pablo 97, 07720 ***Tel*** *971 354 950*

Built around a pretty interior courtyard, Sa Foganya has a menu dedicated entirely to local produce cooked on its grill – try the specials of *buey* (bull), beef entrecôte, breast of duck, country sausages and beef. Grilled vegetables are also served – in the sturdy *tostadas* of country bread with olive oil, tomato and island cheeses.

Key to Price Guide *see p159* **Key to Symbols** *see back cover flap*

ES CASTELL Son Granot €€€€

Carretera Sant Felip s/n, 07720 ***Tel*** *971 355 555*

Located on a hilltop, 500 m (1,600 ft) from Es Castell, this rural hotel and restaurant is set in a colonial-style house dating back to 1712. The traditional Menorcan cuisine is based on old family recipes and the ingredients sourced from their own kitchen garden. Choices include *caldereta de llagosta* (lobster stew), stuffed squid and chicken in champagne sauce.

ES MERCADAL Es Moli d'es Racó €€

C/Major 53, 07740 ***Tel*** *971 375 392*

As the name implies, this is a renovated windmill, refurbished as an unfussy country restaurant dedicated to traditional food. At simple tables under vaulted stone ceilings, you can feast on Menorca rarities such as chicken with spider crab, onions stuffed with rape, calamares in wine, and oven-baked aubergines (eggplant). A good selection of island wines.

ES MERCADAL Ca N'Aguedet ***Tapas*** €€€

Lepant 23–30, 07740 ***Tel*** *971 375 391*

This large, airy restaurant has become a shrine to Menorcan food and is commensurately popular. Its menu of fine country dishes is wide, but snails with crab, suckling pig, rabbit with beans and Menorcan spicy sausages (*sobrasada* and *carn i xua*) are especially recommended. Try the house wines, which are made specifically for Ca N'Aguedet.

ES MERCADAL Ca'n Olga €€€

Pont Na Macarrana s/n, 07740 ***Tel*** *971 375 459*

One of the most sophisticated restaurants in Es Mercadal, in terms of menu, decor and clientele, Ca'n Olga is housed in a 150-year-old town mansion, with a lovely patio area. The chef eschews a traditional menu in favour of rarities such as quail in an onion and vinegar liqueur, scorpion fish, tender baby goat, and mussels in a cheese sauce.

ES MIGJORN GRAN 58, S'Engolidor €€€

C/Major 3, 07749 ***Tel*** *971 370 193*

The name comes from the previous address of this renovated 18th-century townhouse. A plain façade conceals a four-room hotel with a tiny restaurant and a small terrace. The white-and-powder-blue walls feature works by local artists, and the menu includes Menorcan dishes such as tender baby lamb and aubergine (eggplant) stuffed with fish. Closed Nov–Apr.

FERRERIES El Mirador €€€

Platja Cala Galdana s/n, 07750 ***Tel*** *971 154 503*

Blessed with a stunning setting on a small rocky headland with views all around, El Mirador is best booked early. The house specials are paella (check if they need advance warning) and fresh fish of the day cooked in various ways. It also has some prime steak and cutlet options in pepper, cheese and other sauces. An excellent wine list.

FERRERIES Liorna €€€

C/Econòm Florit (C/de Dalt) 9, 07750 ***Tel*** *971 373 912*

Damia Coll's trendy designer restaurant doesn't just look like an art gallery: it is an art gallery, with modernist furniture and a shaded patio. The excellent menu features touches of sushi and Thai fused with Bulli-style flourishes on *solomillo* (sirloin), *cabrito* (kid) and *bacalao* (cod). Do not leave town without trying it. Closed Mon–Wed (winter); Mon (summer).

FERRERIES Meson el Gallo €€€

Ctra Cala Santa Galdana, km 1.5, 07750 ***Tel*** *971 373 039*

A short walk (1.5 km/1 mile) out of Ferreries, on the Galdana road, this 250-year-old farmhouse has been run as a restaurant for 30 years. Rooster (*gallo*) is available in a paella and in other recipes as the house special. The restaurant is also famed for its local steaks with Mallorcan cheese. The popular terrace is set in mature gardens. Closed Mon; Dec–Jan.

FORNELLS Sa Llagosta €€€

Gabriel Gelabert 12, 07748 ***Tel*** *971 376 566*

Sa Llagosta is rated the best among Fornells's fish restaurants, with some reports suggesting you need to book one month ahead for a table on the terrace. The menu is based on Mediterranean seafood, with interesting new ways with *caldereta* (stew), freshly caught fish and a particularly fine foie gras. The quality matches the prices. Closed Oct–Easter.

FORNELLS Es Cranc Pelut €€€€€

Paseo Marítimo 98, 07748 ***Tel*** *971 376 743*

Not to be confused with Es Cranc in the village, this seafront restaurant is in the top three of Fornells's seafood haunts. Chef Diego Coll has won applause for dishes such as octopus meatballs, mussels in tramontana sauce, and wild rice with lobster or shellfish. The covered terrace has sea views and is perfect for unwinding. Closed Tue; Nov–Apr.

FORNELLS Es Pla €€€€€

Passeig des Pla, 07748 ***Tel*** *971 376 655*

Yet another Fornells fish palace where it is advisable to book well in advance, especially in high season, when you could be competing with King Juan Carlos for a table. Es Pla is laid-back, with a large bar and a wooden deck just above the waves. It has a wealth of fresh fish options, but the star dish is the paella with crayfish.

MAÓ Cap Roig €€

Urb Cala Mesquida s/n, 07701 ***Tel*** *971 188 383*

Named after the star of its menu, Cap Roig (scorpion fish) is said to be the finest restaurant in Maó. It is highly recommended for its *caldereta de llagosta* (lobster stew), plus the usual selection of freshly caught fish, but also, when available, for its Norway crab or crayfish. Booking is advised, especially if you are hoping for a terrace table. Closed Mon.

MAÓ Casa Sexto €€€

C/Vassallo 2, 07703 ***Tel*** *971 368 407*

Specializing in Galician cuisine, all fresh ingredients are brought in directly from Galicia and include seafood, shellfish, farmed beef and cheese. Traditional dishes such as *lacón con grelos* (pork shoulder with turnip tops) and Padrón peppers, small green peppers fried in olive oil, are served with home-made *Ribeiro* (white wine). Closed Sun eve.

MAÓ Sa Vinya €€€€

Cami de Baix 47, 07701 ***Tel*** *971 369 382*

This lovely country house just outside Maó was carefully restored by the owner/chef, who has also planted a garden to supply the kitchen. It is a very peaceful place, offering specials such as *escalivada* (a classic Catalan vegetable bake), black pasta, local prawn dishes and *albondigas* (meatballs) in house sauce. Closed Mon; weekends Jul–Aug; lunch.

MAÓ La Minerva €€€€€

Moll de Llevant 87, 07701 ***Tel*** *971 351 995*

The most stylish restaurant in Maó, and the place to be seen, particularly if you are lucky enough to get a table on the floating terrace in the harbour. On the menu (the longest on Menorca) is a wide range of meat dishes, as well as fish options, notably a seafood *zarzuela* (stew). The home-made ice cream is made with Maó cheese. Closed Jan; Mon (winter).

MAÓ Varadero €€€€€

Moll de Llevant 4, 07701 ***Tel*** *971 352 074*

This restaurant would not look amiss on some trendy Barcelona *passeig*. It mixes post-modern design with historic port architecture, and the menu is just as daring. Chiefly known for its creative rice and noodle dishes, Veradero also has its own unusual take on meat (sirloin of pork) and fish (*llomo de bacalao*, or cod steak). Desserts are inventive, too.

SANT CLIMENT Es Molí de Foc €€€€

C/Sant Llorenç 65, 07703 ***Tel*** *971 153 222*

Es Molí has developed a reputation as one of the finest restaurants on Menorca. The menu, like the townhouse decor, is classical, with a meat and fish list that extends to quail and rabbit, and duck or salmon in exotic country sauces. The interior patio is perfect for dinner under the stars. Closed Mon & eve Sep–Jun; mid-Dec–mid-Jan; 2 wks in Mar.

IBIZA

CALA LLONGA La Casita €€€

Urbanización Valverde – Cala Llonga 60, 07840 ***Tel*** *971 330 293*

A pleasant country restaurant with a garden, fountain and shaded terrace in a valley near the beach. In summer the menu changes weekly, but typical plates include green fig soup, goat's cheese and pesto salad, meat and fish carpaccio, and an unusual hot fruit curry. On Thursdays you can sample barbecued suckling pig, beef and lamb. Closed Tue; lunch.

EIVISSA Ca n'Alfredo €€€

Paseo Vara de Rey 16, 07800 ***Tel*** *971 311 274*

Housed in a mansion in the port, this is the oldest restaurant in Eivissa (established 1934). It is much loved by visitors (and the VIPs whose photos adorn the walls). Ca n'Alfredo's menu is mainly based around fish, and specials include scorpion fish in prawn sauce, fish and potato stew, hake with caviar, and pork with melon. Closed Mon; Sun eve.

EIVISSA El Faro €€€

Plaza Sa Riba 1, 07800 ***Tel*** *971 313 233*

With a large terrace and a palm-shaded garden at the end of the harbourfront, this is one of the best places to eat fish and take in the quayside atmosphere. In addition to one of the largest *viveros* (live-fish tanks) in Ibiza, El Faro offers, depending on availability, lobster, clams, oysters, seafood, steaks, grills and roasts. It also has a full kids' menu.

EIVISSA El Portalón €€€

Plaça dels Desemparats 1, 07800 ***Tel*** *971 303 901*

Another Balearic eatery claimed to be popular with Spanish royalty, this is an elegant classic town mansion restaurant, close enough to the port to have established a connection with the best fish and seafood suppliers on the quay. Its signature rape cooked in herbs is famous, and the wine list is truly remarkable. Closed Sun lunch; Feb.

EIVISSA Es Caliu €€€

C/Sant Joan, km 10, 8, Santa Eularia Des Riu, 07840 ***Tel*** *971 325 075*

A fixture on Ibiza's culinary map, this country-style restaurant specializes in grilled meats. Its star dish is *lomo de buey* (prime beef), but other delicacies include kid, suckling pig, rabbit and stone-sizzled chops. Starters are less meaty, and there is a wide range of side salads. Closed lunch Jul–Aug; end Dec–end Jan.

EIVISSA La Brasa €€€

Carrer de Pere Sala 3, 07800 ***Tel*** *971 301 202*

The dress code is more a warning to dress up, since your fellow diners certainly will. This smart villa-style house in the old town has tables indoors or out, in the palm-shaded garden. The menu is international and fresh from the market: lobster, salmon, game, duck. Home-made desserts include cactus fruit pudding. Book ahead if eating after 10pm.

Key to Price Guide *see p159* **Key to Symbols** *see back cover flap*

EIVISSA La Masia d'en Sord €€€

Ctra de Sant Miquel, km 1, 07814 ***Tel*** *971 310 228*

There is an interior patio and garden for outdoor eating at this handsome country house restaurant a short stroll from the town centre. The menu offers upmarket versions of island classics with a gourmet touch: try the wild mushroom terrine, rape with Catalan *escalivada* (veg bake), grilled turbot and fish in salt crust. Closed Nov–Mar; lunch Jul–Aug.

EIVISSA Can den Parra €€€€

C/San Rafael 3, 07800 ***Tel*** *971 391 114*

Hidden in a pretty alleyway in the Dalt Vila and open only for dinner, Can de Parra is an atmospheric, if busy, place to eat. Starters include goat's cheese and spinach, and beef carpaccio; among the fish specialities are sea pike, skate and bass; and meat dishes include steaks, rabbit and lamb cutlets. Desserts are home-made. Closed lunch.

EIVISSA El Olivo €€€€

Pza de Vila 9, 07800 ***Tel*** *971 300 680*

The menu at this popular restaurant with a trendy terrace in fashionable Dalt Vila is Ibizan-French with a *cocina nueva* edge: sample the cold tomato soup with basil and prawns, local skate with capers, cod with fennel and lemon grass, lamb with herbs and garlic, or pork stuffed with goat's cheese and tarragon. Book ahead, if only on the day. Closed Mon.

EIVISSA Sa Punta €€€€

Es Puet de Talamanca, 07819 ***Tel*** *971 193 424*

A place to see and be seen in, Sa Punta attracts an international jet-set crowd that come for the chill out music and fabulous food. Specialities include sea bass supreme with salt crust and cuttlefish balls with shellfish. Snacks are available throughout the day but the rustic decor and low lighting make it a popular evening destination. Closed Nov–Mar.

FIGUERETAS Soleado €€€€

Paseo Ses Pitiusas s/n, 07800 ***Tel*** *971 394 811*

Right on Figueretas's palm-lined seafront, this large terrace restaurant reflects its French owners' culinary heritage. The menu is chiefly fish-based, with paper-baked sea bass, salmon with hazelnuts and balsamic vinegar, crayfish and asparagus, or brochette of prawns. Soleado is candelit at night, with a sheltered/heated patio for cooler evenings. Closed Nov–Apr.

SANT ANTONI Es Rebost de Ca'n Prats €

Calle Cervantes 4, 07820 ***Tel*** *971 346 252*

This family-run restaurant in the heart of town is regarded as a temple to Ibizan cuisine. Secret family recipes are said to be the success of its superlative paellas and rice dishes. The menu also features octopus fried with onion and tomato, and cod in a tomato sauce or with aïoli. Do not leave town without at least trying it once. Closed Tue; mid-Dec–mid-Jan.

SANT ANTONI Rincon de Pepe ***Tapas*** €

San Mateo 6, 07820 ***Tel*** *971 340 697*

Rincon de Pepe is the original quayside tapas bar and restaurant, and a place to see and be seen. The staff operate a point-at-what-you-want policy with a variety of fish, meat, poultry and vegetable tapas. Main courses include soups and salads, grilled sole, or prawns, mussels and various grills. For dessert, try the island cakes soaked in Cointreau.

SANT ANTONI Rias Baixas ***Tapas*** €€

Cervantes 14–16, 07820 ***Tel*** *971 340 480*

Rias Baixas serves genuine Galician food and is now an Ibizan institution. The authenticity goes as far as flying in fish and shellfish caught off Galicia's Atlantic coast. The restaurant also has various meat dishes: *solomillo* (sirloin), entrecôte and chops. You can try tapas of many dishes before committing to a main meal.

SANT ANTONI Sa Capella €€€

Ctra Santa Ines, km 0.6, 07840 ***Tel*** *971 340 057*

This 16th-century former chapel has been restored as a cool modern restaurant with a great terrace. The menu is dominated by fresh fish such as monkfish, tuna, bream, cod and salmon, and there are some excellent desserts. At night, candles and classical music complete the atmospheric effect. Closed Nov–Mar.

SANT JOSEP El Destino ***Tapas*** €

Calle de Talaia Atalaya 15, 07820 ***Tel*** *971 800 341*

History and waves of trend-setters from hippies to clubbers have made this the most famous tapas bar and restaurant on Ibiza. Tapas and full *raciones* come with a twist of Moroccan cookery (couscous and pulses), plus hints of Asian flavours, crossed with traditional island cuisine. Booking is advised.

SANT JOSEP Ca Na Joana €€€€

Ctra San José, km 10, 07830 ***Tel*** *971 800 158*

Named after its owner, pioneering feminist photographer Joana Biarnés, this country house has played host to celebrities such as Picasso, Dalí and Polanski. The star dish is Ibizan potatoes with fresh Navaleno truffles, but also notable are the foie gras, duck carpaccio, lamb in a house sauce, and oxtail in red wine. Closed Sun eve & Mon Jan–May; Nov–Dec.

SANT JOSEP Can Domingo de Can Botja €€€€€

Ctra San José, km 9, 07830 ***Tel*** *971 800 184*

This is still described as a "secret" by the Spanish media, so try to go while it remains so. This beautiful country house has an austere style to both its decor and menu. Classic island dishes made with a touch of Basque cooking include the goat's cheese salad with rough country bread, turbot in a thyme sauce and delicious desserts. Closed Mon Sep–Jun.

SANT RAFEL Dos Lunas €€€€€

Ctra Ibiza–San Antonio, km 5, 07840 ***Tel*** *971 198 102*

Although this is alleged to be the most exclusive restaurant on Ibiza, you might just be lucky enough to get a table in the garden, with its eccentric collection of sculpture and art. The menu is Italian/Mediterranean; although, of course, you are really paying for the chance to rub elbows with Spanish royalty and celebrities. Closed Oct–Apr.

SANT RAFEL El Ayoun €€€€€

C/Isidor Macabich 6, 07816 ***Tel*** *971 198 335*

Whatever your opinion of bellydancing, this is as authentic as a Moroccan restaurant gets in Ibiza. The decor is all drapes and cushions, the waiters are in authentic dress and the music is a mix of north African sounds and chill. The menu is mainly variations on couscous and tajine dishes, with some spicy starters. A favoured drop-in for clubbers. Closed lunch.

SANT RAFEL El Clodenis €€€€€

Plaza de la Iglesia s/n, 07816 ***Tel*** *971 198 545*

This lovely small eatery, a whitewashed island house with a terrace, has become a favourite of nightclubbers without becoming pretentious. The menu is Provençal mixed with traditional island recipes – simple, unpretentious and good, just like the atmosphere. Choose between a garden courtyard or small farmhouse dining rooms.

SANT RAFEL L'Elephant €€€€€

Plaza Iglesia s/n, 07816 ***Tel*** *971 198 056*

Less outrageous than Living Life *(see p169)*, this is still very much a clubbers' haven, with minimalist decor, a stylish rooftop dining area and a cocktail terrace. The menu is French international, featuring mainly fish: cod, tuna, John Dory, turbot, bass and lobster, though there are also meat and vegetarian options. It hits its stride around midnight.

SANTA EULÀRIA DES RIU Can Cosmi *Tapas* €

Plaza Iglesia, Santa Ines s/n, 07840 ***Tel*** *971 805 020*

More a tapas bar than a proper restaurant, Can Cosmi serves what are claimed to be the best tortillas on the island. Have a drink, admire the work of island artists on the walls, and soak in the atmosphere in this genuinely historic island institution. This eatery was the Republicans' bar during the Civil War and is now almost a shrine to that era. Closed Tue.

SANTA EULÀRIA DES RIU Atzaró €€€

Ctra Sant Joan, km 15, 07840 ***Tel*** *971 338 838*

Part of a stylish spa resort and hidden in olive groves outside Santa Eulària, this follows a philosophy of mixing Ibizan country-house style with modern-day island hedonism. Catalan cook Josep Coronado prepares a decadent mix of modern Spanish and international dishes with flair; food is served on a series of terraces and pergolas. Closed Nov–Apr.

SANTA EULÀRIA DES RIU Casa Colonial *Tapas* €€€

Ctra Santa Eulària, km 2, 07840 ***Tel*** *971 338 001*

Perhaps best described as a garden with a restaurant attached, this establishment is housed, as the name implies, in a large country mansion with extensive gardens, lawns, fountains and statuary. The menu is island traditional with an international twist: fish, meats, pastas and salads. Casa Colonial is popular with pre-clubbers.

SANTA EULÀRIA DES RIU Bambuddha Grove €€€€

Ctra San Juan, km 8.5, 07840 ***Tel*** *971 197 510*

The ultimate chill venue on Ibiza is located in an authentic Balinese meeting hall. This east-meets-west restaurant serves its (copyrighted) mix of "MediterrAsian Cuisine", fusing Thai, Indonesian, Japanese and Mediterranean dishes. The theme recurs in the decor and the gardens, which resemble a Zen temple. Closed lunch; Mon; Nov–Mar.

SANTA EULÀRIA DES RIU Celler C'An Pere €€€€

C/Sant Jaume 63, 07840 ***Tel*** *971 330 056*

Probably the oldest establishment on Santa Eulària's restaurant street, this eatery first opened 50 years ago as a bar, and then became a *marisquería* (shellfish restaurant). It now has four different rooms offering a vast range of shellfish, fresh fish, paellas, steaks, and pasta and poultry dishes. The rose-shaded terrace is a pleasant place to eat.

SANTA GERTRUDIS DE FRUITERA Km 5 €€€

Ctra San José, km 5.6, 07840 ***Tel*** *971 396 349*

In recent years, this has become the clubbers' hangout of choice. Km 5 is a complex of tents and awnings resembling a sheikh's desert camp, with a beautiful open-air restaurant with open kitchen, white drapes and blond wood. The menu is short but traditionally based, with large salads, fish with pasta, grills and good vegetarian options. Closed lunch; Oct–Apr.

SANTA GERTRUDIS DE FRUITERA Ama Lur €€€€

Ctra Sant Miguel, km 2.3, 07814 ***Tel*** *971 314 554*

This smart country house restaurant with ample terrace has been favoured by the "in" crowd for many years. The name and decor are Basque, but the menu is Ibizan and international. Star dishes include mozzarella and tomato soup, bass with almond sauce, lamb baked in honey and herbs, and spiced calamares. Closed lunch; Wed; mid-Nov–mid-Mar.

SANTA GERTRUDIS DE FRUITERA Ca'n Pau €€€€

Ctra de San Miguel, km 2.9, 07814 ***Tel*** *971 197 007*

Ca'n Pau is difficult to find but well worth the hunt for its mix of Catalan, Ibizan and a touch of French cuisine. Resembling a country house more than a restaurant, it is noticeable for the unusual sculptures dotting the garden. The menu is traditional, with good country chicken, steaks and spicy island sausages. Booking advised. Closed lunch Jul–Sep.

Key to Price Guide *see p159* **Key to Symbols** *see back cover flap*

FORMENTERA

ES CALÓ Es Rafalet €

Calo de Sant Agusti s/n, 07860 ***Tel*** *971 327 016*

A certain remote atmosphere is attached to Formentera's ultimate dropout beach haunt. Part of the same-name *hostal* on a rocky outcrop above the beach, Es Rafalet is a laid back fish and seafood beach bar. Bob Dylan and Pink Floyd used to hang out here; Kate Moss and others still do. Closed Nov–Mar.

ES CALÓ Restaurante Pascual €€€

Ctra de Mola 12, 07860 ***Tel*** *971 327 014*

With a large terrace and mature gardens, surrounded by pine trees and just a few metres from the sea, Pascual offers a beautiful setting for lunch or dinner. The menu revolves around fresh fish and seafood, including a *caldereta* (stew) of lobster caught in Formentera waters. The atmosphere is laid-back and slightly chaotic, but that is part of the charm.

ES PUJOLS Sa Palmera €€

Playa Es Pujols s/n, 07871 ***Tel*** *971 328 356*

Dating from 1968, this is one of the very first, original beach restaurants. Its star dish is *zarzuela de mariscos* (shellfish stew), but it is also worth trying the fish of the day, grilled or in a green herb sauce. As well as the inevitable, and excellent, paella, Sa Palmera also specializes in beef grilled with onions and tomatoes. Closed Nov–Feb.

ES PUJOLS Caminito €€€€

Camí Es Pujols-La Savina, 07871 ***Tel*** *971 328 106*

One of the smartest restaurants on the island, Caminito is devoted to Argentinian cuisine, specifically grilled meat. The range of cuts is impressive: beef, ox, lamb and an array of tasty sausages; there is also a menu of oven-cooked specials, not least a spicy Creole beef, and aubergines (eggplant) in a bitter vinegar and citrus marinade (*escabeche*).

LA MOLA Es Mirador €€€

Carretera de la Mola, km 14.3, 07870 ***Tel*** *971 327 037*

Es Mirador boasts the most spectacular setting on Formentera, above the easternmost promontory of the island, with views of Ibiza in the distance. As a consequence, booking is advisable and essential in high summer. The menu is good island fare with paellas, fresh fish and oven specialities. Transport, if only two wheels, is essential.

LA SAVINA Bellavista €€€

La Savina, 07870 ***Tel*** *971 322 236*

Below the hotel of the same name *(see p156)*, with a large terrace offering views of the port and the nearby Estany Pudent lagoon, this is one of the best restaurants away from the beach. Bellavista specializes in fish and seafood dishes, with lobster and spider crab, fish stews and grills, all fresh from the port. There is also a range of meat dishes.

PLATJA ILLETES Juan y Andrea €€€€€

Platja Illetes s/n, 07860 ***Tel*** *971 187 130*

Dine on beautifully fresh fish and shellfish, including lobster, caught by the restaurant's own fishing boat, in this wonderful beach restaurant. It overlooks the Playa de Illetas, one of the wildest and most beautiful beaches in the Mediterranean. Local rice dishes are a speciality here. Open daily 1–8pm and closed Oct–Apr.

PLATJA LLEVANT Tanga €€€

Platja Llevant s/n, 07860 ***Tel*** *971 187 905*

Quieter than its northerly neighbours on Platja Illetes, this large open-air beach restaurant has the benefit of a sizeable interior dining area, with a high roof supported by a crooked tree trunk, offering respite from the sun. It serves the usual selection of paellas, *caldereta* (stew) and fresh fish, either on the sundeck or inside. Closed eve except Aug; Nov–Apr.

PLATJA MIGJORN Sa Platgeta €

Sa Playeta, 07860 ***Tel*** *971 187 614*

In an idyllic beach setting – under palm trees and just metres from the sea, with La Mola and Cap Barbaria to the east and west – this terraced restaurant offers a long menu, with pork fillets cooked in a variety of ways, steak, grilled hake or dorado, and two types of paella. The dessert special is apple doughnuts in different sauces. Closed Nov–Apr.

SES ILLETES Blue Bar €

Platja Es Migjorn Gran s/n, 07860 ***Tel*** *971 187 011*

One of the original 1960s hippy *chiringuitos* (beach fish restaurants), Blue Bar has updated itself to the era of ambient chill. Less frenetic than its Ibiza counterparts – the dance floor is the beach itself – it also has a decent restaurant, with salads, pasta dishes, fish, seafood, grills and vegetarian options, and a terrace overlooking the beach. Closed Nov–Apr.

SES ILLETES Es Moli de Sal €€

Platja de Ses Illetes s/n, 07860 ***Tel*** *971 187 491*

The best restaurant at Illetes. Unfortunately, the day ferries from Ibiza know this as well and make a beeline for it. Nevertheless, the cooking at Es Moli de Sal is superb, with a *caldereta* (stew) that is said by some to be the envy of both islands. Its paellas and fresh grilled fish are also highly regarded.

SHOPPING IN THE BALEARIC ISLANDS

As elsewhere in Spain, the islands produce a wide variety of good leatherware, with Inca, in Mallorca, having a worldwide reputation for footwear. Items of clothing including hippy jewellery found on market stalls are most in evidence on Ibiza, which is also known for its fashion trend, 'ad-lib'. Locally produced ceramics also make good souvenirs and are available on all of the islands, as are other island crafts including embroidery and basketwork. Local produce should also not be ignored, and bringing home a string of garlic, some spicy sausages or a good bottle of Mallorcan wine is as good a way as any of remembering the holiday.

Ceramic lantern

Ceramics shop in Maó, Menorca

WHERE TO BUY

Souvenirs of the Balearic Islands can be bought almost anywhere and the number of small shops offering all sorts of knick-knacks and mementos is truly amazing. They can be found in the historic parts of towns, in tourist centres and near harbours and beaches. Almost every hotel has its own boutique. There are also numerous shops selling clothes and anything that may be useful on the beach, including mattresses, mats, hats, beach balls and sun-block creams.

The items offered by boutiques can also be found in larger shopping centres, where you can buy food and various factory products. Palma has the largest choice of shops while Maó, in Menorca, has quite a few outlets and can cater for most holidaymakers' tastes.

Factory shops are good places to buy souvenirs. They offer slightly lower prices and a much larger selection of goods. The specialist centres are also great places to hunt for souvenirs including pottery or synthetic pearls.

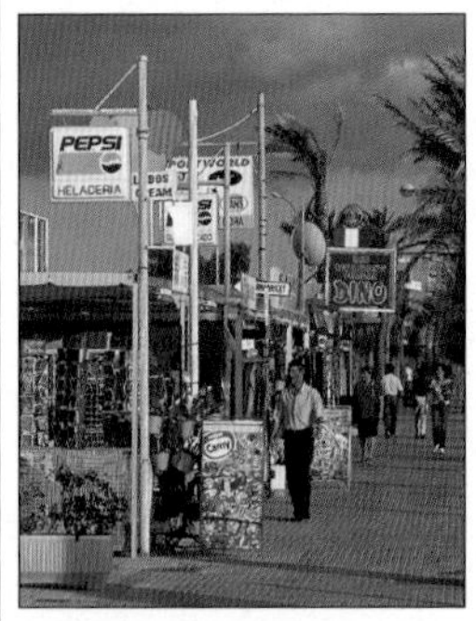

Boutiques and restaurants along a seaside promenade

OPENING HOURS

The large shops in tourist centres are usually open from 9am until 9pm. Some close for a siesta between 2pm and 5pm. Boutiques have similar opening hours. Shops along the beaches open virtually non-stop. These are the most reliable places to buy food and other basic articles. During high season most shops remain open seven days a week.

Provincial towns and villages do not have such regular opening hours and are more attuned to the pace of life of the local people than to holidaymakers. Shops in small villages may also close at weekends.

HOW TO PAY

When shopping in boutiques, small shops, food stores and markets it is customary to pay in cash. Only some larger stores, such as hypermarkets or factory shops, or those selling jewellery, cosmetics and books will accept payment by credit cards.

MARKETS

Markets are an integral feature of the Mallorcan scenery. They are held at weekly intervals, mostly in the provincial towns and villages of the island. They mainly serve the local population, although during high season they also offer many goods aimed at tourists. Besides everyday domestic items, most of them sell fruit, vegetables and sometimes locally produced sauces and preserves. Markets tend to start in the mornings and end early in the afternoon.

Hippy markets are held mainly on Formentera and Ibiza. Aimed squarely at visitors, they offer colourful clothes reminiscent of the fashions popular in the 1960s, as well as every type of ornament, including brooches, earrings, necklaces, belts and bracelets made of shells. These bustling markets are organized during the high season only and, unlike traditional Mallorcan markets, they are held every day.

Hippy bazaar in San Francesc on Formentera

FOOD

The Balearic Islands offer a number of unique food products that are specific to the region. The delicious *ensaimada* pastry, popular with tourists, is packed in distinctive octagonal boxes, making it easy to transport. Gourmets may be tempted by *sobrasada* – a spicy pork sausage produced in several varieties and used in many Balearic dishes. Strings of dried peppers, or olives prepared in a variety of ways, attract those who wish to bring back culinary souvenirs. All these products can be bought in markets and food stores. Shops that sell exclusively Balearic food are very attractive. The sheer number and variety of colourful products on display will tempt anyone to step inside.

The most popular alcohols produced on the islands include gin from Maó and herb liqueurs. You can taste the local gin in the Maó distillery *(see p96)*. Liqueurs are produced in a great number of varieties on all the islands and can be sampled in the shops that sell them. Balearic wines are also well worth trying. The best wines come from the Binissalem region on Mallorca, where a grand wine festival is held every year in September. There are two main wine producing regions in the Balearic Islands – Binissalem and Pla i Llevant, both on Mallorca. Wines that are especially worth sampling include those from the cellars of Jaume de Punitró, Marcià Batle, Vins Nadal, Herederos de Ribas, Pere Seda and Miguel Gelabert.

Shop selling local delicacies in Palma

SOUVENIRS

These days it can be difficult to buy genuine local handicrafts on the Balearic Islands. Sometimes you can find them in markets, but you may find they have been largely replaced by factory-made articles that imitate handicrafts. These include ceramics decorated with traditional patterns, typical of the islands. The most characteristic pottery items – the *siurells* produced mainly on Mallorca – are colourful whistles in the shape of people or animals, painted in white, red and green. They can be bought in many places at the markets, in small shops and in large stores that sell Balearic pottery. Popular, but expensive, is the glassware produced by the three glassworks on Mallorca. At the Gordiola glassworks near Algaida you can witness the production process *(see p87)*. Equally popular are articles made of olive wood, such as bowls and mortars produced by the Olive-Art factory near Manacor.

Dried peppers

Also close to Manacor is a factory producing high-quality simulated pearls that can be bought in many souvenir shops, as well as in smart boutiques all over Europe *(see p81)*.

Among the most popular souvenirs are espadrilles (traditional footwear) from Ibiza. Souvenirs from Menorca include leather goods such as wallets, handbags, jackets and sandals. T-shirts and baseball caps with humorous slogans and pictures are also popular.

What to Buy in the Balearic Islands

The choice of souvenirs in the Balearic Islands is vast, but it can be difficult to find genuine local handicrafts among them. However, it is still possible to buy items from each of the islands that is characteristic of the place. In Mallorca, these include simulated pearls, glassware, dolls and wines from the Binissalem region; in Menorca – leather goods, textiles and local gin; in Ibiza – hippy souvenirs or club clothes.

Doll in regional costume

Ceramics

Ceramic items are among the most popular souvenirs. The variety of forms and designs is staggering. Many of those on offer have not actually been produced on the islands and it is best to buy from one of the local manufacturers.

Plate decorated with cobalt

Colourful plate

Condiment container

Glass

The high quality glassware produced on the Balearic Islands was once as popular as that made in Venice. To this day, the most popular articles of glassware are modelled on traditional designs.

"Gordioli" goblet

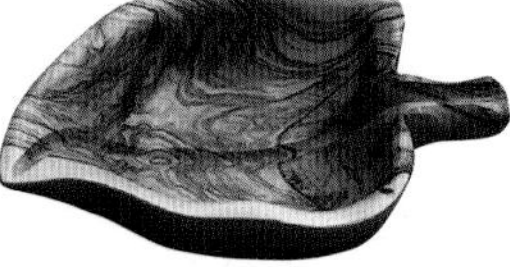
Leaf-shaped bowl

Pestle and mortar

Wooden Articles

Articles made of olive wood are very popular with visitors to the islands. They have a distinctive colour and are very durable. The choice is, however, limited to a few designs.

"Lafiore" pots

Sandals

Leather wallet

Leather Goods

Menorca is famous for its leather goods. The factory shops sell virtually everything that can be made of leather including wallets, coats and jackets. Many articles are made to order for large international companies.

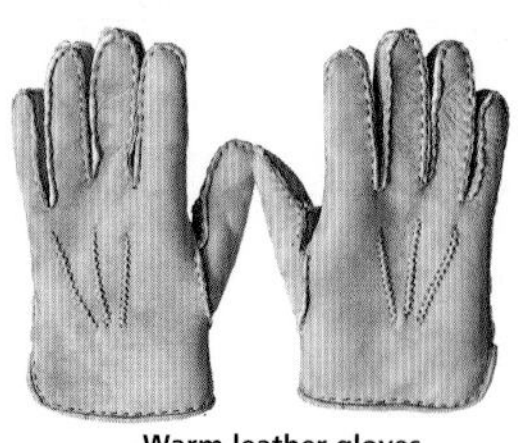
Warm leather gloves

Woman's handbag

Hippy Jewellery

A large number of hippy products sold in Ibiza and Formentera have been produced by a flourishing cottage industry, though less authentic products are beginning to dominate. Even so, it is still worth visiting these markets, if only for their atmosphere.

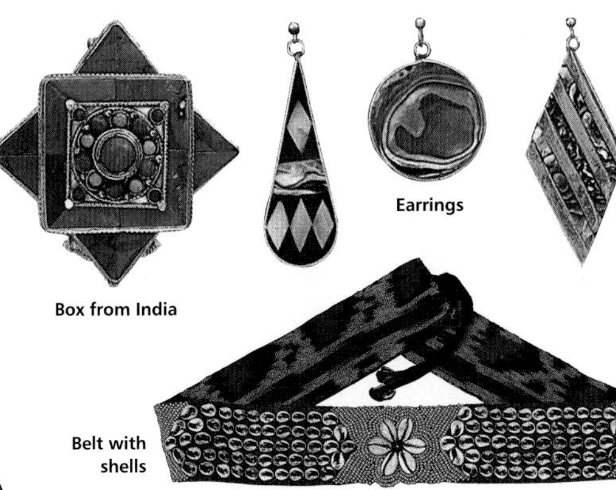

Earrings

Box from India

Belt with shells

Black pearl necklace

Ring

Simulated Pearls

Simulated pearls are Mallorca's signature item. Though expensive, every item comes with a certificate of authenticity. You can buy ready-made jewellery as well as single pearls that you can use to make your own necklace or bracelet.

Necklace of simulated pearls

Wickerwork

Wickerwork is very popular with visitors to the Balearics and wickerwork items are among the most genuine Balearic products. The baskets of various shapes and sizes are particularly attractive.

Beach basket

Straw hat

Clothes

Clothes, including T-shirts with a variety of slogans and original designs, such as the ones sold on Menorca with the "Ecológica de Menorca" sign, are also popular. Club clothes likewise make interesting souvenirs.

Cap with "Mallorca" inscription

Printed T-shirts

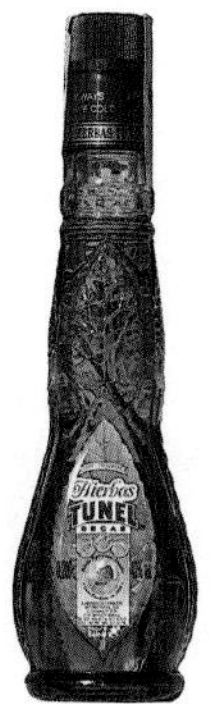

Herb liqueur

Almond liqueur

Alcohol

A large selection of alcoholic drinks is on offer. Each island produces its own herb liqueur (hierbas). *All adult visitors to Menorca might try the local gin. Connoisseurs will not miss the chance to try Mallorcan wines, particularly the best of them – the red wine from Binissalem, but also white and rosé varieties from the same vineyards.*

Local red wine

Handicrafts in the Balearic Islands

A hippy earring

Ceramics are extremely popular in the Balearic Islands, just as in the rest of Spain. One of the most characteristic items of Mallorcan handicrafts is the *siurell* – a statuette-whistle that is made of painted clay. Sa Cabaneta, one of the Mallorcan parishes, is known as "clay country" due to the large number of pottery workshops that can be found there. Weaving and embroidery are also very popular and leather goods are plentiful, especially in Menorca. Mallorca has become famous for its production of simulated pearls.

Ceramic lamps on display in one of Mallorca's markets

CERAMICS

The art of making pottery on the Balearic Islands goes back thousands of years. It was greatly influenced by the art of the Moors, who ruled the archipelago for several centuries.

The item you are most likely to see is the *siurell*, a statuette-whistle made of clay and painted white, with green and red decorations. It usually depicts a man sitting on a donkey or playing a guitar; but it can also be styled as a bull, a dog, a peacock, a rooster or even the devil. The origin of the *siurell* is uncertain; already known in Moorish times, it was most likely inherited from the Phoenicians. The Spanish artist Joan Miró was particularly taken with these little toy whistles and drew inspiration from them. The *siurell* was once a highly important item; a man would hand it to the lady of his choice – if she blew on it, it meant "yes", but if she put it aside, it meant that the suitor had been rejected. The Romeria de Sant Marçal (*see p27*), a lively fair held at the end of June in Sa Cabaneta, is dedicated to these clay whistles.

Original ceramic products with distinctive yellow and green glazing are produced in Felanitx in Mallorca. At the busy Sunday market in this small town, you can also purchase blue-and-white bowls and jugs, decorated with delicate floral or arabesque motifs.

In Pòrtol, near the small town of Santa Maria del Camí, there are a few remaining potters who produce traditional bulging pots made of red clay *(ollas)* and shallow bowls *(greixoneras)*.

In Ibiza, in the small village of Sant Rafael situated on the route from Eivissa to Sant Antoni de Portmany, there are many pottery workshops producing beautiful bowls, vases and jugs based on ancient Carthaginian designs. Ceramic copies of the terracotta figurines dating from the Punic era (3rd century BC) displayed in archaeological museums in Eivissa – particularly busts of women – are popular as souvenirs from Ibiza.

GLASSWARE

The earliest glass vessels found on the Balearic Islands date as far back as Roman times. In the 16th century, glassware from Mallorca competed successfully with popular Venetian products. Even today, the best-selling products tend to be copies of ancient designs.

Traditional condiment pot

There are three factories of artistic and household glass in Mallorca; the best known of these is the Can Gordiola glass museum near Algaida, on the road from Palma to Manacor. The oldest glass-works on the island, it has been run by the same family since 1719. Here, it is possible for visitors to watch the

Clay pot production in a pottery workshop

glassblowers at work. Using long, thin pipes they can produce a variety of objects, from lovely small trinkets to large vases.

SIMULATED PEARLS

The production method for simulated pearls was patented in 1925 by Eduard Heusch, a German engineer. The recipe for producing a thin bead-coating layer is kept secret to this day, for obvious reasons, though it is said to contain fish scales mixed with resin.

Three factories in Manacor and Montuïri produce these simulated pearls, which are of good quality and, to the untrained eye, virtually impossible to distinguish from the real thing.

The beads are immersed repeatedly in a liquid compound, which imitates the natural process of pearl production. Afterwards, each pearl is polished by hand and weighed. The production process can be seen during a visit to the factory. Be aware that the factory shop sells them at much lower prices than those charged by shops elsewhere.

Straw hat, popular in the islands

WOOD AND WICKER PRODUCTS

Artifacts made of olive wood are very popular in the Balearic Islands and can be distinguished by their rich colour and unusual grain. La Casa del Olivio, a shop based in Palma, produces a number of basic household goods, such as bowls and mortars, as well as ornamental items and souvenirs.

The dwarf palm, or palmito, grows on many of the islands' mountain slopes. Its leaves are used, particularly in Artà, to weave chair seats, baskets, bags and the soles of the *espadrille* or *alpargatas*. In addition to this, local craftsmen produce a wide variety of bags and baskets woven from strong grass or jute, and hats that are popular with the locals and tourists alike.

Inside the Gordiola glass factory in Mallorca

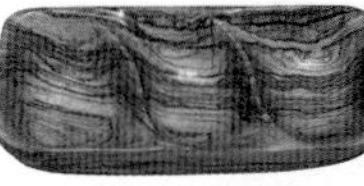

An olive wood household bowl

OTHER LOCAL PRODUCTS

The Balearic Islands, and Menorca in particular, are famous for their production of excellent footwear. In Menorca the centre of the leather industry is Ferreries. Here, you can buy relatively inexpensive shoes, bags and leather clothes. It is worth taking a closer look at some of the sandal designs, which are unique to this island. In Mallorca the cheapest place to buy leather products is Inca.

Weaving and embroidery have a long local history. The traditional *robes de llengues* – print-decorated heavy linen fabrics – are often used to decorate Mallorcan homes, even today. They can be used for curtains and bedspreads as well as wall linings and furniture upholstery.

Clothes that imitate hippy fashions from the 1960s are still very much in vogue, and designs produced in this style continue to create a stir at the annual fashion shows. The three-day fashion show Moda Ad Lib is held in June, at Passeig de Vara de Rey, in Eivissa, Ibiza. Clothes that are shown here can later be bought in Eivissa's fashionable boutiques – at high prices.

Traditional gold and silver jewellery has been produced by local craftsmen on the Balearic Islands for centuries. Although less fashionable now, it is still used as an addition to folk costumes. Similar to the enduringly popular fashion in clothing, the designs of gold jewellery are inspired largely by hippy culture. Silver and metal items can be bought at "hippy markets", particularly in Ibiza and Formentera.

A cobbler at work

ENTERTAINMENT IN THE BALEARIC ISLANDS

Ibiza is listed in the *Guinness Book of Records* as the world's most entertaining place. This is no doubt due to the number of nightclubs, bars and pubs packed into this small island. The other islands of the archipelago have plenty of entertainment on offer, however, and there are many clubs, concerts and shows to choose from.

Horsedrawn cab in Palma

The range of entertainment on available to visitors is much wider than this, however. At the height of the holiday season, the larger resorts open up casinos, concert halls, cinemas and theatres and also organize folklore, theatre and cinema festivals. On top of this, and perfect for the kids, are the many aquaparks and other amusement parks to enjoy.

Shelves of the many liqueurs on offer in a shop

INFORMATION

It is a good idea to find out what is on offer before you leave as local tourist information offices may not always have details of forthcoming cultural events, particularly if they are held in another town. The Internet has a wealth of information on concerts, amusement parks and festivals and may sometimes include first-hand accounts of particular attractions.

Current details may often be found in the local press. Keep your eyes peeled, too, as many events are advertised on posters. Other valuable sources on what is happening are hotel reception areas.

BOOKING TICKETS

Tickets to some of the major nightclubs in Ibiza, such as Amnesia and Privilege, can be booked before you go on holiday, over the Internet or by telephone. It is also advisable to book early for any guided tours. In this case, you must know the organizer's telephone number or go to the local office. The same applies to concerts and music festivals. Hotel receptions will often be happy to do the booking for you. The earlier you book, the better your chances of getting a ticket. In many cases, tickets are only sold a short time in advance. Admission to many open-air events is often free.

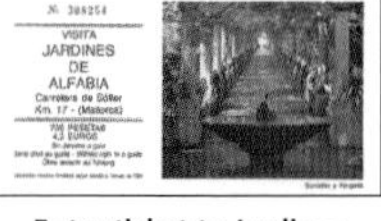

Entry ticket to Jardines d'Alfàbia

NIGHTLIFE

Nightlife flourishes on the islands. Ibiza is particularly famous for it, but Mallorca also has many nightclubs *(discotecas)*. The clubs usually open their doors between midnight and 1am and many remain open all night. Admission to the most famous and fashionable places in Ibiza and Mallorca is relatively expensive. Lesser known venues tempt guests in with various gimmicks or free drinks. Earlier in the evening you can visit bars and pubs.

For those people who do not fancy the nightclubs, there are also casinos and many venues that put on artistic programmes.

MUSIC AND THEATRE

Despite appearances, the cultural life on the Balearic Islands is not limited to pubs, clubs and religious festivals. Classical music, opera and theatre are all very popular with the locals, particularly on Mallorca and Menorca. Theatres and opera houses

Tourist information office in Sant Antoni de Portmany, Ibiza

Partygoers enjoying themselves at Amnesia, Ibiza

can be found in many places. Their repertoire includes mainly modern Spanish drama and there are frequent performances by visiting theatre and opera companies from mainland Spain, as well as from other European countries including Germany, Italy and the UK.

The leading theatres are the **Teatre Principal** in Palma and **Teatre Principal de Maó** in Menorca. During the summer season, when the theatres close, theatre festivals come to take their place. These are mostly international events. Many of these include theatre workshops, which offer plenty of opportunities for audience participation.

Lovers of classical music will also find something on the islands. World-class musicians and orchestras frequently appear in the concert halls, such as the Auditórium de Palma de Mallorca. In addition, many music festivals and concerts are organized during the holiday season. In Menorca, there are three major festivals during the summer season – in Maó, Ciutadella and Fornells. Festivals taking place between June and September are held in concert halls, theatres and churches. Among the important musical events in Mallorca are the classical music festivals held in Palma (Feb–Mar) and the Chopin Festival in Valldemossa (Aug). Other popular events include international festivals of music in Deià and Pollença during the summer.

POPULAR MUSIC

Lovers of jazz and rock have no cause to complain in the Balearic Islands, particularly during the summer season. Occasionally, top rock groups or pop stars make an appearance. You should enquire about dates and venues in the local tourist information office or look up events in the local press. There are also numerous local regular events, such as a Rock 'n' Roll Festival in Maria de la Salut, in Mallorca, while cities such as Palma have many live music venues.

Some events have become a permanent fixture in the islands' cultural calendar. Anyone who loves jazz may know about Sant Climent in Menorca. Twice a week during the summer months and less frequently during the winter season, "jam sessions" are held here. Another extremely popular event in Mallorca is the International Jazz Festival held every year during May and June, in Cala d'Or.

Sign for a horse show

FIESTAS

When visiting the islands, it is worth including one of the fiestas in your itinerary. These are held not only as celebrations of patron saints, but may also commemorate historic events or celebrate important harvests (such as the grape harvest festival in Binissalem and the melon festival in Vilafranca de Bonany). These colourful, bustling celebrations, accompanied by music, dancing and feasting, can continue for several days during which time the town's business life grinds to a halt as the local population joins in the fun.

Street processions with people dressed in regional costumes or their Sunday best are often spiced up by the *dimonis* – devils that personify evil, which are defeated in the end. This happens during the fiestas in Montuïri and Santa Margalida. An important element of many fiestas are the horse races and shows. The most interesting of these are held during the Sant Joan fiesta in Ciutadella (Jun). The majority of fiestas, as well as other cultural and entertainment events, are held during the summer months, at the peak of the holiday season. Important events taking place outside the tourist season include the Procession of the Three Magi (Jan), the carnival (Feb) and the celebrations associated with Holy Week.

Participants in a colourful fiesta

AMUSEMENT PARKS

No visit to the Balearic Islands would be complete without a trip to a water-park or theme park, especially if you have children. Marineland in Mallorca provides the opportunity to see the performing dolphins and sea lions and look at the colourful fish in the aquarium, while the thrills and spills of the water-parks can be great fun, especially when it is hot.

During the high season there are also many funfairs with carousels and circus troupes with acrobats and magicians. Magnificent horse shows are staged in Menorca.

Another form of entertainment in the islands is afforded by a visit to one of the numerous caves, especially in Mallorca. Some of these have their own light and music shows.

MUSEUMS

The islands' museums are sometimes overlooked since they are not set up as tourist attractions. Some of the collections are quite modest, presenting the history of the town or region and its associated folklore. However, there are museums on the islands that are definitely worth visiting. These include the Museu de Mallorca in Palma *(see pp52–3)*, which displays works of art from prehistoric times up to the present day, illustrating the cultural development of the island. The Museu de Menorca in Maó is of a similar character, but its collection is more limited in its scope *(see p96)*.

Another worthwhile museum is the Museu de la Natura de Menorca, found in Ferreries *(see p106)*. It has a modern display showing all that is typical of the island's natural environment, culture and traditions. It is a nice idea to pop in here before you start exploring the island.

Children will probably be more interested in visiting the Waxwork Museum in Binissalem, in Mallorca. Here, they will be able to see wax likenesses of a number of famous people who are in one way or another associated with the island.

Logo of Menorca's natural history museum

Glass-bottomed boat ride

EXCURSIONS

Those looking for an active holiday will have no trouble finding plenty of outlets able to provide details of walking or cycling trails, and even organize excursions. For anyone looking for a less strenuous excursion, there are plenty of coach tours. It is, of course, possible to hire a car and drive to some of the most interesting places around the islands. You can also ask at tourist offices about guided tours. You might, however, bear in mind that some groups may contain a number of nationalities and you should be prepared to listen to a commentary in a variety of languages. Of all the tours and excursions on offer, possibly the most pleasant are boat cruises. These include glass-bottomed boat rides, and even submarine trips. The most pleasurable of these are sailing trips to remote little bays. This way it is possible to circumnavigate the whole of Ibiza or Menorca.

CHILDREN

The Spanish are famously fond of children, and kids are welcomed in restaurants, especially at lunchtimes.

In terms of attractions, Mallorca has the lion's share, with waterparks, dolphin shows, caves and long promenades for cycling. Fun shows, including regular mock pirate battles and jousting tournaments, are organized for the enjoyment of younger visitors. Out of season, there are visits by circuses and fairs to the islands and some of the larger clubs runs special youth afternoons at the weekends.

Although the other islands have fewer attractions, there is still plenty to keep children entertained. Menorca has pony rides and riding shows, for example, while Ibiza's beaches and all the associated seaside attractions, such as snorkelling, beach games and banana rides, will keep most children happily occupied for the duration of your holiday.

Slides in a water-park in Ibiza

DIRECTORY

NIGHTCLUBS

BCM
Avda S'Olivera, Magaluf. ***Tel*** *971 711 856.* **www**.bcm-planetdance.com
British-run entertainment complex – the biggest club on the island.

Menta
Avda Tucan, Alcúdia. ***Tel*** *971 891 972.*
Two dance floors, seven bars and an indoor pool.

Palladium Palace
C/Gaviotas 1, Peguera. ***Tel*** *971 686 557.*
A smaller club that gets packed at the weekends.

Tito's
Paseo Maritímo, Palma. ***Tel*** *971 730 017.* **www**.titosmallorca.com
Upmarket club with a cocktail bar and a great view of the bay from the club's glass elevator.

See pp120–21 for details of clubs on Ibiza.

THEATRES

Café Teatre Sans
C/Can Sanç 5, Palma, Mallorca. ***Tel*** *971 727 166.*

Centro Dramático di Marco
Patronato de asistencia Palmesana. C/Ramon Llull 11, Palma, Mallorca. ***Tel*** *971 726 008.*

Fundació Teatre Principal de Maó
C/Costa d'en Deià 40, Maó, Menorca. ***Tel*** *971 355 603.* **www**.teatremao.org
See p94 for further details.

Orfeó Maonès
C/de Gràcia 155, Maó, Menorca. ***Tel*** *971 363 942.*

Teatre De Vilafranca
Sant Martí 26, Vilafranca de Bonany, Mallorca. ***Tel*** *971 832 072.*

Teatre del Mar
Capitàn Ramonell Boix 90, "Es Molinar", Palma, Mallorca. ***Tel*** *971 248 400.*

Teatre Municipal de Manacor
Avda del Parc s/n, Manacor, Mallorca. ***Tel*** *971 554 549.*

Teatre Principal
Plaza Hospital 4, Palma, Mallorca. ***Tel*** *971 713 346.*
See p49 for further details.

MAJOR CONCERT HALLS

Auditori d'Alcúdia
Plaça de la Porta de Mallorca 3, Alcúdia, Mallorca. ***Tel*** *971 897 185.*

Auditórium de Palma de Mallorca
Paseo Marítimo 18, Palma, Mallorca. ***Tel*** *971 734 735.*

Auditórium Sa Màniga
C/Son Galta 4, Cala Millor, Mallorca. ***Tel*** *971 587 373.*

Centro Cultural Andratx
C/Estanyera, Andratx, Mallorca. ***Tel*** *971 137 770.*

SHOWS

Casino Mallorca
Urb Sol de Mallorca s/n, Magaluf, Mallorca. ***Tel*** *971 130 000/012.* **www**.casinodemallorca.com

Club Escola Menorquína
Ctra Ferreries–Cala Galdana, Menorca. ***Tel*** *971 155 059/497.*

Es Foguero
Crta. Palma–Santanyi, 11 km (6 miles), Mallorca. ***Tel*** *971 265 260.* **www**.esfoguero.com
Flamenco, ballet & cabaret.

Pirates Adventure Show
Magaluf, Mallorca. ***Tel*** *971 130 411.* **www**.piratesadventure.com

Son Amar
Ctra de Sóller, 10 km (6 miles), Palmañola, Mallorca. ***Tel*** *9007 12345 (free).* **www**.sonamar.com

Son Martorellet
Ctra Ferreries–Cala Galdana, 1.5 km (1 mile), Menorca. ***Tel*** *609 049 493 or 649 922 335.* **www**.sonmartorellet.com

AMUSEMENT PARKS

Acuario de Mallorca
C/Gambí 7, Porto Cristo, Mallorca. ***Tel*** *971 820 971.*

Aguamar
Playa d'en Bossa, Ibiza. ***Tel*** *971 396 790.*
May–Oct.

Aqua Center
Urb Los Delfines, Ciutadella, Menorca. ***Tel*** *971 388 705 or 971 388 251.* **www**.aquacenter-menorca.com

Aqualand El Arenal
Autopista Palma–S'Arenal, exit 13, Mallorca. ***Tel*** *971 440 000.* **www**.aqualand.es/elarenal/mallorca
One of the world's largest water-parks, which includes a mini-zoo.

Aqualand Magaluf
Ctra de Cala Figuera, Magaluf, Mallorca. ***Tel*** *971 130 811.* **www**.aqualand.es/magaluf/mallorca
Long-established water-park on the edge of town.

Aquarium Cap Blanc
Ctra De Cala Gració, Sant Antoni de Portmany, Ibiza. ***Tel*** *971 342 206.*

Auto-Safari – Cala Millor
Ctra Porto Cristo–Son Serva, 5 km (12 miles). ***Tel*** *971 810 909.*

Club Hipico Son Gual
Ctra Establiments–Puigpuñyent, 2 km (1 mile), Mallorca. ***Tel*** *971 798 578.*

Golf Fantasía
C/Tenis 3, Palma Nova–Calvià, Mallorca. ***Tel*** *971 135 040.* **www**.golf-fantasia.com
Crazy golf with a choice of three circuits.

Jumaica Tropical Park
Ctra Portocolom–Porto Cristo, Mallorca. ***Tel*** *971 833 355.*

Marineland
C/Gracillaso de la Vega 9, Costa d'en Blanes, Calvià, Mallorca. ***Tel*** *971 675 125.*
See p59 for further details.

Natura Parc
Santa Eugènia, Mallorca. ***Tel*** *971 144 078.* **www**.naturaparc.net

Safari-Zoo Reserva Africana
Sa Coma, Mallorca. ***Tel*** *971 810 909.* **www**.safari-zoo.com
See p80 for further details.

Western Water Park
Ctra Cala Figuera–Sa Porrassa 12–22, Mallorca. ***Tel*** *971 131 203.* **www**.westernpark.com

Xiqui Park
Joan Miró 3, Palma, Mallorca. ***Tel*** *971 283 888.*

HORSE RIDING

Calvià Pony Club
Finca Sa Punta, Calvià, Mallorca. ***Tel*** *609 646 248.* **www**.ponyclubcalvia.com
Special courses for children.

CRUISES

Barcos Azules
Passeig Es Travès 3, Port de Sóller, Mallorca. ***Tel*** *971 630 170.* **www**.barcosazules.com
Island boat trips.

Excursions a Cabrera
Colònia de Sant Jordi, Mallorca. ***Tel*** *971 649 034.*
See p85 for further details.

Nemo Submarines
Av. de Perevaquer, Magaluf, Mallorca. ***Tel*** *971 130 227. Two-hour exploration by submarine. Expensive.*

OUTDOOR ACTIVITIES

The warm climate and diversity of the landscape on the Balearics make them an excellent place for all types of sport. The most popular of these are, of course, water sports and you will find windsurfing, sailing and diving are all well catered for. Those looking for an activity holiday of this kind will have the chance to practise their favourite sports under professional supervision. Cycling, horseriding and golf are also popular in the islands and many travel bureaux and agents offer equipment hire, from yacht charter to bicycle rental. Some hotels also have their own facilities and can often hire out equipment.

Tourist trail signpost

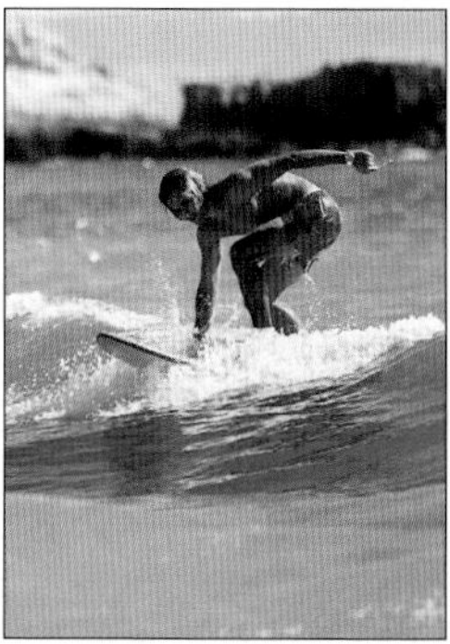

Surfer in Cala Major, in Mallorca

WINDSURFING

The conditions for windsurfing are not as impressive here as they are in the Canary Islands because the local winds are not strong enough for advanced surfers. As a consequence, the Balearic Islands are not popular with professionals, but this makes them a very good place for beginners to pick up some of the basic techniques.

Alhough the number of schools is rather limited, all of the islands have at least one school that teaches basic windsurfing and offers equipment hire. Surfing enthusiasts will also be able to find suitable spots in the Balearic Islands, however do not expect the "ultimate wave".

SAILING

Sailing is the most popular water sport in the Balearic Islands. Major international regattas include the King's Cup and the Princesa Sofia Trophy held in Mallorca. These are high-profile events and attract many of the world's leading sailors; King Juan Carlos is a frequent competitor. The Trofeo Conde Barcelona, held in August, features regattas with classic sailing boats. Almost every coastal town has its own marina and these are visited by yachts from all over Europe. Many vessels remain here for the winter.

Of course you do not have to own a yacht in order to cruise the Balearic Islands. Many firms offer sea-going vessels for charter. Smaller inshore catamarans can be rented by the hour on local beaches. You can also find many clubs or schools that are able to teach you the rudiments of sailing.

The popularity of sailing is so great that during the high season the marinas tend to be very busy, even though the mooring charges are extremely high. Some boats moor in sheltered bays, accessible only by sea.

FISHING

Despite the fact that the local waters teem with fish, fishing is not a popular sport here. A few agents organize trips, however. Further information is available from the Asociación Balear de Pesca *(see p185)*.

BEACH ACTIVITIES

During the high season, beaches employ lifeguards so it is safer to bathe and swim. Most beaches are sandy and situated in small bays. Sailing yachts and fishing boats sometimes anchor at the mouth of the bay and these are only a hazard if you swim out too close to them. The beaches can be busy and are sometimes short of space for beach sports. Nevertheless, a few of them have areas designated for volleyball, and even on busy beaches you can still find space to kick a ball around or play frisbee.

Catamarans on Es Pujols beach in Formentera

Beach volleyball, popular throughout the islands

DIVING AND SNORKELLING

The clear, clean coastal seawaters combined with the diversity of underwater flora and fauna create ideal conditions for diving and the sport is as popular as sailing throughout the islands. Every seaside resort has at least one diving centre *(centro de buceo)* where you can hire equipment, go for a test dive with an instructor or enrol on a course. A one-week stay would be sufficient to complete the beginners' course in scuba diving. The organizers ensure proper supervision by a qualified instructor and provide all the necessary equipment.

People hoping to dive in deeper waters must hold a proper diving certificate, such as PADI, CUC, CMAS/FEDAS or SSI. Holders of these certificates can join expeditions, some of which explore underwater caves. One of the best places to dive is the water around Cabrera, about 18 km (11 miles) off the coast of Mallorca. In 1991, Cabrera and its surrounding waters were awarded the status of a national park – the first park of its kind in Spain. Diving here requires the permission of the park ranger.

A much cheaper but equally exciting way of getting a glimpse of underwater life is to go snorkelling. A snorkeller can observe the wonders of the deep while floating on the surface of the water almost anywhere. Perhaps the most interesting places are the small bays rarely visited by tourists, where nature has hardly been touched by the hand of humans. A word of warning: snorkelling can be dangerous if you are distracted and collide with nearby rocks.

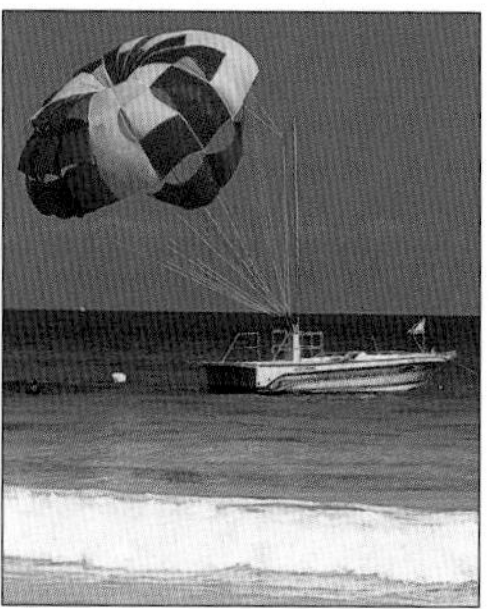

Motorboat with parachute waiting for the adventurous to paraglide

OTHER WATER SPORTS

Other water sports that are popular with visitors include taking out a high-speed water-bike or paragliding. Paragliding behind motor-boats (similar to hang-gliding) offers a wonderful way to see the islands. You can also take water-skiing lessons or (an easier option) bump along on a rubber raft, towed by a speeding boat.

Alternatively, visitors might like to join a sea trip by kayak. The most interesting routes go to the islands such as Conillera, near Ibiza, or Dragonera, off Mallorca. Equally exciting are trips to the waters of Formentor (Mallorca) and Cavalleria (Menorca).

HIKING

Hiking around the islands is becoming popular. The best area for hiking is probably the mountainous regions of Mallorca. The trails leading through the Serra de Tramuntana are difficult, however they offer a wonderful experience and breathtaking scenery. Trekking across the mountains along rough paths requires suitable footwear and clothing and this activity should not be undertaken alone as there are potential hazards such as sudden changes in the weather and unexpected ravines.

Menorca also offers many hiking trails. Most of these lead through the local nature reserves, of which the island has 18. The regions of S'Albufera, Cap de Favaritx and Cap de Cavalleria are truly magnificent areas for hiking. Many agents organize themed excursions, such as bird-watching trips. If setting off without a guide, you should make sure you have a good map, as many tourist trails are not signposted.

Snorkelling in shallow waters in Menorca

TWO-WHEELED SPORT

Cycling is very popular here, and renting a bicycle from one of the numerous hire firms is inexpensive. Cycling is an excellent way to explore the towns or get to a nearby beach. On the island of Formentera it is the most popular form of transport, along with the scooter.

More ambitious cyclists may want to undertake longer trips and all types of terrain can be encountered on the islands, from long, flat stretches of coast through to steep mountain roads. The islands also offer many interesting trails for mountain bikes, although the routes leading through the wild mountain terrains on Mallorca, or the coastal crags of Menorca, are best undertaken with a guide. Agents who organize these tours generally offer guides and equipment.

Climber on a rock face near Valldemossa, Mallorca

HORSE RIDING

Horse riding is another popular island sport and there are several riding centres on the islands that provide facilities for beginners as well as for advanced riders. The riding areas and trails are deliberately set amid beautiful scenery but you should not expect romantic gallops along the beach. All horse riding is done under the supervision of an instructor. There are many riding centres in Menorca and this is where they breed the famous Menorcan black horses that play such a prominent part in many fiestas. As well as riding lessons and outings, many centres also stage displays of horse breaking. For those who fancy a flutter, regular horse races are held on Mallorca and Ibiza.

Cyclists in a boulevard in Playa de Palma, Mallorca

CAVING

Caving and associated pursuits, such as canyoning and rock climbing, are still in their infancy in the Balearics but growing in popularity.

Only a handful of Mallorca's caves, including the Drac and Hams *(see p80)*, are open to all; most are reserved for experienced pot-holers. Adventurers can therefore explore the caves of the Tramuntana mountains and, on Menorca, try sea-cave diving as well. Organized caving expeditions offer anything from a half-day guided starter's cave trip, to day- and even week-long caving holidays, with all equipment provided.

The steep rocks along the coast of Mallorca and the inland regions are good places for rock climbing, too, providing various degrees of difficulty. Companies such as **Rock Sport Mallorca** offer walking, canyoning and rock climbing at beginner and advanced levels.

Diving Center Ciutadella offers sea-cave diving training at various sites around the Menorca. Cave exploration can be dangerous and is only recommended for trained people with the proper equipment. Before embarking on any adventure sport, check your insurance cover.

Sea-cave diving – growing in popularity

OTHER SPORTS

The warm climate and varied terrain mean that most sports can be enjoyed somewhere in the islands. Surprisingly, for such a dry region, there are even places that are good for canoeing, a very popular sport in Spain but one that requires a high level of fitness. When planning these expeditions you should seek advice from the organizers, who will not only inform you about the best routes but will also ensure suitable supervision.

The good aerodynamic conditions on Mallorca make the island suitable for hang-gliding and paragliding *(see p183)*. These sports are not popular in the other islands of the archipelago. The best lifting currents are found in the inland regions. This is where beginners' courses are held and where you can also meet experienced hang-gliders. The islands' weather conditions are also favourable for ballooning. A number of companies and some of the more exclusive hotels on the island can organize hot-air balloon flights.

DIRECTORY

BALLOONING

Mallorca Ballons
Tel *971 818 182.*
www.mallorcaballoons.com

CAVING

Diving Center Ciutadella
Ciutadella,
Menorca.
Tel *971 386 030.*
www.menorcatech.com

Rock Sport Mallorca
Tel *629 948 404.*
www.rocksportmallorca.com

DIVING

Big Blue
C/Marti Ros García 6,
Palma Nova,
Mallorca.
Tel *971 681 686.*
www.bigbluediving.net

Blue Water Scuba
Cala'n Bosch,
Menorca.
Tel *971 387 183.* **www**.bluewaterscuba.co.uk

Diving Center San Miguel
Port de Sant Miquel,
Ibiza.
Tel *971 334 539.*
www.divingcenter-sanmiguel.com

Octopus
Canonge Oliver 13,
Port de Sóller,
Mallorca.
Tel *971 633 133.*
www.octopus-mallorca.com

Skualo
Passeig Cap d'Es Toll 11,
Porto Cristo, Mallorca.
Tel *971 822 739.*
Fax *971 822 739.*
www.skualo.com

Sub Menorca
Club Elité Falcó,
Son Xoriguer.
Tel *971 387 834.*
Fax *971 387 809.*
www.submenorca.de

Vellmari Formentera Diving
Avda del Mediteraneo 90,
Puerto de la Savina,
Formentera.
Tel *971 322 105.*
www.vellmari.com

FISHING

Asociación Balear de Pesca
C/Rey Sancho 17, Palma,
Mallorca.
Tel *678 454 146.*

Federación Española de Pesca y Casting
Navas de Tolosa 3,
Madrid.
Tel *915 328 352.*
www.fepyc.es

HIKING

Dia Complert
Passeig Marítim 41,
Fornells,
Menorca.
Tel *609 670 996.*
www.diacomplert.com
@ info@diacomplert.com

Ecoibiza
Paseo Marítimo s/n,
Edificio Transat,
Eivissa,
Ibiza.
Tel *971 302 347.*
www.ecoibiza.com

Mallorca Activa
Son Pereto 9,
Palma,
Mallorca.
Tel *971 783 160.*
Fax *971 783 159.*
www.mallorcaactiva.com

HORSE RIDING

Ca'n Paulino
Ctra Vieja de Algaida s/n,
Llucmajor,
Mallorca.
Tel *971 121 002.*

Club Escola Menorquina
Ctra Cala Galdana,
Menorca.
Tel *971 155 059.*
Fax *971 373 497.*
www.showmenorca.com

Equus Balearic Mallorca
C/General Riera 3, Palma,
Mallorca.
Tel *971 571 909.*
Fax *971 756 195.*
http://equusbalearic.com

Pony Club Calvià
Finca Sa Punta, Calvià,
Mallorca.
Tel *609 646 248.*
www.ponyclubcalvia.com
Children's lessons only.

Rancho Ca'n Dog
Ctra Sant Joan,
14 km (9 miles),
Ibiza.
Tel *639 574 046.*

SAILING

Centro Wet Four Fun
Platja d'Es Pujols,
Formentera.
Tel *971 321 809.*
www.wet4fun.com

Club Náutico el Arenal
C/Roses s/n, S'Arenal,
Mallorca.
Tel *971 440 142.*
www.cnarenal.com

Club Náutico Ciutadella
Cami de Baix s/n,
Ciutadella, Menorca.
Tel *971 383 918.*
www.cncciutadella.com

Club Náutico Porto Cristo
C/Vela 29, Porto Cristo,
Mallorca.
Tel *971 821 253.*
www.cnportocristo.com

Club Náutico Sant Antoni
Paseo Marítimo s/n,
Sant Antoni de Portmany,
Ibiza.
Tel *971 340 645.*
www.nauticsantantoni.com

Escuela Balear de Náutica
C/Aragón 28 bajos,
Palma,
Mallorca.
Tel *971 909 060.*
www.escueladenautica.com

Real Club Náutico de Palma
Muelle de Sant Pere s/n,
Palma,
Mallorca.
Tel *971 726 848.*
www.realclubnauticopalma.com

WINDSURFING

Cesar's Watersports
Playa S'Arganassa,
Santa Eulalia del Rio,
Ibiza.
Tel *971 330 919* or
670 629 961 (mobile).
www.watersportscesars.com

Club Náutico Sa Ràpita
Explanada del puerto s/n,
Sa Ràpita,
Mallorca.
Tel *971 640 001.*
Fax *971 640 821.*
www.cnrapita.com

Windsurf Fornells
Bahia Fornells,
Menorca.
Tel *971 188 150.*
Fax *971 376 458.*
www.windfornells.com
@ wfornells@excellence.es

Golf in the Balearics

Golf is a relative newcomer in the Balearics, but it is catching up fast, with a growing number of modern and environmentally sensitive golf courses on Mallorca, Menorca and Ibiza. Blessed with a mild climate and boasting excellent facilities, these courses attract golfers all year round. The Federación Balear de Golf oversees a total of 25 courses on the three larger islands, as well as an ever-expanding range of competitions and trophies, training and practise facilities, and junior championships. Formentera has a ferry link that makes a round of golf on Ibiza a viable possibility.

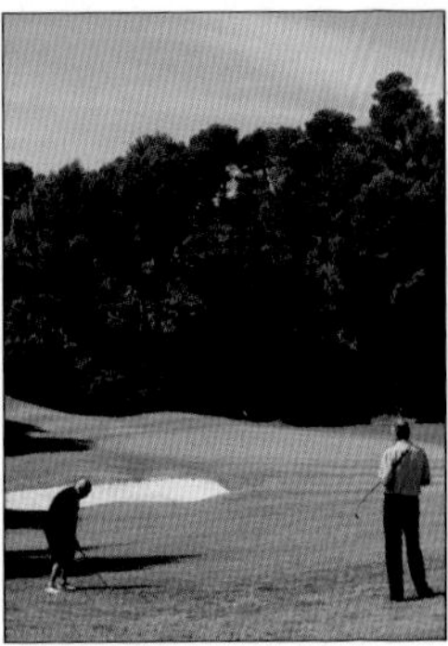

Teeing off on one of the many courses in the Balearic Islands

GENERAL INFORMATION

The Balearic Islands' golf culture is just over 40 years old, which means that courses have been designed to meet the demands of the modern golfer. They are also mindful of the fact that golfers are here for a holiday. Consequently, in addition to training and activities (some organize tournaments, for example), all courses offer extensive leisure amenities – clubhouses, restaurants, bars and shops.

Spain's proactive attitude towards the disabled has also seen the Balearics' disabled sports council **FEBED** (Federació Balear d'Esports per a Persones amb Discapacitat) active in promoting access, facillities, training and tournaments for disabled golfers at the **Real Golf de Bendinat** course in Mallorca.

There are golf tournaments every week of the golf year, although the most important date is the Baleares Doubles, held at Mallorca's **Golf Santa Ponsa II** course in June.

Green fees range from 50 to 150 euros a day, depending on the course and the season. Many clubs and holiday agencies offer discounts on fees and equipment hire. All of the golf courses included in the directory listings are recommended by the **Federación Balear de Golf**.

MALLORCA

The first-ever golf course in Spain opened on Gran Canaria in the Canary Islands only in 1891, some 200 years after St Andrews in Scotland. The first golf course in the Balearics was the **Golf Son Vida**, opened in 1964 a few kilometres outside Palma, in an idyllic valley setting with views of the sea and the Serra de Tramuntana mountains.

Most Balearic golf courses offer extensive and modern facilities, in addition to advanced grounds-maintenance technology. Already considered one of the key golf destinations in Europe, Mallorca is drawing leading course design architects such as Robert Trent Jones Jr, Bradford Benz, Falco Nardi and José Gancedo.

Beautiful views across Bahia de Alcúdia from Golf Alcanada

In 1967, Son Vida was followed by the **Golf Son Servera** course, designed by John Harris, near Artá. It was another ten years before the next golf course opened; the first of the (now three) **Golf Santa Ponsa** courses, designed by Falco Nardi, is still the largest on the island. It was followed in 1978 by another John Harris course, **Golf de Poniente**, still regarded as one of the toughest on Mallorca. Laid out among pine and olive groves, the par-72 Poniente has 18 holes and a number of "character-building" bunkers planted along its *recorrido* (course).

The 1980s and '90s saw another 23 courses open in quick succession in the Balearic Islands – and there are more planned: at least nine more courses are due to open during the next couple of years. Perhaps the ultimate so far is the exclusive **Golf Son Muntaner**, opened in 2000 and winner of two awards for sensitive ecological course management. **Golf Son Termens** has also been praised for its sympathetic approach to pre-existing landscape in its planning.

Most courses cater to all levels of player ability, although a few are designed to put even the most experienced enthusiast through their paces. **Golf de Pollença**, for example, integrated among ancient olive groves on a gentle hill overlooking the Bahia de Pollença, admits that "none of the holes is easy", and deems most to be suitable for mid- to high-experience players and professionals. The Robert Trent Jones Jr-designed **Golf Alcanada**, opened in 2003, is blessed with sea views of the splendid Bahia de Alcúdia from every hole, although players are advised to beware the 58 bunkers Jones has included in the design of this idyllic but testing course. **Golf de Andratx** has declared each of its holes a *reto*, or challenge, while the course at **Golf de Canyamel** is still considered the toughest on the island.

Landscape and climate make Mallorca an ideal setting for golf. It is impossible to say which golf course boasts the most impressive architecture, although Son Muntaner is the most exquisitely manicured. **Golf de Capdepera** is set in a lush valley surrounded by scenic mountains, while the Poniente is set among mature pine and olive woodlands.

The most striking course is **Pula Golf**, whose grounds, located in an old country estate, are shared with some of the most important Talayot structures on the island.

MENORCA

Menorca and Ibiza are still a considerable way behind Mallorca, however it is only a matter of time until they catch up. Menorca's main course, **Golf Son Parc**, is an unusual course with a 69 par and an ingenious course by Dave Thomas that requires strategic thinking to negotiate rocky bunkers, several lakes, reed beds and, not least, a resident colony of peacocks.

IBIZA

The only golf course on the island of Ibiza, **Golf de Ibiza** is something of an oddity. The old Roca Lisa nine-hole course has now been absorbed into the larger, neighbouring Golf de Ibiza, with a new 18-hole course, giving it a 27-hole total. The shorter course is said to be the easier terrain; however, all 27 holes are still described as difficult.

The challenging course of Golf de Ibiza

DIRECTORY

GENERAL INFORMATION

Federación Balear de Golf
Avda Jaume III 17, Entresuelo, Despachos J&K, 07012 Palma de Mallorca.
Tel *971 722 753.*
Fax *971 711 731.*
www.fbgolf.com

FEBED
Avda Joan Miró 327, 07015 Palma de Mallorca.
Tel *971 701 481.*
www.febed.es

MALLORCA

Golf in Mallorca
www.golfinmallorca.com

Golf Alcanada
Carretera del Faro s/n, 07400 Puerto de Alcúdia.
Tel *971 549 560.*
Fax *971 897 578.*
www.golf-alcanada.com

Golf de Andratx
Carrer Cromlec 5, 07160 Camp de Mar.
Tel *971 236 280.*
Fax *971 236 331.*
www.golfdeandratx.com

Golf de Canyamel
Avda dęs Cap Vermell s/n, 07589 Canyamel.
Tel *971 841 313.*
Fax *971 841 314.*
www.canyamelgolf.com

Golf de Capdepera
Carretera Artá–Capdepera, km 3.5, 07570 Artá.
Tel *971 818 500.*
Fax *971 818 193.*
www.golfcapdepera.com

Golf de Pollença
Carretera Palma–Pollença, km 49.3, 07460 Pollença.
Tel *971 533 216.*
Fax *971 533 265.*
www.golfpollensa.com

Golf de Poniente
Carretera Cala Figuera s/n, 07182 Magalluf.
Tel *971 130 148.*
Fax *971 130 176.*
www.ponientegolf.com

Golf Santa Ponsa
Urbanización Santa Ponça, 07184 Calvià.
Tel *971 690 211.*
Fax *971 693 364.*
www.habitatgolf.es

Golf Santa Ponsa II
Urbanización Santa Ponça, 07180 Calvià.
Tel *971 232 531.*
Fax *971 237 041.*
www.habitatgolf.es

Golf Son Muntaner
Urbanización Son Vida, 07013 Palma.
Tel *971 783 030.*
Fax *971 783 031.*
www.sonmuntanergolf.com

Golf Son Servera
Urbanización Costa de los Pinos, 07550 Son Servera.
Tel *971 840 096.*
Fax *971 840 160.*
www.golfsonservera.com

Golf Son Termens
Carretera S'Esglaieta, km 10, 07110 Bunyola.
Tel *971 617 862.*
Fax *971 617 895.*
www.golfsontermens.es

Golf Son Vida
Urbanización Son Vida, 07013 Palma.
Tel *971 791 210.*
Fax *971 791 127.*
www.sonvidagolf.com

Pula Golf
Carretera Son Servera–Capdepera, km 3, 07550 Son Servera.
Tel *971 817 034.*
Fax *971 817 035.*
www.pulagolf.com

Real Golf de Bendinat
C/Campoamor s/n, Urb Bendinat, 07015 Calviá.
Tel *971 405 200.*
Fax *971 700 786.*
www.realgolfbendinat.com

MENORCA

Golf Son Parc
Urbanización Son Parc s/n, 07740 Es Mercadal, Menorca.
Tel *971 359 059.*
Fax *971 359 591.*
www.golfsonparc.com

IBIZA

Golf de Ibiza
Carretera Jesús a Cala Llonga s/n, 07840 Santa Eulària des Riu.
Tel *971 196 059.*
Fax *971 196 051.*
www.golfibiza.com

el Pato
Bar Waikiki

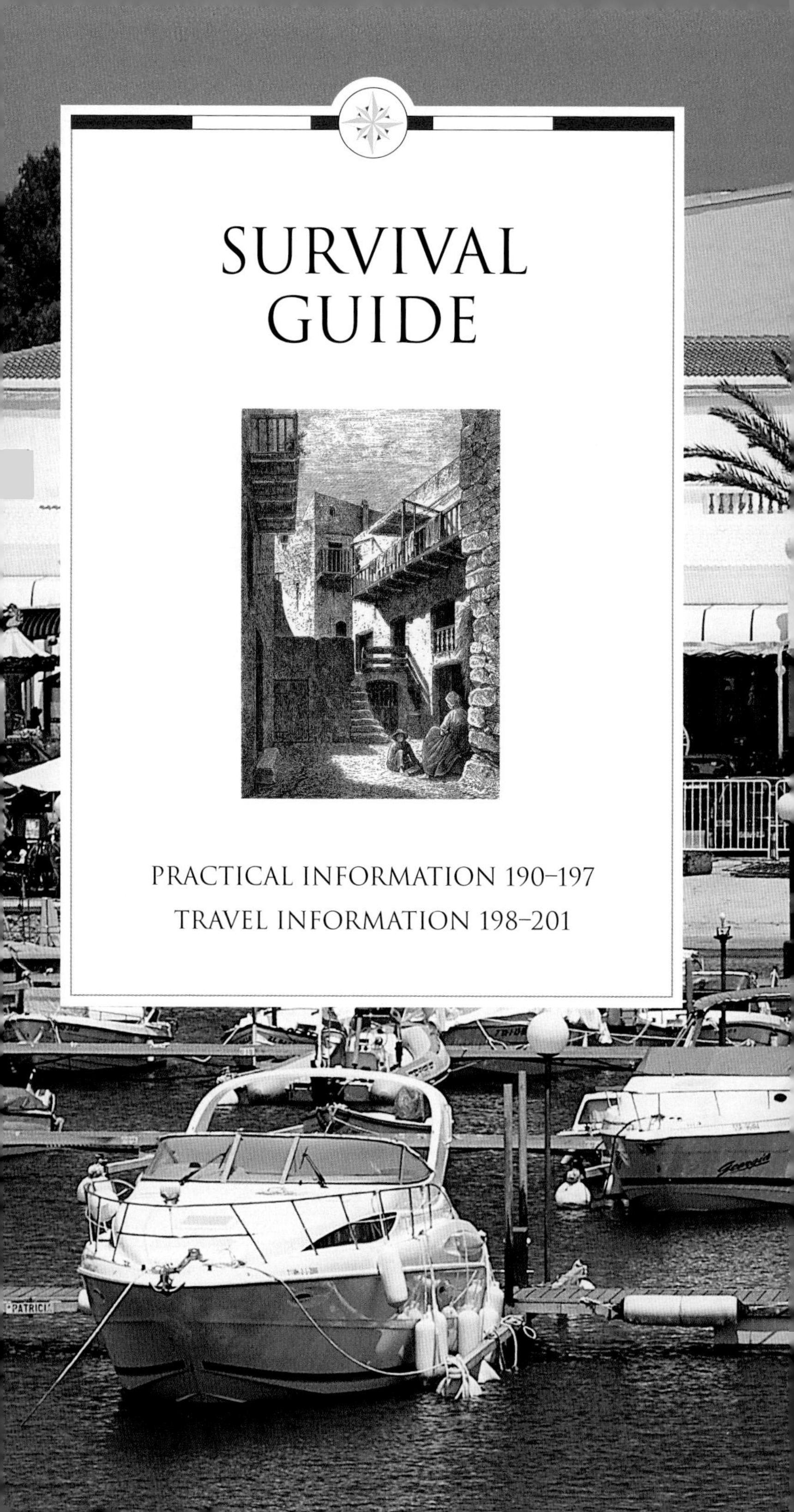

SURVIVAL GUIDE

PRACTICAL INFORMATION

The Balearic Islands are one of Europe's most popular holiday destinations. The islands have invested heavily in tourism and are geared up to receive multitudes of visitors. Hotel and catering facilities are extensive and there are plenty of attractions for the whole family to enjoy. In general, the islands are safe for visitors, although as with any other busy resort destination, holidaymakers are vulnerable to crimes such as bag-snatching. Such crimes can be avoided if you take sensible precautions. A well-developed information service, especially on the Internet, makes researching and planning a trip here a relatively straightforward business. During the peak period tour operators tend to snap up the available accommodation, but outside the summer season it is fairly easy to book a room in advance.

Tourist information sign

WHEN TO VISIT

Each season has something to offer. Nevertheless, the tourist season is at its busiest from July until September. It peaks in August, which coincides with the hottest weather on the islands. The hotels, bars and restaurants fill up, beaches are full of sun-lovers and the clubs are crowded. At the height of the season you are more likely to hear German or English being spoken than Spanish or Catalan.

Anyone who dislikes crowds should plan their visit for the period before the high season or when things begin to quieten down. In May, June, late September and early October, the weather is still warm enough for sunbathing. Springtime is between January and April. This is the best time for hiking as the flowers are in bloom although there can be heavy rain and storms at this time of year. The islands are quietest during the autumn months and December.

West End in Sant Antoni de Portmany, Ibiza

VISAS

Regulations covering admission to the Balearic Islands are the same as for the rest of Spain. Nationals of all the European Union member states do not require a visa to enter the Balearic Islands. People from other non-EU countries including Australia, Canada, Ireland, Israel, Japan, New Zealand and the USA are likewise not required to obtain a visa before entry for tourist visits of up to 90 days. If in doubt, you should contact the Spanish Embassy or seek advice from a travel agent. Anyone who does require a visa must apply in person at the consulate in their own country.

Strolling through Ciutadella, Menorca

CUSTOMS REGULATIONS

Customs regulations state in detail the limits on goods imported to and exported from the Balearic Islands. Such information may be obtained from Spanish Embassies and travel agents. Specific customs queries may be referred to the *Departamento de Aduanas e Impuestos Especiales* (Customs and Excise Department) in Madrid. Remember that only adults are entitled to export alcohol and cigarettes in the quantities allowed by the regulations.

Nationals of non-EU countries may apply for VAT refunds on goods purchased in any of the islands' shops bearing the sign "Duty Free for Tourists". The refund is worked out on the basis of the *formulari*, stamped by the Customs Officer at the point of departure. The refund can be claimed at the airport, at any branch of Banco Exterior, or on returning home, by post or via bank transfer.

◁ The marina in Cala d'en Bosch harbour, Menorca

LANGUAGE

The official joint language of the Balearic Islands is Spanish (Castilian). For many locals, however, the everyday language is Catalan. This bilingual culture can be felt when using local maps, where the names of places may be given in one or the other language. Catalan, in its turn, is divided into variants specific to each of the islands. In Mallorca it is known as *Mallorquín*, in Menorca as *Menorquín* and in Ibiza as *Eivissenc*.

During Franco's regime Catalan was banned and you risked a prison sentence if you were caught speaking it. Nevertheless, the local population has never abandoned its use and learning a few courtesy phrases in Catalan is a good way to win over the locals.

In tourist areas English and German are readily understood. Information signs and restaurant menus are generally multilingual. Greater problems with communication may be experienced away from the busiest areas. But even in the provinces, increasing numbers of people can speak at least one major European language as well as Spanish.

TOURIST INFORMATION

You will find Tourist Information offices *(Informació turística)* in all of the larger towns and resorts. These offer free maps and information packs; they also have details of current cultural events, entertainment and available accommodation. However, the information they provide may be somewhat general in nature and it is usually limited to the town where the tourist office is located or to its immediate vicinity. If you want to go on an organised hike or cruise it is best to enquire with the agent who organizes them *(see p181)*.

Horse-cab ride in Palma, Mallorca

A valuable source of information is the Internet. Individual islands, towns, tourist offices, hotels, car hire firms and museums all have their own websites *(see p193)*. They usually include photographs with text written in several languages. It is therefore much simpler to do your research before leaving home, than once you are already there. While using websites you should check when they were last updated because some may quote last year's prices. The best websites are those which are run by the provincial government of the Balearic Islands and the Tourism Promotion Department "Ibatur" *(Institut Balear del Turisme)*.

Signposts on Menorca

YOUTHS/STUDENTS

The Balearics are an ideal destination for young holidaymakers. The fine weather, great beaches and clubs attract thousands of young people from all over Europe. Some also come in search of seasonal employment, combining work with pleasure. Holders of the International Student Identity Card (ISIC) and the Euro under-26 card are entitled to many benefits when visiting the Balearic Islands.

They can get discounts on ferry travel, entrance charges to museums and galleries and tickets to some of the other tourist attractions. Some travel agents offer cheap flights to cardholders.

CHILDREN

As with much of Europe, children are welcome in most places except the big clubs, which of course, have age restrictions for obvious reasons. Most hotels can provide cots, some have all-day care, babysitting and special entertainment for youngsters. It is nevertheless worth checking in advance what facilities are available at any given hotel.

Restaurants in hotels and in towns are also good at providing for the needs of children. They have high-chairs and have special menus for children. When hiring a car, you should have no problem getting a child seat.

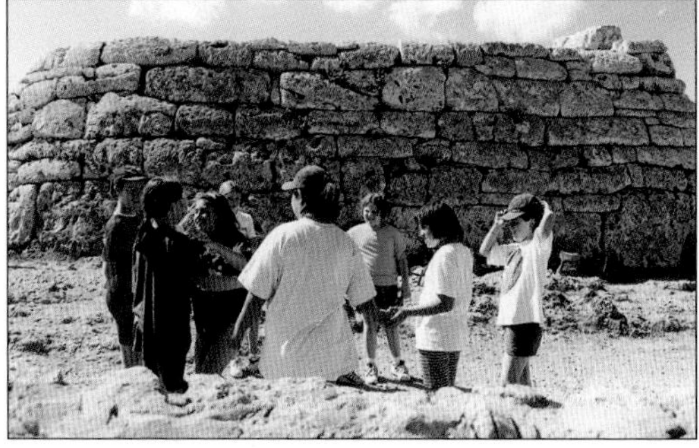

Children visiting one of Menorca's historic sights

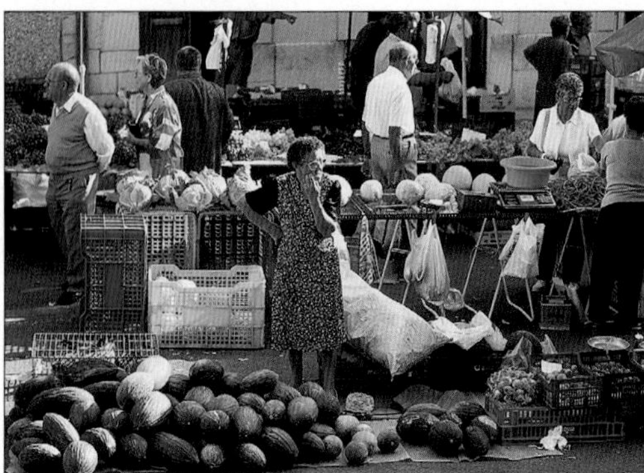

Market in Inca, Mallorca, with local produce

FACILITIES FOR THE DISABLED

The Balearic Islands are not particularly hospitable towards disabled people. Most hotels and restaurants are not adapted to serve guests who use wheelchairs. Many public places such as museums, galleries and shops are also inaccessible. When planning a visit, it is useful to use the services of an organization that deals with the problems of disabled people. **Turismo @ Polibea** is a good first stop for advice. Or you can approach **COCEMFE** (The Spanish Association for the Disabled). Another helpful agency is **Viajes 2000**.

Public transport also presents problems for people in wheelchairs and moving from town to town can be difficult. Disabled visitors to Mallorca are able to use the services of a specialized company, such as EMT Special Bus Service.

EXCURSIONS

Travel agents who sell holidays to the Balearic Islands usually also offer a choice of excursions for an additional fee. These are mostly day-long sightseeing trips, cruises, safaris, or visits to casinos, theatres or clubs. However, the prices you pay for these may be higher than those quoted by local tourist agents, and it is worth browsing through leaflets displayed at the hotel reception desk, or calling in at one or two local tourist offices to check what is on offer.

ISLAND TIME

All the islands are one hour ahead of Greenwich Mean Time (GMT), six hours ahead of Eastern Standard Time and nine hours ahead of Pacific Standard Time. The changeover to summer time, as with mainland Spain, takes place on the last Sunday in March. The clocks are put back on the last Sunday in September.

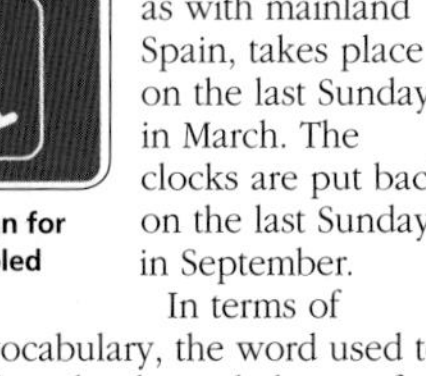

Parking sign for the disabled

In terms of vocabulary, the word used to describe the early hours after midnight is *la matinada*. *El mati* means morning (up to 1pm); late afternoon and evening are translated as *la tarda*, while night is referred to as *la nit*.

OPENING HOURS

Museums and historic monuments are generally open from Tuesday to Sunday, from 10am to 2pm and again from 4pm to 6pm. As with most offices, they close for public holidays and fiestas. Tourist information offices have similar opening hours.

Some sectors of business are reassessing their traditional opening hours. Big department stores, for example, and hypermarkets tend to forgo the siesta and are generally open until 9 or 10pm, though most still close on Sundays.

Theme parks and gardens are open seven days a week and they do not close for siesta. Most clubs open their doors late at night and stay open until morning. Many offices associated with tourism work shorter hours during the winter; some close altogether.

ELECTRICAL SUPPLY

The mains voltage on the islands is generally 220V AC. A three-tier standard travel convertor will enable you to use foreign equipment. Mains sockets require the European-style two-pin, round-pronged plugs.

RELIGION

Like the rest of Spain the Balearic Islands are Roman Catholic and religion plays an important part in community life. All religious festivals are lavishly celebrated and at these times the offices in town remain closed. Church opening hours vary. Some, like the cathedral church in

Tourists resting in Dalt Vila, in Eivissa

Eivissa, have set sightseeing hours. Others, including Palma cathedral, expect a donation or charge an admission fee. Many churches are open only for services, i.e. early mornings or evenings (6pm–9pm).

When planning to visit a particular religious building, you should check its opening hours in advance. Hotel reception desks and tourist information centres can sometimes provide details.

Church statue

TOILETS

Public toilets are few and far between, even in large towns. Bars and restaurants will usually allow non-guests to use their toilet facilities, but it is polite to ask permission first. When looking for a toilet you should ask for *servicios* or *aseos*. Doors leading to the men's toilets are marked *señores* or *caballeros*; to the ladies', *señoras* or *damas*. If there are no written signs, the doors will be marked with a picture of a male or female silhouette. (Sometimes you might see an amusing cartoon of a pipe-smoking man or a long-haired women with a fan.)

Special toilets designed for the disabled are a rarity on the islands, even in hotels, to say nothing of restaurants. In the future things should improve, however, as all newly-built hotels and restaurants must by law be fully accessible to travellers with disabilities.

Customers relaxing at a café in Plaza Mercal, Palma

DIRECTORY

EMBASSIES IN MAINLAND SPAIN

Australia
Paseo de la Castellana 259D, 28046 Madrid.
Tel *913 536 600.*
Fax *914 425 362.*

United Kingdom
Paseo de la Castellana 259D, 28046 Madrid.
Tel *917 146 300.*
Fax *917 146 301.*

CONSULATES

France
Mallorca: C/Mateu Enrique Lladó 2, 07002 Palma.
Tel *971 730 301/302.*
Fax *971 780 099.*

Menorca: C/Deià 30, 07702 Maó.
Tel *971 354 387.*
Fax *971 366 262.*

The Netherlands
Mallorca: C/San Miquel 36, 6th floor, 07002 Palma.
Tel *971 716 493.*
Fax *971 726 642.*

Menorca: C/Angel 12, 1st floor, 07703 Maó.
Tel *971 354 363.*
Fax *971 362 408.*

Germany
Mallorca: C/Porto de Pi 8, 3rd floor, 07015 Palma.
Tel *971 707 737.*
Fax *971 707 740.*

Menorca: C/Des Negres 32, 07703 Maó.
Tel *971 361 668, 971 365 812.*
Fax *971 369 012.*

Ibiza: C/D'Antoni Jaume 2, 2–9th floor, 07800 Eivissa.
Tel *971 315 763.*
Fax *971 315 763.*

United Kingdom
C/Convent dels Caputxins 4, Edif Orisba B, 40D, 07002 Palma de Mallorca.
Tel *971 712 445.*
Fax *971 717 520.*

Ibiza: Avda/ Isidoro Macabich 45, 1st floor, 07800 Eivissa.
Tel *971 301 818.*
Fax *971 301 972.*

ORGANIZATIONS FOR THE DISABLED

Turismo @ Polibea
Ronda de la Avutarda 3, 28043 Madrid.
Tel *917 595 372.*
www.polibea.com/turismo

Viajes INSERSO
Ginzo de Limia 58, 28029 Madrid. ***Tel*** *901 109 899.*
Pensioner travel.

Viajes 2000
C/Forners 7, 07006 Palma de Mallorca.
Tel *902 107 243.*
For blind travellers.

TOURIST INFORMATION

Mallorca
Plaça de la Reina 2, Palma.
Tel *971 173 990.*
Av. Argentina 1, Palma.
Tel *902 102 365.*

Menorca
Muelle de Llevant 5, Maó.
Tel *902 929 015.*
Fax *971 352 674.*
Plaça Catedral 5, Ciutadella.
Tel *902 929 015.*

Ibiza
Passeig Vara de Rey 1, Eivissa.
Tel *971 301 900.*
Fax *971 301 740.*
Passeig de ses Fonts. Sant Antoni de Portmany.
Tel *971 343 363.*

Formentera
Port de la Savina.
Tel *971 322 057.*

TOURIST INFORMATION WEBSITES

www.balearics.com
www.spain.info
www.balearweb.com
www.caib.es
www.visitbalears.com

Mallorca
www.mallorcaworld.net
www.infomallorca.net
www.a2zmallorca.com

Menorca
www.menorca.net
www.e-menorca.org
www.visitmenorca.com

Ibiza
www.ibizaes.com
www.ibiza.travel
www.ibiza-online.com
www.ibiza-spotlight.com
www.ibizaholidays.com

Formentera
www.formentera.es
www.guiaformentera.com
www.formenteraonline.net

Personal Security and Health

The crime level on the Balearic Islands is lower than in other regions of Europe. Thefts do occur in the most crowded places and even in hotels, but they can be minimized by taking sensible precautions. Credit cards and money are best hidden away. Never leave anything visible in your car when you park it. It is also advisable to avoid carrying excessive amounts of cash. When in need, you can always ask a policeman for help. Basic medical help and advice is usually provided by a pharmacist. Holders of valid medical insurance can receive treatment in public hospitals and clinics.

PERSONAL PROPERTY

Before travelling abroad it is wise to make sure you have adequate holiday insurance in order to protect yourself financially from the loss or theft of your property. Even so, it is also advisable to take common-sense precautions against loss or theft in the first place. Travellers' cheques are a far safer option than cash. If you have two credit cards, do not carry them together and make sure you keep a separate note of credit card cancellation numbers. Particular care should be exercised in crowded places such as airports and bus stations. Patrolling policemen often remind visitors about the need to be careful. There are also cases of tourists falling victim to theft when drunk. Never leave a bag or handbag unattended and do not put a purse or wallet on a tabletop in a café. The moment you discover a loss or theft, report it to the local police. The police will give you a *denuncia* (written statement), which you will need to make an insurance claim. If you have your passport lost or stolen, report it to your consulate.

SPANISH POLICE

The island police are friendly towards tourists. They are always ready to give advice and help. However, in case of any infringement of the law, they can be very firm and it is best not to try to argue with them.

As in the rest of Spain there are three types of police on the islands. The *Policía Nacional* (state police), the *Policía Municipal*, also known as the *Policía Local* (local police), and the *Guardia Civil* (National Guard). The force encountered most frequently by tourists is the *Policía Municipal*. Their officers are mostly encountered in small towns, and patrol the streets of crowded tourist resorts; they have a separate branch for traffic. The *Policía Nacional* wear brown uniforms. They deal with more serious incidents and matters concerning foreign visitors; they also guard various important buildings in large cities. The *Guardia Civil*, dressed in green uniforms, patrol rural areas. You can see them while travelling the roads and wild areas of the Balearic Islands.

Beach notice board in Cala Millor

State police car or *Policía Nacional*, frequently seen around the islands

Lifeguard on duty at Sant Elm beach, Mallorca

BEACHES

During the high season most beaches have lifeguards. Many beaches have swimming areas marked by buoys, although this does not mean that swimming outside these areas is prohibited. Many beaches have Red Cross stations. Notice boards at the entrance to the beach give information on facilities such as showers or wheelchair access *(see left)*. Many smaller beaches do not have lifeguards. Nevertheless, swimming is usually safe, as beaches are generally situated in small coves with calm waters.

The majority of the Balearic Islands' beaches are sandy. However, those along the northern shores of the islands are often rocky. You should exercise special care when swimming off rocky beaches. It is also recommended that you use footwear when entering the water and that you watch out for underwater rocks when snorkelling.

The sun should be taken seriously while on the beach. Between noon and 6pm it is best not to stay exposed for too long. It can take only minutes to get sunburnt and children are especially vulnerable. Be sure to apply a high-factor sunblock cream and also make use of an umbrella. Deckchairs and umbrellas can often be hired for a fee. Drink plenty of water to avoid dehydration.

MEDICAL CARE

The UK Foreign Office advises all travellers to buy medical insurance. However, visitors from EU countries are entitled to free national health treatment if they travel with a European Health Insurance Card (EHIC), which can be obtained in the UK from the Department of Health or from a post office before you travel. Note that Spanish healthcare does not cover all expenses, such as the cost of dental treatment. Having private health insurance can also avoid time-wasting bureaucracy. Visitors from outside the EU should always carry valid medical insurance.

In case of illness, you should report to a hospital or clinic. At night, patients are seen by the *Urgencias* (Emergency). You can also telephone the Cruz Roja (Red Cross) for help.

PHARMACIES

Pharmacies have the same opening hours as other shops. They carry a green or red cross with the word *farmàcia*, or sometimes *apotecaria*. Details about those open at night and on public holidays can be found in the windows of all

Firefighting airplane on Ibiza

Ambulance on Formentera

pharmacies. Most pharmacists in large towns speak at least one foreign language. This is important, since when dealing with minor medical problems, pharmacists are entitled to give advice and even dispense necessary medicines. In this instance, consulting a pharmacist may be enough. Balearic pharmacies sell several medicines over the counter that in other countries are available only on prescription. Away from the big towns, a *farmàcia* may be found in any small town or village. Here, opening hours may be shorter and they are not often open at weekends. In smaller towns and villages the pharmacist may be less used to dealing with tourists and communication may be a problem as a result.

Decorative pharmacy sign

FIRE HAZARDS

The Balearic Islands have a dry Mediterranean climate, with mild winters and hot summers. The summer heat often causes droughts since rain falls sporadically between October and February. This creates conditions where fire can spread extremely quickly. Parched woodlands, combined with the general layout of the land, makes firefighting very difficult. Often fire fighting necessitates airplanes and helicopters dropping vast amounts of water. It is vital, therefore, when travelling on the islands or using picnic facilities, to remember to take great care to prevent a fire from starting. Before leaving, carefully check the remains of any bonfire and be sure to pick up glass, particularly bottles, that may also cause fire. It goes without saying that you should be especially careful when extinguishing cigarettes in country areas.

The island Fire Brigade is called *Bomberos*, and as elsewhere in the world, it has an easy-to-remember emergency telephone number *(see below)*.

DIRECTORY

EMERGENCY NUMBERS

Police, Guardia Civil, Red Cross, Ambulance & Fire Brigade
Tel *112.*

PHARMACIES

Mallorca
Farmacia La Rambla C.B.
Rambla Ducs de Palma,
Palma de Mallorca.
Tel *971 711 511.*

Menorca
Farmacia Segui Puntas
Avda Vives Llull 16, Maó.
Tel *971 360 993.*

Ibiza
A.M. Marí Tur
Annibal 11, Eivissa.
Tel *971 310 371.*

Formentera
Climent Gonzalez A.M.
Avda Constitucion 36.
Tel *966 792 311.*

Communication and Banks

Logo of a local bank

The quality of telephone services in the Balearic Islands is high. Thanks to the transfer to digital technology in 1998 the line quality is generally good. The banking services on the islands are equally efficient and many foreign banks, mainly German, have branches here. The Spanish postal system does not function quite so well and it may take a week or more for a letter posted in the Balearic Islands to reach its destination. When communicating with Spanish companies it is best to use fax or e-mail.

Bright and easy-to-spot post box belonging to the Spanish *correos*

TELEPHONES

Most of the telephones in the Balearic Islands are owned and maintained by the Spanish company Telefónica, although in some of the busier resorts you may see telephones belonging to other companies. This competition means that even in a small place you should have no problem finding a public telephone – if not in a street kiosk, then in a bar or restaurant.

The most common phones are coin- or card-operated types. Since 2001, telephones that once accepted Spanish pesetas have been adapted to take euros. The card-operated telephones are of various types, as there are two types of phonecards. One has a black magnetic strip with an encoded value. The other has a PIN number that must be entered before the connection can be made.

When dialling a number you should remember that in Spain you must always dial the full nine-digit number, even if you are in the same area. The code for the Balearic Islands is 971. A call from Mallorca to Menorca will cost the same as one from Palma to Andratx. When telephoning the Balearic Islands from the UK, Ireland and New Zealand you must first dial 0034 (the country code for Spain) and then the subscriber's number starting with the area code (i.e. 971). When calling a mobile phone number you should dial the country code, followed by the subscriber's number. To phone the UK from the Balearic Islands dial 0044, then area code (minus the 0) then number; to phone Ireland dial 00353, then area code (minus the 0) then number; to phone the US or Canada dial 001, then area code then number.

Telephone kiosk

Logo of Telefonica

There are four tariffs for international calls. These apply respectively to EU countries, other European countries and northwest Africa, North and South America, and the rest of the world. International calls are cheapest at night, between 10pm and 8am, on Saturdays after 2pm and on Sundays. A call from a public telephone costs 35 per cent more than one made from a private phone, but is still cheaper than from a hotel.

POSTAL SERVICE

The Spanish postal system is one of the worst in Europe and you should not be surprised if postcards and letters sent from the islands take a week or more to reach the addressee. If a message is urgent, it is much better to send it by fax or e-mail. It is also possible to send express *(urgente)* or a registered *(certificado)* mail.

Post offices are open between 8:30am and 2:30pm Mondays to Fridays (some offices are open to 10pm), and between 9:30am and 1pm Saturdays. If you only want stamps, these are also sold at kiosks bearing the sign *timbre* or at tobacconists; or, ask at your hotel reception. Postal charges depend on where the item is being sent to and fall into bands that include the EU, the rest of Europe, the USA and the rest of the world. Post offices also accept telegrams, registered mail and parcels. Letters and cards can be mailed in a yellow post box.

Many hotels, as well as some shops, offer services of companies other than the Spanish post. They are, however, no more efficient. If you use one of these and buy an appropriate stamp, remember to post your letter in the correct box.

CURRENCY

The Euro (€) is the common currency of the European Union. It went into general circulation on 1 January 2002, initially for twelve participating countries. Spain was one of those twelve countries, and the Spanish peseta was phased out in January 2002. Euro notes, in denominations of €5 to €500, are identical throughout the Eurozone countries while the coins have one side identical (the value side), and one side with an image unique to each country.

BANKS AND CASH DISPENSERS

Most banks are open from 9am until 2pm. Some have longer opening hours or work in the afternoons on a rota system. After the switch to the euro, most bureaux de change closed. Now the easiest way to change currency is in a bank, at the counter marked *cambio*.

To do this you will need to show your passport or other ID. Most banks charge a small commission for this.

Alternatively, you can withdraw money from one of the many cash dispensers that work 24 hours. They accept all major credit cards and do charge a commission but the exchange rate is usually better than at banks.

One of the many cash dispensers available on the islands

CREDIT CARDS AND TRAVELLER'S CHEQUES

The most popular credit cards are Visa and MasterCard. However, most cash dispensers, as well as shops, hotels and restaurants, will also accept American Express or Diners. When you pay with a card, cashiers will usually pass your card through a reading machine. Sometimes you may be asked to punch in your PIN number. Some smaller places, such as market stalls and independent shops may not accept credit cards.

Traveller's cheques are by far the safest way of carrying money. When you lose a cheque you don't automatically lose the money and it can be quickly replaced. These may be cashed in banks and bureaux de change. The most popular traveller's cheques are American Express, Visa and Thomas Cook. Banks charge a commission for cashing a cheque.

RADIO AND TELEVISION

Numerous pubs and cafés have a television and it is easy to watch major sporting events live, including many English and German league soccer matches. Hotels have a larger selection of TV channels. Besides Spanish national TV, such as TVE1, TVE2, there are a number of local channels including Catalan TV3 and Canal 33. These broadcast mainly Spanish news and light entertainment programmes.

You can tune into the BBC's World Service 24 hours a day on 648kHz medium wave and also on 98.5FM.

NEWSPAPERS

Several local newspapers are published on each of the islands. These cover mainly local issues and they can also be valuable sources of information for visitors who want to find out about forthcoming cultural and sporting events. They also publish useful addresses and telephone numbers. Some of the local newspapers have foreign language supplements.

In many towns, kiosks and hotels sell Spanish national papers as well as British and German newspapers, which are available all of the time. The majority of the popular EU publications arrive on the Balearic Islands with a minimum delay.

Diario de Mallorca

MENORCA
DIARIO INSULAR

El Camí de Cavalls abre paso a un plan especial

Ultima Hora

El sector turístico exige que la huelga del 20-J no paralice Son Sant Joan

La Fira del Llibre saca a la calle 50.000 libros

Popular dailies published in the Balearic Islands

Kiosks selling papers in Passeig d'es Born in Palma, Mallorca

DIRECTORY

POST OFFICES

Mallorca
Constitucio 6, Palma.
Tel *971 228 610.*

Menorca
C/Bon Aire 15, Maó.
Tel *971 356 629.*
Pl Borne 9, Ciutadella.
Tel *971 380 081.*

Ibiza
Avda Isidor Macabich 67, Eivissa. ***Tel*** *971 399 769.*

LOST OR STOLEN CREDIT CARDS

American Express
Tel *900 994 426.*

Diners Club
Tel *902 401 112.*

MasterCard
Tel *900 971 231.*

VISA
Tel *900 991 124.*

TRAVEL INFORMATION

Most visitors arrive on the Balearic Islands by air. This is not only the fastest but often also the cheapest way of getting here. The airports are on Mallorca, Menorca and Ibiza. Served by intertional airlines, these are mostly charter flights, though there are also regular scheduled flights from the UK. Alternatively, you can fly to mainland Spain and change planes. During peak season, Palma's airport is one of the busiest in Europe. Sea links are equally convenient, but you must first get to the Spanish coast. The routes from Barcelona, Dénia and Valencia to the Balearic Islands are served by large ferries that may carry cars, and also by fast catamarans.

Iberia's logo

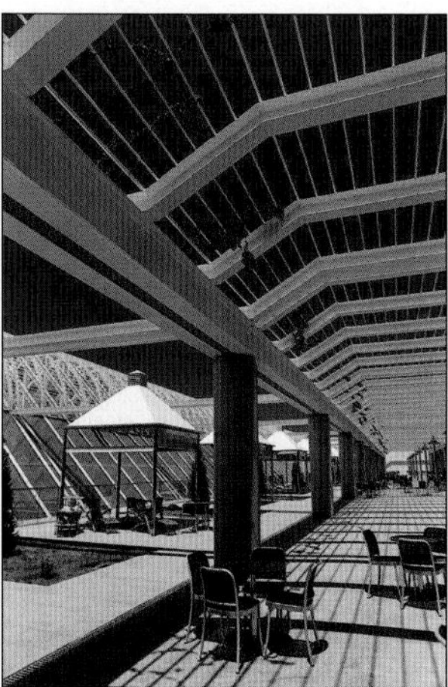

Palma Airport's departure hall, Mallorca

AIR TRAVEL

Regular links between large Spanish cities and the Balearic Islands are provided by the Spanish carriers **Iberia**, **Vueling**, **Spanair** and **Air-europa**. There are also regular flights between the Balearic Islands (mainly Mallorca) and countries that provide the greatest numbers of visitors such as Germany and Britain, as well as Austria, Switzerland, France and the Netherlands.

The Balearic Islands are featured by a wide range of European tour operators – ask your travel agent for advice. Package holidays operate year-round and feature both scheduled and charter flights. Palma is also served by low-cost airlines **easyJet** and **bmibaby** with flights from London Gatwick, Stansted, Luton, Bristol, East Midlands, Manchester and Liverpool.

Flights from the UK take under three hours. These relatively short flight times mean that the islands are popular for annual holidays as well as "mini-breaks". Flights from the US require changing planes in London, Barcelona or Madrid.

FLIGHTS BETWEEN THE ISLANDS

The only carrier providing flights between the islands is **Iberia**. The flight from Mallorca to Menorca takes only 30 minutes. For that reason this is a convenient way of travelling. Before island hopping, it is a good idea to find out what type of aircraft you are going to fly in. Some are quite small and you may not be able to take large hand luggage. Travelling in a small, packed and stuffy light aircraft can be a little unpleasant for anybody who suffers from claustrophobia or other health problems. Even in the best of weather, the flight may be bumpy and a small aircraft makes this more noticeable. However, flying between the islands will not only save you time but will also give you the chance to see magnificent views of the archipelago.

Multi-lingual information sign at Palma's airport

AIRPORTS

Son Sant Joan airport on Mallorca is situated on the outskirts of Palma, around 11 km (7 miles) from the centre of the island's capital. The nearby motorway provides a fast road link to Palma. Terminal A is used for scheduled flights; Terminal B is for charter flights. The airport has many shops, car hire agents and tourist information centres.

Over the last few years the airport has been constantly extended for the needs of tourists. Despite its size, it is difficult to get lost here. Individual zones are well sign-posted, but be prepared for long walks when making your way from one sector of the airport to another. Menorca's airport is near the island's capital – Maó. This is

Colourful aircraft at Ibiza's airport

Ferries in Maó's harbour, Menorca

the smallest of the Balearic airports. Ibiza's airport is a dozen or so kilometres from Eivissa and is far busier. The traffic increases particularly during weekends, when club-goers from all over Europe arrive for the Saturday-Sunday revel. The aircraft touching down here are often painted in the most fantastic designs. When taking off or landing in Eivissa you get a bird's-eye view of the town and of Dalt Vila. Frequent bus services operate from all the main airports and can take you straight to the city centres.

FERRIES

Anyone who plans to take their own car or motorcycle to the islands must use a ferry. These run frequent and regular services between large towns on the Spanish mainland and the harbours of Mallorca, Menorca and Ibiza. Journey times are quite reasonable; it takes seven hours by ferry from Barcelona to Palma for example.

The large ferries operated by **Trasmediterranea** sail from Barcelona and Valencia to Palma and Maó. They also provide transport to Ibiza. The latter may be reached from Barcelona (11 hours) or Valencia (about four hours). **Balearia**, a smaller ferry company, also has services to the islands. If you're in a hurry, you can also use Trasmediterranea's new high-speed ferry service, which carries up to 900 passengers and 265 cars and can take you from Valencia to Ibiza in three hours.

BALEARIA

Logo of Balearia ferry lines

Inter-island services are equally diverse. You can choose a fast Trasmediterranea catamaran or a slower ferry run by a company like **Iscomar**. Both of them have bars for passengers.

Using ferries to hop from island to island will always be cheaper than flying and it can be a very pleasant option. Arriving by sea and catching your first glimpse of Maó's ancient harbour is an unforgettable experience. Some islands can only be reached by sea. These include Cabrera, Formentera and Dragonera. A journey by ferry from Ibiza to Formentera takes about an hour; by catamaran it takes about 30 minutes.

Ticket prices for ferries providing links between the islands are reasonable, but going by a catamaran will cost you more. Price differences between the competing companies are greater for longer routes, but prices depend mostly on the time of year. The lowest prices can be obtained after high season, from October until December, and again from the end of January until the end of March. In the period from Easter until the beginning of July – known as the "half-season" – the ferry prices tend to go up again. Children up to the age of 12 are entitled to a 50 per cent reduction, and infants travel free.

DIRECTORY

AIRPORTS

www.aena.es

Mallorca – Son Sant Joan
Tel *971 789 655.*

Menorca
Tel *971 157 000.*

Ibiza
Tel *971 809 000.*

AIRLINES

Aireuropa
www.aireuropa.com

bmibaby
www.bmibaby.com

easyJet
www.easyjet.com

Iberia
www.iberia.com

Spanair
www.spanair.com

Vueling
www.vueling.com

FERRY LINES

Balearia
www.balearia.net

Iscomar
www.iscomar.com

Trasmediterranea
www.trasmediterranea.es

Pleasure boat – an enjoyable way to travel to smaller ports

Getting Around the Islands

The Balearic Islands have only two railway lines, both of which are in Mallorca. The first is an historic line from Palma to Sóller; the other links Palma with Manacor, via Inca. To explore the more remote parts of the island, as well as the remaining islands of the archipelago, you will need a car, a scooter or a bicycle. On Formentera, a scooter and bicycle are the best means of transport. When travelling round the islands, you should pay particular attention to the numerous motorbike riders. Weekend motorbike rallies and races are held in Mallorca, although they are strongly opposed by the *Guardia Civil.*

Scenic, winding road leading to Sa Calobra, Mallorca

ROADS

Roads and signage on the Balearic Islands are generally good, although there is a shortage of hard shoulders. As a consequence, stopping along the road in order to admire the scenery can be difficult and dangerous and is not recommended. The only free motorway runs along the coast of Badia de Palma, encircling Mallorca's capital. Its second segment links Palma with Inca. To use the segment between Alfàbia and Sóller that passes through the tunnel under Serra de Tramuntana, you have to pay a toll. During the morning and afternoon rush hour in the areas around Palma and other industrial towns like Inca or Manacor, you may experience traffic jams.

Take great care when you are trying to reach some beaches or sights off the beaten track. The roads leading to them can be narrow, steep and winding. Problems can arise when two cars try to pass each other. Some beaches and sights inland can only be reached along unmade, bumpy roads and to travel to these requires a four-wheel drive vehicle.

MAPS

When hiring a car you will normally be given an outline road map of the island. It will show the main roads on which it is safe to drive. Unfortunately the maps are not always up to date and it is advisable to buy one of the maps sold in bookshops, souvenir shops or petrol stations. The folding B&B Maps are particularly good. Please note that town and street signs now appear in Catalan rather than Spanish (Castilian), so make sure you get a map marked in Catalan.

CAR AND SCOOTER HIRE

Companies will be falling over themselves to rent you a car almost as soon as you have landed, as all major car hire companies, **Avis, Hertz** and **Europcar** have their desks at the airports. It is, however, worth taking your time to search for a small local firm that may offer you a better price.

The price of car hire depends on the time of year, the size of the car and the length of hire. Advance booking can also affect the price. It is worth not only comparing the prices quoted by the various companies but checking exactly what the quote includes.

When hiring a car, you will have to show your passport and valid driver's licence. You should also carefully check the conditions regarding insurance and any restrictions about driving on rough tracks or taking the car from one island to another. Be sure to inspect the condition of the car, as you will have to return it in the same condition or pay a fine. The terms and conditions of hire can vary greatly from company to company. Check carefully before signing any contract.

Scooters are a very popular form of transport, particularly on Formentera and Ibiza. Hire

Scooters on the streets of Eivissa, Ibiza

Petrol station run by the Cepsa chain

rates for these are much lower and they can transport you to places that cars cannot reach. Many people learn to ride a scooter during their holidays.

RULES OF THE ROAD

Driving on the Balearic Islands is no different to driving in any other European country. You should remember the speed limits, which are 120 km/h (74 mph) on motorways, 90 km/h (55 mph) on major roads and 40 km/h (30 mph) in towns. The fines for breaking the speed limits are high, just as they are for drunken driving. The highest permitted blood alcohol level is 0.05 per cent.

Sign for a parking meter

BUYING PETROL

Petrol station pumps are generally operated by the staff. Only a few are automatic and open 24 hours. Menorca, Ibiza and Formentera have very few petrol stations. The same applies to the Serra de Tramuntana region of Mallorca. When touring these areas you should remember that a car uses more fuel on mountainous terrain than on a flat road. It is therefore worth filling the tank before setting off.

TOWN DRIVING

If at all possible, you should avoid driving in large town centres and popular resorts. Many streets in historic towns are narrow, with one-way traffic. Cars parked alongside pavements make driving conditions even more difficult. Popular resorts are always crowded and it can be hard to find a parking space.

Most car parks charge fees, and there are fines for non-payment. Paid car parking spaces along pavements are marked with a blue line. Generally, the parking fees apply from 9am to 1pm and from 5pm to 8pm on weekdays, and from 9am to 1pm on Saturdays. In many towns, such as Eivissa, parking in these spaces is limited to a set time. A yellow line painted along the pavement means that parking is prohibited. In Palma and Maó use one of the underground car parks. Here, there is no time limit on parking, but you may have to wait in a long queue.

BUSES

Bus links between major towns as well as between large and small towns are very good. Links between small towns and villages are less efficient. Of the large towns, only Palma has its own municipal bus network. Bear in mind that during weekends bus services are less frequent. When planning a further journey, particularly on Mallorca, check your options for the return journey.

Ibiza has a special night bus service during high season, taking guests to the most popular clubs and ferrying them between Sant Antoni de Portmany and Eivissa.

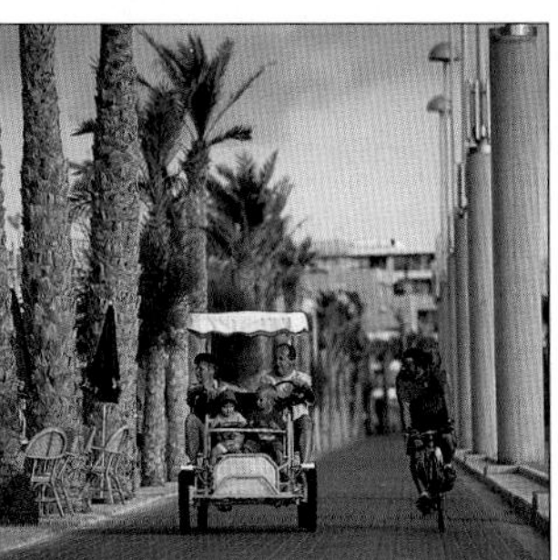
Bicycle and "quadcycle" on a promenade

TAXIS

For travelling around town it is best to hire a taxi. Most taxis in Palma have a black and cream colour scheme. The driver is obliged to turn on the meter at the start of the journey and the sum displayed is the one you pay. For disabled people, taxi transport is by far the most convenient, as you can order a specially adapted vehicle. Taxis to the airport may charge an additional airport and luggage fee. For taxis on Mallorca call 971 755 440, on Menorca call 971 367 111 and on Ibiza call 971 398 4833.

DIRECTORY

HIRING A CAR

Avis
www.avisworld.com

Europcar
www.europcar.es

Hertz
www.hertz.com

Spain Car Rental
www.rentspain.com

BUS STATIONS

Empresa Municipal de Transportes Urbanos de Palma
Plaça Espanya, Palma, Mallorca
Tel *971 177 777.*

Transportes Menorca
Vassallo s/n, Maó, Menorca.
Tel *971 360 475.*

Autobuses
Sant Antoni de Portmany, Ibiza.
Tel *971 340 510.*

TRAIN STATIONS

Palma-Inca
Tel *971 177 777.*

Tren de Sóller
Tel *902 364 711.*

General Index

Page numbers in bold type refer to main entries.

Q

R

T

U

V

W

X

Y

Z

Acknowledgments

Dorling Kindersley would like to thank the following people whose contributions and assistance have made the preparation of this book possible.

Consultant Chris Rice

Factcheckers Paula Canal, Bernat Fiol, John Gill

Proofreader Stewart Wild

Indexer Helen Peters

Additional Contributors Tony Kelly, Andrew Valente, Jeffrey Kennedy

Additional Photography Joe Cornish, Neil Lucas, Ian O'Leary, Coline Sinclair

Additional Design & Editorial Assistance Sonal Bhatt, Jo Cowen, Gadi Farfour, Anna Freiberger, John Gill, Alison McGill, Caroline Mead, Marianne Petrou, Mani Ramaswamy, Lucinda Smith, Susie Smith, Sylvia Tombesi-Walton, Hugo Wilkinson, Conrad Van Dyk

Senior Editor Jacky Jackson

Managing Editor Helen Townsend

Publishing Manager Kate Poole

Special Assistance

Wiedza i Życie would like to thank the following people for their help in creating this guide.

Martin & Toni Cornell, Zbigniew Dybowski, Joanna Egert-Romanowska, Christiane Hagen, Martin Hagmüller, Javier Lopez Silvosa, Barbara Sudnik.

The publisher would also like to thank the people and institutions who allowed photographs of their property to be reproduced, as well as granting permission to use photographs from their archives:

AENA, Gabinete de Comunicación-Aeropuertos de Baleares; Aeropuerto de Palma de Mallorca (Elisabet Royo Romero); AFP in Warszawie (Piotr Ufnal); Aguamar in Platja d'en Bossa; Amic Hotels in Palma (Andreu Llabrés); Amnesia in Sant Rafael (Stéphane Schweitzer, Aymeric Huot-Marchand); Banys Àrabs in Palmie (Doña Pilar); National Library in Warsaw (Iwona Grzybowska); Centre Perles in Palma (Lluc Antonio Bibiloni, Carolina Gato); Corbis – Agencja Free in Warsaw (Gabriela Ściborska); Coves de Campanet (Maria Antònia Siquier); Eden in Sant Antoni de Portmany (Gemma); El Divino in Eivissa; Els Calders (Javier Marqués); Es Paradis in Sant Antoni de Portmany; Fundació Pilar i Joan Miró in Cala Major (Núria Sureda, Joan Insa); Grupo Aspro-Ocio (Omar García Melcon); Ibatur (Esteve Rigo Ribas); La Granja (Manuel Moragues Marqués); La Residencia in Deià (Arantza Zamora); La Reserva Puig de Galatzó (Heike Killisch); Modas Leather in Ferreries (Suzanne Sparkes-Keeble); Museu d'Art Espanyol Contemporani in Palma (Antonio Barcelo); Museu de Lluc in Monasteri de Luc (Elvira González); Museu de Mallorca in Palma (Guillem Rosselló Bordoy); Museu de Menorca in Maó (Anna Fernandez); Naviera Universal Española, S.L. in Barcelona (Núria Alvarez); paulunderhill.com (Paul Underhill); Safari-zoo Mallorca (Miquel Brunet Alós)

Picture Credits

t=top; tl=top left; tc=top centre, tr=top right; c=centre; cl=centre left; cr=centre right; cb=centre below; ca=centre above; clb=centre left below; crb=centre right below; cla=centre left above; cra=centre right above; b=bottom; bl=bottom left; bc=bottom centre, br=bottom right, ba=bottom above, la=left above

Works of art have been reproduced with the permission of the following copyright holders: *Personage and Bird* and *Mosaic in Parc de la Mar, Palma* Joan Miró © Succession Miró/ADAG, Paris and DACS, London 2006: 58c/48b; *La Eustacia* Guillermo Perez Villalta © DACS, London 2006 56tl.

The publisher is grateful to the following individuals, companies and picture libraries for permission to reproduce their photographs:

4Corners Images: SIME/Schmid Reinhard 11br, 11c; AENA: 198cl; AFP 195b; Alamy Images: allOver photography/TPH 10tc; Paul Bourdice 158cl; imagebroker/White Star/Monica Gumm 187cr; islandspics 11tl; nagelestock.com 10cl; Wolfgang Pölzer 184bc; The Geoff Williamson Image Collection 186tr; Amic Hotels: 142t; Amnesia:120t, 179t.

Biblioteca Naradowa in Warsaw: Krzysztof Konopka 67clb; Club de Golf Alcanada: 186bl; Corbis: 34c, 35c, 35bl, 120ca, 121b; Franz-Marc Frei 29t; Roger Halls 111t; Bob Krist 19b; Kelly-Mooney 37ca; Vittoriano Rastelli 133b; Hans Georg Roth 31c, 91b; James A. Sugar 21b, 29c, 37cb; Cueva des Hams 79 tl.

El Divino: 120b; Fundació Pilar i Joan Miró: 58b; La Granja: 65bc, Grupo Aspro-Ocio: 41bl, 59tl, 59bl, 59br, 87t, 88cb, 89b; Hemispheres Images: Michel Gotin 10br; Ibatur: 26b, 27c, 28t, 179b; Iberia: 198tc.

Piotr Kiedrowski: 157bc, 175cb; Julius and Hanna Komarniccy: 14, 20c, 26c, 175la; Wesley Kutner: 17b, 18c, 19t, 156c. Andrzej Lisowski: 16c, 17t, 19c, 21br, 23br, 28b, 96ca, 120cb, 121c, 129b, 143c, 155t, 155c, 183t, 190b, 191b, 192b, 198b, 200b.

Carlos Minguel: 24ca, 24cb, 25c, 25cb, 25bl, 25br; Pawel Murzyn: 12c, 12b, 15b, 20bl, 20br, 23ba, 25tl, 29b, 40ca, 89tl, 119b, 128c, 178cl, 182c, 190c; Museu de Mallorca: 52c, 52cb, 52tr, *Paris i Helena* Ca. 1665 Mattia Preti 52cla, 53bl, 53c, 53cb, *Cabeza de Mercurio* Jaume and Rafael Blanquer Ca 1630–1650 53 ca.

Robert Pasieczny: 22 cb, 34b, 37bl, 41t, 45, 64t, 64ca, 66t, 68b, 70cp, 178t, 180t; Paulunderhill.com: 120t; La Reserva Puig de Galatzó: 61t, 61c; Biel Salas Servera: 22t, 23c, 23ca, 23cb, 24t, 24b, 25tr, 84tl, 84b, 85t; Telfonica: 196c.

Andrzej Zygmuntowicz and Ireneusz Winnicki: 5c, 101b, 156tr, 156cla, 156ca, 156cra, 156crb, 156br, 157bl, 157tc, 157tr, 157ca, 157cb, 157cr, 157bl.

Jacket: Front – 4Corners Images: SIME/Schmid Reinhard main image; DK Images: Barrlomiej Zaranek clb. Back – DK Images: Ian Aitken cla, clb; Joe Cornish tl; Colin Sinclair bl. Spine – 4Corners Images: SIME/Schmid Reinhard t; DK Images: Barrlomiej Zaranek b.

Phrase Book

In Emergency

Help!	**Auxili!**	*ow-**gzee**-lee*
Stop!	**Pareu!**	***pah**-reh-oo*
Call a doctor!	**Telefoneu un metge!**	*teh-leh-fon-**eh**-oo oon **meh**-djuh*
Call an ambulance!	**Telefoneu una ambulància!**	***teh**-leh-fon-**eh**-oo oo-nah ahm-boo-**lahn**-see-ah*
Call the police!	**Telefoneu la policia!**	***teh**-leh-fon-**eh**-oo lah poh-lee-**see**-ah*
Call the fire brigade!	**Telefoneu els bombers!**	***teh**-leh-fon-**eh**-oo uhlz boom-**behs***
Where is the nearest telephone?	**On és el telŹfon més proper?**	***on**-ehs uhl tuh-leh-**fon mehs** proo-**peh***
Where is the nearest hospital?	**On és l'hospital més proper?**	***on**-ehs looss-pee **tahl mehs** proo-**peh***

Communication Essentials

Yes	**Si**	*see*
No	**No**	*noh*
Please	**Si us plau**	***sees plah**-oo*
Thank you	**Gràcies**	***grah**-see-uhs*
Excuse me	**Perdoni**	*puhr-**thoh**-nee*
Hello	**Hola**	***oh**-lah*
Goodbye	**Adéu**	*ah-they-**oo***
Good night	**Bona nit**	***bo**-nah **neet***
Morning	**El matí**	*uhl muh-**tee***
Afternoon	**La tarda**	*lah **tahr**-thuh*
Evening	**El vespre**	*uhl **vehs**-pruh*
Yesterday	**Ahir**	*ah-**ee***
Today	**Avui**	*uh-**voo-ee***
Tomorrow	**Demà**	*duh-**mah***
Here	**Aquí**	*uh-**kee***
There	**Allà**	*uh-**lyah***
What?	**Què?**	***keh***
When?	**Quan?**	***kwahn***
Why?	**Per què?**	*puhr **keh***
Where?	**On?**	***ohn***

Useful Phrases

How are you?	**Com està?**	*kom uhs-**tah***
Very well, thank you	**Molt bé, gràcies.**	*mol **beh grah**-see-uhs*
Pleased to meet you.	**Molt de gust.**	*mol duh **goost***
See you soon.	**Fins aviat.**	*feenz uhv-**yat***
That's fine.	**Està bé.**	*uhs-**tah beh***
Where is/are ...?	**On és/són?**	***ohn ehs/sohn***
How far is it to ...?	**Quants metres/ kilòmetres hi ha d'aquí a ...?**	***kwahnz meh-truhs**/kee-**loh**-muh-truhs **yah** dah-**kee** uh*
Which way to ...?	**Per on es va a ...?**	*puhr **on** uhs **bah** ah*
Do you speak English?	**Parla anglès?**	***par**-luh an-**glehs***
I don't understand	**No l'entenc.**	*noh luhn-**teng***
Could you speak more slowly, please?	**Pot parlar més a poc a poc, si us plau?**	***pot** par-**lah mehs pok** uh **pok sees plah**-oo*
I'm sorry.	**Ho sento.**	*oo **sehn**-too*

Useful Words

big	**gran**	***gran***
small	**petit**	*puh-**teet***
hot	**calent**	*kah-**len***
cold	**fred**	***fred***
good	**bo**	***boh***
bad	**dolent**	*doo-**len***
enough	**bastant**	*bahs-**tan***
well	**bé**	***beh***
open	**obert**	*oo-**behr***
closed	**tancat**	*tan-**kat***
left	**esquerra**	*uhs-**kehr**-ruh*
right	**dreta**	***dreh**-tuh*
straight on	**recte**	***rehk**-tuh*
near	**a prop**	*uh **prop***
far	**lluny**	***lyoon**yuh*
up/over	**a dalt**	*uh **dahl***
down/under	**a baix**	*uh **bah**-eeshh*
early	**aviat**	*uhv-**yat***
late	**tard**	***tahrt***
entrance	**entrada**	*uhn-**trah**-thuh*
exit	**sortida**	***soor**-tee-thuh*
toilet	**lavabos/ serveis**	*luh-**vah**-boos sehr-**beh**-ees*
more	**més**	***mess***
less	**menys**	***men**yees*

Shopping

How much does this cost?	**Quant costa això?**	***kwahn kost** ehs-**shoh***
I would like ...	**M'agradaria ...**	*muh-grad-uh-**ree**-ah*
Do you have?	**Tenen?**	***tehn**-un*
I'm just looking, thank you	**Només estic mirant, gràcies.**	***noo**-mess ehs-**teek** mee-**rahn grah**-see-uhs*
Do you take credit cards?	**Accepten targes de crèdit?**	*ak-**sehp**-tuhn tahr-**zhuhs** duh **kreh**-deet*
What time do you open?	**A quina hora obren?**	*ah **keen**-uh oh-ruh **oh**-bruhn*
What time do you close?	**A quina hora tanquen?**	*ah **keen**-uh oh-ruh **tan**-kuhn*
This one.	**Aquest**	*ah-**ket***
That one.	**Aquell**	*ah-**kehl***
expensive	**car**	***kahr***
cheap	**bé de preu/ barat**	***beh** thuh **preh**-oo/ bah-**rat***
size (clothes)	**talla/mida**	***tah**-lyah/**mee**-thuh*
size (shoes)	**número**	***noo**-mehr-oo*
white	**blanc**	***blang***
black	**negre**	***neh**-gruh*
red	**vermell**	*vuhr-**mel***
yellow	**groc**	***grok***
green	**verd**	***behrt***
blue	**blau**	***blah**-oo*
antique store	**antiquari/botiga d'antiguitats**	*an-tee-**kwah**-ree/ boo-**tee**-gah/dan-**tee**-ghee-**tats***
bakery	**el forn**	*uhl **forn***
bank	**el banc**	*uhl **bang***
book store	**la llibreria**	*lah lyee-bruh-**ree**-ah*
butcher's	**la carnisseria**	*lah kahr-nee-suh-**ree**-uh*
pastry shop	**la pastisseria**	*lah pahs-tee-suh-**ree**-uh*
chemist's	**la farmàcia**	*lah fuhr-**mah**-see-ah*
fishmonger's	**la peixateria**	*lah peh-shuh-tuh-**ree**-uh*
greengrocer's	**la fruiteria**	*lah froo-ee-tuh-**ree**-uh*
grocer's	**la botiga de queviures**	*lah boo-**tee**-guh duh keh-vee-**oo**-ruhs*
hairdresser's	**la perruqueria**	*lah peh-roo-kuh-**ree**-uh*
market	**el mercat**	*uhl muhr-**kat***
newsagent's	**el quiosc de premsa**	*uhl kee-**ohsk** duh **prem**-suh*

post office	**l'oficina de correus**	*loo-fee-**see**-nuh duh koo-**reh**-oos*
shoe store	**la sabateria**	*lah sah-bah-tuh-**ree**-uh*
supermarket	**el supermercat**	*uhl soo-puhr-muhr-**kat***
tobacconist's	**l'estanc**	*luhs-**tang***
travel agency	**l'agència de viatges**	*la-**jen**-see-uh duh vee-**ad**-juhs*

Sightseeing

art gallery	**la galeria d' art**	*lah gah-luh **ree**-yuh **dart***
cathedral	**la catedral**	*lah kuh-tuh-**thrahl***
church	**l'església**	*luhz-gleh-**zee**-uh*
	la basílica	*lah buh-zee-lee-kuh*
garden	**el jardí**	*uhl zhahr-**dee***
library	**la biblioteca**	*lah bee-blee-oo-**teh**-kuh*
museum	**el museu**	*uhl moo-**seh**-oo*
tourist information office	**l'oficina de turisme**	*loo-fee-**see**-nuh thuh too-**reez**-muh*
town hall	**l'ajuntament**	*luh-djoon-tuh-**men***
closed for holiday	**tancat per vacances**	*tan-**kat** puh bah-**kan**-suhs*
bus station	**l'estació d'autobusos**	*luhs-tah-see-**oh** dow-toh-**boo**-zoos*
railway station	**l'estació de tren**	*luhs-tah-see-**oh** thuh **tren***

Staying in a Hotel

Do you have a vacant room?	**¿Tenen una habitació lliure?**	***teh**-nuhn **oo**-nuh ah-bee-tuh-see-**oh** **lyuh**-ruh*
double room with double bed	**habitació doble amb llit de matrimoni**	*ah-bee-tuh-see-**oh** **doh**-bluh am **lyeet** duh mah-tree-**moh**-nee*
twin room	**habitació amb dos llits/ amb llits individuals**	*ah-bee-tuh-see-**oh** am **dohs lyeets**/ am **lyeets** in-thee-vee-thoo-**ahls***
single room	**habitació individual**	*ah-bee-tuh-see-**oh** een-dee-vee-thoo-**ahl***
room with a bath	**habitació amb bany**	*ah-bee-tuh-see-**oh** am **bahn**yuh*
shower	**dutxa**	***doo**-chuh*
porter	**el grum**	*uhl **groom***
key	**la clau**	*lah **klah**-oo*
I have a reservation	**Tinc una habitació reservada**	***ting oo**-nuh ah-bee-tuh-see-**oh** reh-sehr-**vah**-thah*

Eating Out

Have you got a table for...	**Tenen taula per...?**	***teh**-nuhn **tow**-luh puhr*
I would like to reserve a table	**Voldria reservar una taula.**	*vool-**dree**-uh reh-sehr-**vahr** **oo**-nuh **tow**-luh*
The bill please.	**El compte, si us plau.**	*uhl **kohm**-tuh **sees plah**-oo*
I am a vegetarian	**Sóc vegetarià/ vegetariana**	***sok** buh-zhuh-tuh-ree-**ah** buh-zhuh-tuh-ree-**ah**-nah*
waitress	**cambrera**	*kam-**breh**-ruh*
waiter	**cambrer**	*kam-**breh***
menu	**la carta**	*lah **kahr**-tuh*
fixed-price menu	**menú del dia**	*muh-**noo** thuhl **dee**-uh*
wine list	**la carta de vins**	*lah **kahr**-tuh thuh **veens***
glass of water	**un got d'aigua**	*oon **got dah**-ee-gwah*
glass of wine	**una copa de vi**	***oo**-nuh **ko**-pah thuh **vee***
bottle	**una ampolla**	***oo**-nuh am-**pol**-yuh*
knife	**un ganivet**	*oon gun-ee-**veht***
fork	**una forquilla**	***oo**-nuh foor-**keel-yuh***
spoon	**una cullera**	***oo**-nuh kool-**yeh**-ruh*
breakfast	**l'esmorzar**	*les-moor-**sah***
lunch	**el dinar**	*uhl dee-**nah***
dinner	**el sopar**	*uhl soo-**pah***
main course	**el primer plat**	*uhl pree-**meh** **plat***
starters	**els entrants**	*uhlz ehn-**tranz***
dish of the day	**el plat del dia**	*uhl **plat** duhl **dee**-uh*
coffee	**el cafè**	*uhl kah-**feh***
rare	**poc fet**	***pok fet***
medium	**al punt**	*ahl **poon***
well done	**molt fet**	*mol **fet***

Menu Decoder *(see also pp30-31 & 144-5)*

l'aigua mineral	***lah**-ee-gwuh mee-nuh-**rahl***	mineral water
sense gas/ amb gas	*sen-zuh gas/ am gas*	still/sparkling
al forn	*ahl **forn***	baked
l'all	***lahl**yuh*	garlic
l'arròs	*lahr-**roz***	rice
les botifarres	*lahs **boo**-tee-fah-rahs*	sausages
la carn	*lah **karn***	meat
la ceba	*lah **seh**-buh*	onion
la cervesa	*lah-sehr-**ve**-sah*	beer
l'embotit	*lum-boo-**teet***	cold meat
el filet	*uhl fee-**let***	sirloin
el formatge	*uhl for-**mah**-djuh*	cheese
fregit	*freh-**zheet***	fried
la fruita	*lah froo-**ee**-tah*	fruit
els fruits secs	*uhlz froo-**eets** **seks***	nuts
les gambes	*lahs **gam**-bus*	prawns
el gelat	*uhl djuh-**lat***	ice cream
la llagosta	*lah lyah-**gos**-tah*	lobster
la llet	*lah **lyet***	milk
la llimona	*lah lyee-**moh**-nah*	lemon
la llimonada	*lah lyee-moh-**nah**-thuh*	lemonade
la mantega	*lah mahn-**teh**-gah*	butter
el marisc	*uhl muh-**reesk***	seafood
la menestra	*lah muh-**nehs**-truh*	vegetable stew
l'oli	*truh **loll**-ee*	oil
les olives	*luhs oo-**lee**-vuhs*	olives
l'ou	***loh**-oo*	egg
el pa	*uhl **pah***	bread
el pastís	*uhl pahs-**tees***	pie/cake
les patates	*lahs pah-**tah**-tuhs*	potatoes
el pebre	*uhl **peh**-bruh*	pepper
el peix	*uhl **pehsh***	fish
el pernil salat serrà	*uhl puhr-**neel** suh-lat sehr-**rah***	cured ham
el plàtan	*uhl **plah**-tun*	banana
el pollastre	*uhl poo-**lyah**-struh*	chicken
la poma	*la **poh**-mah*	apple
el porc	*uhl **pohr***	pork
les postres	*lahs **pohs**-truhs*	dessert
rostit	*rohs-**teet***	roast
la sal	*lah **sahl***	salt
la salsa	*lah **sahl**-suh*	sauce
les salsitxes	*lahs sahl-**see**-chuhs*	sausages
sec	*chuhs **sehk***	dry
la sopa	*lah **soh**-puh*	soup
el sucre	*uhl-**soo**-kruh*	sugar

la taronja	*lah tuh-**rohn**-djuh*	orange
el te	*uhl teh*	tea
les torrades	*luhs too-**rah**-thuhs*	toast
la vedella	*lah veh-**theh**-lyuh*	beef
el vi blanc	*uhl **bee blang***	white wine
el vi negre	*uhl **bee neh**-gruh*	red wine
el vi rosat	*uhl bee roo-**zaht***	rosé wine
el vinagre	*uhl bee-**nah**-gruh*	vinegar
el xai/el be	*uhl **shah**ee/ uhl **beh***	lamb
el xerès	*uhl shuh-**rehs***	sherry
la xocolata	*lah shoo-koo-**lah**-tuh*	chocolate
el xoriç	*uhl shoo-**rees***	red sausage

Numbers

0	**zero**	***seh**-roo*
1	**un (masc)**	***oon***
	una (fem)	***oon**-uh*
2	**dos (masc)**	***dohs***
	dues (fem)	***doo**-uhs*
3	**tres**	***trehs***
4	**quatre**	***kwa**-truh*
5	**cinc**	***seeng***
6	**sis**	***sees***
7	**set**	***set***
8	**vuit**	***voo**-eet*
9	**nou**	***noh**-oo*
10	**deu**	***deh**-oo*
11	**onze**	***on**-zuh*
12	**doce**	***doh**-dzuh*
13	**tretze**	***treh**-dzuh*
14	**catorze**	kah-**tohr**-dzuh
15	**quinze**	**keen**-zuh
16	**setze**	**set**-zuh
17	**disset**	dee-**set**
18	**divuit**	dee-voo-**eet**
19	**dinou**	dee-**noh**-oo
20	**vint**	***been***
21	**vint-i-un**	*been-tee-**oon***
22	**vint-i-dos**	*been-tee-**dohs***
30	**trenta**	***tren**-tah*
31	**trenta-un**	***tren**-tah **oon***
40	**quaranta**	*kwuh-**ran**-tuh*
50	**cinquanta**	*seen-**kwahn**-tah*
60	**seixanta**	*seh-ee-**shan**-tah*
70	**setanta**	*seh-**tan**-tah*
80	**vuitanta**	*voo-ee-**tan**-tah*
90	**noranta**	*noh-**ran**-tah*
100	**cent**	***sen***
101	**cent un**	***sent oon***
102	**cent dos**	***sen dohs***
200	**dos-cents (masc)**	*dohs-**sens***
	dues-centes (fem)	***doo**-uhs **sen**-tuhs*
300	**tres-cents**	***trehs-senz***
400	**quatre-cents**	***kwah**-truh-**senz***
500	**cinc-cents**	***seeng-senz***
600	**sis-cents**	***sees-senz***
700	**set-cents**	***set-senz***
800	**vuit-cents**	***voo**-eet-**senz***
900	**nou-cents**	***noh**-oo-**cenz***
1,000	**mil**	***meel***
1,001	**mil un**	***meel oon***

Time

one minute	**un minut**	***oon** mee-**noot***
one hour	**una hora**	***oo**-nuh **oh**-ruh*
half an hour	**mitja hora**	***mee**-juh **oh**-ruh*
Monday	**dilluns**	*dee-**lyoonz***
Tuesday	**dimarts**	*dee-**marts***
Wednesday	**dimecres**	*dee-**meh**-kruhs*
Thursday	**dijous**	*dee-**zhoh**-oos*
Friday	**divendres**	*dee-**ven**-druhs*
Saturday	**dissabte**	*dee-**sab**-tuh*
Sunday	**diumenge**	*dee-oo-**men**-juh*

Ferry Routes to the Balearic Islands
N1 A2
A2 AP2 E90
A7 AP7 E15
C32
N232
N420
Reus
Tarragona
N211
N232
C12
Tortosa
A7 AP7 E15
Costa Daurada
SPAIN
CV10
A7 AP7 E15
Mediterranean Sea
Costa de Azahar
CV20
Benicàssim
Castellón de la Plana
A23
Sagunto
A3 E901
Valencia
A7 AP7 E15
Palma
IBIZA
A34 N430
Sant Antoni de Portmany
C733
Santa Eulàr del Riu
Gandía
Eivissa
Dénia
Xàbia
Alcoi
Sa Savina
Sant Francesc
FORMENTE
N340
A7 AP7 E15
Palma
Benidorm
Alicante
Costa Blanca
0 km
30
0 miles
30